QuarkXPress

by Jay J. Nelson

for **dummies**®
A Wiley Brand

QuarkXPress For Dummies®

Published by: **John Wiley & Sons, Inc.**, 111 River Street, Hoboken, NJ 07030-5774, www.wiley.com

Copyright © 2017 by John Wiley & Sons, Inc., Hoboken, New Jersey

Media and software compilation copyright © 2016 by John Wiley & Sons, Inc. All rights reserved.

Published simultaneously in Canada

No part of this publication may be reproduced, stored in a retrieval system or transmitted in any form or by any means, electronic, mechanical, photocopying, recording, scanning or otherwise, except as permitted under Sections 107 or 108 of the 1976 United States Copyright Act, without the prior written permission of the Publisher. Requests to the Publisher for permission should be addressed to the Permissions Department, John Wiley & Sons, Inc., 111 River Street, Hoboken, NJ 07030, (201) 748-6011, fax (201) 748-6008, or online at http://www.wiley.com/go/permissions.

Trademarks: Wiley, For Dummies, the Dummies Man logo, Dummies.com, Making Everything Easier, and related trade dress are trademarks or registered trademarks of John Wiley & Sons, Inc. and may not be used without written permission. QuarkXPress is a trademark of Quark Software, Inc. All other trademarks are the property of their respective owners. John Wiley & Sons, Inc. is not associated with any product or vendor mentioned in this book.

For general information on our other products and services, please contact our Customer Care Department within the U.S. at 877-762-2974, outside the U.S. at 317-572-3993, or fax 317-572-4002. For technical support, please visit https://hub.wiley.com/community/support/dummies.

Wiley publishes in a variety of print and electronic formats and by print-on-demand. Some material included with standard print versions of this book may not be included in e-books or in print-on-demand. If this book refers to media such as a CD or DVD that is not included in the version you purchased, you may download this material at http://booksupport.wiley.com. For more information about Wiley products, visit www.wiley.com.

Library of Congress Control Number: 2016957973

ISBN: 978-1-119-28598-4

ISBN 978-1-119-28599-1 (ebk); ISBN ePDF 978-1-119-28600-4 (ebk)

Manufactured in the United States of America

10 9 8 7 6 5 4 3 2 1

Table of Contents

Introduction

At the height of its worldwide popularity, QuarkXPress had almost 4 million users. That proved too tempting a plum for the competing Adobe juggernaut not to pluck from the desktop publishing pie, so over the course of 10 years, Adobe was able to draw many graphic designers to InDesign by providing it for free in bundles with Photoshop and Illustrator. Meanwhile, Quark underwent a complete metamorphosis, changing ownership and management to become the company that created this jewel of digital publishing: QuarkXPress 2016.

Meanwhile, the publishing industry itself experienced major changes, embracing multiple ever-changing digital formats — and QuarkXPress evolved along with these changes. QuarkXPress 2016 is not your father's, mother's, or grandparents' QuarkXPress: Although the program has maintained its trademark efficiency and focus on the day-to-day needs of real-world publishers, it has also become a multifunction, platform-agnostic publishing engine capable of efficiently producing documents for any medium today — or that may present itself in the future.

Many graphic designers lost track of QuarkXPress, and they wonder what kind of organizations have continued to use it year after year. The simple answer is this: companies that value time and efficiency over bells and whistles. Financial organizations, pharmaceutical companies, manufacturing industries, newspapers and magazines, book publishers, multilingual publishers, and especially East Asian publishers all rely on QuarkXPress because it saves them time.

QuarkXPress is happily experiencing a resurgence of interest from publishers and graphic designers, partly because it remains efficient, practical, and elegant, but also because it combines the features of several competing programs. You can use it for most tasks that publishers habitually use Adobe Illustrator for — but with a more efficient interface. (In fact, if you preferred Aldus FreeHand's efficient, task-based interface over Illustrator's byzantine tool-based interface, you might find yourself using QuarkXPress as if it were FreeHand!)

Another reason is cost: QuarkXPress is still sold with a perpetual license — there are no monthly fees to use it, and its year-over-year cost is significantly lower than Adobe's InDesign or Creative Cloud suite. And now it can convert PDF, Illustrator, EPS, InDesign, and Microsoft Office content into native QuarkXPress items — a first in the industry.

I'm proud to have been asked to contribute a book to this successful book series. But, don't be fooled by the series title. If you are using or considering using QuarkXPress, you are far from being a dummy. This is world-class software that will efficiently and effectively support your creative work for years to come.

About This Book

The purpose of *QuarkXPress For Dummies* is to clearly explain the fundamentals of how to use all the tools in QuarkXPress. Whether you're new to QuarkXPress or upgrading to the latest version, you get answers to your real-world questions about how stuff works. If you're looking for a comprehensive book on how to do absolutely everything in QuarkXPress inside out, backward and wearing heels, this is not it. That book doesn't exist — and if it did, it would be three times the size of this one. This book was written to QuarkXPress 2016 and should be useful to anyone using QuarkXPress versions back to 8.

To help you absorb the concepts, this book uses the following conventions:

>> Web addresses appear in monofont. If you're reading a digital version of this book on a device connected to the Internet, you can click the live link to visit a website, like this: http://www.dummies.com.

>> When I tell you to enter text into a field or or some other element, the text you enter appears in **bold.**

>> I list keyboard shortcuts for both Mac and Windows, in that order. For example, Command-K means press the Command and K keys at the same time on a Mac; Ctrl+K means press the Ctrl and K keys at the same time time on a Windows PC. Here's how I say this in the book: "Press Command-K (Mac) or Ctrl+K (Windows)." Modifier keys on a Mac include Shift, Option, Command, and Control; modifier keys in Windows include Shift, Alt, and Ctrl. (The Control key on a Mac is rarely used for keyboard shortcuts.)

>> When you need to choose an item from the QuarkXPress menu bar, you see them separated by a special arrow, like this: File ⇨ New File, which tells you to click File and then click New File.

Foolish Assumptions

The first assumption is that you're familiar with Mac OS or Windows, because the book doesn't provide any guidance in this regard. This book doesn't discuss any platform-specific issues. You need to know how to work with your chosen platform before you begin working with this book.

Icons Used in This Book

As you read this book, you encounter icons in the margins that indicate material of special interest. Here's what the icons mean:

TIP

Tips help you save time or perform a task in a clever way.

REMEMBER

Remember icons mark the information that's especially important to know.

TECHNICAL
STUFF

The Technical Stuff icon marks information that provides a more technical explanation than is absolutely necessary for you to accomplish the task explained in that section. If you're deeply interested in the topic, read these. Otherwise, you can skip them without missing important how-to information.

WARNING

The Warning icon tells you to watch out! Some stuff that QuarkXPress lets you do may not be in your best interest, and these warnings help you identify them before causing irreparable harm to yourself and the fabric of the universe. Or something less drastic.

Beyond the Book

The great Internet contains a couple of additional resources for readers of this book:

>> **Cheat Sheet:** QuarkXPress is all about efficiency, and nothing is more efficient than using your keyboard to accomplish tasks. That's why there's a keyboard shortcut for just about every important operation in the program. The ones that power users find most useful are collected in the Cheat Sheet at www.dummies.com (search for *QuarkXPress For Dummies Cheat Sheet*).

>> **Updates:** If Quark changes something important about QuarkXPress between the time this book is published and the next major revision of QuarkXPress, look for updates at www.dummies.com.

Where to Go from Here

This book isn't linear — you can start almost anywhere if you already understand the basics of how QuarkXPress works. However, if you're new to QuarkXPress, Chapters 1 and 2 familiarize you with its overall purpose and interface. Chapters 3 and 4 explain how to create Items and work with them. Chapter 5 explains how to use master pages to ensure uniformity across multiple pages. QuarkXPress has a unique approach to sharing content across pages, layouts, and even multiple users, and Chapter 7 explains that. Most users spend 80 percent of their time in QuarkXPress working with text, so Chapters 8 through 11 dive deeply into the realm of text. Tables, pictures, and colors are explained in Chapters 12 through 15. Printing gets its own chapter (16), followed by a deep immersion into all the ways you can enhance and export your projects for digital media such as PDF and e-books. As you complete different kinds of projects in QuarkXPress, you may think: "There has to be an easier/better way!" so Chapter 18 points you to additional resources for help with specific topics. And finally, Chapter 19 attempts to smooth your QuarkXPress path with ten do's and don'ts that are easy to forget but powerful if you remember them.

1
Getting Started with QuarkXPress

IN THIS PART . . .

Understanding QuarkXPress

What's new in QuarkXPress 2016

Getting to know the interface

Creating and working with boxes, lines and text paths

Converting InDesign, Illustrator, PDF, and Microsoft Office files to native QuarkXPress items

Building a layout, a project, and a book

Syncing and collaborating with the sharing features

IN THIS CHAPTER

» Getting acquainted with QuarkXPress

» Finding out what's new in QuarkXPress 2016

» Catching up with recent versions' enhancements

» Knowing how to manage your files from the get-go

» Opening, creating, and saving files

Chapter **1**

Meeting QuarkXPress 2016

QuarkXPress 2016 is not your daddy's QuarkXPress. It may not even be *your* QuarkXPress if you haven't used it since version 7. QuarkXPress has evolved far past its spectacular first incarnation as the world's greatest tool for laying out pages for print. Adobe may have infiltrated the desktops of graphic designers by giving away InDesign, but QuarkXPress is still the industry's most efficient engine for producing documents for multiple media. It's currently in use by more than a million customers worldwide, especially in markets that value efficiency, such as manufacturing, financial, real estate, and pharmaceuticals, as well as book publishers, magazines, newspapers, and a wide variety of retailers and smart graphic designers.

In this chapter, I give you a brief overview of some QuarkXPress fundamentals and bring you up to speed on the new features in QuarkXPress 2016 as well as the major enhancements added to recent versions. Also, I provide some real-world advice for creating, naming, and organizing your files, opening older QuarkXPress documents, and saving your QuarkXPress 2016 document so that it can be read by

QuarkXPress 2015. And finally, I point you to a hidden feature that saves backup copies of your files.

Understanding What QuarkXPress Does

QuarkXPress is a page layout program. To build a page, you draw a few *boxes* (containers) and fill them with *content* (text, pictures, and other stuff). Add a few *rules* (lines) and *frames* (picture edges) and you have a *layout*. If you're clever, you link your page to a *master page* (which holds items such as page numbers and headers that repeat on multiple pages) and organize your page *items* on *layers* (to cluster related items together for viewing or printing).

REMEMBER

Everything on a QuarkXPress page is referred to as an *item*.

Over the years, QuarkXPress has evolved to support the needs of publishers and designers with major new capabilities such as interactive and animated items, Bézier (pen) tools that rival Adobe Illustrator, real-time collaboration with others working on the same document, creating e-books and even mobile apps, supplying powerful table-creation tools, converting content from other programs into native QuarkXPress items, creating anchored callouts, and providing support for dozens of languages in the same document.

In case the built-in features aren't enough for you, you can buy and add third-party XTensions to QuarkXPress, which are plug-ins that add new capabilities ranging from one feature to an entire automated database publishing system.

REMEMBER

Quark is the company's name. QuarkXPress is the product's name. Quark has other products besides QuarkXPress. Just as you would never say "Adobe" when referring to Photoshop or Acrobat, or "Microsoft" when referring to Word or Excel, you don't refer to QuarkXPress as "Quark." That said, you commonly hear people say "Quark" when referring to QuarkXPress. Use your social judgment to decide which name you want to use.

TIP

Quark was founded by a science geek who named the company after the elementary particle that is a fundamental constituent of matter. In keeping with that science nerdiness, one XTension (QuarkXPress plug-in) developer cleverly named his company Gluon, which is the elementary particle that "glues" quarks together to form protons and neutrons.

HOW QUARK REVOLUTIONIZED PUBLISHING

Quark was founded in 1981 in Denver, Colorado, by Tim Gill. After writing several successful programs for the Apple II and Apple III computers (including Word Juggler and Catalyst), Gill saw Apple's Macintosh computer and realized that it could change the world of publishing. Until that time, publishing systems were available to only the wealthiest members of society, at a cost of several hundred thousand dollars. But in the late 1980s, all publishing required was a Macintosh, QuarkXPress, and a LaserWriter — at a total cost of less than $10,000.

This tenfold reduction in the price of publishing indeed created a new worldwide industry that came to be known as Desktop Publishing. But most important, it put publishing into the hands of those formerly without a voice. This was the idea that most excited Gill, who in 1986 took on a financial partner named Fred Ebrahimi. Together, they conquered the publishing world in several ways: by building QuarkXPress into the tool that 90 percent of publishers wanted to use; by extending its reach into historically disenfranchised areas of the world such as India, Latin America, and portions of East Asia; and by supporting a cottage industry of trainers and XTension developers.

Being a programmer himself, Gill had a special place in his heart for independent programmers who wanted to make a difference in the world but wanted to work for themselves. He held training events for XTension developers, invited them to Quark's events, and even helped set up a worldwide marketing distributor for XTensions so that the developers could spend their time coding instead of marketing. Quark benefitted, of course, by being able to focus on improving the core set of features in QuarkXPress needed by most users, and allowing the XTension developers to provide solutions for specific needs. When some of those XTensions later became features in QuarkXPress, Gill always tried to take care of the developers. (When Quark released a Windows version of QuarkXPress, Gill cleverly released free XTensions to give features to Mac users that weren't possible to create in Windows.)

In 2000, Gill sold his half of Quark to Fred Ebrahimi to focus on philanthropic endeavors such as The Gill Foundation. Quark and QuarkXPress never fully recovered from Gill's departure, but still maintain a strong presence in enterprise and vertical markets that value efficiency. (In 2006, Fred Ebrahimi gave all his shares of Quark Inc. to his children, with his daughter Sasha taking the position of Chairman. In 2006, Quark also hired Raymond Schiavone, former CEO of Arbortext, as its new CEO. In 2011, the Ebrahimi family sold all its shares to Platinum Equity, a California-based private equity firm that focuses on underperforming companies with high potential.)

Getting a Feel for What's New in QuarkXPress 2016

The biggest new feature in QuarkXPress 2016 is the capability to convert imported PDF, EPS, and Adobe Illustrator files to native, editable QuarkXPress objects. You can even convert objects or entire pages from Adobe InDesign, Adobe Illustrator, Microsoft Office (including Word, Excel, and PowerPoint), CorelDRAW, Affinity Designer, and other apps.

The program sports many other new features as well. You can export any QuarkXPress layout as an HTML5 publication, enabling you to create an app-like experience in a web browser or mobile device — complete with interactive objects and all the typographic control in QuarkXPress. You can create multicolor blends (gradients), each color with its own level of opacity. The new Fit Box to Text feature resizes a text box so that if your text is shorter than the box, or if it overflows the box, the box resizes to fit the text. This feature even balances text in boxes that have multiple columns of text. The new Color Picker (formerly only available as an XTension) lets you click any item (including imported pictures) to add new color swatches to your layout. You can access Stylistic Sets included in advanced OpenType fonts. You can enlarge the icons and labels on the Measurements palette by 50 percent.

QuarkXPress 2016 also offers improvements to existing features. In previous versions of QuarkXPress, for example, dynamic guides appear as you drag an item to show you its spacing in relationship to other items. This feature lets you easily align and uniformly space items. In QuarkXPress 2016, guides now appear that show when the edges and centers of text columns and gutters align with other items in multicolumn text boxes. The Find/Change feature now remembers your most recent searches; also, it allows you to search for and change nonbreaking spaces and characters. Content variables can now wrap onto multiple lines just as regular text does, which is useful for longer headers and for created/modified/printed slugs. Print experts will appreciate full support for ICCv4 color profiles. And the QuarkCacheCleaner app now deletes the QuarkXPress Preferences file as well as the font and picture cache files used by QuarkXPress.

Windows users will be happy to have the modern, efficient user interface that Mac users have enjoyed in previous releases. And if you use a Mac, you can now pinch, zoom, and rotate items using gestures on your Mac's touchpad.

Installing QuarkXPress 2016 on a Mac is now blissfully easy: Just drag it into your Mac's Applications folder. In contrast to previous versions, which required XTensions to be rewritten for each new version of QuarkXPress, XTensions written for QuarkXPress 2015 also work with QuarkXPress 2016 (as long as the XTension doesn't conflict with a new function). And as opposed to Adobe InDesign, QuarkX-Press doesn't require payment of an ongoing subscription — its perpetual license lets you use the program forever.

If you forget which features are new, choose Help ⇨ What's New to be taken to Quark's website to find an explanation of the new features.

Introducing the Big Features in Recent Versions

If you skipped a release or three, you're not alone — but you've missed some efficiency-enhancing improvements. Conveniently, Quark has provided a chart of new features that stretches back to version 7 and has allowed me to include it in the appendix of this book. Here are some of the most exciting and useful new features introduced since version 7:

» Intelligent palettes that adapt to your work

» Layers on master pages

» The capability to drag and drop from other apps, the desktop, and Adobe Bridge

» Having a page size larger than 48 inches

» Having multiple page sizes in one document

» Crisp display of all images

» The capability to scale images up to 5000 percent

» An 8000 percent zoom

» The capability to import native Photoshop (PSD) and Illustrator (AI) files

» The capability to relink images in Usage dialog

» Format painter

» Item Find/Change

» Item Styles

» A page thumbnail navigator (Mac only)

» Cloner utility copies items or pages across layouts

» Intelligent scaling: You choose the attributes to scale

- » Footnotes/Endnotes

- » Table styles

- » Sound, video, and interactivity

- » The capability to synchronize text, pictures, and formatting automatically

- » Conditional styles

- » Callouts

- » Hanging punctuation

- » Bullets and numbering

- » Story Editor

- » Redlining

- » Notes

- » Glyphs palette

- » Job Jackets for automated document creation

- » Print previews

- » The capability to export to ePub, iPad, Kindle, Android

- » The capability to export items and pages as images

- » Advanced east Asian typography

- » Global language support built in (35+ languages)

- » Spotlight and QuickLook support (Mac only)

- » Cross-platform dual-licensing (Mac and Windows)

REMEMBER

In the bad old days, you couldn't edit a document created in a different language edition of QuarkXPress. Now, a project created in any language edition of QuarkXPress can be edited, printed, and saved in any other language edition of QuarkXPress — no more language-specific projects!

Managing Your Files

If you haven't used a page layout program before, you soon discover that managing files for QuarkXPress projects is a bit different from how you may have managed them with other kinds of programs. For example, QuarkXPress changes its file format with every version, so older versions can't open projects saved by newer versions. Also, a QuarkXPress project usually has several parts and pieces that are best stored together in a folder. You learn about these important topics next.

Futzing with file formats

QuarkXPress 2016 can directly open documents that were last saved by QuarkX-Press 7 and higher; documents earlier than version 7 require conversion first, as explained in the next paragraph. You can also copy entire pages from Adobe InDesign or Illustrator as well as import pages from PDF files, and convert them to native QuarkXPress items. See Chapter 3 for more on importing and converting those files.

TECHNICAL STUFF

Every version of QuarkXPress has allowed you to "downsave" a copy of your document to the format understood by the previous version. That way, you can hand off your QuarkXPress 2016 document to someone using QuarkXPress 2015. To downsave to the previous version, open your document and choose File ⇨ Export ⇨ Layouts as Project. In the resulting dialog box, choose 2015 from the Version pop-up menu. Unless you want to replace your existing project, give the new one a different name — perhaps add "qxp2015" to the end. QuarkXPress 2015 then happily opens the exported document just as if it had created it. However, any page items that use features not in that version will be either translated to something that version can understand or removed entirely. (For example, multicolor blends are converted to two-color blends, cross references are lost, and variables with line wraps are lost.) Use with caution!

TIP

If you use a Mac, you can use its QuickLook feature to preview QuarkXPress documents that were last saved by version 9 or higher. To do that, click once on the file in the Finder and then press the spacebar on your keyboard. The first page of the document appears in a preview window.

Opening projects

Opening an existing project in QuarkXPress is no different from opening a file in any other application: From within QuarkXPress, choose File ⇨ Open and navigate to the file. But QuarkXPress also has a handy Welcome screen (see Figure 1-1) that appears when no project is open, or when you choose Window ⇨ Welcome Screen.

The Welcome screen has three sections:

>> **Open a Recent Project:** Lists your most recently opened projects. Click one to open it. To open a different project, click the Other Projects folder icon. This opens your computer's standard Open File dialog box.

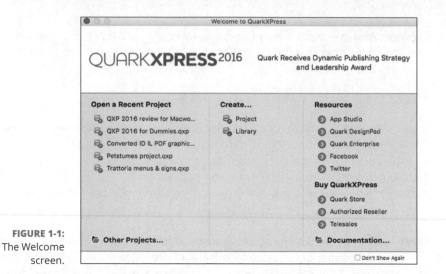

FIGURE 1-1:
The Welcome
screen.

>> **Create. . .:** Lets you create a new project or a new library. (Libraries are explained in Chapter 4.)

>> **Resources:** These Quark-related online resources are updated whenever Quark feels the need to change them. Click a resource to be taken to its web page. Below the Resources section is a list of ways to buy QuarkXPress. You also find a handy Documentation folder icon that opens the folder on your hard drive containing the QuarkXPress Getting Started reference PDF (in many languages) along with comprehensive documentation for creating AppleScript scripts (if you're on a Mac). See Chapter 18 for more on AppleScripts.

Opening older QuarkXPress projects

QuarkXPress 2016 can open documents last saved by QuarkXPress 7 and higher. (Version 7 is when Quark dramatically modernized the document format.) To open QuarkXPress documents last saved by versions 3.1–6, first convert them with the free QuarkXPress Document Converter, available at Quark's website. (The easiest way to find it is to type **QuarkXPress Document Converter** in your web browser's search field.)

TIP

On a Mac, the File menu in QuarkXPress has a handy Open Recent item that lists recently saved QuarkXPress projects. To make a similar feature available in Windows, QuarkXPress includes the DejaVu XTension, which is installed automatically. To adjust the number of items it shows, choose Edit ⇨ Preferences and click the File List pane. If you find yourself repeatedly opening projects, saving projects, and retrieving text and pictures from the same folder, you can also use DejaVu to designate default folders for those actions. That way, whenever you choose the File ⇨ Open, File ⇨ Save, File ⇨ Import, or File ⇨ Export commands, the resulting dialog will already be directed to your chosen default folder for that action. To assign default folders, choose Edit ⇨ Preferences and click the Default Path pane.

Understanding and creating a project

In contrast to most other programs, QuarkXPress documents often rely on external files that have been imported and linked. For example, when you import a picture, QuarkXPress inserts a preview of the picture on your page and remembers where the original picture file is. It then grabs that picture file whenever you export or print the QuarkXPress document. This feature can be tremendously handy for at least two reasons. First, picture files can be enormous, so by not including them inside your QuarkXPress document, your document doesn't balloon to an unworkable file size. Equally important, if you edit the picture file after importing it into a QuarkXPress page, the updated version of the picture is used when printing or exporting the document.

Therefore, before you create a new QuarkXPress project, it's smart to create a new project folder to hold it. A handy naming convention for the folder might be as follows: *client name-project name-year-month,* which would look like this:

petstumes-2017 catalog-16-11

You can then create a folder inside that folder for linked pictures, which keeps them handy for your project. You may also want to create a folder for files related to the project, such as the original word processing files given to you, notes about the project, and other files related to your project but that aren't necessary for printing it.

Understanding Projects versus Layouts

Back in QuarkXPress 7, Quark changed the way files are structured. Previously, QuarkXPress documents were similar to those by other applications: Each document had one page size and orientation. But in QuarkXPress 7 and beyond, you no longer have "documents." Instead, QuarkXPress creates what it calls a *project* that can include multiple *layouts.* (You can think of a layout as what was previously a document.)

Each layout can be a different size and orientation (portrait or landscape), so you can keep different parts of a project or campaign together. For example, a client's business card, letterhead, and envelope can each be a layout within the same project. Or, for another example, a restaurant's menu, table tents, happy-hour specials, and signage can each be a layout within one project.

A QuarkXPress project can contain two types of layouts: print and digital. This allows you to use one project to create content for various media — such as print, PDF, ePub, native apps, Kindle books, and HTML5 publications.

By grouping them together like this, QuarkXPress also lets you share content among these layouts. For example, the colors and fonts can be consistent across those layouts, and you can even use QuarkXPress's Synchronization features to ensure that if you change, say, an address or phone number on one layout, that address or phone number changes on all of them. (See Chapter 7 for more on synchronization.)

Because of this fantastic capability, every project has at least one layout. Each layout has its own name (similar to how documents in other applications have their own names), and you can add new layouts to the open project by choosing Layout ⇨ New.

TECHNICAL
STUFF

Each layout can contain as many as 2,000 pages, and can be as large as 224" × 224" in size (or 112" × 224" for a two-page spread). A project can contain an unlimited number of layouts.

REMEMBER

You can work with multiple open projects, each containing multiple layouts. Feel free to open as many projects as you need, although you are likely to work on only one or two at a time.

Creating a new project

To create a new project, follow these steps:

1. **Click Project in the Create panel of the Welcome screen that appears when no projects are open, or choose File ⇨ New ⇨ Project.**

    Either way, the dialog box shown in Figure 1-2 appears.

2. **Enter a name for your layout in the Layout Name field.**

    As explained previously, a project can have multiple layouts, and each layout can have a different name. At the moment, you're entering a name for the first layout in your project.

3. **In the Layout Type drop-down menu, select the type of layout you want.**

    If you intend to print the layout you design, choose Print. If you intend your layout to be viewed onscreen, perhaps as a fixed-layout e-book or reflowing e-book, an HTML5 publication, or an app, choose Digital. (If in doubt, choose Print — you can always convert it to Digital later, as explained in Chapter 17.)

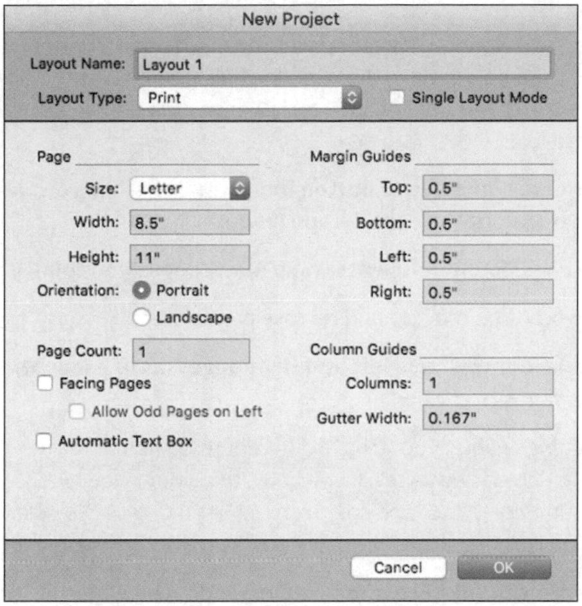

New Project

Layout Name: Layout 1

Layout Type: Print ☐ Single Layout Mode

Page

Size: Letter

Width: 8.5"

Height: 11"

Orientation: ● Portrait
○ Landscape

Page Count: 1

☐ Facing Pages
☐ Allow Odd Pages on Left

☐ Automatic Text Box

Margin Guides

Top: 0.5"

Bottom: 0.5"

Left: 0.5"

Right: 0.5"

Column Guides

Columns: 1

Gutter Width: 0.167"

Cancel   OK

FIGURE 1-2:
The New Project dialog box.

4. **Select the Single Layout Mode check box if you think you won't be adding any further layouts to this project.**

   Selecting this check box hides the layout's name (Layout 1) from the project, which simplifies filenames if you export your layout as a PDF or other digital document. As you learn in Chapter 17, when you export your layout to PDF or other formats, the new file is named *Project_Layout,* using the project and layout names you assigned to them. (The project name is the same as the name of your file when you save it.) When in Single Layout Mode, the name of the exported file is simply the project name, which is the name of the QuarkXPress file on your computer.

   TIP

   If you find yourself creating projects with just one layout most of the time, you can change QuarkXPress's Preferences so that every new project has Single Layout Mode enabled by default. To do that, first close all QuarkXPress projects. Then, choose Preferences from either the QuarkXPress menu (Mac) or the Edit menu (Windows). In the Preferences dialog, scroll down to Project and click General. Select the Single Layout Mode check box. After that, every time you create a new project, the dialog box will already have the Single Layout Mode check box selected for you. To create a multi-layout project, just deselect that check box and a field will appear for you to name your first layout in the project.

5. **In the Page box, type a width and height for your layout or choose a preset size from the Size pop-up menu.**

TIP

You can save your own preset page sizes. To do that, choose New from the Size pop-up menu, and in the resulting dialog box, enter the dimensions of the page size that you want to save and give your preset page size a name, such as Postcard-6x4.

6. **For Orientation, select a button indicating whether you want your page to be Portrait (tall) or Landscape (wide).**

7. **In the Page Count field, enter how many pages you think you'll need.**

   Don't worry: You can add and remove pages later.

8. **If your layout will have left and right pages (as in a magazine), select the Facing Pages check box.**

   This setting enables you to have different margins and Master Pages for the left- and right-facing pages. If you know that your layout will require having odd page numbers (1, 3, 5, and so on) on the left-facing pages, select the Allow Odd Pages on Left check box. Normally, you keep this unselected.

9. **If you want QuarkXPress to be able to add new pages automatically as your text grows (for example, in a long document), select the Automatic Text Box check box.**

   This setting places a text box within the margins of the Master pages and applies that text box to every page based on that Master page. (You can learn all about Master pages in Chapter 5.)

10. **Set the Margin Guides as needed.**

    These special guides indicate the "live" area of your layout, where your main content will be (text, pictures, and so forth). Items such as your page numbers, headers, and footers will normally be in the Margin area, so be sure to leave room for them if you plan to use them.

11. **If your layout will have several columns, enter the number of columns in the Columns field under Column Guides.**

    The Gutter Width field determines the space between the columns. QuarkXPress then does the math for you and places guides within the Margins on each page, as necessary for the number of columns and gutter width you entered. If you enabled the Automatic Text Box check box (see Step 9), the text box will have these columns as well; otherwise you need to set the number of columns for each text box manually.

12. **Click OK to create your new layout with these specifications.**

REMEMBER

Conveniently, QuarkXPress remembers these specifications and fills them in for you the next time you create a new layout or project. Of course, you can also choose all new specifications when you create a new layout or project.

Closing and saving projects

To close an open project, choose File ⇨ Close Window or click the red button in the title bar of its window. If you've made changes to the project, or it hasn't yet been saved, the Save dialog box opens. In the Save As field, enter a name for your file along with a location to save it, and click Save to save and close your project.

Conversely, if you know you haven't yet saved your project and want to continue working on it, you can choose File ⇨ Save to open the Save dialog box. Give your project a name, choose a location in which to store it, and click Save. Your project remains open, yet it's safely saved on your computer.

TIP

If you've made changes to your project and want to keep the old version as well as the new version, choose File ⇨ Save As instead of File ⇨ Save. The Save As command lets you save the new version of your project with a new name and location.

TIP

To save a copy of your QuarkXPress 2016 project that can be opened in QuarkX-Press 2015, choose File ⇨ Export Layouts as Project. In the resulting dialog box, choose 2015 from the Version pop-up menu. Unless you want to replace your existing project, give the new one a different name. QuarkXPress 2015 can open this new project, but any page items that use features not in that version will be either translated to something QuarkXPress 2015 can understand or removed entirely. For example, multicolor blends will be converted to two-color blends, cross-references will be lost, and variables with line wraps will be lost. Use with caution!

Using Auto Save and Auto Backup

If you're paranoid, or simply don't trust yourself to save your projects often enough as you work on them, you can enable QuarkXPress's Auto Save, or the Auto Backup feature, or both.

When you enable Auto Save, it automatically saves a temporary copy of your project in the background as you work, at whatever time interval you set in Preferences. If your computer crashes, QuarkXPress offers to open the automatically saved version the next time you open your project.

Auto Backup creates a new copy of your project every time you save it and keeps each of the previous copies you've saved (up to the number you enter in Preferences). If you decide that your recent changes to a project are awful, you can close it and open one of the previously saved versions, which are stored either in the same folder as your project or in a different folder that you specify in Preferences. To enable these features and adjust their settings, choose QuarkXPress ⇨ Preferences (Mac) or Edit ⇨ Preferences (Windows). In the Application area of the Preferences dialog box, click Open and Save. Choose the Auto Save and Auto Backup settings you prefer and click OK.

In any case, even if you don't enable Auto Save or Auto Backup, QuarkXPress 2016 silently saves a backup of your last ten opened documents. You find them in the Quark_Backup folder that QuarkXPress creates for you in the Documents folder on your hard drive.

TIP

If you change your Preferences settings while a project is open, these preferences will apply to only this project. If you change them while no project is open, these preferences will apply to all new projects.

Using templates

If you find yourself creating a similar document repeatedly, you may be tempted to duplicate it and replace its content. Instead, consider saving it as a template. A *template* is simply a QuarkXPress document that duplicates itself before opening into QuarkXPress as a new document. To save a document as a template, choose File ⇨ Save As, and in the Save As dialog box, go to the Type drop-down menu and choose Project Template.

To use the template, choose File ⇨ Open and navigate to it on your computer. When you open the template, QuarkXPress 2016 creates a new project from the template file. After making your changes, you can then save it with any name and be confident that you haven't replaced the original.

Chapter **2**

Getting to Know the Interface

S mart designers and publishers value QuarkXPress for its efficiency. Before each revision of the program, Quark's design team watches how users perform tasks, and the team comes up with clever ways to reduce the number of mouse clicks required to accomplish those tasks. But still, the first time you launch QuarkXPress, you may think that you're staring at the cockpit of a commercial jet. Not to worry! The layout is logical, and after you read this chapter, you'll be pointing and clicking without even thinking about it.

The most important idea to understand is that some interface items relate to only the current layout you're working on; others relate to QuarkXPress itself; and still others change depending on the active item on your page. For example, if you have multiple layouts open, the layout controls attached to the project window let you view each layout at a different view percentage, with different ruler measurements and (optionally) split windows. In contrast, the free-floating palettes don't change as you switch among projects and layouts. And amazingly, although the menu bar at the top of your display hosts menu items that can affect anything in QuarkXPress, those menu items change depending on what kind of page item is active.

TIP

The little icons you see scattered throughout QuarkXPress will seem cryptic until you use them a few times. Fortunately, when you hover your mouse pointer over any of them, a tooltip appears with the name of the control. For example, when you hover over a tool in the Tools palette, the tooltip displays that tool's name and shortcut key.

In this chapter, I take you through an overview of each of the QuarkXPress menus so that you know the purpose of each one. But first I tell you a little about the Application and Project interfaces. Later, you see how to do everything you need to do with palettes, how to navigate your layout by zooming and scrolling, and how to switch around among your various layouts.

Getting a Feel for the Application Interface

The palettes you see at the left, right, and bottom of QuarkXPress (see Figure 2-1) are free floating — you can drag them anywhere that's convenient for you. In contrast to the palettes, the menus in the menu bar are glued in place: You must always take your mouse up to the menu bar to access them. However, a context-sensitive subset of menu items is also available in the context menu that appears directly under your mouse pointer whenever you Control-click (Mac) or right-click (Windows) anywhere in QuarkXPress.

You also encounter dialog boxes, which appear whenever you choose a menu item that has an ellipsis (. . .) after its name. For example, when you choose File ➪ Open. . ., a dialog box appears that lets you navigate to a file to open, and if you choose File ➪ Print. . ., a dialog box appears so that you can set your printing options.

REMEMBER

In QuarkXPress, each project may contain multiple layouts. Each layout may have a different size and orientation as well as a different output intent: print or digital. When this book uses the word *project*, it means a QuarkXPress project; when it says *layout*, it means a QuarkXPress layout. See Chapter 1 to learn about projects and layouts.

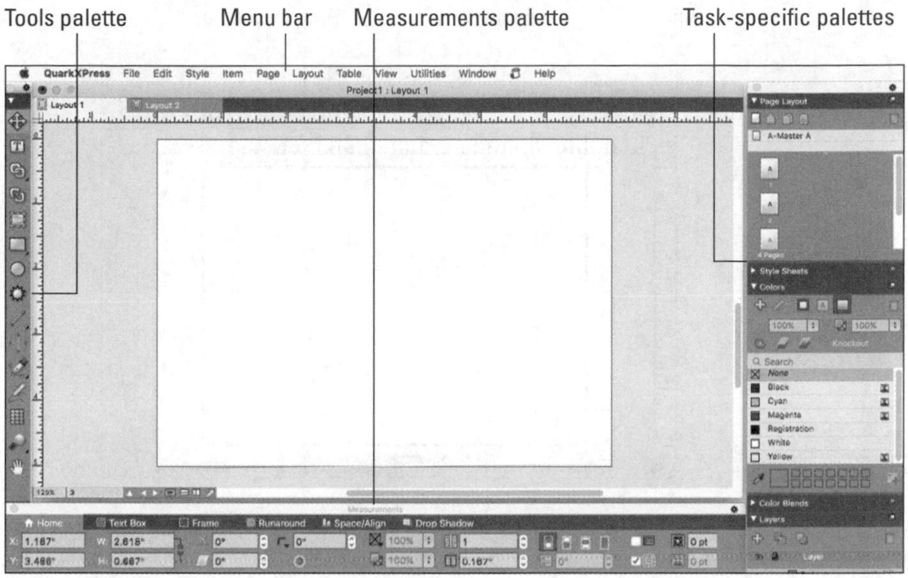

Tools palette   Menu bar   Measurements palette   Task-specific palettes

FIGURE 2-1:
The Application interface controls.

Surveying the Project Interface

Although the vast majority of interface items don't change when you switch among projects, a few relate only to the currently active project, as follows:

» **Scroll bars:** The scroll bars on the right edge and bottom edge of your project window let you see other areas of your current layout.

» **Rulers:** The units of measurement for the horizontal and vertical rulers (inches, centimeters, picas) are also specific to your current layout.

» **Layout tabs:** Click the tabs between the top ruler and your project's title bar to move among the layouts in your project.

» **Pasteboard:** The rectangle in the center is your active page, and the gray area around it is called the Pasteboard, on which you can store picture boxes, text boxes, or any other page items until you're ready to position them on that page. If your layout has multiple pages, the Pasteboard around your currently active page appears lighter than the Pasteboard around the other pages.

Items that are contained completely on the Pasteboard don't print. However, if any part of a Pasteboard item overlaps onto the page, that part will print (if you don't explicitly forbid this in the Print or PDF Export dialog box).

» **Layout controls:** The Layout controls attached to the bottom left of your project window let you change the view percentage of your project, navigate to other pages within it, and print or export that layout, as shown in Figure 2-2.

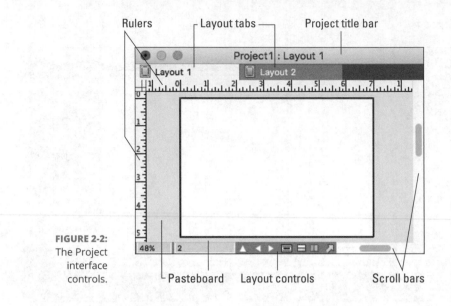

Rulers — Layout tabs — Project title bar

Project1 : Layout 1

Layout 1   Layout 2

FIGURE 2-2:
The Project
interface
controls.

48%   2

Pasteboard   Layout controls   Scroll bars

Marching through the Menus

The original Macintosh interface (and later, Windows) was designed to accommodate a very small display. (The original Macs had a 9-inch display, and a 13-inch display was state of the art for years after that.) To get the interface out of the way so that you had space to work in, all the commands were tucked into the menu bar at the top of the display. The menu items that people used most were given a keyboard shortcut, and that tradition continues to this day.

In the sections that follow, I briefly explain the purpose of each menu and highlight a few of the menu items it contains. You can explore the other menu items later in the book as they apply to appropriate topics — otherwise, this section would be completely overwhelming!

TIP

Pay attention to the keyboard shortcuts for commands that you use frequently, and memorize them if you can. The less you have to use the mouse, the more productive you'll be! I include a handy list of QuarkXPress's most popular keyboard shortcuts on this book's Cheat Sheet (go online to www.Dummies.com and search *QuarkXPress For Dummies Cheat Sheet*), but if your favorite menu item lacks a shortcut (and you're using a Mac), you can assign your own: Choose QuarkXPress ⇨ Preferences and scroll down to Key Shortcuts.

The QuarkXPress menu

Application-level information such as your license code is here, along with application-level controls such as Quark Update settings and hiding or quitting the app. On a Mac, the all-powerful Preferences are here, too. (On Windows, Preferences is in the Edit menu.)

The File menu

File-level controls such as Open, Print, Save, and Close reside in this menu. The File menu is also where you go to create new projects or libraries, import text or graphics, append colors and style sheets from other projects, export text, layouts or pages to other formats, collect linked files for output, and use Job Jackets. (I explain Job Jackets in Chapter 7.)

TIP

The File menu includes a Revert to Saved menu item, which you can use for creative explorations. First, save your document; then make some changes you may or may not like to keep. If you hate, hate, hate the result, choose File⇨Revert to Saved, and your project goes back to how it looked when you last saved it.

The Edit menu

This very long menu hosts options to cut, copy and paste items, find and change text or page items, define repeatedly used resources such as colors, style sheets, hyperlinks, lists, color management, output styles (collections of output settings), and play with some wonderfully esoteric font controls. On Windows, the all-powerful Preferences controls are here, too. (On a Mac, Preferences is in the QuarkXPress menu.)

The Style menu

Most of the items in this menu are also available in QuarkXPress palettes. (See the section "Mastering palettes," later in this chapter, for a detailed explanation of palettes.) The Style menu holds font style controls, picture box formats and controls, item styles, cross references, and hyperlinks.

TIP

The items you see in the Style menu change, depending on what kind of page item is currently active. This feature is another way QuarkXPress tries to help you be more efficient. Most of these menu items are also available in various palettes.

The Item menu

This menu gives you the power to make changes to an entire page item. (Page items include text boxes, picture boxes, lines, paths, and shared items such as Composition Zones.) You can duplicate the active item, delete it, lock it, group or align it with other items, and change its shape or content type. If you have a path selected, you can edit its segments or anchor points. You can convert editable text to picture boxes. This menu also lets you set up sharing and synchronization of items and their content, create nonprinting notes, and scale one or more items and control how their content and attributes are scaled. If you're building an e-book from a complex layout, this is where you add text for reflowing.

TIP

QuarkXPress provides two different menu items to remove selected page items or text: Edit ⇨ Cut and Item ⇨ Delete. What's the difference? Edit ⇨ Cut moves the item or text to your computer's clipboard so that you can then choose Edit ⇨ Paste to paste that item somewhere else. However, the clipboard can hold only one item or chunk of text at a time. So what if you have some text on the clipboard and want to remove a page item — without losing the text on the clipboard? Choose Item ⇨ Delete instead! Also, even if you're currently using the Text Content or Picture Content tool (instead of the Item tool), you can still click an item and use Item ⇨ Delete to remove it. Smart QuarkXPress users memorize the Command/Ctrl-K shortcut for Item ⇨ Delete. You can easily remember this command if you think of this: "Kill this item!"

The Page menu

This one's simple: Use the Page menu for inserting, deleting, or moving pages, for going directly to a page, or for displaying the Master page assigned to the current page. The Page menu is also where you create or edit a section, which is useful for controlling page numbering in a long document. If you're working on setting up a Master page, this is where you access its margin guides, column guides, and gridlines.

The Layout menu

Commands related to managing an entire, multipage layout are here, such as deleting an entire layout, duplicating it, or adding a new layout to the project. The Layout menu is also where you can change layout properties you set initially when you created the project, such as the layout's name, page size, orientation, and output intent (print or digital). You can share your layout so that others can work on it, and create a new Layout Specification for Job Jackets. (Job Jackets are a collection of requirements and limitations for specific kinds of projects; they ensure that your layouts will output properly. I tell you more about Job Jackets in Chapter 7.) If you're making an e-book, you can enter its metadata here and add the entire content of a layout to the reflow in the e-book. And last, in case you're not fond of clicking the Layout tabs to switch to a different layout, you can choose a layout from a list, or switch to the previous, next, first, or last layout in the project.

The Table menu

When you're working with a table, you find all the ways to change it on this menu. You can select, insert, or delete rows and columns, select gridlines, combine cells, break the table into pieces, and create headers and footers. This menu is also where you convert tabbed text to a true table, convert a table into text boxes, and link text cells so that text flows from one to the other.

The View menu

The View menu controls all aspects of what you see on your page and how you see it. Use this menu to control the view percentage, and how you see guides and grids, rulers, invisible characters, and item tags. You can turn on highlighting for content variables (text that is automatically created based on its location in the layout, such as running headers or footers) and cross references (as used in books), and edit text in a special Story Editor that's like a word processor.

Because QuarkXPress lets you extend items off the edge of the page (also known as a *bleed*), you can view your page as if the bleed were trimmed off. (A bleed is necessary when a page item extends to the edge of a printed page, because a commercial printer will print your page on larger paper and then trim off the excess — just in case the cutter isn't accurate.) And because QuarkXPress lets you set any item to be suppressed when printing or exporting, you can hide any suppressed items. (A *suppressed* item appears in the layout but is not included when exporting or printing. Some items are suppressed automatically, such as non-printing Notes). In a Print layout, the View menu is also where you go to preview how a layout's colors will print on various devices (color spaces).

And finally (but very important), you use the View menu to save, manage, and choose among View Sets, which are combinations of View settings. Some examples are Authoring view, which helps when you're working on page content, and Output Preview, which lets you quickly see how the page will look when printed. You learn all about View Sets later in this chapter.

The Utilities menu

Longtime QuarkXPress users may forget the first time they discovered the spell-checking tools in the Utilities menu and concluded that this menu holds a hodge-podge of commands and tools that don't fit under the other menus. New users are about to have that same "a-ha!" experience. If you're a wordsmith, you'll want to remember that the spell-checking, word count, and content variable controls are here (not in the Edit menu). The Usage utility is also here, which every user needs to manage fonts and linked pictures.

Following are the tools on the Utilities menu:

- » **Insert Character:** Lets you insert special characters such as breaking and nonbreaking spaces.

- » **Content Variable:** A content variable is text that is automatically created based on its location in the layout, such as a running header or footer. This tool lets you create, edit, insert, and remove a content variable or convert one to text.

- » **Check Spelling:** Check the spelling of a word, a selection of text, a story, a layout, or all Master pages in a layout. On a Mac, Auxiliary Dictionary and Edit Auxiliary are here, too — see explanations in the next two items.

- » **Auxiliary Dictionary (Windows only):** Lets you specify an auxiliary dictionary for use in spell checking. (You create an auxiliary dictionary and add words to it that you want QuarkXPress to spell check and hyphenate in addition to the words in the built-in dictionary. For example, you might add industry-specific or discipline-specific terms.)

- » **Edit Auxiliary (Windows only):** Lets you edit the auxiliary dictionary associated with the active layout. This is where you add, edit, and hyphenate words in the auxiliary dictionary.

- » **Word and Character Count:** Displays the number of words and characters in the active layout or story.

- » **Line Check:** Finds widows (a lone word on a line at the top of a page), orphans (a lone word at the bottom of a page), loosely justified lines, lines that end with a hyphen, and overflow text.

- » **Suggested Hyphenation:** Displays the suggested hyphenation for the current word when it breaks at the end of a line.

- » **Hyphenation Exceptions:** Lets you view and edit the exceptions as well as import and export lists of language-specific hyphenation exceptions.

- » **Convert Project Language:** Lets you convert all the characters in the active project that use a particular character language to a different character language.

- » **Usage:** Lets you view and update the status of fonts, pictures, color profiles, tables, Composition Zones, and assets used in layouts.

- » **Item Styles Usage:** Lets you view and update applied Item Styles.

- » **Job Jackets Manager:** Job Jackets are a collection of requirements and limitations for specific kinds of projects; they ensure that your layouts will output properly. This menu item displays the Job Jackets Manager dialog box.

- ⟫ **Build Index:** Creates an index from the contents of the Index palette.

- ⟫ **Insert Placeholder Text:** Generates random text in the active text box.

- ⟫ **Cloner:** Displays the Cloner dialog box, which lets you copy items or pages to one or more other layouts and projects.

- ⟫ **ImageGrid:** Displays the ImageGrid dialog box, which lets you create a grid of picture boxes and fill them with pictures from a folder.

- ⟫ **Tracking Edit (Windows only; under Edit menu on Mac):** Lets you control tracking (letter spacing for a selection of text) for installed fonts.

- ⟫ **Kerning Table Edit (Windows only; under Edit menu on Mac):** Lets you control kerning, or the spacing between each specific pair of letters, for installed fonts.

- ⟫ **Linkster:** Displays the Linkster dialog box, which lets you link and unlink text boxes in various ways. You learn much more about working with text boxes in Chapter 8.

- ⟫ **ShapeMaker:** Displays the ShapeMaker dialog box, which creates boxes in a mind-boggling number of different shapes.

- ⟫ **Remove Manual Kerning (Windows only; under Style menu on Mac):** Lets you remove all manual kerning applied between characters.

- ⟫ **Font Mapping:** Lets you create and edit rules for substituting a new font for a font that is requested when you open a project, but which is not active on your computer.

- ⟫ **Component Status (Windows only):** Lets you view the status of required software components.

- ⟫ **PPD Manager:** Lets you control which PostScript Printer Description files (PPDs) are loaded in the Print dialog box.

- ⟫ **Convert Old Underlines:** Converts all underlines in the active story from QuarkXPress 3.*x* (Stars & Stripes) format to Type Tricks format.

- ⟫ **XTensions Manager:** Lets you control which XTensions are loaded when you launch QuarkXPress.

- ⟫ **Profile Manager:** Lets you control which color profiles are loaded in QuarkXPress.

- ⟫ **Make QR Code:** Lets you generate Quick Response (QR) codes directly within QuarkXPress and then style and color them the way you want.

- ⟫ **Redline:** Enable and disable automatic tracking and highlighting of text changes or display the Redline palette.

>> **Check Out License/Check In License:** If you have installed Quark License Administrator (QLA), this tool lets you check licenses in and out.

The Window menu

The Window menu lets you manage how you view the projects that are currently open and which palettes are displayed. You can tile multiple projects to see them all at one time, and split one project window into multiple panes (which is useful for working on one part of a layout while also viewing another part of it). The Window menu is also where you control whether your palettes display all the time or only when you move your mouse to the edge of your display. In addition, you can manually invoke the Welcome screen, which lets you open your recently opened projects, create new projects, and access information resources about QuarkXPress.

Using Context Menus

You may have heard of "feature bloat," which happens when an application's developers keep adding new features until the interface is impossible to navigate. Quark's solution to this is twofold: First, QuarkXPress often displays only the controls you need for your current task; and second, it uses context menus.

Context menus are huge timesavers when you haven't yet memorized the shortcut key for a command. Rather than using the mouse to navigate to the menu bar and search for the command, just Control-click (Mac) or right-click (Windows) anything in QuarkXPress. For example, if you right-click a text box, you see the context menu for a text box, as shown in Figure 2-3. If the Item tool is active, you see the menu on the left, which includes only menu items for tasks that you might want to accomplish when the box itself is selected. If the Text tool is active, you see the menu on the right, which includes additional menu items related to formatting or inserting text.

You can even use context menus to help with using palettes. For example, if you are editing text and right-click the name of a style sheet in the Style Sheets palette, the context menu displays options for applying the Style Sheet to the text in various ways, along with options to edit, duplicate, or delete that style sheet, or to create a new style sheet (see Figure 2-4).

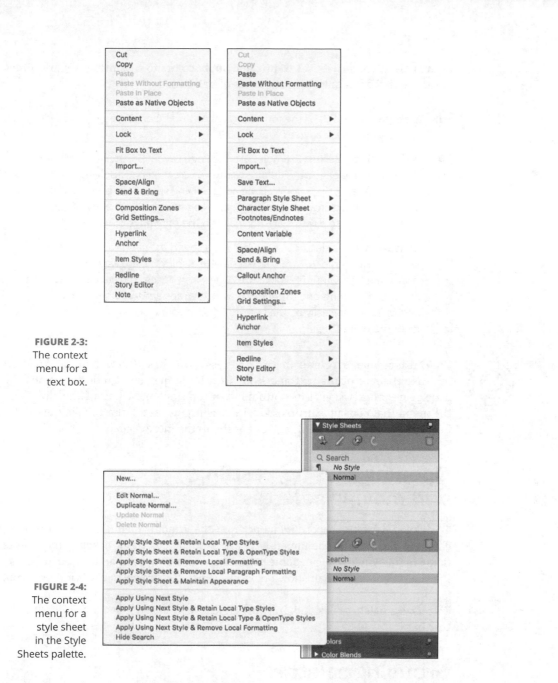

FIGURE 2-3:
The context
menu for a
text box.

FIGURE 2-4:
The context
menu for a
style sheet
in the Style
Sheets palette.

Mastering Palettes

In QuarkXPress, you use palettes to create, edit, and apply attributes to everything on your page. (Quark named them palettes because they're the digital equivalent of the palettes an artist uses to mix and apply colors to a painting.) QuarkXPress has three fundamentally different kinds of palettes:

>> **Tools palette:** Holds all the tools for creating and managing page items. It's normally on the left edge of your display.

>> **Task-specific palettes:** Examples are the Page Layout palette, for creating and rearranging pages; the Colors palette, for creating and applying colors; the Style Sheets palette, for creating and applying sets of attributes to text; and the Layers palette, for clustering items together in layers above or below other items. These palettes are normally on the right edge of your display.

>> **Measurements palette:** This is where you spend the vast majority of your palette-clicking time. This very smart palette displays all the ways you can change the attributes of text, pictures, lines, and boxes. You also use it to align and distribute items and to control how text wraps around other items. For Mac users, it's normally on the bottom edge of your display; Windows users might prefer it at the top.

TIP

The Measurements palette in QuarkXPress 2016 has a new feature: You can increase the size of the text and icons in it by 50 percent. To do that, click the little gear sprocket icon at its bottom left or top right and choose Large Size from the menu that pops up. Surprisingly, increasing the size doesn't make the palette itself very much bigger — it just makes the items more readable.

Opening, closing, resizing, and moving palettes

To display a palette, choose its name from the Window menu. To close a palette, click the close box in the upper-left corner of the palette or deselect the palette name in the Window menu. Some palettes can also be opened and closed by pressing the keyboard shortcut shown next to the palette's name in the Window menu.

To resize a palette, click and drag any edge or corner. To move a palette, drag its title bar.

Grouping palettes

Because QuarkXPress has almost 30 different palettes you can open, it also lets you glue them together into palette groups that stay together as you move them. The steps to create a palette group depend on whether you're using a Mac or Windows:

>> **On a Mac:** Click the gear icon at the top right of any palette. A menu appears that lists every palette in QuarkXPress. Choose one to add it to the top of this palette group. If you choose a palette that's already open, it moves to become part of this palette group. To remove a palette from the palette group, choose it again from the gear icon menu.

>> **In Windows:** Right-click the title bar of a palette and choose any palette name. If you choose a palette that's already open, it moves to become part of this palette group. To remove a palette from the palette group, right-click the palette name and choose Detach *palette name*.

Docking palettes

You can dock a palette or palette group to the left or right edge of your display by dragging it until a blue area appears around it. When you release the mouse, that palette (or palette group) positions itself in the optimum location against that edge. This docking feature also makes palette hiding possible (see the next section).

WARNING

Because of the Measurements palette's width, you can dock it only horizontally, to the upper or lower edge of your display. You can dock the Tools palette either vertically or horizontally.

Hiding palettes (Mac only)

When it comes to working with palettes, Mac users have an advantage over their Windows-using counterparts. After docking a group of palettes, Mac users can hide the group by choosing Window ⇨ Turn Hiding On and then choosing which docked palettes to hide. When you do that, the palettes disappear beyond the edge of your display. When you move your mouse over that area again, the palettes reappear. If you have a small display, hiding palettes is a great way to keep those palettes handy but out of the way to maximize your project space.

Using palette sets

After working on a few projects in QuarkXPress, you may find that you keep some palettes open and others closed while performing certain tasks such as editing text, working with tables, designing a publication, or adding interactivity. By all means, make use of palette sets! This feature lets you store and recall the position and status of all open palettes and libraries so that you can easily switch among different palette arrangements. (To learn about libraries, see Chapter 4.)

To create a palette set, you first display all the palettes that you need for a particular task and hide all other palettes. Then you choose Window ⇨ Palette Sets ⇨ Save Palette Set As and enter a name for your set in the Save As dialog box that appears. If you think that you'll frequently switch to this palette set, you might also want to assign a keyboard shortcut to it (as explained in the next paragraph). To retrieve a palette set, choose Window ⇨ Palette Sets ⇨ *name of palette set* or press the keyboard shortcut for that palette set.

To delete, rename, or assign a keyboard shortcut to an existing palette set, open the Edit Palette Sets dialog box by choosing Window ⇨ Palette Sets ⇨ Edit Palette Sets. Select the palette set in the Edit Palette Sets dialog box and either give it a new name or click the minus (−) icon to delete it. To assign a keyboard shortcut to a palette set, select the set in the dialog box, click the Add Shortcut button, and then press your preferred combination of modifier keys along with a letter, number, or F-key. (Modifier keys on a Mac include Shift, Option, Command, and Control; modifier keys in Windows include Shift, Alt, and Ctrl.) To edit a keyboard shortcut, click the shortcut next to its name and then press your new shortcut keys.

Oddly, QuarkXPress doesn't include a default palette set. So, before you go creating new ones, you may want to save the default palette arrangement as its own set. That way you can get back to what Quark believes is a basic set of useful palettes. Call it "the Palette Set Quark should have included" or maybe just "Default Palette Set."

Searching palettes

You may find that some projects use a ridiculous number of style sheets, colors, or hyperlinks. Thankfully, those three palettes have a search feature that helps you find the one you need. To use it, click the Search field at the top of the list of items in the palette and type in part of the name of the item you want. The list will shorten to display only those items that contain the letters you type.

Organizing with View Sets

The View menu lets you show and hide many combinations of helpful indicators, such as guides, grids, invisible characters, rulers, and so on. When you discover a combination of View menu settings that works especially well for a particular task, you can save that combination as a view set. To do that, first turn on only the view options that you want to store in that view set. Then choose View ⇨ View Sets ⇨ Save View Set As, and in the resulting dialog box, enter a name and optionally assign a key command.

The View menu settings that are remembered in a View Set are the following: Guides, Page Grids, Text Box Grids, Rulers, Ruler Direction, Visual Indicators, Invisibles, Trim View, and Hide Suppressed.

To switch to a view set, do one of the following things:

>> Choose View ⇨ View Sets ⇨ *name of view set.*

>> Press the keyboard combination for the View Set.

>> Display the View Sets palette by choosing View ⇨ View Sets ⇨ Manage View Sets and then double-clicking the name of the View Set in the palette.

To manage your view sets, open the View Sets palette by choosing View ⇨ View Sets ⇨ Manage View Sets. You can then use the Edit, Apply, and Delete buttons at the top of this palette for the selected view set.

QuarkXPress includes three prebuilt view sets that help you get your work done:

>> Authoring View: Displays guides, invisibles, visual indicators, and rulers

>> Default: The set of view options that displays when you create your first layout after launching QuarkXPress for the first time

>> Output Preview: A preview of your layout, as described in the following section

Visualizing with Output Preview

QuarkXPress can display many things that don't appear when you print or export your layout (such as invisible characters, Pasteboard items, guides and gridlines, hyperlink and index markers, and items and layers that have Suppress Output enabled). Fortunately, you have an easy way to preview exactly what will appear when you print or export your layout: Output Preview. Choose View ⇨ View Sets ⇨ Output Preview and you see only the items that will print. Output Preview also trims off anything that extends beyond the edge of the page, so you can see exactly how your layout will look after being printed and trimmed. To get back to seeing your guides, Pasteboard items, invisibles and any page items that have Suppress Output enabled, choose View ⇨ View Sets ⇨ Authoring View. (Items that you want to see onscreen but not export or print can be set to Suppress Output by enabling the Suppress Output check box in the Measurements palette.)

THE FULL-SCREEN MAC EXPERIENCE

If you're using a Mac, you can switch QuarkXPress to Full Screen mode, which minimizes distractions and provides the maximum space for working in QuarkXPress. Here are three ways to get to Full Screen mode:

- Choose View⇨ Enter Full Screen.

- Press Control-Command-F.

- Click the green dot in the top left of your project's title bar.

Full Screen mode hides everything on your display that isn't part of QuarkXPress and causes QuarkXPress's interface items to scurry to the edges of your display. (Even though Full Screen hides the menu bar, you can make it temporarily appear by hovering your mouse pointer at the top of your display.) To exit Full Screen mode and get back to your original view, press Control-Command-F again or hover your mouse pointer at the top of your display to show the menu bar and choose View⇨ Exit Full Screen. Here are two helpful ways to remember the Control-Command-F keyboard shortcut: Press the two absolute highest-level modifier keys (Control and Command), along with F for Full Screen; or be a smug Mac user and remember that because this is a Mac-only feature, and Windows users have only Ctrl as their highest-level modifier, Mac users get to use both Control and Command!

Zooming around Your Layout

The two navigation techniques that you use the most when laying out pages in QuarkXPress are zooming in and out of a page (also known as changing view percentage) and panning around a page. Because these actions are so common, you find tools for them at the bottom of the Tools palette. The Zoom tool looks like a magnifying glass and the Pan tool looks like a hand.

Using the Pan tool

Using the Pan tool is as simple as can be: Hold your mouse button down on the page and drag around. This is handy when you're zoomed in so far that you can't see the entire page.

Using the scroll bars

Just as you do in any window on your computer, if you have more to see than can fit in the window, you can drag the scroll box in the vertical and horizontal scroll bars to see what's out of sight. You can also click the empty area outside the scroll box to jump one screenful in that direction.

Using the Page Up and Page Down keys

If your keyboard has special keys marked Page Up and Page Down, you can use those keys to quickly scroll through your layout pages:

>> **Page Up:** Scroll one screenful up

>> **Page Down:** Scroll one screenful down

>> **Shift+Page Up:** Go to previous page

>> **Shift+Page Down:** Go to next page

Using the Zoom tool

The Zoom tool works as you might expect: Click on the page to zoom into that area. (It zooms 25 percent at a time, but you can change this amount in the Tools section of the QuarkXPress Preferences.) But the Zoom tool also has a couple of hidden tricks:

>> To zoom out of a page, hold down the Option (Mac) or Alt (Windows) or key while clicking with the Zoom tool.

>> To enlarge a particular area to fill your document window, click and drag with the Zoom tool around that area, rather than simply clicking that area. A marquee appears as you drag, and when you let go of your mouse, that area fills your window.

Zooming (even better) with your keyboard and mouse

Although you can also choose various view percentages from the View menu, or use the Zoom and Pan tools, a faster way to zoom in and out of your page is to use your keyboard and mouse instead. Here's how:

>> **Zoom into an area:** Hold down Control (Mac) or Ctrl+Shift (Windows) and drag a marquee around an area of your page. QuarkXPress magnifies that area to fill your window, or to 8000 percent, whichever comes first.

» **Pan around your page:** Press Option (Mac) or Alt+spacebar (Windows) and drag. This gives you the Pan tool until you let up on the key.

» **Zoom into an item:** You can also zoom in by pressing Command/Ctrl++ (plus sign) and zoom out with Command/Ctrl+- (minus sign). The + and – sign keys are to the right of the 0 key on your keyboard. Each time you press these keys, you zoom in or out in 25 percent increments, but you can change that amount in the Zoom Tool setting in the Tools section of the QuarkXPress Preferences.

» **Zoom to a precise view percentage:** Press Control/Ctrl+V to highlight the View Percentage area at the bottom-left corner of your document window and then type any view percentage you'd like.

TIP

The View Percentage field isn't limited to numbered percentages; you can type **T** to view your document as Thumbnails!

» **Fit page in window:** Press Command-0 (Mac) or Ctrl+0 (Windows).

» **Fit the Pasteboard and the page (or spread if there is one) in window:** Press Option-Command-0 (Mac) or Alt+Ctrl+0 (Windows).

» **100% (Actual Size) view:** Press Command-1 (Mac) or Ctrl+1 (Windows).

THE FASTEST NAVIGATOR IN THE WEST

With all these options available for zooming, there is one technique that most users find to be the fastest and most useful. It combines the three best tricks from the previous section and goes like this:

1. **Hold down Control (Mac) or Ctrl (Windows) along with Shift and drag a marquee around the area that you want to work on within your page.**

   QuarkXPress magnifies that area to fill your window.

2. **Make your edits.**

   If you need to make edits nearby, press Option-spacebar (Mac) or Alt+spacebar (Windows) and drag to pan to that area.

3. **Press Command-0 (Mac) or Ctrl+0 (Windows) to zoom back out and see your entire page.**

   In shorthand for Mac/Windows:

   Control/Ctrl+Shift-drag. Option/Alt+spacebar-drag. Command/Ctrl-0. Repeat, repeat, repeat!

On a Mac that has a trackpad, you can zoom out by pinching with two fingers, or zoom in by spreading two fingers apart. When a picture box is selected and the Picture Content tool is active, you can use two fingers to rotate the picture inside its box.

Moving through pages

As with almost everything in QuarkXPress, you have several ways to navigate from page to page as follows:

>> **Page menu:** You can choose Previous, Next, First, Last, or Go To. Go To is incredibly useful when you know the page number you want to, well, go to. QuarkXPress power users use Go To's keyboard shortcut all day long: Command/Ctrl-J. Soon, muscle memory takes over and you're typing Command/Ctrl-J followed by a number to get to the page you need — no mousing required!

>> **Page Layout palette:** Double-click a page on the Page Layout palette to go to that page.

>> **Scroll bars:** Drag the scroll box to watch pages fly by your document window.

>> **Layout controls:** The layout controls are at the bottom-left corner of your document window. To go to a specific page, click the Page Number field and type in a new page number. To choose from thumbnail previews of the pages, click the upward-pointing triangle to the right of the Page Number field. To go to the previous page, click the left-pointing triangle. To go to the next page, click the right-pointing triangle.

Using Split Views

By splitting a window into two or more panes, you can display multiple views of a project at the same time, which has these benefits:

>> You can see your edits in all panes simultaneously.

>> You can view several pages at the same time.

>> You can view several layouts at the same time.

>> You can use a different view mode in each pane.

>> You can view your work at different magnifications at the same time.

Splitting a window

You have three ways to split a window:

>> Choose Window ⇨ Split Window ⇨ Horizontal or Window ⇨ Split Window ⇨ Vertical.

>> (Windows only) Click the split bar to the right of the scroll bar (for a vertical split) or at the top of the scroll bar (for a horizontal split).

>> Click the split window icons in the layout controls area at the bottom left of the project window (refer to Figure 2-2).

After a window has been split, you can change the width and height of the splits by dragging the bars between the splits.

You can split panes multiple times horizontally or vertically within a pane, to see several views of your project at the same time. To do that, use the same window-splitting techniques mentioned previously in this section.

Removing splits and panes

To remove one pane, click the Close button (X) in the top-right corner of the pane. To remove all split panes from a window, choose Window ⇨ Split Window ⇨ Remove All.

Switching among Layouts

If your project has multiple layouts, you can switch among them in two ways:

>> Each layout is represented by a tab just below the project's title bar. Click the one with the name of the layout you want to switch to.

>> The Layout menu lets you choose to go to the Previous, Next, First, or Last layout in the order they appear in the layout tabs. Or, choose Go To and choose a layout by name from the list that appears.

On a Mac, the order of the layout tabs isn't fixed — you can drag them left or right to change their order.

IN THIS CHAPTER

» **Creating boxes, lines, and arrows**

» **Using the Bézier Pen tool**

» **Formatting frames and lines**

» **Flowing text along text paths**

» **Converting text to outlines**

» **Using ShapeMaker for shapes**

» **Converting PDF, EPS, or Illustrator files to native QuarkXPress items**

» **Converting objects from InDesign, Microsoft Office, and other apps to native QuarkXPress items**

Chapter **3**

Creating Items

QuarkXPress calls the building blocks of a page — boxes and lines, for example —*items.* If an item has something inside it, such as text or a picture, QuarkXPress calls this material *content.* To create a layout, you usually draw a few text boxes and picture boxes, and then insert text and pictures into those boxes.

In this chapter, you find out how to create all the essential items that you can use in a layout in QuarkXPress. The chapter introduces you to working with the tools that enable you to create text boxes, picture boxes, lines, and tables, and text paths for your text. You also see how to go beyond the basic shapes by working with Bézier lines and shapes, converting live text to boxes (containers), making arrows, and using the powerful ShapeMaker to generate beautiful, complex shapes.

Plus, QuarkXPress has the unique capability to convert objects from other applications and manipulate them exactly as if they were created in QuarkXPress! You can copy and paste anything from Microsoft Word, Excel, PowerPoint, and other Office apps, or even entire pages from Adobe InDesign or Illustrator, and then use the powerful tools in QuarkXPress to customize those items to match your corporate brand. You can also convert a PDF file from *any* application into native QuarkXPress items — an unprecedented feature for a page layout application. In this chapter, you learn how to import content from all these places, with some tips for improving the process.

Using the Item and Content Tools

The basic types of items that comprise a layout in QuarkXPress are the following:

>> **Boxes:** Text boxes, picture boxes, and no-content boxes, which are useful for creating decorative items. Boxes can take any imaginable shape, from rectangular to wavy.

>> **Lines:** Simple lines, arrows, and paths for text. Lines can be straight or Bézier (flexible).

>> **Groups:** Sets of items that have been stuck together so that they behave like a single item.

>> **Tables:** Can contain both text and pictures.

The tools for creating all these items are (not surprisingly) in the Tools palette, shown in Figure 3-1. (For an overview of all the palettes in QuarkXPress, see Chapter 2.) In fact, the principles of *item* and *content* are so basic to QuarkXPress that almost all the tools in the Tools palette are dedicated to making or adjusting items and their content. For example:

>> The Item tool lets you move, resize, rotate, reshape, cut, copy, and paste items.

>> The Text Content tool lets you create rectangular text boxes, as well as select text in text boxes or on text paths.

>> The Picture Content tool lets you create rectangular picture boxes, manipulate pictures in picture boxes, and cut, copy, and paste pictures in picture boxes.

I tell you about the Picture Content tool in the upcoming section, and explain the Item, Text Content, and other tools in the Tools palette in this and other chapters as they become relevant to the tasks being explained.

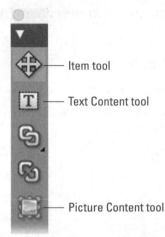

— Item tool

— Text Content tool

— Picture Content tool

FIGURE 3-1:
Tools in the
Tools palette.

Creating Boxes

Boxes in QuarkXPress can have any shape that you want to give them, and there are three kinds:

>> **Text box:** This type of box is a container for text. You can optionally link text boxes together so that a story flows from one to the next, as shown in Figure 3-2.

>> **Picture box:** This box serves as a container for a picture, illustration, or PDF.

>> **"No-content" box:** This is just what it sounds like: An empty box, which is often used to create an area of color or a multicolor blend.

TIP

If you accidentally make a text box when you need a picture box (or vice versa), don't worry — you can easily change it. One way is to select the box, choose Item ⇨ Content, and then choose Picture, Text, or None. Another way is to ignore what kind of box it is and import whatever you want into it. For example, if you import a picture into a text box, it becomes a picture box; if you import text into a picture box, it becomes a text box.

FIGURE 3-2:
Three linked
text boxes.

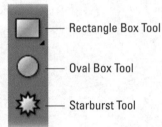

As you might guess, you use different tools to create different types of boxes, as follows:

>> **Rectangular Text box:** Click and drag with the Text Content tool.

>> **Rectangular Picture box:** Click and drag with the Picture Content tool.

>> **"No-content" box:** Click and drag with the Rectangle Box tool, the Oval Box tool, or the Starburst tool (depending on what shape you want), as shown in Figure 3-3.

Rectangle Box Tool

Oval Box Tool

Starburst Tool

FIGURE 3-3:
The "no-
content" tools.

TIP

You can also create a square with the Rectangle Box tool, or a circle with the Oval tool, by holding down the Shift key while creating the item. For extra fun, hold down the Option (Mac) or Alt (Windows) key along with the Shift key to draw the square or circle out from its center! This is handy when you want to draw a box or circle around another item.

TIP

You can use the no-content Rectangle, Oval, and Starburst box tools to create a text box or picture box in those shapes. To make a text box, press T as you draw one of these boxes, or choose Item ⇨ Content ⇨ Text after creating it. To make a Picture box, press R as you draw a no-content box, or choose Item ⇨ Content ⇨ Picture after creating it.

That's all there is to creating rectangular and oval boxes! In later sections, you learn to create boxes with infinite shapes, including how to convert text to shapes you can fill and distort.

Creating Lines and Arrows

The second most common shape in most layouts is a line. In QuarkXPress, you can format lines with an almost infinite variety of stripes, dashes, and dots, and if you apply an arrowhead to a line, you get an arrow. Read on to learn how to create and format lines and arrows.

Creating lines

The Tools palette contains four tools for creating lines: two for straight lines and two for curvy lines. I tell you how to create curvy lines later in this chapter, in the "Building Bézier boxes and lines" section, but you're in the right place to find out how to create a straight line, which you do by using one of these two tools, shown in Figure 3-4:

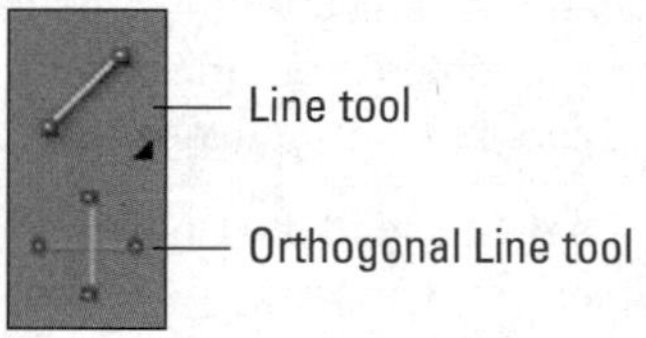

FIGURE 3-4:
The two straight-line tools.

— Line tool

— Orthogonal Line tool

>> **Line tool:** Produces a straight line at any angle. To use the Line tool, click and hold the mouse button, drag, and release the mouse to create a line. To constrain the angle to perfectly horizontal, perfectly vertical, or 45-degree lines, hold down the Shift key while drawing the line.

>> **Orthogonal Line tool:** Produces only a vertical or horizontal straight line and lines at a 45-degree angle.

Chances are, you'll want to do more with your lines than simply plunk them down on your layout, so keep reading for more details about working with lines.

Changing line attributes

To change the line thickness, style, color, or transparency, or to change the line to an arrow, you can use either the Style menu or the controls in the Home (Mac) or Classic (Windows) tab of the Measurements palette, as shown in Figure 3-5. The following sections give you the details.

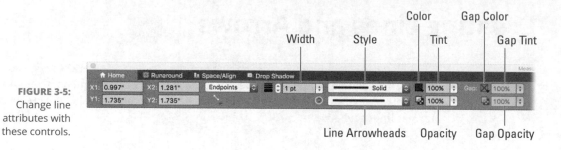

FIGURE 3-5:
Change line
attributes with
these controls.

Changing line width

From the Measurements palette, you can change the line width in three ways:

>> Click the up or down arrow on the left of the Line Width field (see Figure 3-6). Each click changes the width to the next preset size.

>> Click the Line Width field and type in a new width. To use inches, centimeters, or millimeters instead of points, enter the unit after the number. For example, enter **.25"** for .25 inches, **1cm** for 1 centimeter, or **5mm** for 5 millimeters. QuarkXPress converts the value to points when you leave the Line Width field.

>> Click the up or down arrows on the right end of the Line Width field and choose a preset width from the menu that appears.

TIP

One of the width presets is Hairline, but it's best to avoid that one because its printed width varies with the output device. On a PostScript imagesetter, for example, the width is .125 pt; other printers usually print a hairline as the thinnest line they can print.

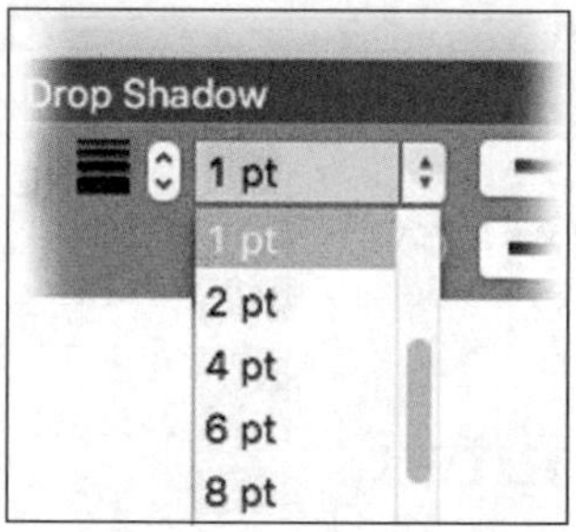

FIGURE 3-6:
The Line Width
control.

REMEMBER

Instead of using the Measurements palette, you can choose preset line attributes from the Style menu. However, you can't enter your own values as you can when you're working in the Measurements palette.

Changing line style

QuarkXPress offers several time-tested line styles, and you can add new ones by choosing Edit ⇨ Dashes & Stripes. If you choose a dotted or dashed style, you can customize the color and opacity of the spaces between the dots or dashes (the "gap") with the controls that appear at the right of the controls that you use to set the color and opacity of the solid dots or dashes, as shown in Figure 3-7.

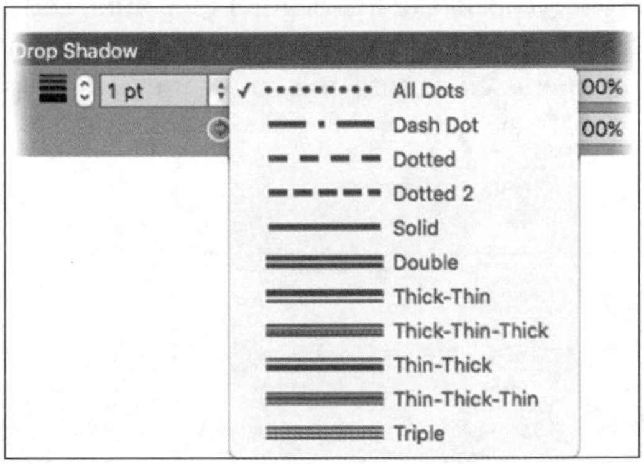

FIGURE 3-7:
The Line Style control.

Creating an arrow

To make an arrow, choose a style from the Line Arrowheads control shown in Figure 3-8. Note that some have tail feathers and others don't, and the last one has an arrowhead at both ends!

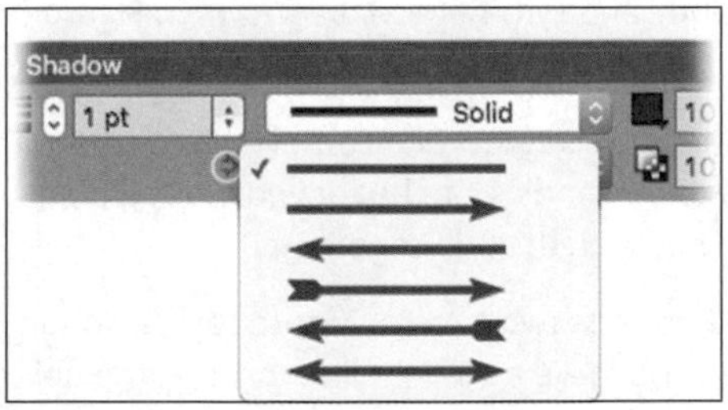

FIGURE 3-8:
The Line Arrowheads control.

Building Bézier Boxes and Lines

When you want to create a box or line that's more complex than a simple rectangle, oval, or starburst, you enter the realm of the Bézier path. (Pierre Bézier was an engineer at the French automaker Renault who patented and popularized a way to control smooth curves.) If you've used the Pen tool in Adobe Illustrator or Photoshop, you already understand Bézier paths. If not, read on — it takes some practice and a relaxed mind to grasp how to use Bézier tools, so don't be surprised if you feel a little frustrated at first.

Understanding Bézier shapes

A Bézier shape (or path) consists of line segments, points, and curve handles. Line segments connect at points. Handles are attached to the points and control the shape of the line segments going into and out of the points. Figure 3-9 shows an example of a Bézier path and shape.

FIGURE 3-9: A Bézier path (left) and Bézier shape (right), with curve handles attached to the point connecting two line segments.

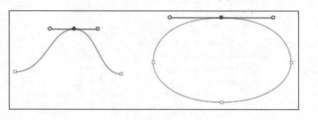

Here's a breakdown of the terms used to describe the various parts of a Bézier shape:

>> **Point:** A point connects two line segments. QuarkXPress has three kinds of points: corner, smooth, and symmetrical, as shown in Figure 3-10:

- **Corner point:** Connects two straight lines, a straight line and a curved line, or two curved lines that connect at a corner. When connecting curved lines, a corner point's curve handles can be moved independently to form a sharp transition between the two segments.

- **Smooth point:** Connects two curved lines to form a continuous curve. The curve handles always make a straight line through the point, but they can be lengthened independently.

- **Symmetrical point:** As with a smooth point, a symmetrical point connects two curved lines to form a continuous curve. However, the curve handles are always equidistant from the point.

>> **Curve handles:** Extend from both sides of a point and control a curve's shape.

>> **Line segments:** Straight or curved line sections connecting two points.

FIGURE 3-10:
A corner
point (left),
smooth point
(center), and
symmetrical
point (right).

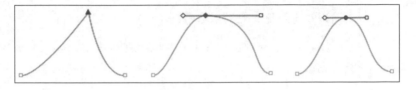

Drawing a Bézier box

To draw a Bézier box, follow these steps

1. **Activate the Bézier Pen tool in the Tools palette and then click to drop the first point anywhere on the page.**

2. **Move the pointer to where you want the next point.**

3. **Click to create additional points and line segments.**

   To create a straight line and corner point, click without dragging. To create a curved line segment and smooth point, click and drag where you want the next point positioned. A point with two curve handles appears, and you can control the curve's shape by dragging a curve handle. To create a point that connects a curve to a straight segment, press Option (Mac) or Alt (Windows) while dragging a smooth point. This creates a curved segment and corner point.

4. **To edit the Bézier shape while you are still drawing it, do the following:**

   - **To add a point to an existing segment:** Click the segment where you want the point to be.

   - **To delete a point from the shape while you are drawing it:** Click the point.

5. **To complete the box, close the path by positioning the mouse pointer over the beginning of the path; then click when the pointer changes to the Close Box pointer.**

   The Close Box pointer looks like a pen nib with a tiny diamond at its bottom right, as shown in Figure 3-11.

FIGURE 3-11:
The Close Box
pointer.

When any of the drawing tools are active, you can temporarily switch to the Select Point tool by pressing Command (Mac) or Ctrl (Windows). When the Select Point tool is active, you can temporarily switch to the Item tool by pressing Command–Option (Mac) or Ctrl+Alt (Windows).

TIP

Using the Pen tools

Each Pen tool (see Figure 3-12) has a different purpose. Here's what each one does:

>> **Bézier Pen:** This is the main tool for creating Bézier lines and boxes. To constrain its angle to 45 degrees, press and hold Shift while drawing. To adjust or edit a Bézier path, use the tools described next.

>> **Add Point:** Adds a point to an existing line segment. Adding a point to a regular (non-Bézier) content box automatically turns the content box into a Bézier item.

>> **Remove Point:** Removes a point from a path.

>> **Convert Point:** Automatically converts corner points to curve points, and curve points to corner points. Click and drag to change the position of a point, the curve of a curved-line segment, or the position of a straight-line segment. Click a rectangular box or straight line to convert it to a Bézier box or line.

>> **Scissors:** Cuts an item into separate paths. You can use the **Scissors** tool to cut the outline of a box and turn it into a line, or to cut a line or text path into two. When you cut a picture box, it is converted to a Bézier line and its content is removed. When you cut a text box, it is converted to a text path. When you cut a text path, it is converted into two linked text paths.

>> **Select Point:** Selects curves or points so that you can move them or delete them. Shift-click to select multiple points. Hold down Option (Mac) or Alt (Windows) and click a point to make it symmetrical.

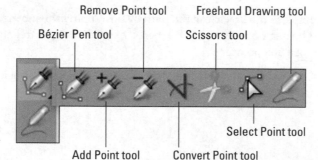

FIGURE 3-12: The Bézier Pen tools.

Remove Point tool   Freehand Drawing tool

Bézier Pen tool   Scissors tool

Select Point tool

Add Point tool   Convert Point tool

Using the magic Freehand Drawing tool

If you can't get the hang of using the Pen tools, try the Freehand Drawing tool, which creates a smooth curve as you drag your mouse around the page. If you finish a drawing by ending on the beginning point, the drawing becomes a box;

otherwise it remains a line. To automatically close a freehand drawing with a straight-line segment, press Option (Mac) or Alt (Windows) before you release the mouse button.

Editing Bézier shapes

QuarkXPress gives you several different ways to edit the shape of a Bézier shape, including choosing one of the standard QuarkXPress shapes from the Item menu and using the Select Point tool or Bézier Pen tool in the Tools palette. I describe these three techniques in the next sections.

Changing a Bézier shape to a standard shape

To change the shape to a standard rectangle, oval, or line, choose Item ➪ Shape and choose the desired shape from the Shape menu.

Editing with the Select Point tool

To select curves or points so that you can move or delete them, use the Select Point tool, shown in Figure 3-12. Shift-click to select multiple points. Hold down Option (Mac) or Alt (Windows) and click a point to make it symmetrical.

Editing with the Bézier Pen tool

>> To add a point to a Bézier box while working with the Bézier Pen tool, click a line segment or use the Add Point tool.

>> To remove a point from a Bézier box while working with the Bézier Pen tool, click the point or use the Remove Point tool.

>> To convert a point to another kind of point while working with the Bézier Pen tool, Option-click (Mac) or Alt-click (Windows) the point or use the Convert Point tool.

>> To move a point or change the shape of a line segment while working with the Bézier Pen tool, hold down Command (Mac) or Ctrl (Windows) and drag the point or line segment.

TIP

To pan the layout while a Pen tool is selected, press Shift+Spacebar and then click and drag.

Converting an existing box or line to Bézier

Now that you're all hot about making and editing Bézier shapes, here's a trick to converting an existing box or line so that you can reshape it with the Pen tools:

With the item selected, choose Item ⇨ Shape. If your item is a box, choose the shape from the Shape submenu that looks like a painter's palette. If your item is a line, choose the curvy line. After that, you can use any of the Pen tools to reshape your item to infinity and beyond.

TIP

You can also convert a regular box or line into a Bézier item with either of two Pen tools: Just click a line segment with the Add Point or Convert Point tool.

Applying Frames, Dashes, and Stripes

In QuarkXPress, a *frame* is a decorative border that you can place around any kind of box. Frames and lines have the same choices for style, width, color, and opacity — the only difference is where you access them:

>> To access frame controls for an active box, click the Frame tab of the Measurements palette.

>> To access attribute controls for an active line, click the Home/Classic tab of the Measurements palette.

Use the controls in Figure 3-13 to specify style, width, color, and opacity. If the frame or line style contains gaps, you can also specify gap color and opacity.

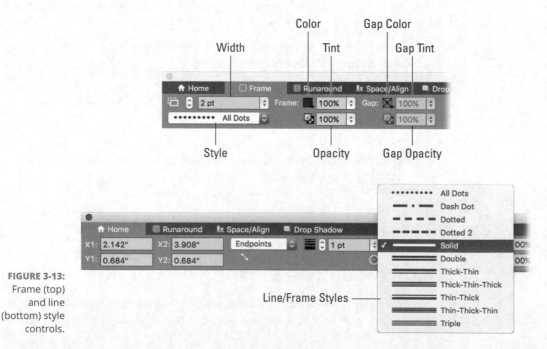

FIGURE 3-13:
Frame (top)
and line
(bottom) style
controls.

WARNING

When applying a "Scotch rule" style (any of the thick-and-thin combinations), be sure to choose a width that's wide enough to be clearly seen when printed. Try a minimum of 6 points for a double line and 9 points for a triple line.

REMEMBER

Frames always extend from the edge of a box to the inside of the box unless you reverse this behavior in the Framing Preferences. (The purpose of this behavior is to keep boxes aligned regardless of whether they have a frame.) To change the frame position to Outside, choose QuarkXPress ⇨ Preferences (Mac) or Edit ⇨ Preferences (Windows) and scroll down to the Print Layout or Digital Layout section (depending on whether you're working on a Print or Digital layout). In the Layout section, go to the General section and locate the Inside and Outside radio buttons next to Framing. When you select one of these radio buttons, you get the following:

>> **Inside:** The frame on a picture box overlaps the picture, and the frame on a text box insets the text farther into the box.

>> **Outside:** The frame is placed outside the box, increasing the box's width and height.

TIP

You can create your own frame styles by choosing Edit ⇨ Dashes and Stripes.

Creating Text Paths

When you want a string of text to follow a line or a shape, you add that text to a text path. You can adjust the following: how text rides the path; the attributes of the text (font, color, size and so forth); and the attributes of the path.

To add text to a line or path, double-click the line or path with the Text Content tool. Then either begin typing or paste in any text you previously copied to the Clipboard. You can format the text using any of the controls in the Measurements palette.

TIP

To convert a selected box (of any shape) to a text path, first change its content to text by choosing Item ⇨ Content ⇨ Text. Then choose Item ⇨ Shape and choose the squiggly line icon to convert the box to a path.

To control the starting point of the text, use the usual text formatting techniques such as left indent, tabs, or spaces.

To control how the text rides the path, select the path and then use the controls in either the Text Box tab of the Measurements palette (Mac) or the Text Path tab of the Measurements palette (Windows). Using the controls shown in Figure 3-14, you can make the text bend along the path in four different ways, flip it to the other side of the path (good for running text *inside* the path), and control where the text sits vertically on the path.

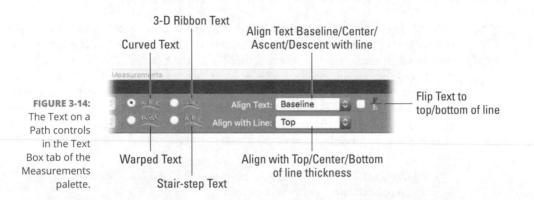

FIGURE 3-14:
The Text on a Path controls in the Text Box tab of the Measurements palette.

3-D Ribbon Text

Curved Text

Align Text Baseline/Center/
Ascent/Descent with line

Flip Text to
top/bottom of line

Warped Text

Align with Top/Center/Bottom
of line thickness

Stair-step Text

PUTTING TEXT ON A CIRCLE

Text on a circle — that is, text following the outside of a circle or oval — is a common design element. This is really easy to do in QuarkXPress, but it's not at all obvious how. Just follow these steps:

1. **Get the Oval tool from the Tools palette and draw out an oval the size you need on your page, and then hold down the Shift key to draw a perfect circle.**

   This creates a "no content" oval or circle.

2. **With the oval selected, choose Item ⇨ Content ⇨ Text.**

   The no-content oval converts to a text box.

3. **Get the Text Content tool from the Tools palette and type your text into the oval.**

4. **Click and hold the Bézier Pen tool in the Tools palette to display the array of Pen tools; then slide over to the Scissors tool to select it.**

5. **Click the oval at the location where you want the text to start, end, or be centered.**

   If the text is left-aligned, click where you want it to start. If the text is right-aligned, then click where you want it to end. If the text is center-aligned, then click where you want the text to be centered.

6. **If the oval (which is now a path) has a frame and you want to remove it, change its color to None in the Measurements palette.**

7. **Adjust the position of the text on the path using the Text on a Path controls (refer to Figure 3-14).**

If (for some strange reason) you want text to flow from a text path to other text paths, text boxes, or text cells in a table, you can use the Text Linking tools, as explained in Chapter 8.

Converting Text to Outlines for Special Effects

The text formatting controls in the Measurements palette are fantastic, but there are some effects you can't create on live text, such as filling text with a picture or a color blend (gradient), or reshaping the outline of an individual character. To achieve these effects, you need to convert the text to Bézier boxes, which you can easily do by following these steps:

1. Select the character or characters you want to convert.

2. Choose Item ➪ Text to Boxes and one of these options from its submenu:

- **Unanchored:** To convert selected text to unanchored Bézier boxes, choose Unanchored. The text is copied, converted to boxes, and placed lower on the page.

- **Anchored:** To convert selected text to anchored Bézier boxes, choose Anchored. This option converts the text to boxes and replaces the text with anchored boxes within the story. (For more on anchored items, see Chapter 14.) This technique is handy when you want to convert a small amount of text, such as a drop cap, and keep it within the flow of text.

- **Convert Entire Box:** To convert all the characters in a text box or multiple text boxes to unanchored Bézier boxes, choose Convert Entire Box. This option removes the text from its box, converts each line to a merged set of boxes, and places each merged set in the same location on the page as the original lines of text. The original text box (now empty) remains below the converted text.

After your text is converted to Bézier boxes, you can treat them exactly like other boxes: Fill them with pictures or color blends, use the Pen tools to reshape them, and so on.

If you paste or import a picture into the converted text, the entire string of text acts as a combined mask for the picture. If you want to put a different picture in each letter, separate them by choosing Item ➪ Split ➪ Outside Paths or Item ➪ Split ➪ All Paths. Splitting "outside paths" maintains the counters (holes) in the letters, to see through them to whatever is behind. Splitting "all paths" unmerges the holes from their surrounding letters, causing them to be shapes on top of the letters.

REMEMBER

After you convert text to boxes, it is no longer editable as text — you can't type new letters to replace old ones. Those original letters have been converted into boxes shaped like the original letters.

Using ShapeMaker to Generate Boxes and Lines

If you've absorbed the many techniques in this chapter for creating and editing the shape of boxes, you may be thinking "This is all very complicated if all I want is a triangle, a rectangle with just two rounded corners, or a spiral-shaped text path." And you would be absolutely correct! That's why QuarkXPress includes Shape-Maker, which automatically creates complex geometrical boxes and lines for you.

TIP

If you select an existing box or line before launching ShapeMaker, you can apply all the magic in ShapeMaker to that box or line. Otherwise, ShapeMaker creates a new box or line for you.

ShapeMaker's many controls are beyond the scope of this book, but they are explained completely in *A Guide to QuarkXPress 2016* at (`http://www.quark.com/Support/Documentation/QuarkXPress/2016.aspx`). However, to get you started, this chapter covers the basics.

To launch ShapeMaker, choose Utilities ➪ ShapeMaker. The dialog box shown in Figure 3-15 appears.

The tabs at the top of the ShapeMaker dialog box let you switch to the different shape-making options (waves, polygons, spirals, and rectangles) as well as a Presets tab for creating and managing preprogrammed shapes that you commonly make. You can start with these preset shapes and modify as you like. The shape preview in each tab is live, and as you make changes to the controls, the shape reflects those changes.

The bottom area of the dialog box is the same on all the tabs and contains these controls:

>> **Item:** Lets you choose whether you want to create a text box, picture box, no-content box, text path, or rule path (line).

>> **Width** and **Height:** Let you enter a width and height for the box or path.

>> **Columns** and **Gutters:** When you select Text Box from the Item menu, these fields let you specify how many columns you want in the text box and how wide the gutters between them should be.

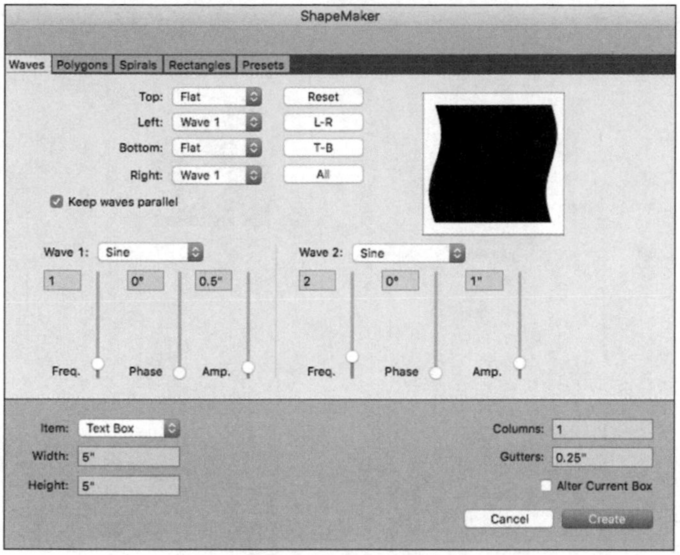

FIGURE 3-15:
The
ShapeMaker
dialog box.

>> **Lines** and **Spacing:** When you select Text Path is selected from the Item menu, you can specify how many lines to create and how much space you want between them.

>> **Alter Current Box:** If a box is selected when you choose Utilities ⇨ ShapeMaker, ShapeMaker updates that box instead of creating a new box.

Creating shapes from scratch

As mentioned previously, the ShapeMaker dialog box provides tabs for creating waves, polygons, spirals, and rectangles. On the Waves tab, you create boxes with wavy sides by choosing from drop-down menus how you want the top, bottom, left, and right sides of the box to appear. The buttons to the right of the drop-down menus let you reset or apply shapes to various combinations of sides.

Figure 3-16 shows the Waves tab in the ShapeMaker dialog box.

The Polygons tab lets you create boxes with multiple straight sides, as shown in Figure 3-17. The settings on this tab require you to choose what type of polygon you want (polygon, star, polygram, spirogram, golden rectangle, and double square) and then set parameters for that shape. The Golden Rectangle shape is particularly useful when you want to create a rectangle based on the golden mean. Even if you don't know what a golden mean is, it's fun to play around with the options in the Polygons tab!

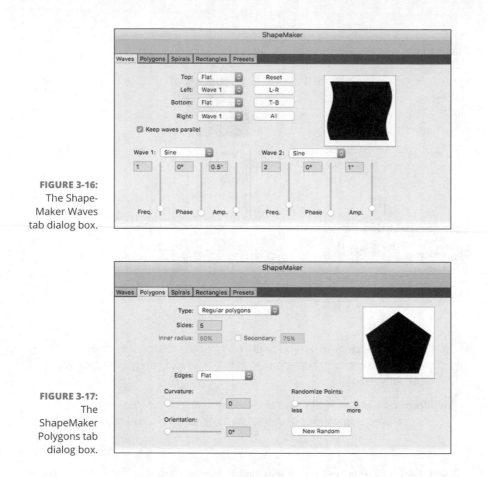

FIGURE 3-16:
The Shape-Maker Waves tab dialog box.

FIGURE 3-17:
The ShapeMaker Polygons tab dialog box.

The Spirals tab lets you create spiral lines, as shown in Figure 3-18. Among the options in the Type drop-down menu are Archimedes (for a uniform distance between arms) and Golden, which you can use to create your own snail or nautilus shell. To make the resulting spiral be a path you can add text to, choose Text Path from the Item menu.

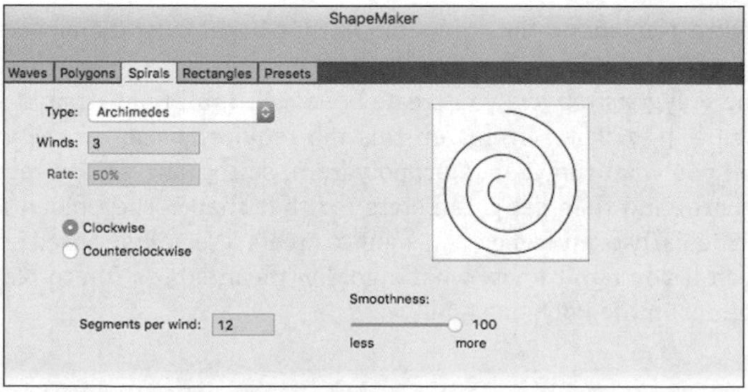

FIGURE 3-18:
The ShapeMaker Spirals tab dialog box.

The Rectangles tab lets you create rectangular boxes with customized corners, as show in Figure 3-19. The drop-down menu lets you choose a corner type (Normal, Rounded, Beveled, Concave, Pointed, or Inset) and a diameter for the corner effect. If you want to create a rectangle that has fewer than four rounded corners, use ShapeMaker — it's far easier than trying to draw one with the Pen tool or trying to combine shapes with the Item ⇨ Merge Or Split Paths menu item.

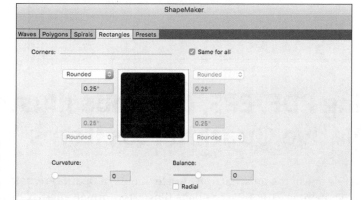

FIGURE 3-19: The ShapeMaker Rectangles tab dialog box.

Working with shapes found on the Presets tab

The Presets tab lets you save and manage combinations of settings you want to use again later, as shown in Figure 3-20 below. To create and use your own preset, first make all the changes you want to save in each of the tabbed areas. (Your preset will store all the settings in all the tabs.) Then you can do the following:

>> **To store all the settings in all the tabs:** Type a name in the Name field and click Save. A named preset is added to the list on the left, with (oddly) an image of the shape from the last tab you were looking at.

>> **To load a set of saved settings:** Select it in the list on the left, click Use Settings, and then click any tab to use those saved settings.

>> **To replace the settings in a preset with the settings currently in the ShapeMaker tabs:** Select the preset and click Replace.

>> **To delete a preset:** Select it and click Delete.

>> **To rename a preset:** Select it and click Rename.

>> **To restore all tabs to the settings they had when you opened the ShapeMaker dialog box:** Click Revert All.

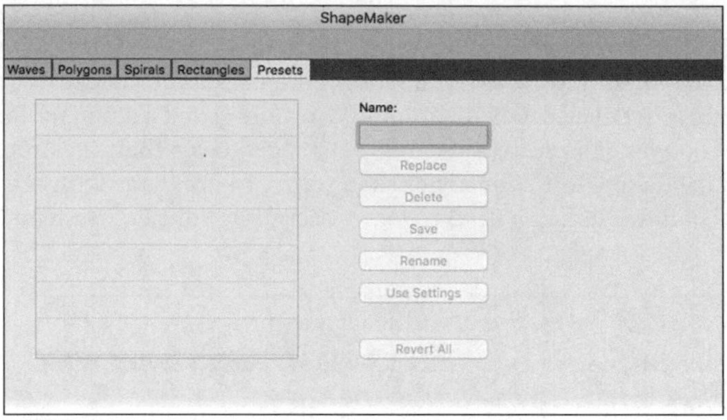

FIGURE 3-20:
The
ShapeMaker
Presets tab
dialog box.

Converting PDF, EPS, or Adobe Illustrator Files to Native QuarkXPress Items

Here's one of the most exciting developments in QuarkXPress: If you already have a document in PDF, EPS, or Adobe Illustrator format, QuarkXPress 2016 can convert all its objects to native QuarkXPress items for you in just a few seconds. You can then work with those items just as you can with any other items in QuarkXPress. To convert entire files from another format into QuarkXPress items, follow these steps:

1. **If the PDF, EPS, or AI file is already in a picture box on your QuarkXPress page, select it; if not, choose File ⇨ Import.**

2. **Navigate to the file you want to import and click Open; and if the file is a multipage PDF, choose the page you want to import.**

   QuarkXPress creates a new picture box containing the file.

3. **With the new picture box selected, choose Style ⇨ Convert to Native Objects (or right-click and choose Convert to Native Objects).**

4. **In the Convert to Native Objects dialog box, select the Retain Source Picture Box check box if you want to keep the original picture box as well as make a converted copy.**

   QuarkXPress converts the pictures, text, shapes, and lines in that file to native QuarkXPress items. If some of the items overlap in unexpected ways, try deselecting the other two options in that dialog box (Ignore Soft Masks and Ignore Transparent Blend Modes) and then convert again.

5. **To edit individual items, choose Item ⇨ Ungroup.**

   If you have many items, you may need to repeat the Item ⇨ Ungroup command, or choose Item ⇨ Ungroup All to ungroup all groups within groups.

You don't have to convert an entire document. If you import the file into a QuarkXPress picture box and crop it, only the area showing in the box is converted. (See Chapter 13 to learn all about importing and cropping pictures.)

I can't overstate the usefulness of this capability. Designers often work with charts, graphs, and PowerPoint slides that almost never use the correct colors or fonts for a company's brand. Conveniently, when you convert these items to native items in QuarkXPress 2016, their colors are added to the Colors palette, where you can replace them all at one time with your brand-approved colors. The text in these graphics is also converted to native QuarkXPress text, so you can easily format it to match the brand by using style sheets.

After they've been converted, vector graphics become native QuarkXPress items and Adobe Illustrator paths become QuarkXPress paths with the exact same Bézier anchor points as in Illustrator. You can then use the Bézier (pen) tools in QuarkXPress to adjust them. (See "Building Bézier Boxes and Lines," earlier in this chapter, to learn about using Beziér paths.)

Here's a time-saving use for these conversions: Publications almost always receive advertisements in PDF format, and after they're converted to native QuarkXPress items, the publication can update prices, dates, and colors inside the ad. That capability has never existed in a page layout program before.

Also, publishers who import charts or maps now have a unique trick available to use. After converting to native QuarkXPress items, you can resize the chart or map without changing the size of the text within it. The Scale feature (choose Item ⇨ Scale to use it) in QuarkXPress lets you choose which attributes to scale, as described in Chapter 4.

Product labels and packaging are another good candidate for conversion. Many packaging designers use Adobe Illustrator and provide art to their clients in native Illustrator or PDF format. But if you're more comfortable in QuarkXPress, you can convert the art to native QuarkXPress items and easily update them. (Plus, the onscreen preview in QuarkXPress is much more clear and accurate than Illustrator's!)

To convert your QuarkXPress layout back to Adobe Illustrator, export it in PDF format (File ⇨ Export ⇨ Layout as PDF) and then open the PDF in Illustrator. However, do this *only* if absolutely necessary, because Illustrator won't recognize your QuarkXPress layers, and many items will break into smaller parts, making editing very difficult.

TIP

QuarkXPress currently imports only one page at a time from a PDF file. If you want to import multiple pages simultaneously, try PDF Importer XT from www.creationauts.com. This $20 XTension lets you choose which pages to import from a PDF: selected pages, or only the even or odd pages. When importing the

PDF, the XTension creates a new QuarkXPress page for each page in the PDF and optionally converts its objects to native QuarkXPress items.

TIP

If you don't want to invest in the PDF Importer XTension mentioned in the preceding tip, you can still import multiple pages of a PDF simultaneously. The trick requires Adobe Acrobat and using the ImageGrid utility in QuarkXPress, using the steps that follow:

1. **Open the PDF in Acrobat and find where Acrobat lets you extract multiple pages as separate PDF files.**

   The location is different in each version of Acrobat, so look for the area containing the Pages tools and then look for Extract.

2. **After extracting all the pages as separate PDFs, rename the first nine so that the number in their filename has a 0 before it (for example, change 1 to 01, 2 to 02, and so on).**

   That way the pages are imported in the correct order.

3. **In QuarkXPress choose Utilities ➪ ImageGrid to open the ImageGrid dialog box.**

4. **In the ImageGrid dialog box, select the Autosize To radio button and enter 1 into both the rows and columns fields, as shown in Figure 3-21.**

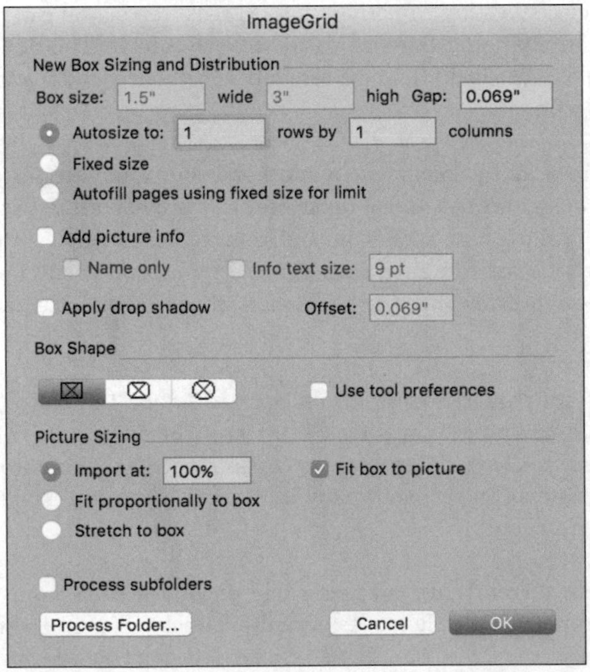

FIGURE 3-21:
The ImageGrid
dialog box.

5. **Click the Process Folder button in the ImageGrid dialog box and choose the folder that contains your separate PDF page files.**

6. **Watch while QuarkXPress builds a new page for each PDF file and imports the PDF into a picture box on it.**

7. **(Optional) Select the picture box on each page and choose Style⇨ Convert to Native Objects to convert the PDF to native QuarkXPress items.**

Converting Objects from InDesign, Microsoft Office, and Other Apps to Native QuarkXPress Items

You can copy objects from many other applications and paste them into QuarkX-Press as native QuarkXPress items, including Adobe InDesign, Illustrator, Corel-DRAW, Affinity Designer, Word, Excel, PowerPoint, and Apple Pages. And yes, you can successfully convert an entire InDesign page to QuarkXPress. Here's how:

1. **Copy the items in their original application.**

   Copying the items places them on your computer's clipboard.

2. **Switch to QuarkXPress and choose Edit⇨ Paste as Native Objects (or right-click and choose Paste as Native Objects).**

   QuarkXPress converts the pictures, text, shapes, and lines in that file to native QuarkXPress items. If some of the items overlap in unexpected ways, try deselecting the two options in that dialog box (Ignore Soft Masks and Ignore Transparent Blend Modes) and then convert again.

   The original objects are converted to a group of QuarkXPress items.

3. **To edit individual items, choose Item⇨ Ungroup.**

   If you have many items, you may need to repeat Item⇨ Ungroup, or choose Item⇨ Ungroup All to ungroup all groups within groups.

This capability to convert objects from other applications opens a whole new world of graphic possibilities. For the first time, you can use the Smart Art tools in Microsoft Office applications to create flowcharts and then fine-tune them in QuarkXPress. Same for charts and graphs in Illustrator, CorelDraw, or Microsoft Office. This capability could fundamentally change the relationship between corporate chart producers and page layout artists, because now a page layout artist can customize the charts created elsewhere without having to master the goofy appearance tools in Microsoft products.

TIP

For Windows users: When copying objects from some applications, you may get a better result if you copy them as a PDF file into the Windows Clipboard, with the most prominent example being Adobe InDesign. So make sure that you select the Copy PDF to Clipboard check box in the Clipboard Handling section of InDesign's preferences before attempting to copy objects from InDesign and pasting them as native objects in QuarkXPress.

TIP

If you get only an image when you choose Paste as Native Objects in QuarkXPress (instead of an editable object), the application you're copying from may be copying its objects only as images, and therefore QuarkXPress cannot paste them as items. To work around this problem, export the page from the original application as a PDF file and then import that PDF file into QuarkXPress, at which point you then convert to native items as described in the preceding section. This process will typically give you the items you want.

Chapter **4**

Working with Items

I f you've ever been faced with a blank wall and several pieces of framed art to hang, you know the importance of mastering your hanging skills. The digital equivalent in QuarkXPress is your skill at manipulating page items: The faster you master these skills, the faster and more creative you'll be with every project! In this chapter, you learn the smartest and fastest ways to move, duplicate, and align objects, stack them, group them onto layers, store them in libraries, and use Item Styles for speed and consistency.

Selecting Items

Although you *can* select an item with the Text Content tool or Picture Content tool, don't do it. Using the Item tool instead is usually more efficient. Here are two ways to select items with the Item tool:

» **Click or Shift-click:** Click once on top of an item to select it. To add more items to your selection, Shift-click each one.

>> **Drag across an area:** Drag the Item tool from an empty area of the page across any edge of the item. To add more items to your selection, Shift-drag until you touch its edge with the Item tool. This is the fastest way to select multiple items, but it works best if the items are on an empty background. You don't have to surround the item when dragging — just touching an edge selects it.

To deselect an item in a bunch of selected items, Shift-click the item. You can also Shift-drag with the Item tool from an empty area of the page until you touch its edge.

To deselect all selected items, click outside them. When using the Item tool, you can press Tab to deselect all selected items — which is another reason to use the Item tool! When using the Text Content tool, press Esc instead (otherwise you might create a tab in a text box).

TIP

If you're using the Picture Content tool, you can quickly switch to the Item tool by pressing the V key on your keyboard. This trick also works with the Text Content tool, but be sure to click outside the box or press Esc before pressing V so that you don't type a V in your text box!

Manipulating Items

After they've been selected, most kinds of items display an outline (called a *bounding box*) and handles for reshaping.

TIP

When moving, resizing, or rotating a box, pause a moment after clicking (and before dragging) to see the content of the box change as you drag. Otherwise, you see only the bounding box change. When you release the mouse, you see the box content update.

Moving items

You can move a selected item or items in any of several ways:

>> **Drag it:** With the Item tool active, click and drag the item to its new location. Be sure not to click and drag the bounding box of the item, or you change its shape instead of moving it.

>> **Use the Measurements palette:** To move the item to a new location, type new values in the X and Y fields on the Home/Classic tab in the Measurements palette. To move the item a specific amount, type the plus sign (+) or minus sign (–) after the existing value and then type the distance you want to move the item. QuarkXPress will do the math for you and move the items.

>> **Nudge it:** With the Item tool active, press the arrow keys on your keyboard to nudge the item or items by one point. To nudge by ten points, press Shift while pressing the arrow keys.

TIP

You can change the Shift+nudge amount in the Item Tool preferences: Choose QuarkXPress ➪ Preferences (Mac) or Edit ➪ Preferences (Windows) to open the Preferences dialog box. In the Preferences dialog box, click Item Tool in the left pane (it's in the Tools section of the Print Layout section in the left pane). Type a new value into the Shift + Nudge Increment field.

TIP

When nudging items, you can see them more clearly if you turn off their bounding box (selection outline). To do that, choose View ➪ Hide Selection.

Resizing and reshaping items

Resizing and reshaping items in QuarkXPress can be an enjoyably fluid experience, after you master where to point, click, and drag, along with knowing a few modifier keys to hold down while doing so. The following techniques take you several steps closer to QuarkXPress nirvana. (I'm not kidding!)

Resizing an item

You can resize a selected item in several ways:

>> **Drag the sides or handles:** Drag the side of a selected item or its handles to make it larger or smaller.

>> **Use the Measurements palette:** To resize a selected item to a specific size, type new values in the X and Y fields on the Home/Classic tab in the Measurements palette.

>> **Use the Scale feature:** Choose Item ➪ Scale to enter a scaling percentage and control which attributes of the item are scaled. See the "Scaling Items or Layouts, Intelligently" section, later in this chapter.

TIP

The easiest way to scale the content of a box along with the box itself is to hold down the Command (Mac) or Ctrl (Windows) key while dragging a side or handle. To maintain the original proportions of the box while resizing it, hold down the Shift key while dragging. To resize an item from its center outward, hold down the Option (Mac) or Alt (Windows) key while dragging. You can use these modifier keys in any combination to achieve your intended result. For example, Shift-Option-Command-drag (Mac) or Shift+Alt+Ctrl+drag (Windows) to maintain the proportions of the box and its content, while growing or shrinking it from the center of the item.

Locking box and picture proportions

When resizing a box, you normally want the freedom to change its height and width separately. However, when resizing a picture box, you usually don't want to change the proportions of the picture inside the box. So by default, QuarkXPress locks the proportions of the content of a picture box but allows you to change the box shape however you like.

To lock or unlock the proportions of a text or picture box, in the Home/Classic tab of the Measurements palette, click the chain-link icon next to the W and H fields (see Figure 4-1). To lock or unlock the proportions of a picture, click the chain-link icon next to the X% and Y% fields.

When resizing a text box, the text normally doesn't change its shape or size — unless you hold down the Command (Mac) or Ctrl (Windows) key while dragging a box handle. QuarkXPress therefore doesn't offer a way to lock the proportions of text.

FIGURE 4-1:
The proportion lock controls: unlocked (left) and locked (right).

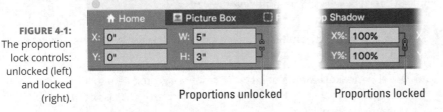

Proportions unlocked   Proportions locked

Fitting a box to a picture

To fit a box to a picture inside it, or to scale the picture to fit its box, use either the Style menu or the context menu (open it using Control-click on the Mac or right-click on Windows). If you choose Scale Picture to Box, the picture fills the box so that the picture isn't squished or stretched in either dimension. You'll therefore almost always have some blank space on left/right or top/bottom. To remove the empty space, choose Fit Box to Picture.

Fitting a box to text

To fit a box to the text inside it, choose Fit Box to Text from the Item menu or the context menu. If the text is shorter than the box, the box shortens. If the text overflows the box, the box expands vertically so that it displays all the text.

Changing the corner shape of a box

You can change the corner shape of rectangular boxes to rounded, concave, and beveled corners by choosing Item ⇨ Shape or by using the Box Corner Style menu in the Measurements palette. To adjust the radius of nonsquare corners, go to the Home/Classic tab of the Measurements palette and change the value in the Box Corner Radius field, or click the up or down arrows next to the Box Corner Radius field. Figure 4-2 shows the Box Corner Radius controls.

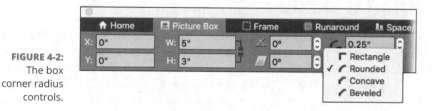

FIGURE 4-2:
The box corner radius controls.

Changing the overall shape of a box

In QuarkXPress, a box is a box is a box, and you can freely switch among box shapes. To change the shape of a box, choose Item ⇨ Shape and choose a different shape from the submenu that appears, as shown in Figure 4-3. The bottom four shapes are particularly interesting: The artist's palette converts your box shape to a Bézier shape, the angled line converts the box to a line angled at 45 degrees, the crossed lines convert the box to a single horizontal line, and the squiggly line converts the box to a Bézier path. If the box contained text when you convert it to a line, the text flows along the new line. If the box contained a picture when you convert it to a line, the picture is removed.

TIP

A fast way to put text on a path is to type or paste it into a text box and choose Item ⇨ Shape and choose one of the lines at the bottom of the submenu shown in Figure 4-3 to convert the box to a line. See the previous section for details.

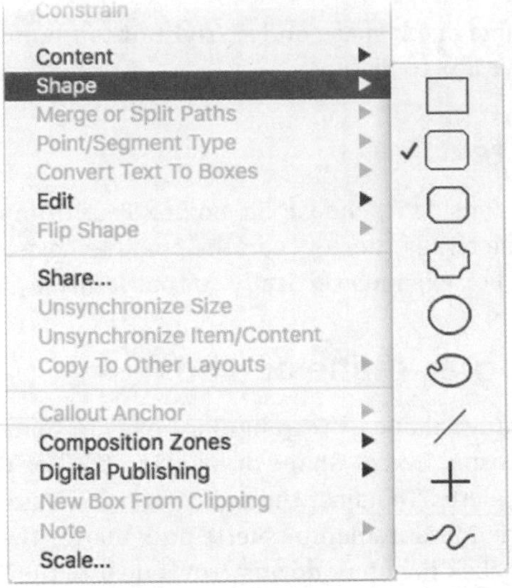

Constrain

Content ▶
Shape ▶
Merge or Split Paths ▶
Point/Segment Type ▶
Convert Text To Boxes ▶
Edit ▶
Flip Shape ▶

Share...
Unsynchronize Size
Unsynchronize Item/Content
Copy To Other Layouts ▶

Callout Anchor ▶
Composition Zones ▶
Digital Publishing ▶
New Box From Clipping
Note ▶
Scale...

FIGURE 4-3:
The box shape
options in the
Shape menu.

Rotating boxes

You can rotate a box with either the Item or Content tools. When you position your mouse pointer outside a corner handle, but near the box, the pointer changes to a curved arrow. Click and drag to rotate the box. You can also rotate a box by going to the Home/Classic tab of the Measurements palette and changing the value in the Box Angle field, or by clicking the up or down arrows next to the Box Angle field (see Figure 4-4).

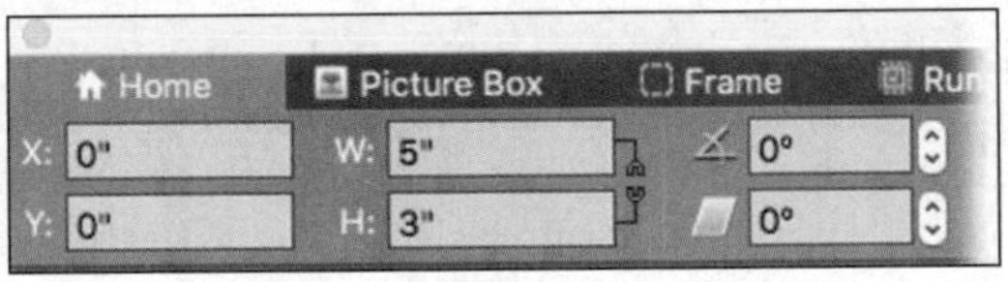

FIGURE 4-4:
The Box Angle
field (top
right) and Box
Skew field
(bottom right).

♠ Home	🖬 Picture Box	⬚ Frame	🗐 Ru
X: 0"	W: 5"	∡ 0°	⬍
Y: 0"	H: 3"	╱ 0°	⬍

Skewing boxes

To skew a box and its content, go to the Home/Classic tab of the Measurements palette and change the value in the Box Skew field, or click the up or down arrows next to the Box Skew field (refer to Figure 4-4). Positive values slant items to the right; negative values slant them to the left.

KEYBOARD SHORTCUTS FOR MODIFYING BOXES

You can use the following table as a reference for efficiently modifying your boxes:

Task	Mac	Windows
Resize box, constraining shape	Shift-drag box handle	Shift+drag box handle
Resize box, maintaining aspect ratio	Option-Shift-drag box handle	Alt+Shift+drag box handle
Resize box and scale picture/text	Command-drag box handle	Ctrl+drag box handle
Resize box and scale picture/text, constraining shape	Command-Shift-drag box handle	Ctrl+Shift+drag box handle
Resize box and scale picture/text, maintaining aspect ratio	Command-Option-Shift-drag box handle	Ctrl+Alt+Shift+drag box handle

KEYBOARD SHORTCUTS FOR CREATING, RESIZING, AND ROTATING ITEMS

The following table can help you efficiently work with your items:

Task	Shortcut for Mac/Windows
Constrain proportions while resizing	Shift+drag handle
Scale contents while resizing item	Command/Ctrl+drag handle
Resize relative to center	Option/Alt+drag handle
Resize multiple items	Press Command/Ctrl before dragging handle
Constrain item rotation to 0°/45°/90°	Press Shift while rotating
Constrain straight line angle to 0°/45°/90°	Press Shift while creating or resizing line
Rotate picture content relative to center	Option/Alt+drag rotation handle
Duplicate item while dragging	Press Option/Alt while dragging item

Flipping box content

You can flip the content of a Text or Picture box from left to right and from top to bottom, but the controls are in slightly different places:

>> **Picture Box:** Choose Style ⇨ Flip Horizontal or Style ⇨ Flip Vertical or go to the Home/Classic tab or Picture Box tab of the Measurements palette and click the Flip Horizontal or Flip Vertical buttons (see Figure 4-5).

>> **Text Box:** In the Measurements palette, go to the Text Box tab and click the Flip Horizontal or Flip Vertical buttons.

FIGURE 4-5:
The Flip Horizontal (top) and Flip Vertical (bottom) buttons.

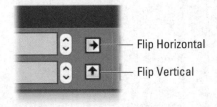

Flip Horizontal

Flip Vertical

Locking items

To keep from accidentally moving or changing the content of a text or picture box, you can lock the position or the content of the box. Choose Item ⇨ Lock and then choose Position or Picture (for a picture box), or Story (for a text box). You can also Control-click (Mac) or right-click (Windows) the box and use the context menu to choose these options.

Suppressing item output

Sometimes you may want to place an item on a page but not include it when you print or export your project. For example, you may want to make a note for a coworker without using the Notes feature (which I explain in Chapter 11). Or perhaps you're having trouble printing a page and want to eliminate certain items when troubleshooting. Whatever the reason, you can keep an item from printing or exporting by setting it to Suppress Output. Note that the controls are different for Mac and Windows, as follows:

>> **On the Mac:** In the Measurements palette, go to the Home tab and click the Suppress Output button. It looks like a green arrow in a circle and is on the bottom row of the palette (see Figure 4-6).

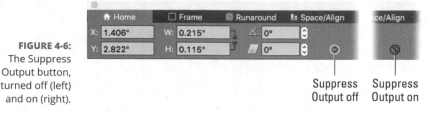

FIGURE 4-6:
The Suppress Output button, turned off (left) and on (right).

Suppress Output off   Suppress Output on

>> **In Windows:** Choose Item ⇨ Modify, and in the Modify dialog box, go to the appropriate pane (Box, Line, Picture, or Layout) and then select the Suppress Output check box.

On Mac or Windows, you can also suppress the output of an entire layer. To do that, select the Suppress Output check box in that layer's Attributes dialog box, as explained later in this chapter.

TIP

After you've suppressed an item or items, to quickly see what your project will look like when exported or printed, choose View ⇨ Hide Suppressed. This command tells QuarkXPress to hide all items for which the Suppress Output box is selected. It also hides underlines on hyperlinks, hyperlink anchors, index markers, and the text overflow symbol.

Suppressing picture output

Picture boxes have a special suppress feature: Suppress Picture Output. When enabled, the frame, background, and drop shadow of a picture box prints or exports, but the picture in the box doesn't. The control appears in different places on Mac and Windows:

>> **On the Mac:** In the Measurements palette, go to the Picture Box tab and click the Suppress Picture Output button. It looks like a green arrow in a circle and resides at the far right end of the controls.

>> **In Windows:** Choose Item ⇨ Modify, and in the Modify dialog box, go to the Picture pane and select the Suppress Picture Output check box.

Duplicating items

In addition to the standard technique of copying and pasting an item to duplicate it, QuarkXPress offers several others.

- **Paste In Place:** After you copy an item or items by choosing Edit ⇨ Copy, you can paste the copy directly on top of itself or navigate to another page and paste it in exactly the same location on that page. To do so, choose Edit ⇨ Paste In Place.

- **Duplicate:** If you need a copy of an item or items and don't want to replace the last thing you copied (for example, if you copied some text and want to paste it into a copy of a text box), choose Item ⇨ Duplicate. This command creates a copy of the item(s), and the copy is offset a little down and to the right of the original.

- **Option-drag or Alt+drag:** Hold down the Option (Mac) or Alt (Windows) key while you drag one or more items to instantly create a duplicate at the new location.

- **Super Step & Repeat:** Read about this powerful feature in the upcoming section, "Using Super Step & Repeat for Super Duplication."

- **Cloner:** Read about this powerful feature in the "Cloning Items with Cloner" section, also upcoming.

Deleting items

QuarkXPress offers several ways to delete one or more selected items:

- **Edit ⇨ Cut:** With the Item tool active, this menu command (or its keyboard shortcut Command-X on the Mac or Ctrl+X in Windows) removes the item and places it on your computer's Clipboard. You can then choose Edit ⇨ Paste (shortcut: Command-V on the Mac or Ctrl+V in Windows) to paste it into the center of the QuarkXPress document window. If the Picture Content tool is active, this command cuts the picture out of the active Picture box. If the Text Content tool is active, this command cuts selected text in the active text box.

- **Delete key:** With the Item tool active, press the Delete key on your keyboard. If the Picture Content tool is active, this command deletes the picture within the active Picture box. If the Text Content tool is active, this command deletes the previous character in the active text box.

TIP

- **Item ⇨ Delete:** This menu item and its keyboard shortcut (Command-K on the Mac or Ctrl+K in Windows) is your friend! No matter what you're doing to an item, you can always press this keyboard shortcut to zap the item from the page without switching to the Item tool. You can remember it as Command-KILL or Ctrl+KILL.

Using Super Step & Repeat for Super Duplication

When you need to duplicate an item more than once or twice, or if you want to duplicate an item and change its attributes with each duplicate, try Super Step & Repeat. This feature is useful for creative effects, but it's especially handy when you need to duplicate a logo or other art in a variety of sizes.

To use it, select a picture box, text box, text path, or line. Then choose Item ⇨ Super Step and Repeat. The dialog box shown in Figure 4-7 appears.

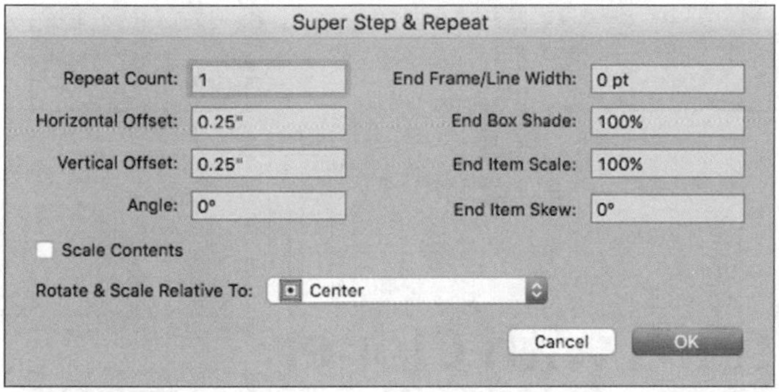

FIGURE 4-7:
The Super Step & Repeat dialog box.

The options in the Super Step & Repeat dialog box let you specify the following:

>> Number of duplicates you want (up to 100)

>> Horizontal distance from the original (negative values place the copy left; positive values place it right)

>> Vertical distance from the original (negative values place the copy above; positive values place it below)

>> Rotation of each copy (all rotation is counterclockwise)

>> Thickness of the final frame or line

>> Background color shade of the final box or line color shade of the final line

>> Scale of the final duplicated item (from 1 percent to 1000 percent)

>> Skew amount of the final item (from 75° to –75°)

To scale the content of a picture box, text box, or text path along with scaling the item itself, select Scale Contents.

And finally, to specify the point around which rotation or scaling will take place for the item, choose an option from the Rotate & Scale Relative To drop-down menu, shown in Figure 4-8. Note that Selected Point is available as a choice only when a point on a Bézier item is selected.

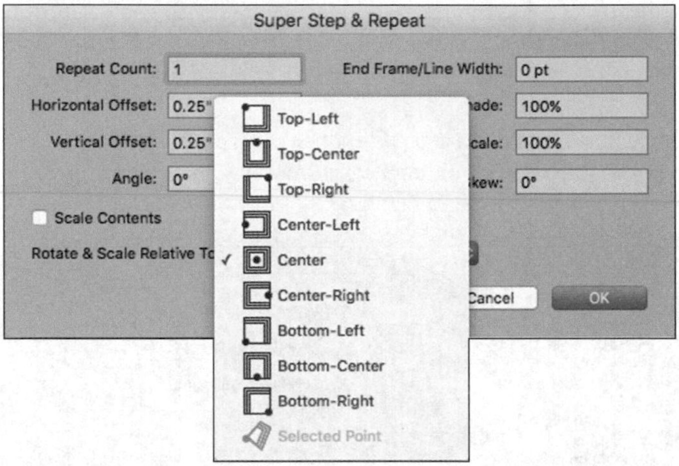

FIGURE 4-8:
The Rotate & Scale Relative To drop-down menu in the Super Step & Repeat dialog box.

Cloning Items with Cloner

Another supercharged duplication tool in QuarkXPress is Cloner (see the preceding section for the other especially handy way to duplicate items). Cloner lets you copy selected items to the same location on different pages or into a different project. You can also copy pages into a different project.

To use Cloner, you first select the items you want to clone, or deselect all items if you want to clone entire pages. Next, choose Utilities ⇨ Cloner to display the Cloner dialog box, shown in Figure 4-9.

Here's what you find in the Cloner dialog box:

>> **Clone Source area:** Lets you choose what you want to clone. Click Selection to clone the selected items, or Pages to clone a range of pages.

>> **Clone Destination area:** Lets you choose where the cloned content goes. Choose an option from the Destination drop-down menu shown in Figure 4-10.

FIGURE 4-9:
The Cloner
dialog box.

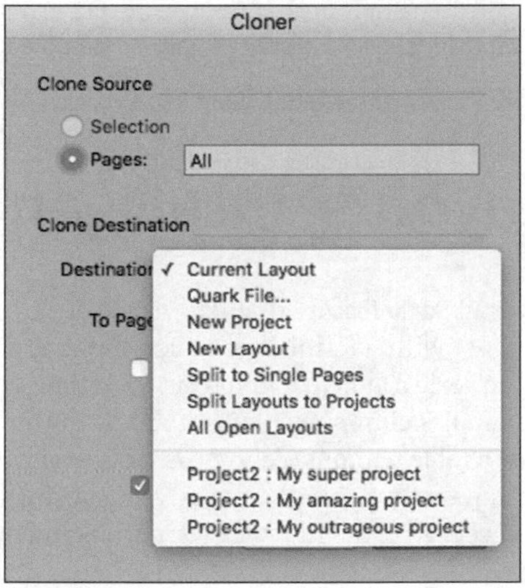

FIGURE 4-10:
The Clone
Destination
menu.

>> **Clone Destination drop-down menu:** Lets you copy selected items to a different location in the active layout, copy the selected items or pages into an existing QuarkXPress project on your computer, copy the selected items or pages to a new QuarkXPress project, or copy the selected items or pages to a new layout in the active QuarkXPress project. Other options create a one-page project file from each page, create a single-layout project from each layout in the active project, copy the selected items to all layouts in this project, or copy the selected items or pages into a specific layout in an open QuarkXPress project.

>> **To Page field:** Lets you indicate the target page to copy the selected items into. If you're copying pages, indicate the page number you want the copied pages to begin on in the target layout.

>> **Copies field:** If you're cloning a selection, use the Copies field to enter the number of copies you want to make. For example, if To Page is set to 21 and Copies is set to 5, copies will be created on pages 21, 22, 23, 24, and 25.

>> **Make Section(s):** If you're cloning pages, and those pages include section breaks (you learn about sections in Chapter 5), select Make Section(s) to create sections in the new page copies; then choose an option:

- **Keep Contiguous:** Puts all the page copies in a single section in the destination layout, even if the original includes different sections.

- **Multiple Sections:** If the pages you're copying include section breaks, the section breaks are preserved in the copies.

>> **Copy Style Sheets:** Select Copy Style Sheets to include all the style sheets from the source layout in the new project or projects. Otherwise, only style sheets that you're using in text on the source pages are copied.

Scaling Items or Layouts, Intelligently

QuarkXPress has a powerful Scale feature that lets you scale not only items but also entire multipage layouts — with control over which items and attributes change size. For example, you can scale a bunch of items but keep their frame or line widths intact. Or you can scale a multicolumn text box but not its gutter width or text inset value. You can even scale a table without scaling the table grid within it. When scaling text, you can scale the text but not the paragraph spacing, and then you can update the text's style sheets with the new size (or not). So many possibilities!

To scale items, first select those items. To scale an entire multipage layout, you don't need to select any items. Oddly, you have two ways to access the Scale feature: by choosing Item ⇨ Scale and using the Scale Settings dialog box, or by choosing Window ⇨ Scale and using the Scale palette, as shown in Figure 4-11. The Scale palette is more flexible for several reasons, including its capability to scale an entire layout, so you may prefer to use that.

To scale using a percentage of the original size of the items, choose Percent from the pop-up menu. To scale to a specific final size, choose Units instead.

To scale without maintaining the original proportions of the item(s), click the chain-link icon at the far right of the Width and Height drop-down menus to break it. You can then enter any value in the Width and Height fields.

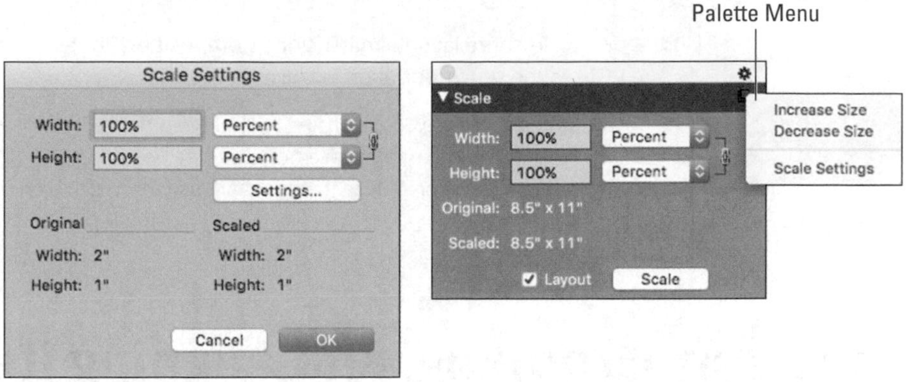

Increase Size
Decrease Size

Scale Settings

FIGURE 4-11:
The Scale
Settings dialog
box (left) and
the Scale
palette (right).

To scale an entire multipage layout, select the Layout check box in the Scale palette.

To control which items or attributes get scaled, click the Settings button in the dialog box or choose Settings from the palette menu in the upper right of the Scale palette. Either way, the dialog box in Figure 4-12 appears, with a multitude of choices. Make your choices and click OK.

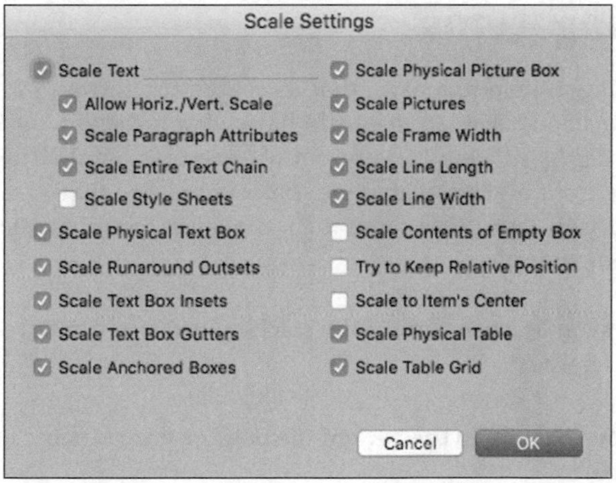

FIGURE 4-12:
The Scale
Settings
dialog box.

WARNING

The Scale feature has four limitations to be aware of:

>> Scale lets you scale an item so that it is smaller or larger than QuarkXPress otherwise allows. The scaled item will print correctly, but if you attempt to modify it with QuarkXPress tools or commands, an error message displays.

>> Scale does not work completely with synchronized items. (See Chapter 7 for more about synchronizing items.) Instances of the shared item inherit only width and height changes from Scale.

>> Don't scale entire layouts that include Composition Zones, because doing so confuses the synchronization features in them.

>> Rotated items are scaled according to their original geometry. For example, if you scale the width of a square box that has been rotated 45 degrees, a rotated rectangle is produced (rather than, as you might have wanted, a wider diamond).

Stacking, Grouping, and Aligning Items

Each item on a QuarkXPress page has a spatial relationship with the other items on the page. Not only are items arranged in a left-to-right and top-to-bottom fashion on the page, but the items also have a stacking relationship, like a deck of cards. In addition, you can use layers to keep items together that you may want to show or hide all at one time. All the items on a layer appear above or below the items on other layers. (I tell you about layers later in this chapter, in "Illuminating the Layers Palette.")

Stacking items

As you add each item to a page, that item appears in front of the existing items. Even if items don't overlap, they still have what's called a *stacking order*. You can see this order by moving an item until it overlaps another item; the one that's close to the front of the stacking order blocks out one that's closer to the back. In addition, if your layout has more than one layer, items on each layer have their own stacking order.

The Item menu lets you control the stacking order of a selected item or items in the following ways:

>> **To move an item to the back of the page or layer:** Choose Item ⇨ Send to Back.

>> **To move an item to the front of the page or layer:** Choose Item ⇨ Bring to Front.

>> **To move an item one level backward in the page or layer:** On a Mac, press Option and then choose Item ⇨ Send Backward. On Windows, choose Item ⇨ Send Backward.

>> **To move an item one level forward in the page or layer:** On a Mac, press Option and choose Item ⇨ Bring Forward. On Windows, choose Item ⇨ Bring Forward.

A faster technique is to use the context menu that appears when you or Control-click (Mac) or right-click (Windows) an item. Choose Send & Bring from the context menu and then choose Send to Back, Send Backward, Bring to Front, or Bring Forward.

To activate an item that is hidden behind other items, get the Item tool and press Command-Option-Shift (Mac) or Ctrl+Alt+Shift (Windows) while you click repeatedly where items overlap. Each click activates the next item back in the stacking order.

Grouping and ungrouping items

Grouping in QuarkXPress is incredibly handy when you want to select or move several items at the same time. After you create a group, you can still edit, resize, and reposition individual items within the group. To create a group, select multiple items and choose Item➪Group (or Command-G on the Mac or Ctrl+G in Windows).

A group is also considered an Item, so you can group multiple groups together, and you can even group individual boxes, lines, and text paths with an existing group. Use the following techniques to work with groups:

>> **To move, cut, copy, paste, duplicate, rotate, and color a group:** Select it with the Item tool.

>> **To manipulate an individual item within a group:** Use the Text Content tool or Picture Content tool.

>> **To resize every item in a group:** Click and drag the group's handles.

If you click and drag a group's handles to resize it, the grouped items resize but their frame widths, line weights, pictures, and text don't change size. If you press Command-Shift (Mac) or Ctrl+Shift (Windows) while resizing a group, all frame widths, line weights, pictures, and text do resize proportionally. If you press Command (Mac) or Ctrl (Windows) while resizing a group, frame widths, pictures, and text are still resized, but not proportionally.

>> **To move an item within a group:** Press Command (Mac) or Ctrl (Windows) and select the item with the Item tool, the Text Content tool, or the Picture Content tool.

>> **To ungroup a single group:** Choose Item➪Ungroup (or Command-U on a Mac; Ctrl+U in Windows). To ungroup every group in a group that contains other groups, choose Item➪Ungroup All.

Spacing and aligning items

Both the Space/Align tab of the Measurements palette and the Space/Align menu (choose Item➪Space/Align to get to that menu) let you easily align or evenly space multiple items with one click. You can choose to align or space the items relative to each other, or to the page (or the spread in a Print layout with facing pages). Then you choose whether to use the top, bottom, left, right, or center of the items for your alignment or spacing.

REMEMBER

When aligning or spacing items relative to each other, if you select the items by dragging across them, the topmost item on the page becomes the "key" item (that is, the item that the other selected items align to) and does not move. If two or more items have the same top edges, the leftmost top item becomes the key item and doesn't move. To align or space items to a different key item, select that item first and then select the others. All selected items then align or space relative to that key item.

If you prefer text descriptions of the commands instead of icons, choose Item➪Space/Align to open the Space/Align menu, shown in Figure 4-13. The alignment options shown in the figure are identical whether you choose the Item Relative submenu or the Page Relative submenu.

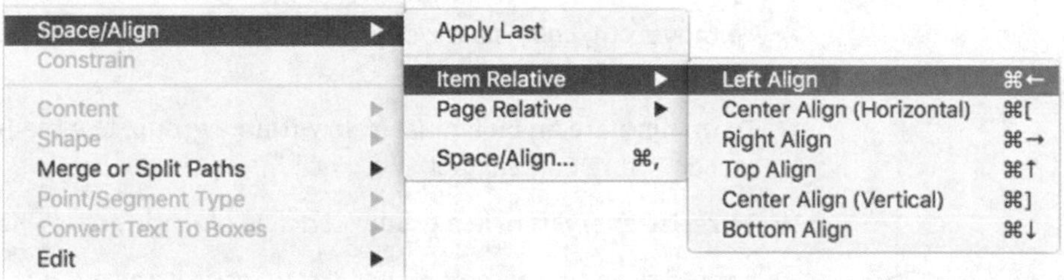

FIGURE 4-13:
The Space/
Align menu.

If you prefer icons for the commands instead of text descriptions, use the Space/Align tab of the Measurements palette. The Space options are clustered on the left, the Align options are clustered in the middle, and the "Relative To" options (Item, Page, or Spread) are clustered on the right, as shown in Figure 4-14. Hover over an icon to see its text label.

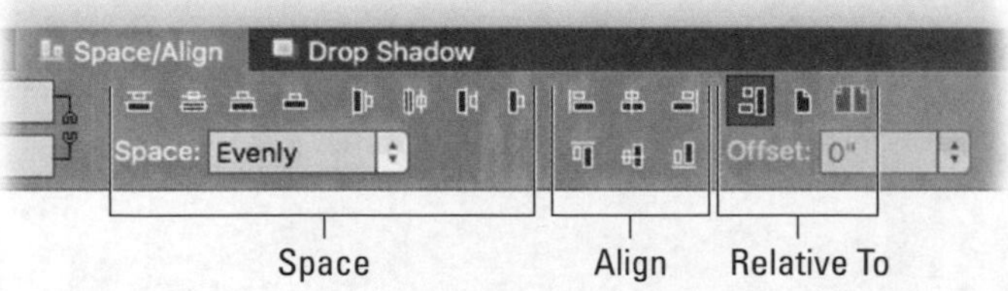

FIGURE 4-14:
The Space/
Align tab of the
Measurements
palette.

Space   Align   Relative To

To apply a specific amount of space between items, enter it into the Space field. Otherwise, the existing amount of space between them is averaged and applied to each of them. (In other words, the items in the two most extreme locations remain in place and the items between them are spaced evenly.)

When aligning items with a page or spread, you can choose to align them with the top, bottom, left, right, or horizontal or vertical center of the page. But you can also enter a value in the Offset field to position them a precise distance away from the edge or center of the page.

TIP

To quickly jump to the Space/Align tab of the Measurements palette, press Command-, or Ctrl+, (that's Command-comma on a Mac and Ctrl+comma on Windows).

KEYBOARD SHORTCUTS FOR ALIGNING ITEMS (MAC ONLY)

Here's a handy reference for you to use while aligning items on a Mac:

Task	Shortcut
Left Align (Item Relative)	Command-Left arrow key
Left Align (Page Relative)	Command-Shift-Left arrow key
Right Align (Item Relative)	Command-Right arrow key
Right Align (Page Relative)	Command-Shift-Right arrow key
Center Align Horizontal (Item Relative)	Command-[
Center Align Horizontal (Page Relative)	Shift-Command-[
Center Align Vertical (Item Relative)	Command-]
Center Align Vertical (Page Relative)	Shift-Command-]
Top Align (Item Relative)	Command-Up arrow key
Top Align (Page Relative)	Command-Shift-Up arrow key
Bottom Align (Item Relative)	Command-Down arrow key
Bottom Align (Page Relative)	Command-Shift-Down arrow key
Display Space/Align tab of Measurements palette	Command-, (comma)

Illuminating the Layers Palette

A QuarkXPress layer is like a clear overlay on your layout. Items you place onto it are always in front of all items on layers below it. You can toggle the visibility and output state of each layer, which makes them useful when creating a layout that's translated into multiple languages. Or you can place different versions of a design on different layers and then switch back and forth among the variations when showing a design to your client.

When working with complex layouts, you can lock individual layers, which makes editing items on other layers easier. Some projects naturally lend themselves to using layers — for example, when designing a package or label, you can put the die lines (cut-and-fold lines) on one locked layer for reference but exclude them from printing. The uses for layers are endless, and they dramatically increase your productivity.

Using layers in QuarkXPress is slightly different (and, in my opinion, superior) from using layers in some other applications such as Adobe Photoshop. For example:

>> You don't have to manually activate a different layer to select an item on it — just click the item to select it and activate its layer.

>> Each layer appears on every page in a layout, rather than on only the active page, which makes controlling the appearance of a long document easy.

>> Text on a rear layer can run around items on a front layer.

Understanding the Layers palette

The Layers palette, shown in Figure 4-15, is the control center for layers. It lets you create layers, edit layer attributes, control whether a layer displays and prints, and move objects between layers. Every layout has a Default layer. You can add items to and remove items from the Default layer, but you cannot delete the Default layer. To display the Layers palette, choose View ⇨ Layers. In the palette, hover over an icon to see its text label.

Here's how to accomplish tasks by using the Layers palette:

>> To create a new layer, click the New Layer button, which looks like a green plus sign. A new layer appears above the active layer.

>> To move a layer (and all the items on it) above or below other layers, drag it up or down in the Layers palette.

New Layer   Palette menu

Move Item to Layer

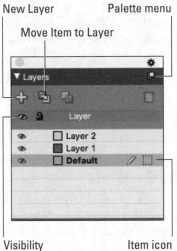

FIGURE 4-15:
The Layers
palette.

Visibility   Item icon

>> To create a new item and place it onto a specific layer, first activate that layer by clicking its name in the Layers palette. A pencil icon appears to the right of the layer's name. Then create the item.

>> When you select an item on the page, its layer becomes active in the Layers palette, and a dotted square (Item icon) appears to the right of the layer's name. If you select items from multiple layers, a dotted square (Item icon) appears next to each layer to which those items belong.

>> Every layer has a different color assigned to it. When you select an item on the page, its bounding box and handles appear in the color assigned to its layer.

>> To move a selected item to a different layer, do one of these things:

- Click the Move Item To Layer icon and then choose a layer from the dialog box that appears.

- Drag the item's Item icon from its current layer to another layer. The item's bounding box and handles change color to match the color of the new layer in the Layers palette.

WARNING

If you move a master page item on a layout page from the Default layer to another layer, those items will no longer be master page items. (Read more about master pages in Chapter 5.)

>> To merge multiple layers into one layer, first select them in the Layers palette. To select consecutive layers, click the first one and then Shift-click the last one. To select nonconsecutive layers, Command-click (Mac) or Ctrl+click (Windows) each layer that you want to select. Click the Merge Layers icon, and a dialog box appears. Choose a target layer from the Choose Destination Layer menu and click OK. All items on all the selected layers move to the

new layer, and they remain in their original stacking order. In other words, the items appear in the same front-to-back order, except that they're all on the new layer. The original layers are deleted.

>> To delete the active layer, click the Delete Layer (trash can) icon.

>> When you group items that are on different layers, all items stay on their layer, even though the group itself belongs to a specific layer.

>> To toggle the visibility of a layer, click the leftmost column. A Visibility (eyeball) icon appears or disappears there. To make only one layer visible, Control-click (Mac) or Ctrl+click (Windows) its Visibility icon.

>> To lock or unlock a layer, click the second column on the left. A Lock icon appears or disappears there. To unlock one layer and lock all the others, Control-click (Mac) or /Ctrl+click (Windows) its Lock icon.

Working faster with the Layers palette menu

Some people like to click visual icons — they make sense to their brains. Some prefer the text-based menus for the same reason. The Layers palette has both, with some additional features in its palette menu. Although you can click icons in the Layers palette to create, edit, duplicate, show or hide, and lock or unlock layers, try using the Layers palette menu instead, as shown in Figure 4-16. To display it, click the little square in the top-right corner of the Layers palette or Control-click (Mac) or right-click (Windows) in the Name column.

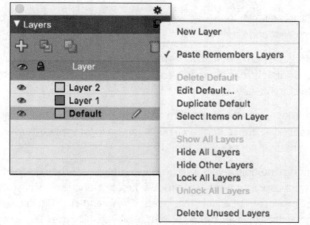

FIGURE 4-16:
The Layers palette menu.

The Layers palette menu is also useful for these operations:

>> Selecting all the items on a layer

>> Deleting all unused layers

>> Showing or hiding and locking or unlocking all layers

>> Controlling whether pasting items will paste them onto the currently active layer or onto the layers they came from

REMEMBER

If Paste Remembers Layers is selected, and you paste items from a different layout, items from layers whose names match layers in the active layout are pasted onto those matching layers. If you paste items from layers whose names don't match those in the active layout, new layers are created with those names, and these items are pasted onto those new layers.

Changing layer attributes

To change the attributes of a layer, such as its name and color, double-click its name. The Attributes dialog box appears (see Figure 4-17), where you can do the following:

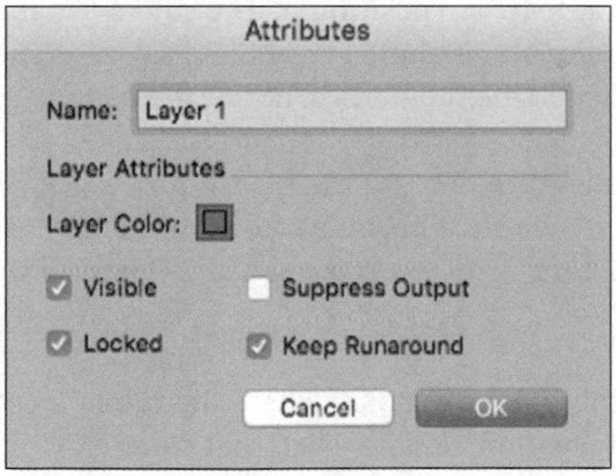

FIGURE 4-17:
The Layer
Attributes
dialog box.

>> **Change the layer's name:** Type a new name in the Name field.

>> **Change the layer's color:** Click the color swatch and choose a new color from the color pickers that appear.

>> **Enable the Suppress Output check box:** Select this check box if you don't want items on that layer to be included when you print or export the layout.

>> **Enable the Keep Runaround check box:** Select this check box if items on that layer cause text to run around them and you want the text to run around them even if the visibility of the layer is turned off.

Using layers on master pages

Beginning in QuarkXPress 10 (and including QuarkXPress 2015, 2016, and higher), you can use layers on master pages. Items on a layer on a master page appear behind items on that same layer on the document page. When possible, try to name layers differently on master pages — just to keep your head from exploding.

Getting Guidance from Rulers and Guides

Precision is one of the strongest qualities of QuarkXPress. Everything from the precise way the pointer interacts with text and page items, pixel-perfect image previews (by far the best in the industry), and a battery of truly helpful guide behaviors combine to give you confidence in positioning items. Don't underestimate the power of precision: Some art directors can see when two items are misaligned by as little as one point (1/72 inch).

Ruling rulers

To display page rulers, choose View ⇨ Rulers. Rulers then appear along the top and left edges of your document window. As you create or move an item, dotted lines appear on the rulers that help you position it. The rulers use the unit of measurement set in the Measurements section of QuarkXPress Preferences. By default, the zero point for both rulers is the top-left corner of the page.

To change the unit of measurement on the fly, Control-click (Mac) or right-click (Windows) the ruler and choose a new unit from the context menu that appears, such as inches, centimeters, or picas. You can use different units for the horizontal and vertical rulers.

To change the zero point, drag the square where the rulers meet onto the page. To return it to its original position, double-click that square.

To reverse the measurement direction of the rulers, Control-click (Mac) or right-click (Windows) the ruler and choose a new ruler direction from the context menu that appears. By default, the direction is left to right for the horizontal ruler and top to bottom for the vertical ruler.

Getting guide-ance

QuarkXPress has three types of guides that help you position page items: ruler guides; column and margin guides; and dynamic guides. All of them are nonprinting, and you can create them on layout pages and master pages.

Using ruler guides

Ruler guides are also simply called *guides.* To create and position a ruler guide manually, click the horizontal or vertical ruler and drag the mouse onto the page. As you drag, a small line appears in the ruler to indicate the guide's current position. The Measurements palette also shows the guide's location in the X or Y field. This guide appears only on the page you drag it onto.

Here's how to use a ruler guide:

» **To create a guide that extends across the pasteboard and all pages of a spread:** Release the mouse button when the ruler guide is positioned over the pasteboard. You can change an existing single-page guide into a pasteboard-spread guide by dragging it onto the pasteboard and then back onto the page.

» **To move a ruler guide:** Click and drag it to a different location. You can also double-click a ruler guide with the Item tool and enter a new location into the Guide Manager Pro dialog box. (See "Using Guide Manager Pro (the Guides palette)," later in this chapter.)

» **To remove a ruler guide:** Drag the guide back onto the ruler.

» **To remove all ruler guides from a page:** Scroll until a portion of the page touches the ruler and then Option-click (Mac) or Alt-click (Windows) the ruler.

» **To remove all ruler guides from the pasteboard:** Scroll until a portion of the pasteboard touches the ruler and then Option-click (Mac) or Alt-click (Windows) the ruler.

» **To create multiple guides at exact locations:** Use Guide Manager Pro, as explained in the upcoming "Using Guide Manager Pro (the Guides palette)" section.

Using margin and column guides

When you create a new project or layout, you enter values in the Margin Guides fields and Column Guides fields in the New Project or New Layout dialog box, shown in Figure 4-18.

Margin guides indicate a page's outside margins. If you want multiple columns on your page, you use column guides to show where they should be placed. If you select the Automatic Text Box check box in that dialog box, the automatic text box fits within the margin guides, and its columns match the column guides.

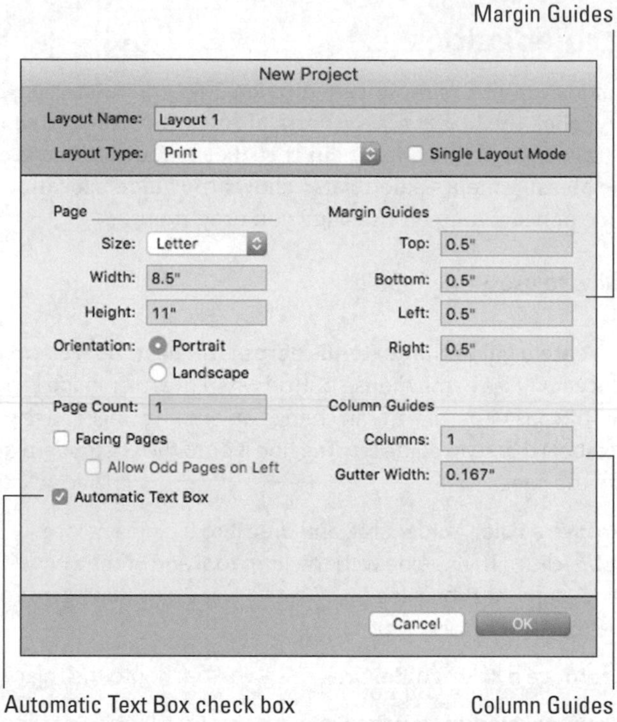

Margin Guides

New Project

Layout Name: Layout 1

Layout Type: Print   □ Single Layout Mode

Page

Size: Letter

Width: 8.5"

Height: 11"

Orientation: ● Portrait
             ○ Landscape

Page Count: 1

□ Facing Pages
    □ Allow Odd Pages on Left
☑ Automatic Text Box

Margin Guides

Top: 0.5"

Bottom: 0.5"

Left: 0.5"

Right: 0.5"

Column Guides

Columns: 1

Gutter Width: 0.167"

Cancel   OK

FIGURE 4-18:
The New
Project dialog
box, which is
identical to the
New Layout
dialog box.

Automatic Text Box check box   Column Guides

To change the placement of the margin guides and column guides after creating a project or layout, display the master page by either double-clicking its icon in the Page Layout palette or by clicking the View Master Page icon at the bottom left of the document window. Then, choose Page ⇨ Master Guides & Grid. In the Master Guides & Grid dialog box that appears, make your changes. If Automatic Text box is enabled for that layout, your changes affect the size, placement, and columns in the automatic text box on every page of the layout that uses this master page.

Snapping to guides

Guides aren't just visual indicators that assist you in aligning items. They can have a "magnetic field" around them so that when you drag an item close to a guide, the item automatically snaps to the guide. To toggle this feature on and off, choose View ⇨ Snap to Guides.

You can also choose View ⇨ Snap to Page Grids to force items to align with the master page grid. See "Using a design grid," later in this chapter, for more about forcing item alignment in this scenario.

Using Guide Manager Pro (the Guides palette)

After you've worked with guides for a while, you may wish for easier ways to create, edit, and copy guides. Look no further than the Guides palette, which is the control center for Guide Manager Pro! To open it, choose Window ⇨ Guides and marvel at the controls, shown in Figure 4-19.

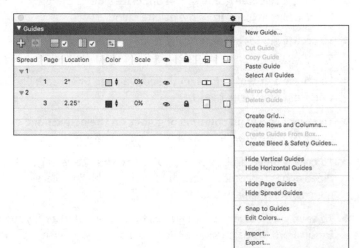

FIGURE 4-19:
The Guides palette, with its palette menu exposed.

The Guides palette lets you not only see all the guides on all the pages of a layout but also control many attributes of a guide, such as its location, orientation, display color, whether it appears on a page or entire spread, and the minimum view scale at which the guide displays. You can edit, copy, and paste guides; mirror guides; create grids, rows, and columns of guides; create guides from a box; and add bleed and safety guides. Wow!

The controls at the top of the palette, from left to right, let you create new guides, mirror guides, show horizontal guides, show vertical guides, show guides only on the current page or spread, and delete guides.

Here are lots more ways to use the Guides palette:

>> **To sort the guides by an attribute:** Click the column heading for that attribute.

>> **To display the page numbers in a spread:** Click the arrow next to the spread number.

>> **To edit a guide:** Double-click it.

>> **To display a context menu of options for a selected guide:** Control-click (Mac) or right-click (Windows) anywhere in the palette.

>> **To display a menu of options for a selected guide or the entire palette:** Click the palette menu at the top right.

>> **To create guides numerically:** Click the Create a New Guide button at the top of the Guides palette or choose New from the palette menu.

>> **To copy a selected guide to the opposite side of the page or spread:** Choose Mirror Guide from the palette menu.

>> **To create guides automatically from the edges of a box:** Select the box and then choose Create Guides from Box from the palette menu.

>> **To create a grid of guides on the active page or spread:** Choose Create Grid from the palette menu.

>> **To create rows and columns of guides on the active page or spread:** Choose Create Rows and Columns from the palette menu.

>> **To create bleed and/or safety guides on the active page:** Choose Create Bleed and Safety Guides from the palette menu. This places guides outside the page, on the pasteboard.

>> **To save your current set of guides for use on another layout:** Choose Export from the palette menu. To load a previously saved set, choose Import.

Using Dynamic Guides

When you create, transform, or move an item, Dynamic Guides automatically appear to help you align the item with other items or the page. To enable or disable them, choose View ⇨ Dynamic Guides ⇨ Show/Hide Dynamic Guides.

The guides are blissfully obvious as you drag your item around the page. They show you when your item aligns to the center or edge of another item, the center or edge of a column in a text box, or the center of the page. They also show when the width or height of your item is equal to that of another item, or when the distance between your item and another item is equal to the distance between other items on the page.

To control which Dynamic Guides appear, choose View ⇨ Dynamic Guides and then choose the type of guide you want to view or hide, as shown in Figure 4-20.

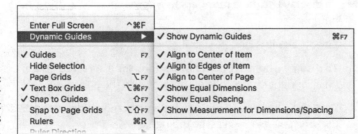

FIGURE 4-20:
The View ⇨ Dynamic Guides submenu.

Using a design grid

A design grid is a set of nonprinting guidelines for aligning text and items. This advanced feature is tremendously useful when designing a publication, or when designing a complex layout for East Asian languages, because it can ensure that everything lines up perfectly on all pages, and within all text boxes. Although this feature is too complex to cover in this book, Quark explains it clearly in the *A Guide to QuarkXPress 2016* at (`http://www.quark.com/Support/Documentation/QuarkXPress/2016.aspx`), as well as in the Help file you can access under the Help menu in QuarkXPress. In the Help file, look for the "Text and typography" category and then open the "Working with design grids" section.

Briefly, design grids work like this: Every page has a design grid that tags along with the master page it's based on. Every text box also has a design grid. Here are some tips for working with a design grid:

» **To view the page grid:** Choose View ➪ Page Grids. To view an active text box's grid, choose View ➪ Text Box Grids. Then Control-click (Mac) or right-click (Windows) the text box and choose Grid Settings from the context menu that appears. Click the Display Settings tab and then select the check boxes next to each of the gridline options that you want to display. Select the Preview check box to see the gridlines appear in the text box.

» **To adjust the page grid for a page:** First display its master page and then choose Page ➪ Master Guides & Grid. To control the placement and spacing of the grid, use the controls in the Text Settings tab. To control the display of the grid, use the controls in the Display Settings tab. To preview changes as you make them, select Preview. To use the specifications of an existing master page grid, grid style, or style sheet, click Load Settings.

» **To save time when working with design grids:** You can create Grid Styles and apply them to new or existing master pages and text boxes. To create and edit grid styles, choose Edit ➪ Grid Styles or choose Window ➪ Grid Styles to display the Grid Styles palette. To apply grid styles, use the Grid Styles palette.

Merging and Splitting Items

For those of us with limited drawing skills, it can be easiest to create a complex shape by combining several simple shapes (just as you can draw a cat's head by drawing a circle with two triangles on top and then merging them into one shape). The Merge or Split Paths menu (choose Item ➪ Merge or Split Paths) gives you the tools for this, and the result is a Bézier box that you can edit with the Pen tools.

TIP

These operations are difficult to comprehend without experimenting, so take a minute to try the different choices with a few basic rectangles and ovals, as shown in Figure 4-21. Try the following: Use Union to create the shapes on the left; Difference to create shapes in the center; and Split Outside Paths to separate the letters that have been converted to boxes.

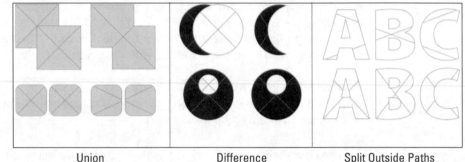

FIGURE 4-21:
Examples
of Merge
and Split
commands.

Union   Difference   Split Outside Paths

Here's how the Merge and Split feature works: You select two or more items and then choose one of the following options from the submenu attached to the Merge or Split Paths menu:

>> **Intersection:** Keeps the areas where the front items overlap the backmost item and removes the rest.

>> **Union:** Combines all the items into one box shaped like the outermost outline of all of them. This is the most-used option by far.

TIP

You can use Union to combine multiple picture boxes into one so that any picture you import gets spread across all the boxes — as if the boxes were windows looking out onto one view.

>> **Difference:** Deletes the front items and cuts out overlapping areas. Use it to punch a hole through one box with another box.

>> **Reverse Difference:** Deletes the back item and cuts out overlapping areas.

>> **Exclusive Or:** Leaves all the shapes intact but cuts out overlapping areas. It creates two points where any two lines originally crossed.

>> **Combine:** Similar to Exclusive Or, but adds no points where two lines intersect.

>> **Split Outside Paths:** Separates the outermost items from each other. For example, when used on text that has been converted to boxes by choosing Item ⇨ Convert Text To Boxes, this option separates each letter in a word.

>> **Split All Paths:** This option is like running Split Outside Paths repeatedly until every box within a complex box has been split. If you use this command on a shape that has a hole in it, the hole becomes solid.

TIP

When you convert text to boxes and then import a picture into the result, the picture shows through all the boxes as if they were windows on a wall looking out onto one scene. To separate the letters so that you can import a different picture into each one, use Split Outside Paths.

Finding and Changing Item Attributes

When you need to change the attributes of a bunch of items at the same time, choose Edit ⇨ Item Find/Change. The window shown in Figure 4-22 appears.

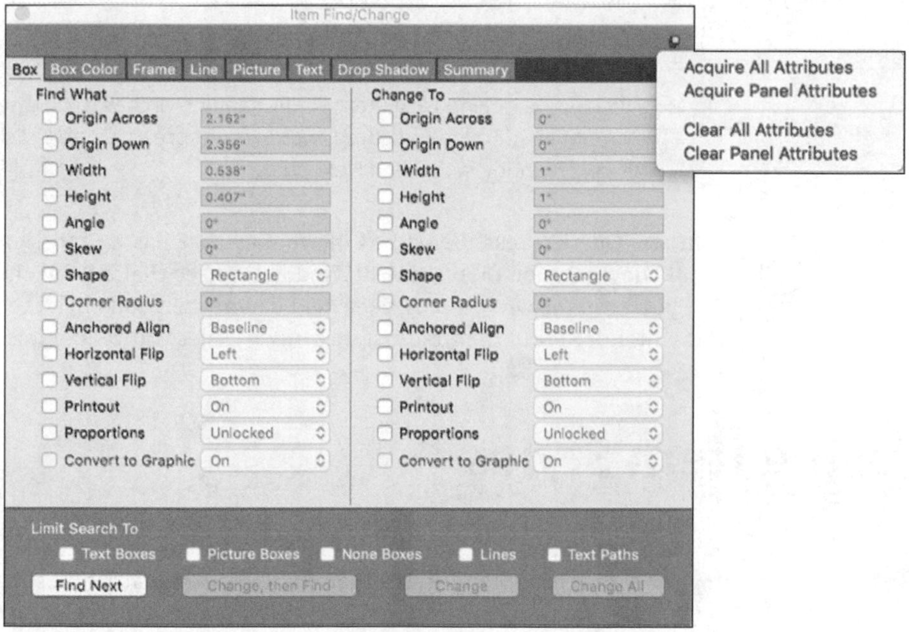

FIGURE 4-22:
The Item
Find/Change
window with
its palette
menu exposed.

The Item Find/Change window works more like a palette than a dialog box, in that you can select and manipulate items on the page while using it.

You can use Item Find/Change on text boxes, picture boxes, no-content boxes, lines, and text paths, but not on tables.

REMEMBER

Here's how you can make use of the Item Find/Change window:

>> To use Item Find/Change, you select the attributes in the Find What column that you want to change; then select those attributes in the Change To column and enter new values into the various fields or choose different options from the pop-up menus.

>> Click the tabs at the top of the Item Find/Change window to see groups of attributes that relate to specific kinds of items. The final Summary tab lists all the changes you've told it to make in all the tabs.

>> To save time, you can add all the attributes of a selected item by choosing Acquire All Attributes from the Palette menu at the top right (refer to Figure 4-22). If you choose Acquire Panel Attributes, only the attributes in that panel are added. If you select multiple items before choosing one of these Acquire options, it adds attributes in the order the items were created; if a newer item's attribute conflicts with an older item's attribute, that attribute is ignored from the newer item.

>> In the area below the attributes, you can limit your search to specific types of boxes or lines. To find and replace all types of items, leave all these boxes deselected.

>> When you click Find Next, Item Find/Change searches the entire layout from start to finish. To limit a search to the active spread, Option-click (Mac) or Alt-click (Windows) the Find Next button.

TIP

In any QuarkXPress dialog box or window that has a Find Next button, you can hold down Option (Mac) or Alt (Windows) to see that button change to Find First. If you keep the Option or Alt key held down when you click the Find First button, it will indeed find the first instance of whatever you're looking for.

Using Item Styles

When consistency is important, or if you value your time when working on a project that has lots of items that share the same attributes, use the Item Styles feature. Conceptually similar to using style sheets for text, Item Styles let you save any combination of item attributes and apply them with one click to a page item. Also, if you need to change one or more attributes across all those items, you can change the item style, and all the items will update. Item Styles can be especially handy for ensuring that drop shadows on related items all look the same. The Item Styles feature works across all the layouts in a project, and you can export and import these styles into different projects.

WARNING

Item Styles has some important limitations: Item Styles do not affect locked attributes of items (position, story, or picture); Item Styles don't work with the Shared Content and Composition Zones features (see Chapter 7 to learn about these features); and Item Styles cannot be used on tables — instead, use Table Styles, as explained in Chapter 12.

Creating and editing Item Styles

To create or edit an Item Style, use either the Item Styles palette (choose Window ➪ Item Styles) or the Edit Item Styles dialog box (choose Edit ➪ Item Styles), shown in Figure 4-23.

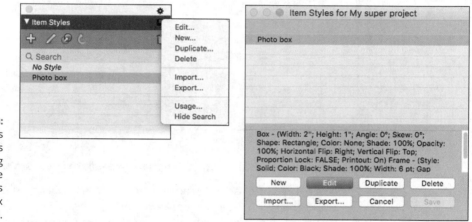

FIGURE 4-23:
The Item Styles palette with its menu showing (left) and the Edit Item Styles dialog box (right).

Using the Item Styles palette

To apply an Item Style to selected items, click its name in the Item Styles palette. The Item Style applied to an item displays in bold.

If the Item Style name has a plus sign (+) next to it, the selected item uses local formatting that is different from what is defined in the Item Style. To remove local formatting from the item, you can click No Style at the top of the Item Styles palette, and then click the Item Style name again. But the quickest way is to Option-click (Mac) or Alt+click (Windows) the name of the Item Style.

To create a new Item Style, follow these steps:

1. **To start with an existing item, select it.**

To start from scratch, make sure that no items are selected.

2. **Click the New button in the Item Styles palette, or choose New from the palette menu.**

   The Edit Item Style dialog box appears as shown in Figure 4-24.

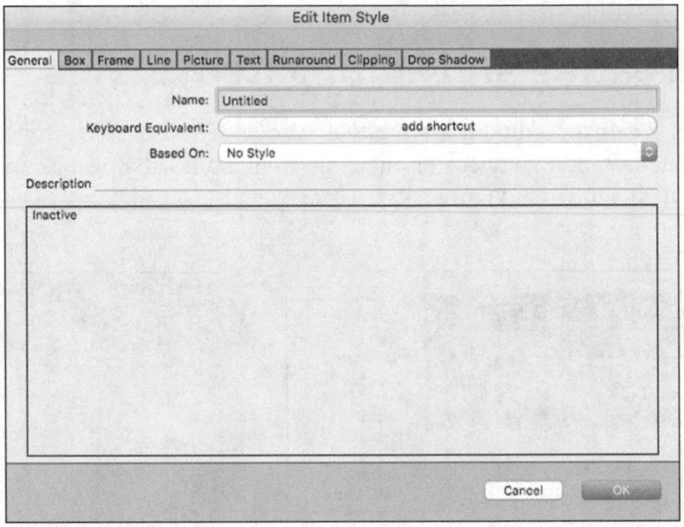

			Edit Item Style					

General | Box | Frame | Line | Picture | Text | Runaround | Clipping | Drop Shadow

Name: Untitled

Keyboard Equivalent: add shortcut

Based On: No Style

Description

Inactive

Cancel   OK

FIGURE 4-24:
The Edit
Item Style
dialog box.

3. **Enter a name for the style, and optionally assign a keyboard shortcut.**

   On a Mac, you can use any combination of Command, Option, Control, and Shift with the numbers on the numeric keypad or the function keys. In Windows, you can use any combination of Control and Alt with the numbers on the numeric keypad, or any combination of Control, Alt, and Shift with the function keys.

   WARNING

   If you use a function key for your shortcut, you override QuarkXPress commands and system-level commands that use that function key.

4. **To base this style on another Item Style, choose its name from the Based On menu.**

   Your new style remembers only the attributes that are different from the Based On style, so if you change attributes of the Based On style, those changes are also applied to this style.

   If you're starting with an existing item, its attributes are listed in the Description field. You can change them by clicking any of the tabs at the top of the dialog box. If you're creating a style from scratch, click those tabs and set the attributes as you want. (See Figure 4-25.) Only the attributes with their check boxes selected are applied. The all-powerful Apply check box at the top left turns all the attributes on or off for that category.

5. **Click OK to save your changes to the Item Style.**

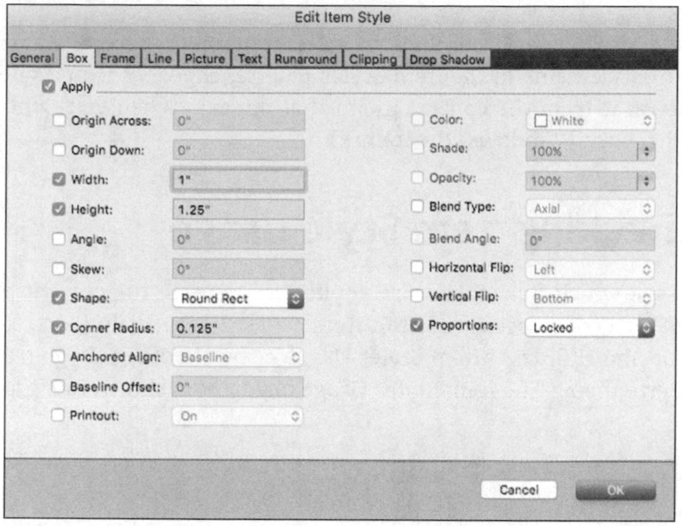

FIGURE 4-25:
Setting attri-
butes in the
Edit Item Style
dialog box.

Here are ways to work with your new or existing Item Style:

>> **To edit a selected Item Style:** Click the pencil icon or choose Edit from the Item Styles palette menu.

>> **To duplicate a selected Item Style:** Click the Duplicate icon next to the pencil icon or choose Duplicate from the Item Styles palette menu.

>> **To search for a style in a long list of styles:** Type part of its name into the Search field.

>> **To export a selected Item Style for use in a different project:** Choose Export from the Item Styles palette menu, navigate to a location on your computer to save the exported Item Style file, and give it a name. To import an Item Style that was exported from a different project, choose Import.

Updating an Item Style from a page item

If you change some attributes of an item that has an Item Style applied to it, and you like those changes so much that you want to apply them to all the other items that use that Item Style, select the item and then click the Update button in the Item Styles palette (it looks like a curved arrow). If you change your mind right after updating the Item Style, you can undo the update by choosing Edit ➪ Undo ItemStyle.

Using the Edit Item Styles dialog box

Choose Edit ➪ Item Styles to open the Edit Item Styles dialog box where you can create, edit, duplicate, delete, import, and export Item Styles exactly as you can by using the palette menu on the Item Styles palette.

TIP

You can apply an Item Style to selected items in several ways: You can click an Item Style name in the Item Styles palette; choose it from Style ⇨ Item Styles; or choose it from the context menu that appears when you Control-click (Mac) or right-click (Windows) the item(s).

Checking Item Style usage

To see which Item Styles are applied to items in the current project, and where local overrides occur, use the Item Styles Usage dialog box. You can open it by choosing Utilities ⇨ Item Styles Usage or by choosing Usage from the Item Styles palette menu. The Item Styles Usage dialog box, shown in Figure 4-26, appears.

Item Styles Usage		
Name	**Page**	**Status**
Photo box	1	OK
Headshot box	1	OK
Photo box	2	Modified
Done	Show	Update

FIGURE 4-26: The Item Styles Usage dialog box.

To see an item on the page that uses an Item Style, click it and then click Show.

If the Status of a selected item is listed as Modified, one or more of its attributes are different from those in the style. Click Update to remove all these local overrides.

Storing Items in Libraries

When you have an item or a group of items that you use frequently, you can store them in a library for easy retrieval into any project. You're not limited to one library; you can have a different library for each client, project type, or any other use. To add an item or group of items to a library, you drag them onto it and optionally give the entry a name. To use an entry, you drag it from the library onto any layout page. Whether you're dragging items into or out of a library, QuarkXPress makes a copy, leaving the original untouched.

REMEMBER

Libraries are platform specific. If you created a library on a Mac, you can use it only on a Mac. If you created it in Windows, you can use it only in Windows. If your workflow is cross-platform, you can't share libraries, so you may want to stop reading this section now.

Here's the scoop on working with libraries:

>> **To create a new library:** Choose File ▷ New ▷ Library. Give the library a name and choose a location to store it on your computer.

>> **To open a library:** Choose File ▷ Open and navigate to that library's file on your computer. You can have multiple libraries open at one time.

>> **To add an entry to an open library:** Select one or more items in your layout and drag them onto the library.

WARNING

If you move an original picture file after importing it into your document or adding it to a library, you have to choose Utilities ▷ Usage and update its location in the Usage dialog box when you copy it from the library onto a layout. Figure 4-27 shows a library on a Mac.

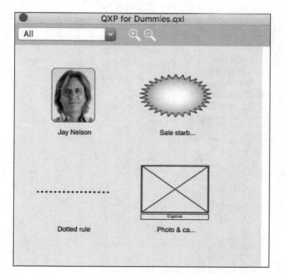

FIGURE 4-27:
A QuarkXPress library on a Mac.

>> **To move an entry within a library:** Click it and drag it to a new position.

>> **To enlarge the entries in the library window:** Click the + magnifying glass icon. To shrink them, click the – magnifying glass icon.

>> **To resize an open library:** Drag one of its edges or corners. For convenience, you can make it wide instead of tall.

>> **To copy an entry from one library into another:** Click it and drag it to the other open library.

>> **To replace an entry in a library:** Select the replacement items in a document and then choose Edit ⇨ Copy. Click the entry in the library to select it and then choose Edit ⇨ Paste.

>> **To remove an entry from a library on a Mac:** Click it and choose Edit ⇨ Clear, or choose Edit ⇨ Cut, or press Delete. To remove an entry from a library in Windows, click the Library palette menu and choose Edit ⇨ Delete or Edit ⇨ Cut.

>> **To manage your entries:** Give each one a label. To add or change a label on an entry, double-click the entry to open the Label dialog box and then enter a new label in the Label field or select an existing label from its drop-down menu and click OK. To see only the entries in the library with one or more specific labels assigned, choose that label from the pop-up menu at the top of the library window, as shown in Figure 4-28. You can choose more than one label to display at one time. To see all the entries again, choose All from that menu.

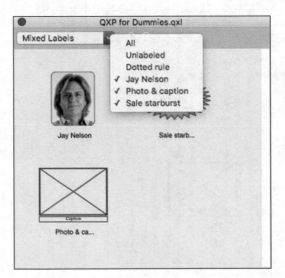

FIGURE 4-28:
The Label
menu in
a library
on a Mac.

By default, QuarkXPress resaves each library every time you make a change to it. However, you can change QuarkXPress Preferences so that the library is saved only when you close it. To make this change on a Mac, choose QuarkXPress ⇨ Preferences; in Windows, choose Edit ⇨ Preferences. In the Open and Save section, deselect Auto Library Save.

Chapter **5**

Building a Layout

As noted in Chapter 1, a QuarkXPress project can contain multiple layouts, and each layout can have any size, orientation, and output intent (print or digital). For information on how to create projects and layouts, please flip back to Chapter 1. This chapter focuses on creating and managing pages within a layout, which includes using master pages to store items that appear on every page, setting up an automatic text box to link long stories across multiple pages, and adding automatic page numbers to every page.

Making and Using Master Pages

If your layout consists of just one or two pages, you can ignore master pages entirely. But if you're using QuarkXPress to publish a newsletter, magazine, book, catalog, or other multipage document, master pages are essential to your pagination happiness.

You may think of a master page as a template for pages, but it's more than that. For example, if you change a master page at any time, your change on the master page ripples throughout your document, affecting every layout page based on that master page. Also, automatic page numbers on a master page will update on layout pages as you add, remove, and rearrange your layout pages.

The most common uses for a master page include headers, footers, background images or colors, and page numbers — any items you want to appear on many pages. If your layout has facing pages (left and right pages of a spread), you can use different content on each side. And your layout isn't limited to just one master page: You can apply different master pages to any combination of layout pages.

When you create a new layout, you automatically generate a master page from the page size, margins, and columns that you choose in the New Layout dialog box. To add content to the master page, or to change its page size, margins, and columns, you need to display the master page instead of a layout page. A layout's master pages (used and unused) are listed in the Page Layout palette, just above the layout pages, as shown in Figure 5-1.

FIGURE 5-1:
The Page
Layout palette.

The master page that is automatically generated when you create the layout is named "A-Master A." In Figure 5-1, the A that you see superimposed on the page 1 icon indicates that this master page was applied to it. Double-click the master page icon to display the master page for editing in the project window.

TIP

The easiest way to display the master page being used by the current layout page is to click the View Master Page button at the bottom left of the project window, as shown in Figure 5-2. When the master page is displaying, you can click that button again to switch back to your layout page. Another way is to choose Page ⇨ Display ⇨ *your master page name.*

FIGURE 5-2:
The View
Master Page
button.

View Master Page

The master page is exactly like a document page, with a few special features:

>> Items that you add to a master page display on every layout page that is based on that master page.

>> All items on the master page are stacked behind the items that you create on the layout page.

>> A master page can have an automatic text box, which allows text to flow from page to page, and can create new pages as you add text to the chain of linked text boxes.

TIP

To control where the new automatic pages are added, open QuarkXPress Preferences, choose Print Layout ⇨ General, and then click the Auto Page Insertion drop-down menu, shown in Figure 5-3. Your choices are Off, End of Story, End of Section, and End of Document. By default, the insertion is set to End of Story, which places your new pages immediately after the page containing the last text box in your current text chain. If your layout is divided into sections (see "Creating a section," later in this chapter), you can choose End of Section instead. End of Document really should be labeled End of Layout instead, because it adds new pages at the end of your current layout.

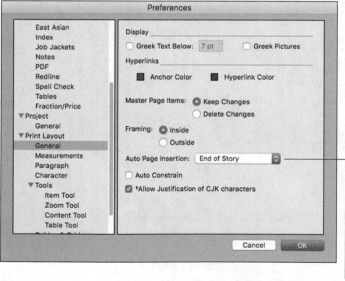

FIGURE 5-3:
Auto page
insertion
options in
QuarkXPress
Preferences.

Auto Page Insertion drop-down menu

The two most common items on a master page are an automatic text box and a text box for an automatic page number.

Creating an automatic text box

Automatic text boxes are most often used in books and other long documents. When an automatic text box is on the master page, QuarkXPress automatically adds new pages as needed whenever long text is imported or typed into a text box. This makes it easy to start with just a few pages and then let QuarkXPress add more as the text gets longer.

With the master page displayed, notice the link icon at the top left of each page (or each page in the spread, if your layout includes facing pages). If the link is broken, that means you didn't enable the Automatic Text Box check box in the New Layout or New Project dialog box when you created your layout. If the link is unbroken, you did enable the Automatic Text Box check box and it's already set up, as shown in Figure 5-4.

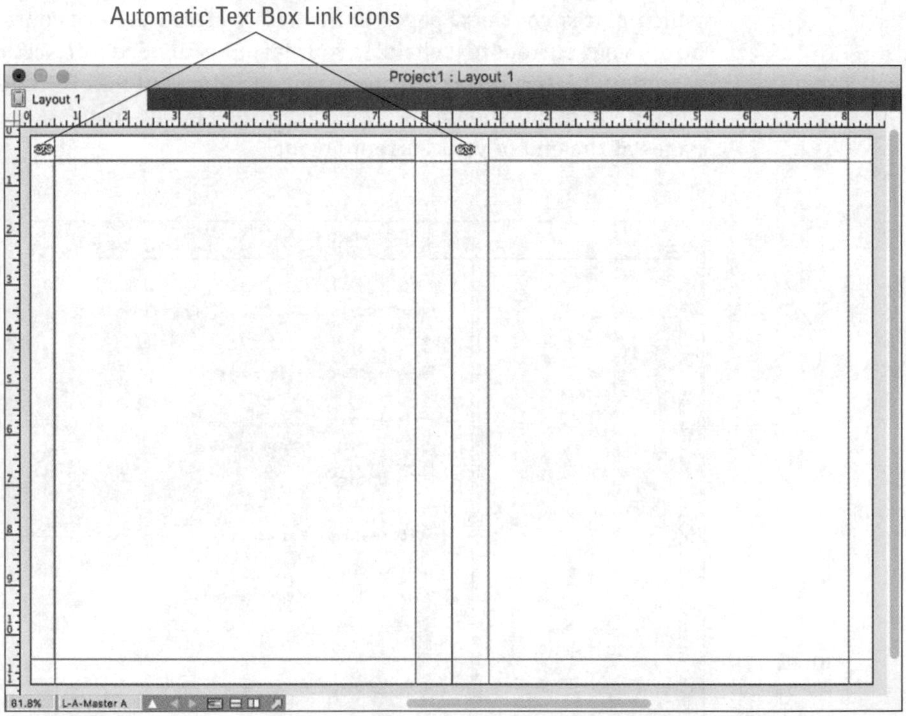

Automatic Text Box Link icons

FIGURE 5-4:
A two-page ("facing") master page with unbroken link icons.

TIP

To verify that your master page is set up with an automatic text box, open the Tools palette, click the Text Linking tool, and then click the text box on the master page. If it's an automatic text box, an arrow appears that connects the link icon to the text box.

If the link icon is broken, you need to create the automatic text box by following these steps:

1. **In the Tools palette, click the Text Content tool, and drag it to create a text box within the margins of the page.**

2. **In the Tools palette, click the Text Linking tool.**

   Your cursor changes to a chain link icon.

3. **Click the broken link icon and then click the text box.**

   An arrow appears that connects the link icon to the text box. Click a blank part of the page to end the linking process.

4. **If your layout has facing pages, repeat the process with the other page in the spread.**

REMEMBER

You can create multiple automatic text boxes on a master page that link to each other. For example, if you want two columns of text with one longer than the other, you need two text boxes. To link the first box to the second box, click the Text Linking tool and then click the first box. Next, click the second box. Text on layout pages then flows from the previous page into the first text box and continues into the second text box. Text that overflows from the second box then flows into the first box on the next page.

Creating an automatic page number

Not all your layouts need page numbers, but at least some certainly will, and you may as well make placing and changing them as easy as possible. Just follow these steps to create a new text box and place page numbers in your document automatically:

1. **In the Tools palette, click the Text Content tool to activate it.**

   Your cursor changes to an I-beam.

2. **Click and drag to create a text box near the top or bottom of each master page.**

   You can position the box on the outside edge of each page, or in the center — whichever design you prefer.

3. **With the Text Content tool still active, click one of the text boxes to select it.**

4. **Choose Utilities ⇨ Insert Character ⇨ Special ⇨ Current Box Page #.**

A character appears that will display as the current page number in layout pages. On the master page, it displays as <#>.

5. **Format and justify the character any way you like.**

Creating a new master page

Most longer documents have multiple sections. For example, a book may have front matter, chapters, appendices, and an index. A magazine may have different page layouts for each section or article. Although QuarkXPress creates your first master page for you, you can create new master pages that have different text box arrangements, page number locations, running headers and footers, or even picture boxes that you want to appear on every page.

You create new master pages in the Page Layout palette. To create a new single-page master page, drag the Blank Single Page icon from the top of the Page Layout palette into the master page area just below it. If your layout was created with the Facing Pages check box enabled, you can also create facing-page master pages by dragging the Blank Facing Page icon from the top of the Page Layout palette into the master page area. Either way, a new master page displays in the palette and is named one letter after the newest existing master page (for example, after "A-Master A" comes "B-Master B").

Duplicating a master page

If you have a master page that you like, but want to change some of it and make a new master page, you can duplicate it and then make your changes. To do so, click the master page in the Page Layout palette and then click the Duplicate button just above it or choose Duplicate from the Page Layout palette menu. When the new master page appears in the palette, double-click its icon to display it in the project window for editing.

Converting a layout page to a master page

QuarkXPress doesn't let you convert a layout page into a master page, but you can work around this limitation by using the Paste In Place feature. To do so, follow these steps:

1. **Select all the items on the layout page that you want to use on the master page.**

One way to select all the items is to click the Item tool in the Tools palette and choose Edit ⇨ Select All.

2. **Choosing Edit ➡ Copy to copy the items to the Clipboard.**

3. **Create a new blank master page or switch to an empty master page and choose Edit ➡ Paste In Place.**

   The items you copied from the layout page are pasted into the exact same position on the master page.

Deleting a master page

To delete a master page, click it in the Page Layout palette and then either click the trash can icon at the top right of the palette or choose Delete from the Page Layout palette menu. Any layout pages that are based on that master page keep all their current items but are no longer associated with a master page.

Changing the name of a master page

As lovely and elegant as "A-Master A" is, you can change the name of any master page to something more meaningful to you. To change the name of a master page, double-click its name in the Page Layout palette to highlight it and type a new name. Always keep the letter-and-hyphen structure at the front of the name, because the letters before the hyphen (up to three) display on the page icons in the Page Layout palette. For example, use "A-Front Matter" or "BDY-Body Page."

Adding new layout pages

As you work with your document, you may be continually adding or deleting pages. Here are the two quickest ways to add new pages to your layout:

>> Choose Page ➡ Insert from the system menu bar or Insert Pages from the Page Layout palette menu.

>> In the Page Layout palette, press Option (Mac) or Alt (Windows) and then drag a master page or blank page icon from the top part to the desired location in the bottom part where the page icons are.

Either way, the Insert Pages dialog box, shown in Figure 5-5, displays. Enter the number of new pages you want, where they should go, and what master page to base them on. If a text box is currently selected on your existing layout page, and the master page has an automatic text box on it, the Link to Current Text Chain check box is available. If you enable that check box, the text boxes on your new pages are linked to the selected text box.

FIGURE 5-5:
The Insert
Pages
dialog box.

Insert Pages

Insert: 3 page(s)

○ before page:
● after page: 2
○ at end of layout

☑ Link to Current Text Chain

Master Page: A-Master A

Cancel   OK

Deleting layout pages

To delete one or more layout pages, select them in the Page Layout palette and then either click the trash can icon at the top right of the palette or choose Delete Pages from the Page Layout palette menu. Nothing to it!

WARNING

To understand what happens when a text box on the deleted page is linked to a text box on a page you're not deleting, see the section in Chapter 8 about linking text boxes.

Moving layout pages

You have several ways to move one or more layout pages to a different position in the flow of pages. First, select any pages you want to move in the Page Layout palette and then do one of the following:

>> Drag the page or pages to a new location in the Page Layout palette. Arrows and page icons appear to let you know where your page(s) will land.

>> Choose either Page ➪ Move Pages or Move Pages from the Page Layout palette menu. The Move Pages dialog box, shown in Figure 5-6, appears.

TIP

Oddly, the Before Page: and After Page: options share the same field for a page number, so don't be confused by the fact that the "after page:" option doesn't seem to have its own number field.

Move Pages

Move page(s): 1   thru: 2   ○ before page: 3
                               ● after page:
                               ○ to end of layout

Cancel   OK

WARNING

Moving pages in a facing-pages layout is fraught with peril. To be safe, move only even numbers of pages, and move them to the same relative left-right position from which they came. For example, if you move a selection of four pages that starts with a right-facing page, be sure to move that set of pages so that the first page you move remains as a right-facing page. Otherwise, your master page items can get scrambled.

Applying a different master page to a layout page

When setting up a layout that uses multiple master pages, you sometimes need to change the master page that a layout page is based on. For example, you may have created several new layout pages and mistakenly based them on the wrong master page. Or, there may be no master page assigned to a layout page because when you created the page, you based it on a Blank Single Page or Blank Facing Page instead of a master page. (See the "Adding new layout pages" section, earlier in this chapter, for details on how to add new pages.)

To apply a master page to a layout page, do one of these things in the Page Layout palette:

» Drag a master page from the top part of the palette onto a layout page in the bottom part.

» Select the target page or pages in the bottom part of the palette, then press Option/Alt and click the desired master page in the top part of the palette.

Either way, the layout page(s) will receive all the items from the master page.

Changing master page items

When you change an item on a master page, that change is automatically copied to any layout pages that are based on that master page. However, unless you locked an item on a master page (by choosing Item ⇨ Lock ⇨ Position or Item ⇨ Lock ⇨ Story — or both), you can change the position and text of that item on a layout page.

If you change the position or text of a master page item on a layout page, the changes you made to the item on the layout page override similar changes you may subsequently make on the master page. For example, if you change the font in a text box on a layout page, and then change the font to something else on the master page, your layout page will keep the font that you used there. Or, if you move an item on a layout page and then move that item somewhere else on the master page, the item on the layout page will not change its position to match the master page.

To force the changes made on a master page to apply to the items on a layout page, drag the master page in the Page Layout palette onto a layout page icon in the bottom part. When you do this, one of two things will happen, depending on a setting in QuarkXPress Preferences (to get to the setting, open QuarkXPress Preferences by choosing QuarkXPress ⇨ Preferences on a Mac or Edit ⇨ Preferences in Windows and then scroll down to Print Layout and click General):

>> If Master Page Items is set to Keep Changes, the changed item is left as it is but is no longer linked with the master page, and a copy of the item from the master page is added.

>> If Master Page Items is set to Delete Changes, the changed item is deleted and replaced with a copy of the item from the master page.

Modifying Page Size and Margins (If You Dare)

After you've set up your layout and added text and other items to its pages, changing the page size, margins, and columns can wreak havoc with the arrangement of items on those pages. So, making these changes is not something you want to do unless you haven't yet put much on the pages and you understand a lot about how QuarkXPress works. If you still want to make these kinds of changes, read on.

Changing page size

Page size is an attribute of the layout, so changing the page size affects all the pages in the layout. To change page size, choose Layout ⇨ Layout Properties. In the dialog box that appears, you can change page width, height, and orientation. To change the margins and columns, you need to switch to the master page, as explained next.

Changing margins and guides

Margins and column guides are an attribute of the master page used by a layout page. To display the master page for the current layout page, click the View Master Page button at the bottom left of the project window, as shown previously in Figure 5-2. While viewing the master page, choose Page ⇨ Master Guides & Grid to display the dialog box shown in Figure 5-7.

The tiny chain icons that connect the Top/Bottom and Inside/Outside guide location fields let you control whether your change in one value also changes the other. If the chain is broken, you can use different values in the two related fields. If it's solid, changing one will change the other as well — this can save you some typing and help ensure that the margins that should be the same width *are* the same width. To change a broken chain to a solid one (or vice versa), click the chain icon.

TIP

Behold the handy Content Dimensions values in the Master Guides & Grid dialog box! As you change the margin sizes, these values also change to indicate the size of the area inside the margins — which is usually also the size of the automatic text box.

Numbering Pages in Sections

Some long documents are traditionally formatted in sections. For example, a book may include the front matter, chapters, and back matter — each of which may have a different page numbering style, such as roman numerals, letters, or Arabic (modern) page numbers. Also, you may need to begin a layout with a page number other than 1. To control the page numbering in this manner, you create a section.

Creating a section

To create a section, make sure that the page you want to be the first page of the section is the currently active page by clicking that page in the project window. That page's Pasteboard then appears lighter than the Pasteboard around the other pages, and its page icon is highlighted in the Page Layout palette. Next, choose Page ⇨ Section or choose Section from the Page Layout palette menu. The Section dialog box appears, as shown in Figure 5-8.

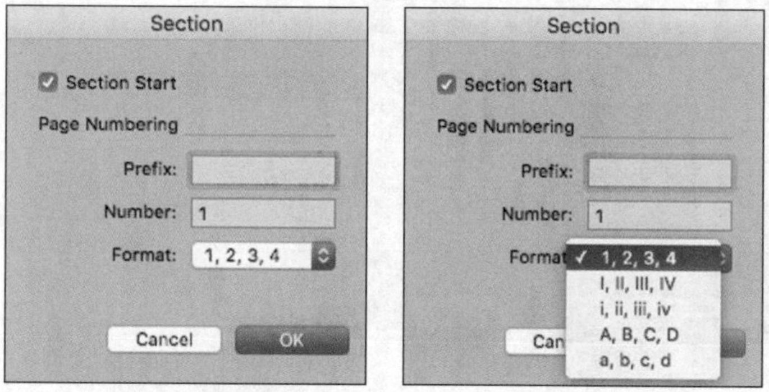

FIGURE 5-8:
The Section dialog box (left) with its Format menu exposed (right).

Click the Section Start check box to enable it; then choose among the following Page Numbering options:

>> **Prefix:** Type anything here that you want to appear before each page number.

>> **Number:** Type the number you want as the beginning page number for this section.

>> **Format:** Choose a numbering format from the menu. Commonly, you use Arabic numbers (1, 2, 3, 4) for chapter pages; you use roman numerals (I, II, III, IV or i, ii, iii, iv) for front matter; and you use alphabetic letters (A, B, C, D or a, b, c, d) for appendices and other back matter. The page numbers on the page can appear in the format you choose.

Changing the starting page number

After you create a section, you can go back and change its starting page number if you need to. First, make sure that the active page is the first page of the section. In the Page Layout palette, the first page of a section has an asterisk (*) after its page number. Double-click that page's icon to make that page active. Then choose Page ⇨ Section or choose Section from the Page Layout palette menu to open the Section dialog box. Type a new page number in the Number field and click OK.

Changing the page numbering style

To change the page numbering style (roman, Arabic, or alphabetic), reopen the Section dialog box as explained in the previous section and choose a new option from the Format menu.

Adding prefixes to page numbers

To add a prefix to each page number, reopen the section dialog box by choosing Page ⇨ Section or choosing Section from the Page Layout palette menu; then type the prefix text into the Prefix field.

Creating a "Continued on Page . . ." Jump Line

You can add an automatic page number to any page of your layout — not just master pages. This feature can be handy when you need a "continued on" or "continued from" message for a story that jumps to another page. The best approach is to create a separate text box for this jump line and position it on top of the linked text box. (If you type your "continued on" message inside the text box, it will move if the other text in the box reflows. Not good.)

Type **continued from page** in the text box and then choose Utilities ⇨ Insert Character ⇨ Special ⇨ Previous Box Page #. To insert the page number of the next box in the chain instead, choose Next Box Page #. Through some magic known only to Quark, this separate text box picks up the page number of the previous or next text box linked to the box beneath it and automatically updates the page number if those boxes should move.

IN THIS CHAPTER

» **Using the Books palette to create a book**

» **Working with chapters**

» **Generating a table of contents**

» **Putting together an index**

» **Including footnotes and endnotes in your chapters**

Chapter **6**

Building a Book

As any book publisher can tell you, building a book involves processes and techniques unique to this craft. Sure, page layout tools are the same regardless of the project, but managing a book's chapters, keeping styles consistent, building a table of contents and an index, and managing multiple documents possibly authored by different people requires book-specific techniques. That's what the Book features in QuarkXPress are all about — and what's covered in this chapter.

In QuarkXPress, a book is a collection of QuarkXPress layouts, from one or more projects, linked together in the Books palette. Each layout becomes a chapter, and you assign one chapter as the master chapter. The master chapter's colors, style sheets, hyphenation, and justification settings, lists, dashes, and stripes can be synchronized with any or all of the other chapters, to maintain consistency throughout the book. Also, the order of the chapters in the Book palette determines the page numbers for each chapter: As you add or remove pages, page numbers adjust in the book's later chapters.

Because each chapter file is a separate document, multiple people can work on a book at the same time. The entire collection of files is used only when you're building a list (for example, a table of contents) or an index, or when you're printing or exporting to PDF format.

This chapter unravels the mystery of how to put a book together. You find out how to start creating a book through the Books palette; how to work with chapters, which QuarkXPress treats as separate project files; and how to include a table contents, index, and footnotes and endnotes.

Starting a Book

You handle all the administrative activities involving a book in the Books palette, which you get to by choosing Window ⇨ Books. You can open only one book at a time, but multiple chapters can be open and edited by one or more people. As those chapters get saved and replaced in their original location, their information gets updated in the Books palette. When someone closes a chapter, it becomes available for others to open and edit. QuarkXPress saves the changes you make to a book in the Book palette when you close the Book palette or quit QuarkXPress.

REMEMBER

A book doesn't include the separate chapter files. QuarkXPress treats those files as separate project files, and they behave just like any other QuarkXPress project file. The book palette simply remembers where those files are on your hard drive or server and can access their content.

To create a new book, follow these steps:

1. **In QuarkXPress, choose File ⇨ New ⇨ Book.**

A dialog box appears that asks you to name your book file and choose a location to store it. This book file is separate from the chapter files that you will add to it, and must be stored on the same hard drive or server with your book chapter files.

2. **In the Save As field, specify a location to save the book file and give it a name.**

The Books palette opens with your new book active in it, as shown in Figure 6-1.

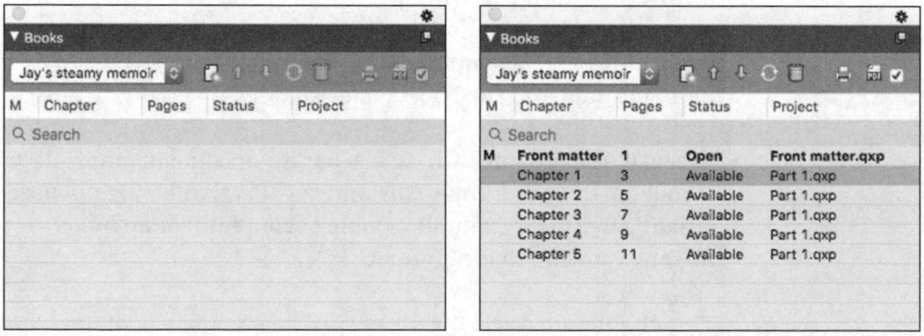

FIGURE 6-1:
The Books palette before adding chapters (left) and after (right).

▼ Books				
Jay's steamy memoir				
M	Chapter	Pages	Status	Project
Q Search				

▼ Books				
Jay's steamy memoir				
M	Chapter	Pages	Status	Project
Q Search				
M	Front matter	1	Open	Front matter.qxp
	Chapter 1	3	Available	Part 1.qxp
	Chapter 2	5	Available	Part 1.qxp
	Chapter 3	7	Available	Part 1.qxp
	Chapter 4	9	Available	Part 1.qxp
	Chapter 5	11	Available	Part 1.qxp

WARNING

If you intend to allow multiple users to edit chapters, you must store the book and its chapter files on a shared network server.

REMEMBER

When you create a book, QuarkXPress creates a Job Jacket XML file with the same name in the same location. This Job Jacket file is automatically attached to each QuarkXPress project that you add to the book as a chapter and enables all the chapters to share style sheets, colors, and other specifications that you want to synchronize across those chapters. If you move or copy your book to another location, you must also include this Job Jacket XML file. For more on Job Jackets, see Chapter 7.

WARNING

QuarkXPress 10 and higher cannot read books created in QuarkXPress 3 to 9. To re-create one of these older books, you must open and save each chapter file in QuarkXPress 10 or higher, and then add them to a new book.

Working with Chapters

Each chapter in a book exists as a separate layout in a QuarkXPress project located on the same volume (hard drive or server) as the book file. To add it as a chapter, the layout must be a print layout, not a digital layout, and it must have last been saved in QuarkXPress 10 format or higher.

Adding layouts to a book as chapters

To add a layout to a book, follow these steps:

1. **In the Books palette, click the Add Chapters button (or choose Add Chapters from the Books palette menu).**

The dialog box in Figure 6-2 appears. (If a chapter is selected in the Books palette when you add new chapters, those chapters are added below the selected chapter — otherwise, they are added at the end of the book.)

2. **Click the project that contains the layout(s) you want to add as chapters.**

The project's layouts are listed in the Layouts area below the file list (refer to Figure 6-2).

3. **Select the check boxes for the layouts you want to add as chapters and then click the Add button.**

The layouts you selected appear as new chapters in the Books palette.

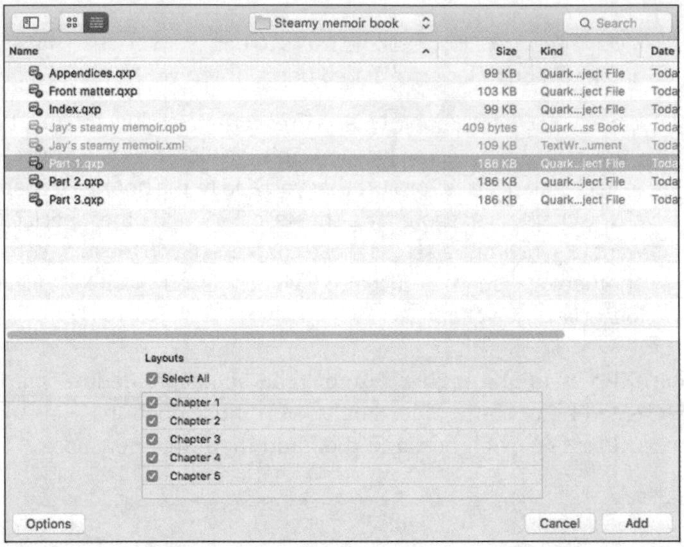

FIGURE 6-2:
The Add
Chapters
dialog box.

Working with chapters in the Books palette

The Books palette, shown in Figure 6-3, is command central for everything related to books you create. The menu at the top left lets you switch among books you've created. The buttons along the top let you do the following:

» **Add Chapters:** Adds new chapters to the open book

» **Move Chapter Up/Down:** Moves selected chapters up and down in the chapter list

» **Synchronize:** Synchronizes selected chapters with the master chapter

» **Remove Chapters:** Deletes selected chapters

» **Print Chapters:** Prints selected chapters

» **Export to PDF:** Exports selected chapters to PDF

The Single File check box next to the PDF icon controls whether multiple chapters are combined into one PDF file or are exported as separate PDF files. When this check box is enabled (turned on?), all selected chapters are combined into one PDF. Many of these controls are also available in the Books palette menu exposed on the right side of the palette.

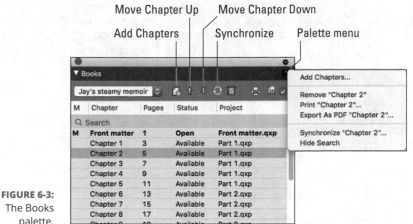

FIGURE 6-3:
The Books palette.

Specifying the master chapter

When you add the first chapter to a book, it becomes the master chapter. The master chapter defines the style sheets, colors, hyphenation and justification specifications, lists, and dashes and stripes that you want to use throughout the book. To choose a new master chapter, click it to select it and then click the leftmost column (under the M heading, for master).

Synchronizing the settings for chapters

As you add new chapters, you may want to synchronize them, which means to adopt the settings from the master chapter. Some examples of settings to synchronize are colors, style sheets, and item styles. To synchronize new chapters, follow these steps:

1. **Click the chapter name and then click the Synchronize button to open the Synchronize Selected Chapters dialog box, shown in Figure 6-4.**

2. **To synchronize all settings, click the Synch All button.**

3. **To choose a specific setting to synchronize, select it from the Synchronize list.**

   All the items in that setting appear in the left box.

   (a) To include all the items, click the Include All button; they move to the box on the right.

   (b) To include one item, click it and then click the right-pointing arrow to move it to the right box.

   (c) To remove an item that you don't want synchronized, click it in the box on the right and then click the left-pointing arrow.

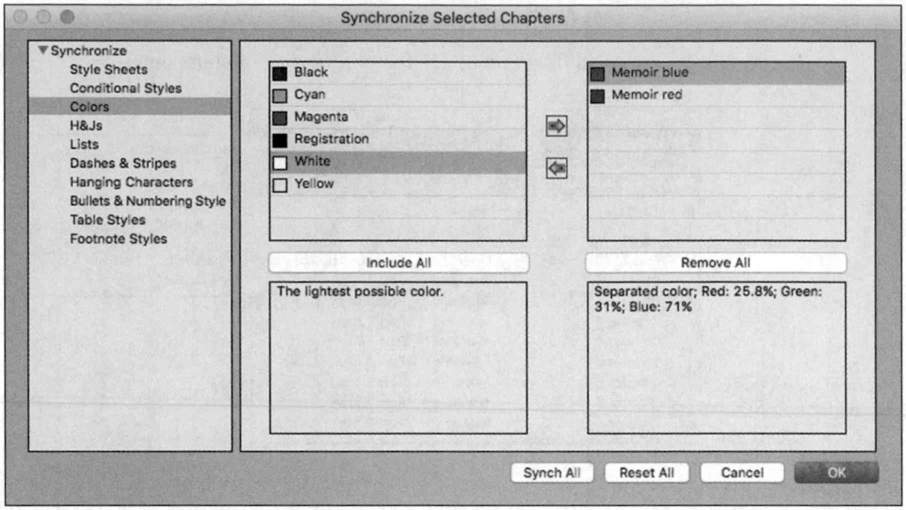

FIGURE 6-4:
The Synchro-
nize Selected
Chapters
dialog box.

Any of the selected settings that exist in the new chapter are redefined using the attributes from the master chapter. Any selected settings in the master chapter that aren't in the new chapter are added to the new chapter.

REMEMBER

Thankfully, any settings in the new chapter that aren't in the master chapter remain in the new chapter, but aren't added to the master chapter. (This is a one-way street.)

Reordering chapters

To move a chapter up or down in the list, click the chapter and then click either the Move Chapter Up or Move Chapter Down button. The selected chapter moves up or down one row. When you reorder chapters, QuarkXPress updates the automatic page numbers.

Numbering pages and sections

As long as your chapters don't include sections (see Chapter 5 for details about sections), QuarkXPress assigns sequential page numbers to all the pages in your book. If a chapter has sections, the sections and page numbers are maintained. Many publishers like to use roman numerals for front matter, regular Arabic numerals for the body pages, and alphabetic letter prefixes for back matter. To create or remove a section marker, you choose Page ⇨ Section while the first page of your section is active.

Opening a chapter

To open a chapter, double-click it in the Books palette. The original QuarkXPress file for that chapter opens in the project window. The Status column in the Books palette shows the current availability of each chapter:

>> **Available** indicates that you can open the chapter.

>> **Open** indicates that you already have the chapter open on your computer.

>> **Modified** indicates that the chapter has been opened and edited independently of the book. To update the status to Available, reopen the chapter through the Books palette and then close the chapter.

>> **Missing** indicates that the chapter's file has been moved since it was added to the book. Double-click the chapter name to display a dialog box for locating the file.

Printing a chapter or book

To print an entire book, make sure that no chapters are selected. To select one chapter, click it. To select consecutive chapters, press Shift while you click them. To select or deselect nonconsecutive chapters, press Command/Ctrl while you click them.

Click the Print Chapters button to display the Print dialog box. For more on print settings, see Chapter 16.

WARNING

If a chapter is missing or in use by someone else, the book will not print.

Exporting a PDF of a chapter or book

To export an entire book, make sure that no chapters are selected. To choose one chapter, click it. To select consecutive chapters, press Shift while you click them. To select nonconsecutive chapters, press Command/Ctrl while you click them.

Notice whether the Single File check box is enabled next to the Export as PDF button. If it is, a single PDF will be generated from all the selected chapters. If it isn't enabled, QuarkXPress generates a separate PDF for each selected chapter.

Click the Export as PDF button to display the Export as PDF dialog box. For more on PDF export settings, see Chapter 17.

If a chapter is missing or in use by someone else, the book will not export to PDF.

When you enter page numbers in the Print or Export as PDF dialog boxes, you must use the complete page number, including any prefix, or an absolute page number. An *absolute page number* is a page's actual position relative to the first page of a document, regardless of the way in which the document is sectioned. To specify an absolute page number in a dialog box, type a plus (+) sign before the number. For example, to display the third page in a document, enter **+3**, regardless of its printed page number.

Generating a Table of Contents

In QuarkXPress, a table of contents is considered one type of list within the List feature. To create a list, you choose a few style sheets that you also use on heads, subheads, and so forth. Any paragraphs or words that have those style sheets applied to them are added to the List. For example, if your project uses style sheets named Chapter Head and Section Head, you can create a two-level List that includes an entry for each paragraph that has those style sheets applied to them, followed by the page number where they appear — a classic table of contents. Another use for a list might be to compile a list of illustrations based on a style sheet that you use for captions, or perhaps a list of products in a catalog, or a list of people in a directory.

Setting up a list

After you apply style sheets to all the text in your book, you need to create a new style sheet to control the appearance of the list. You may want to name this style sheet Table of Contents or TOC.

To create the list, choose Window ⇨ Lists to open the Lists palette, as shown in Figure 6-5.

If you have a book open, its name appears in the Show List For menu. Otherwise, that menu displays only Current Layout. To create a list for the entire book, choose the book name.

When you switch between Current Layout and your book name in the Show List For menu, the list items may disappear. Click the Update button to view the list items again.

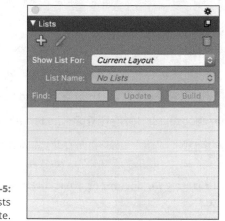

FIGURE 6-5:
The Lists
palette.

To create a new list, follow these steps:

1. **Click the New List (+) button or choose New List from the Lists palette menu.**

   The Edit List dialog box appears, as shown in Figure 6-6.

Edit List

Name: Table of Contents

Available Styles:

Name
¶ Body Text
A Head-big
¶ Normal
A Normal
¶ TOC-1
¶ TOC-2

Styles in List:

Name	Level	Numbering		Format As	
¶ Chapter Head	1 ○	Text only	○ ¶	TOC-1	○
¶ Section Head	2 ○	Page#...Text	○ ¶	TOC-2	○

☐ Alphabetical

Cancel   OK

FIGURE 6-6:
The Edit List
dialog box.

2. **Enter the name for your list.**

3. **To add a style sheet, click its name in the Available Styles box and then click the right-pointing arrow.**

   The style sheet you selected appears in the Styles in List box on the right.

4. **Choose an indent level for each style sheet:**

   ● **Level 1:** Use for your topmost list entries, such as Chapter Head

   ● **Level 2:** Use for your next highest entry, such as Section Head

5. **Choose a Numbering option for each style sheet:**

- **Text** displays only the text of the entry without its page number

- **Text...Page#** displays the text, and then a tab, and then the page number

- **Page#...Text** displays the page number, and then a tab, and then the text

6. **In the Format As column, choose a style sheet from the drop-down menu.**

This style sheet will format the text of each level when QuarkXPress builds it on the page.

7. **Click the OK button to return to your document; then click the Update button in the Lists palette.**

QuarkXPress adds all your list items to the bottom part of the Lists palette, as shown in Figure 6-7.

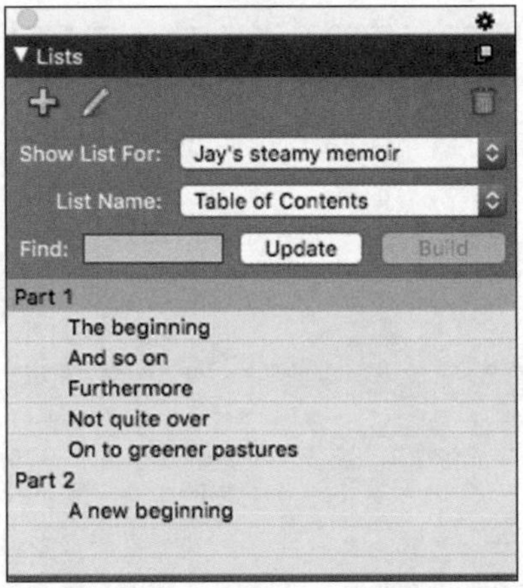

FIGURE 6-7:
The Lists palette with the beginning of a table of contents.

WARNING

The list items in the Lists palette don't update automatically as you make changes to your document. You must click the Update button to force QuarkXPress to reexamine your layout(s) whenever you want to be sure that you're seeing the most current list.

Building a list (collecting the list items into a text box)

After you've set up your list the way you like it and clicked the Update button in the Lists palette to make sure that its content is current, you can let QuarkXPress build it for you inside a text box. To do that, place the text insertion point in a text box and then click Build in the Lists palette. QuarkXPress builds the list automatically and formats it using the style sheets that you chose in the drop down menu of the Format As column in the Edit Lists dialog box.

Rebuilding a list (updating list items in a text box)

To update a formatted list in a text box, click the text box to select it, click Update in the Lists palette (to make sure that the list is up-to-date), and then click Build in the Lists palette. QuarkXPress detects the list in the box and displays a message asking whether you want to insert a new copy of the list or replace the existing version. To update the existing list, click Replace.

TIP

A list can be useful for navigating your document, even if you never build or print it. If you double-click any item in the Lists palette, you jump directly to that text in the layout. It's like having a hyperlinked table of contents for your layout or book!

TIP

When exporting your layout to a PDF file, QuarkXPress can convert your table of contents to bookmarks in the PDF. This lets users quickly navigate to any entry in the table of contents with one click in the Bookmarks panel of their PDF reader.

To convert your TOC to bookmarks, follow these steps:

1. **In the PDF Export dialog box, click the Options button.**

The PDF Export Options dialog box opens, as shown in Figure 6-8.

2. **In the Hyperlinks section, select Export Lists as Bookmarks and choose your Table of Contents list (or any list) from the Use List menu.**

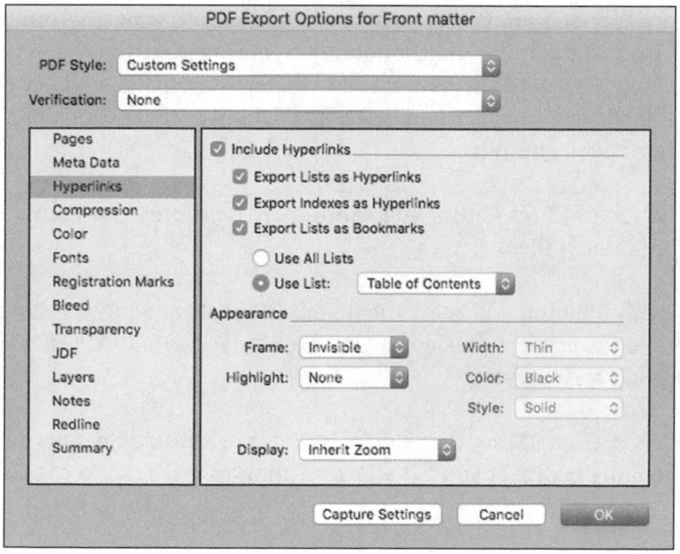

FIGURE 6-8:
The PDF Export Options dialog box.

Creating an Index

Creating an index in QuarkXPress begins with marking words in documents as first-level, second-level, third-level, or fourth-level index entries. You can create cross-references and choose whether index entries cover a word, a number of paragraphs, a text selection, or all the text until the next occurrence of a specific style sheet. To build the index, you specify a format (nested or run-in), punctuation, a master page, and style sheets for the various levels. QuarkXPress then creates and styles the index for you.

Here's a brief overview of the process:

1. Use the Index palette (Window menu) to tag text as an index entry.

2. Specify punctuation for the index in the Index Preferences dialog box (QuarkXPress/Edit ⇨ Preferences ⇨ Index).

3. When your book is complete, generate the index using the Build Index dialog box (Utilities menu).

The process of building an index involves far more details than I can cover in this book. Thankfully, Quark's *QuarkXPress User Guide* guides you through the process.

Using Footnotes and Endnotes

Footnotes and endnotes consist of two linked parts: the reference number that appears in the text, and the footnote/endnote text that appears at the bottom of the text. Footnote text is created at the end of a page, and endnote text is created at the end of a story. As you insert and delete footnotes and endnotes, QuarkXPress automatically numbers them.

As of QuarkXPress 2016, you can import footnotes and endnotes from Microsoft Word (.docx) files.

As with building an Index, the details of creating Footnotes and Endnotes are too detailed to cover in this book. However, Quark's *QuarkXPress User Guide* guides you through the process.

REMEMBER

Quark's *QuarkXPress User Guide* includes additional details about creating and managing books. If you get stuck, turning to this resource is a good idea.

Chapter **7**

Share and Share Alike: Syncing and Collaborating

The ability to share items, groups, and entire layouts adds a virtual third dimension to your layout tools in QuarkXPress. If you've ever used the same text, graphic, or ad in multiple projects, and had to track down every instance of it when a change is made, you understand the kind of headache these synchronization features can relieve.

This chapter explains how to allow text, pictures, groups of page items and entire multipage layouts to be shared, and how to use those shared items on other layouts. It also explains how to allow other QuarkXPress users to contribute content to your layout at the same time as you're working on it. And finally, Quark's revolutionary Job Jackets "preflight done right" feature is briefly explained so that you might consider implementing it into your workflow.

Sharing and Synchronizing Items

When your layout has an item that repeats in multiple places, all the items can share content, attributes, or both. Items that can be shared include pictures, boxes, lines, formatted and unformatted text, and chains of linked text boxes.

You can use synchronization on three different levels of items:

» **Shared item:** You can synch the shape, position, attributes or content of one item across an unlimited number of instances in a project. If you edit any of the instances, all of them change as well!

» **Composition Zone:** A *Composition Zone* is an area of a page that can be used on other pages, layouts, or projects. When you edit the original, all the instances change as well.

» **Shared layout:** A *shared layout* is an entire multipage layout from one project that can appear in other projects. When you edit the original, the changes ripple out to all the instances. (Quark considers this a type of Composition Zone.)

To share and synchronize an item, follow these steps:

1. **Choose Window⇨ Content to display the Content palette, as shown in Figure 7-1.**

2. **Select the item you want to synchronize.**

3. **Click the Add Item (+) button in the Content palette.**

   The Shared Item Properties dialog box displays, as shown in Figure 7-2.

4. **To share the attributes of a selected item, such as its size, frame, color, and so on, select the Synchronize Box Attributes check box.**

5. **To share the actual text or picture in the box, select the Synchronize Content check box for that box.**

   This has two options, depending on whether you want to share the content's formatting or not:

   • **Content and Attributes:** Choose this option to share the text with its formatting or the picture with its formatting.

   • **Content Only:** Choose this option to share the text or picture without its formatting.

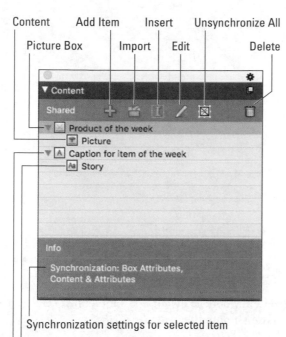

Content   Add Item   Insert   Unsynchronize All

Picture Box   Import   Edit   Delete

Synchronization settings for selected item

Content

Text Box

FIGURE 7-1:
The Content
palette, with
a picture box
and a text box
added.

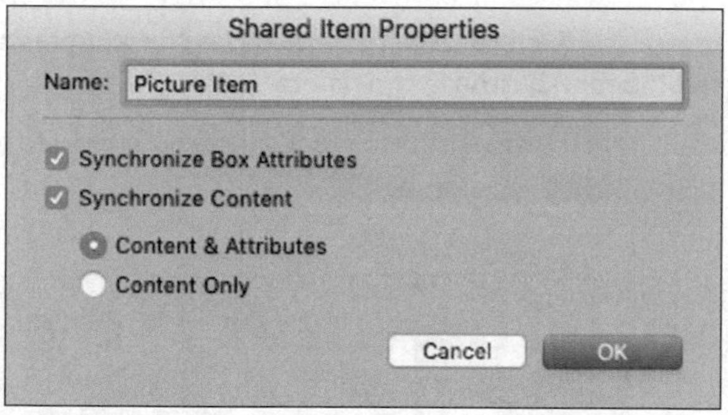

Name: Picture Item

☑ Synchronize Box Attributes
☑ Synchronize Content
   ● Content & Attributes
   ○ Content Only

Cancel   OK

FIGURE 7-2:
The Shared
Item Properties
dialog box.

WARNING

When you share the content in a text box, the complete text is shared. To share only part of the text, use a Content Variable as explained in Chapter 11.

6.   Click OK to add the item to the Content palette.

The item's resizing handles change to squiggles, as shown in Figure 7-3. In this figure, the box on the left is selected; the box on the right is not.

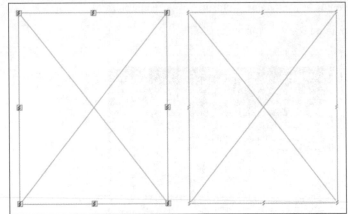

FIGURE 7-3:
A shared
box and its
handles.

Placing shared items and content

Placing a shared item where you want it is simple: Just select the item in the Content palette and drag it onto the page.

Placing shared content is slightly more involved than placing an item, but not by much. To place shared content where you want it, follow these steps:

1. **Select a text box, text path, or picture box on the page.**

2. **Select the text or picture content item in the Content palette and click the Insert (I-beam) button in the palette.**

   The content from the item in the Content palette is placed into the selected box or path.

SHARING MULTIPLE ITEMS AT ONE TIME

If you try to add multiple items or a group of items to the Content palette, those items may be immediately added with all their options turned on: synchronize box, content, and attributes. To control this behavior, open QuarkXPress Preferences and under the Application section click Sharing. There, you can change the default synchronization choices for items added to the Content palette, and you can also enable or disable a check box labeled Do Not Display Dialog When Sharing Multiple Items. When enabled, the items are immediately added to the Content palette when you click the Add Item button. When disabled, the Share Multiple Items dialog box is supposed to display when you click the Add Item button. (However, there may be a bug in QuarkXPress that simply disables the Add Item button instead.) If this works for you and the Share Multiple Items dialog box displays, you can choose the sharing properties for each individual item.

The item's resizing handles change to synchronization symbols (squiggles). You can also drag the text or picture item from the Content palette to an active text box, text path, or picture box.

TIP

Oddly, you can import text or a picture into a shared item by using the Content palette, rather than by choosing File ⇨ Import. Here's how: Select the item in the Content palette, click the Import icon, and then navigate to the text or picture on your computer that you want to import into that item.

Unsynchronizing shared items

To unsynchronize all instances of a shared item, select one instance on the page and click the Unsynchronize All button in the Content palette. All instances will retain their current attributes and content, but any further changes to one of them will apply only to that one item.

To unsynchronize the item and remove it from the Content palette, click the Delete (trash can) icon.

Using Composition Zones

When you want to share an area of a page (or even an entire multipage layout) so that someone else can work on it, you can spin it off as a Composition Zones layout. The Composition Zones layout behaves just like any QuarkXPress document, so others with QuarkXPress can edit and save it. When they give it back to you (or place it back in its original location on a file server), the Composition Zones item on your page updates with their work.

Creating a Composition Zones item

You have three ways to create a Composition Zones item:

>> Select multiple items and then choose Item ⇨ Composition Zones ⇨ Create.

>> Activate the Composition Zones tool, shown in Figure 7-4, and manually drag out the area for your Composition Zones item. To activate the Composition Zones tool, click and hold the Rectangle Box tool in the Tools palette. The tools related to the Rectangle Box tool display, as shown in Figure 7-4. While keeping your mouse button down, drag over to the Composition Zones tool to activate it.

» Designate an entire layout as a Composition Zones item by choosing Layout ⇨ Advanced Layout Properties and selecting the Share Layout check box.

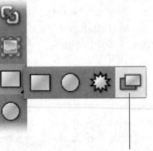

FIGURE 7-4:
The Composition Zones tool.

Composition Zones tool

WARNING

If the position of one or more selected items is locked (you lock an item by choosing Item ⇨ Lock ⇨ Position), you cannot create a Composition Zones item. You must first unlock the locked item(s) by choosing Item ⇨ Lock ⇨ Position again. This removes the check mark in the menu, which indicates a locked item.

After using either of the first two techniques to create a Composition Zones item, you need to select the settings for working in the Composition Zone. To do that, choose Item ⇨ Share and the Shared Item Properties dialog box, shown in Figure 7-5, appears.

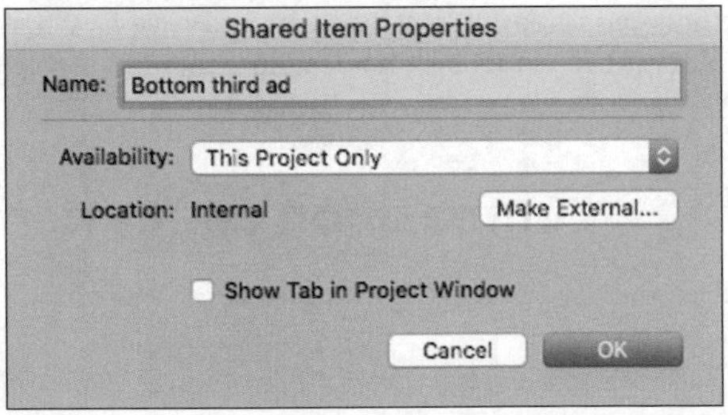

Shared Item Properties

Name: Bottom third ad

Availability: This Project Only

Location: Internal   Make External...

☐ Show Tab in Project Window

Cancel   OK

FIGURE 7-5:
The Shared Item Properties dialog box.

In the Name field, give your Composition Zones item a name, and in the Availability menu, choose This Project Only or All Projects, depending on how you want this item to be available.

If you want someone else to work on this Composition Zones item, click the Make External button and choose a name and location on your computer or network.

A new Composition Zones layout file appears there that can be edited by anyone with QuarkXPress.

To make this Composition Zones layout appear as a separate layout tab in your current project, select the Show Tab in Project Window check box. Enabling this check box makes it easy to edit that layout; otherwise, you must select the Composition Zones item on the page and choose Item ⇨ Composition Zones ⇨ Edit.

When you've completed choosing your settings, click OK. The name of your new Composition Zones item displays in the Content palette, and the items in the Composition Zone are grouped together on the page with one bounding box around them. Conveniently, when you select the Composition Zones item on the page, its name appears on it.

You can also create a Composition Zones item from an entire layout. To do so, follow these steps:

1. **Display the layout you'd like to share.**

2. **Choose Layout ⇨ Advanced Layout Properties.**

   The Advanced Layout Properties dialog box, shown in Figure 7-6, appears.

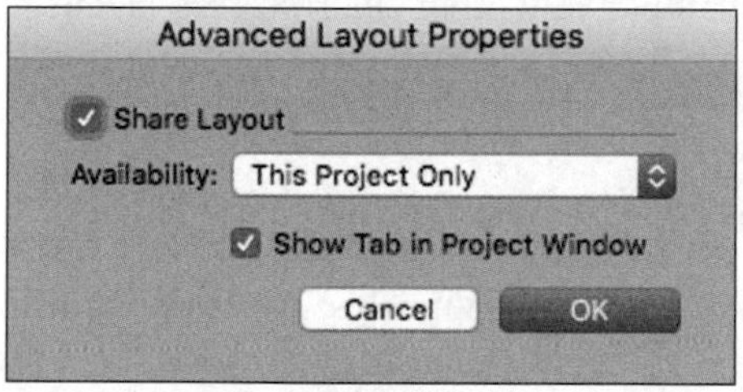

FIGURE 7-6:
The Advanced Layout Properties dialog box.

3. **Select the Share Layout check box.**

4. **In the Availability menu, choose This Project Only or All Projects.**

5. **Select the Show Tab in Project Window check box if you want to make this Composition Zones layout appear as a separate layout tab in your current project.**

   Having your layout appear as a separate tab makes it easy to edit that layout. Otherwise, you must select the Composition Zones item on the page and choose Item ⇨ Composition Zones ⇨ Edit.

6. **Click OK.**

   The Composition layout displays in the Content palette.

Placing, styling, and editing a Composition Zones item

After you establish a Composition Zones item, you can place it where you want it on a page, make changes to its attributes, and edit it as much as you want.

To place a Composition Zones item, select it in the Content palette (choose Window ⇨ Content to open the Content palette) and drag it onto the page. If the composition layout contains multiple pages, you can choose which page you want to show in your current layout. To choose that page, go to the Measurements palette (choose Window ⇨ Measurements to open the Measurements palette), click the Home/Classic tab, and select the page from the Page drop-down menu.

After placing a Composition Zones item onto your page, you can change its attributes to alter its appearance as if it were any normal box. You can make these changes in the Measurements palette: You can change its opacity, add a frame, give it a drop shadow, set its text runaround, and so on.

To edit a Composition Zones item that you've placed on a page, you go to the original Composition Zones layout that's linked to that item and do your editing there. First, select the Composition Zones layout item on your page and then choose Item ⇨ Composition Zones ⇨ Edit. The original layout opens in a new window, and you can edit it just as you can any other QuarkXPress layout. When you close its window, the Composition Zones item on your page updates with the new content.

Unsynchronizing a Composition Zones item

When your publication is ready to be published, you may want to freeze its content so that if someone opens the publication in the future, its content will be exactly the same as when it was published. Or, perhaps for legal reasons, a document needs to be frozen in its current state. To do that, you need to *unsynchronize* the Composition Zones so that they don't accidentally update if the original Composition Zones layout changes.

QuarkXPress gives you two ways to break the link between a selected Composition Zones item that you've placed on your page and the original Composition Zones layout:

>> **Create an external picture file from the Composition Zones item.** Choose Item ⇨ Composition Zones ⇨ Convert to Picture. This creates a picture file and replaces the Composition Zones item with the picture, permanently freezing its content.

>> **Choose Item ⇨ Unsynchronize:** The original Composition Zones layout remains in the Content palette for future use, but subsequent changes to it will not affect this Composition Zones item.

Understanding Job Jackets

A complete design workflow has experts who oversee every technical aspect of a project, such as typesetting, image quality, color management, and output details such as page size, number of pages, page spreads, page bleeds, number of ink colors, and bindery processes. Ideally, all these details are defined and implemented before a layout artist touches the job — which is also when the project can most easily be altered. But all too often, project-stopping problems are encountered just before output. The use of Quark's Job Jackets feature can avoid all these problems.

You can think of Job Jackets as living super-templates, even though Quark doesn't describe their revolutionary feature this way. Quark prefers to say that Job Jackets is "preflighting done right." (*Preflighting* is the process of checking that all the parts and pieces of a project are set up correctly for output.) Both are correct, because Job Jackets lets the output experts in a workflow insert technical requirements to templates that are then used by designers to create and constantly check that their documents are going to output correctly.

TECHNICAL STUFF

Job Jackets aren't considered templates, because they contain only a project's metadata, not actual page geometries. For example, Job Jackets include the number of ink colors allowed in a project, the fonts that are allowed, and the number of pages, but not the size or location of page items such as text boxes and picture boxes. For those things, you would use an actual QuarkXPress template, as explained in Chapter 1.

Before Job Jackets, preflighting occurred just before output, when the pressure was highest to get the job printed or exported. If a problem was discovered, it needed to be fixed as quickly as possible to avoid delaying the job. With Job Jackets, all the specifications are available during the design process, and designers can regularly check the documents against them. This gives the layout artist a chance to fix problems before they become critical.

The details of creating and using Job Jackets are enough to fill a small manual, so I cover just the basics here. For complete details, download Quark's excellent *A Guide to QuarkXPress 2016* at (http://www.quark.com/Support/Documentation/QuarkXPress/2016.aspx).

To quote Quark's user guide, "Technically speaking, Job Jackets are XML structures that include specifications and rules for creating and inspecting QuarkXPress layouts." Job Jackets can provide specifications for literally every consideration that a project might encounter, from colors, fonts, page size, and number of pages allowed in a document to bindery processes, information about whom to contact about any step in the workflow, and detailed requirements for a specific output device.

Here's a rough overview of how the Job Jackets system works. The technical experts in your workgroup create and maintain a Job Jackets file that contains all the specifications for every kind of project the workgroup might create. Then a Job Ticket is generated for each specific type of project, such as a book, manual, directory, sell sheet, ads for various publications, a digital catalog, or even a business card.

A layout artist opens a Job Ticket template, which creates a QuarkXPress layout with all the correct specifications and resources necessary to produce a perfect document — page size and output intent, fonts, style sheets, colors, color management settings, and more. (If you have an existing project, you can also manually link it to a Job Ticket template to add new layouts.)

While developing the layout, the layout artist can check her work against the Job Ticket specifications to avoid unexpected surprises down the road. These inspections can occur manually by choosing File ⇨ Job Jackets ⇨ Evaluate Layout, or automatically when opening, outputting, saving, or closing a project. If QuarkXPress finds problems, the layout artist can use a dialog box that lets her navigate to the design elements that violate the rules defined in the Job Ticket.

When a layout is complete, the layout artist sends it to output by direct printing, Collect for Output, or export to PDF. If the Job Jackets file includes output specifications, the job can output to specific formats using specific settings.

Although the process of creating and maintaining a Job Jackets system is relatively straightforward, there are hundreds and hundreds of details to be considered. Quark's website has several resources dedicated to helping Job Jackets users.

2
Speaking in Text

IN THIS PART . . .

Creating text boxes and importing text

Formatting characters and paragraphs

Using style sheets and Conditional Styles

Editing text

Tracking changes

Managing fonts

Using Content Variables and Notes

IN THIS CHAPTER

» **Creating text boxes**

» **Working with the shape and appearance of a text box**

» **Linking and unlinking text boxes**

» **Importing and exporting text**

» **Working with word processing applications**

Chapter **8**

Creating Text Boxes

QuarkXPress began its life almost 30 years ago with just three kinds of page items: text boxes, picture boxes, and rules (lines). Aside from some additional features to keep up with design trends and new media, it's still all about text, pictures, and rules. If you master these items, you'll have a lot more fun designing layouts.

Among the three, you'll spend the vast majority of your time building text boxes and formatting text. This chapter takes you through building text boxes, linking text boxes, and importing text (and offers a little guidance with exporting text as well). When you're ready to learn all about formatting text, turn to Chapters 9 and 10.

Understanding Why You Need Text Boxes

QuarkXPress is not a word processor. It has many of the features of a word processor, but it is *so much* more. A word processor creates documents that are essentially one long column of text, perhaps with some pictures inserted into it. Any document as complex as a magazine consists of multiple stories, in multiple locations on the page, with multiple areas of color and pictures. Pick up any magazine and ask yourself, "How would I create this in Microsoft Word?" The answer, of course, is you wouldn't. You need a tool like QuarkXPress to arrange those items into a layout.

If you like, you can think of each story in a QuarkXPress layout as a separate word processing document. (In fact, each story often begins its life as a word processing document that is imported into a text box.) Logically, you need a separate text box — or chain of linked text boxes — for each story.

Deciding Which Is Best: Manual or Automatic?

The most common way to create a text box is to use the Text Content tool to drag out an area on a page to contain your text. You can then optionally link several text boxes together so that if your text is too long to fit into the first one, it will flow into the others. If you're creating a short document, such as an ad, a brochure, or even an article in a magazine, creating and linking text boxes can be a fun and satisfying way to work. (Text that doesn't fit into a text box is called *overset text*.)

However, if you're building a long document, such as an entire book or a chapter in a book, you can tell QuarkXPress to automatically add new pages and text boxes as the length of text grows. QuarkXPress links these new text boxes to your current text box, and the new text boxes magically appear whenever you type more text than fits into your current text box (or import text from a text file).

To learn all about automatic text boxes and the master pages that control them, jump back to Chapters 4 and 5. To understand how to manually create text boxes and link them to other text boxes, read on.

Creating a Text Box Manually

Creating a text box is as easy as can be — which is handy because you'll do it 100 million times, or at least as many times as you create new layouts. Just follow these steps:

1. **Select the Text Content tool from the Tools palette, as shown in Figure 8-1.**

   The Text Content tool is a rectangle with a capital T in its center.

   When you move the mouse pointer into the layout page, the mouse pointer changes to look like a crosshair.

2. **Hold down the mouse button and drag the mouse across your page until you've drawn a text box the size you want.**

Height and Width dimensions appear at the bottom right of the text box as you size it. They also appear in the Measurements palette.

Conveniently, alignment guides and dimension arrows appear on the edges of your text box whenever they align with the edges or centers of other items on the page. These guides and arrows also appear when your text box's text columns or gutters align with those in another text box.

3. **Release the mouse button.**

FIGURE 8-1:
The Item tool
and the Text
Content tool.

—— Item tool

—— Text Content tool

TIP

You don't need to worry about the exact size and position as you're creating the new text box. Later, you can drag the text box's side handles or corner handles to adjust its size and position, or use the Item tool to drag the text box around on the page — or even to another page. You can also enter precise measurements into the Measurements palette for the box's location (labeled X: and Y: for horizontal and vertical position, respectively) and size (labeled W: and H: for width and height).

TIP

Smart designers use a grid to determine where to place page items. Using a grid not only ensures that your page items line up with each other and appear to be part of a cohesive whole but also frees your brain to focus on more creative stuff. I tell you how to create and use grids in Chapter 2.

Changing the Shape and Appearance of a Text Box

When a text box is active (click it with the Text Content tool or the Item tool to activate it), you can use the controls in the Text Box tab of the Measurements palette to adjust all kinds of its attributes, as described in the following sections.

Changing the box angle and skew

To rotate a box to a precise angle, enter that angle (in degrees) into the Box Angle field. You can also rotate the box by clicking the up and down arrows next to the Box Angle field. Figure 8-2 shows the Box Angle field.

To rotate a text box visually, get the Item tool or the Text Content tool and mouse over to just outside a corner of the box. The pointer changes to a curved arrow, and if you click and drag around the outside of the text box, it rotates. Release your mouse button when you're satisfied with the position. (The Box Angle field in the Measurements palette updates to indicate the new angle.)

You can also skew the text box as if you'd pushed its top corner to the left or right; the text inside skews along with the shape of the box. This is usually not an attractive effect (yuck!), but should you need to do it, either enter an angle amount into the Box Skew field in the Measurements palette or click the up and down buttons next to it. Figure 8-2 shows the Box Skew field.

FIGURE 8-2:
The Box Angle and Box Skew fields.

Changing the box corner shape

To change the shape of the box's corners, hold your mouse button down on the Box Corner Shape control (it looks like an orange box corner) and choose one of the following options: Rectangle, Rounded, Concave, and Beveled. To control how far the corner intrudes on the text box, use the Box Corner Radius control to the right of the Box Corner Shape control. You can either type in a number or click the up and down arrows to increase or decrease the radius of the corner, respectively. Figure 8-3 shows the Box Corner Shape field.

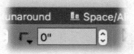

FIGURE 8-3:
The Box Corner Shape field.

Changing the box color and opacity

Every box in QuarkXPress has a background color (even if it's None), and that color can have any level of opacity (or transparency). It can also blend from one color to another in various ways. You can read all about color control in Chapter 11; then you can apply your knowledge to the controls shown in Figure 8-4.

Adding frames and drop shadows

A text box is just like any other box, so you can add various kinds of striped, dashed, and dotted frames to it (see Chapter 3 for more about frames) as well as an impressive drop shadow on either the text itself, the box, or both (see Chapter 13 for more about drop shadows).

Creating other text box shapes

In QuarkXPress, any box can be a text box, even if it began its life as something else. For example, you can put text in any of the following:

>> A picture box

>> A rectangular (no content) box

>> An oval (no content) box

>> A starburst

>> A shape created by ShapeMaker

>> A freeform shape

Chapter 3 explains how to create all these kinds of boxes. The secret to converting one of them into a text box is this: With the item active, choose Item ⇨ Content ⇨ Text. This converts the item to a text box, and you can then type or import text into it.

Controlling the Position of Text in Its Box

The text in each text box has a relationship to its box in much the same way that page items have a relationship with the page. You can control the number of columns of text in the box, the text's nearness to the edge of the box, whether the text aligns to the top or the bottom of the box, and more. Read on to discover the various ways your text and its box can relate to each other.

Setting the columns and margins of a text box

The text in each text box can have its own number of columns, margin between the columns, and inset from the edge of the box. (These settings are separate from the margins and columns of your layout page and apply only to the active text box.) Use the Columns control to choose how many columns of text you want in your text box, and the Gutter Width control to adjust the space between the columns, as shown in Figure 8-5.

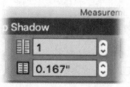

FIGURE 8-5:
Column and margin controls for a text box.

Vertically aligning the text

Your text doesn't have to be glued to the top of the box; it can be attached to the bottom (leaving room at the top), float in the center of the box, or stretch out to fill its height. Figure 8-6 shows the text alignment options. If you choose Justify, QuarkXPress adds space between paragraphs to fill the box, and you can specify the maximum amount of space you want in the Inter Paragraph Maximum field.

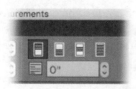

FIGURE 8-6:
The vertical text alignment controls.

Setting the inset of a text box

In QuarkXPress, the text inside a text box never bumps into the edge of the box — it's always inset a tiny amount. Sometimes, such as when a text box is filled with a color or has a frame around it, you may want to increase the amount of inset so that the text isn't cramped by the frame or appear to be pushing its way off the background. To increase the amount of inset, use the Inset controls, shown in Figure 8-7.

For a uniform amount of inset on all sides, enter an amount in the first text inset field. To apply a different inset to various sides, click the Multiple Insets check box and then enter amounts for each side.

FIGURE 8-7:
The text inset controls.

Where should the text start?

You can also control the vertical position of your first line of text in the box. Sometimes a font is so tall that it sticks its neck out of the top of the box, interfering with what's above it. Or maybe you used a big font in one box and a smaller font in a box next to it, but you need their first lines of text to line up in both boxes. That's where the controls in Figure 8-8 can save you.

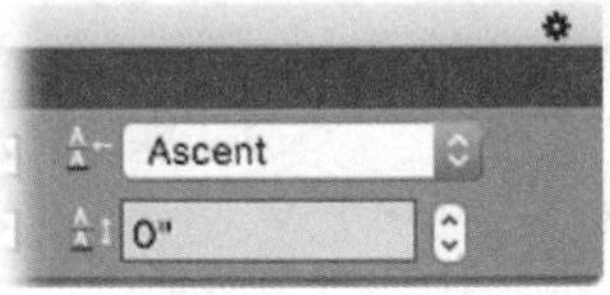

FIGURE 8-8:
The First Baseline alignment controls.

The top control (named First Baseline Minimum) has three options: Cap Height, Cap + Accent, and Ascent. Because not all font designers follow the same rules, you may need to try each of them to achieve the result you want.

The lower control (named First Baseline Offset) simply nudges all the text up and down in the box. Depending on the font and font size, you may need to enter a large number before you see a change.

Setting the text angle and skew

You can achieve some creative text effects by changing the angle of the text within the box (for example, to make it look as though it's marching uphill), or by skewing the text (so that it's leaning over). Figure 8-9 shows the text angle and skew controls.

FIGURE 8-9:
The text angle and skew controls.

Linking and Unlinking Text Boxes

When you have more text than will fit into one text box and you want it to continue in another, it's time to link the boxes together into one long story. For example, newsletter and magazine stories often begin on one page and continue on another (and another). You use the Linking tools to flow a story from one text box to others.

Linking text boxes

To link two text boxes together use the Text Linking Tool, follow these steps:

1. **Create two or more empty text boxes.**

WARNING

You can't link text boxes that already contain text. To do that, you use the Linkster utility (see the "Using Linkster" section, later in this chapter).

2. **Get the Text Linking Tool shown in Figure 8-10.**

As you move your mouse over any text box, your pointer changes to a chain link. (You may have to wiggle your mouse to see it.)

3. **Click the first text box.**

The outline of the text box changes to marching ants.

4. **Click the next text box you want to add to the chain.**

A hollow arrow appears, attached to the bottom-right corner of the first box and pointing to the top-left corner of the second box, as shown in Figure 8-10.

5. **Click the next text box you want to add to the chain.**

Repeat to link to additional boxes.

6. **To end the linking process (after you click the last text box you want to add to the chain), do one of the following:**

- Click anywhere in your document where there isn't a text box.

- Click on another tool in the Tools palette.

- Press the Esc key on your keyboard.

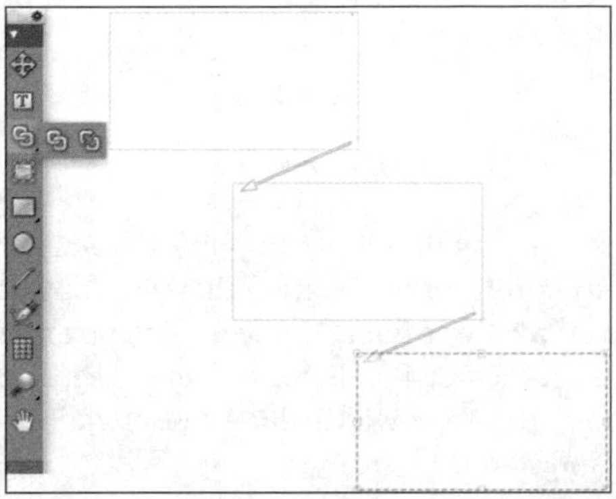

FIGURE 8-10:
The Text Linking tool and the Text Unlinking tool with three linked text boxes.

TIP

When working with text in linked boxes, you can force the text after your text insertion point to start in the next text box by using the Next Box character. To type a Next Box character, hold down the Shift key and press the Enter key on your keyboard's numeric keypad. (On a Mac that doesn't have an extended keyboard, hold down the fn key and press Shift-Return.) Similarly, you can force text to start in the next *column* in a multicolumn text box by pressing the Enter key on your numeric keypad (or fn-Return on a Mac keyboard that doesn't have a numeric keypad). You can find more keyboard tricks like this in the Cheat Sheet for this book (go to www.dummies.com and search for *QuarkXPress For Dummies Cheat Sheet*).

Unlinking text boxes

You can easily click the wrong box when using the Text Linking Tool. To fix your mistake and break the link between two text boxes, use (surprise!) the Text Unlinking Tool and follow these steps:

1. **Get the Text Unlinking Tool.**

   Press and hold on the Text Linking Tool to show the Text Unlinking Tool and then slide over onto it to make it your active tool.

2. **Click any text box in the chain.**

   Arrows appear that connect the boxes.

3. **Click the head or tail of an arrow to break the chain at that location.**

If you click the pointy head of the arrow, the box it was pointing into remains selected. If you click the tail of the arrow, the box it came from remains selected.

If those boxes had text in them, the story stops flowing where you unlinked them and remains in the box(es) in the chain ahead of where you unlinked it.

TIP

If you're having trouble clicking exactly on the arrow head or tail, try zooming into your layout for a closer look.

Copying linked text boxes

Copying linked text boxes is fraught with peril, unless you remember this simple rule: All the text downstream from the box(es) that you copy comes along for the ride. For example, if you have three boxes and you copy box number two, the copy will include box two and all the text inside boxes two, three, four, and so on. If you copy boxes two and three, the copy will include those two boxes and all the text inside boxes four, five and so on.

Deleting linked text boxes

If you delete a linked text box from the middle of a chain, QuarkXPress reflows the story as if the box was never there. For example, if you delete box number two, the story flows from box one to box three.

Using Linkster

If all this linked-box logic makes your head swim, or you need to creatively link and unlink text boxes in ways that QuarkXPress normally doesn't allow, try using the Linkster utility, available in the Utilities menu and shown in Figure 8-11.

You can use Linkster to

>> Link text boxes that already have text in them

>> Unlink text boxes while maintaining the text already in them

>> Unlink text boxes across multiple pages

To use Linkster, first select one or more linked text boxes and then choose Utilities ➪ Linkster. In the Linkster dialog box, choose a scope — either your selected text boxes or all the text boxes on your choice of pages. Then choose an action — either Unlink or Link.

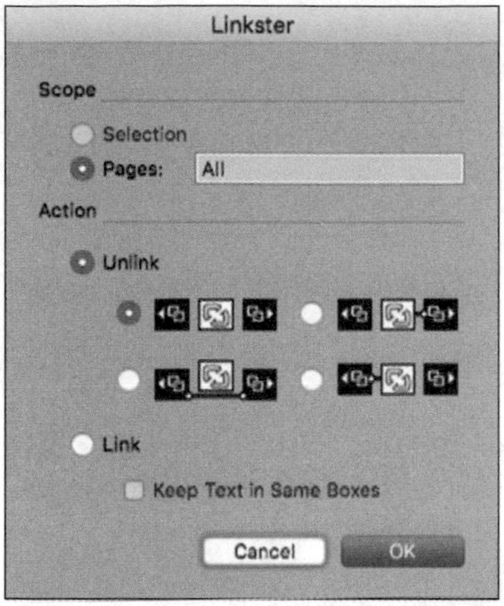

FIGURE 8-11:
The Linkster
dialog box.

WARNING

Linkster has no Undo command, so before using Linkster, always save your document so that if the results aren't what you expect, you can choose File ⇨ Revert to Saved. You can then return to your document as it was before you used Linkster.

Using Linkster for Unlinking

The Unlinking action has four choices:

>> **Top left creates three or more stories:** If you select all the linked text boxes before opening Linkster, this option unlinks all the boxes while maintaining the existing text within each one. If you select fewer than all the linked text boxes, it creates three stories: one for the boxes before the selected boxes; one for the selected boxes; and one for the boxes after the selected boxes.

>> **Bottom left creates two stories:** One for the boxes before and after the selected boxes, and one for the selected boxes.

>> **Top right creates two stories:** One for the boxes before the selected box and the selected box, and one for the boxes after the selected box.

>> **Bottom right creates two stories:** One for the boxes before the selected box, and one for the selected box and the boxes after the selected box.

REMEMBER

A *story* is one or more text boxes that contain text.

Using Linkster for Linking

The Link action links text boxes, even if they already contain text. If Pages is enabled in the Scope section at the top of the dialog box, only those boxes that have been unlinked by Linkster will be relinked. If Selection is enabled, Linkster tries to link the selected boxes in the order you selected them.

Click Keep Text in Same Boxes to keep the existing text in their original boxes after linking. Otherwise, the text from all the boxes is combined into one story that flows from the first box through all the other linked boxes — usually not landing where they originally were.

Importing Text

Although typing text into QuarkXPress is easy (it behaves very much like Microsoft Word), you can also import text from word processing documents and other applications in several ways, including the following:

>> Choose File ⇨ Import and select a text document.

>> Drag a text file from the file system onto a text box.

>> Copy and paste text from another application onto a text box.

>> Drag text from another application onto a text box.

The following sections explain how to get text into a text box using each of these techniques.

Importing text from a word processing document

The most common way by far to import text is from a document created in Microsoft Word or another word processing application. To do so, follow these steps:

1. **Select the Text Content tool.**

2. **Place the text insertion point where you want text to be inserted in the text box.**

3. **Choose File ⇨ Import and navigate to the word processing document.**

4. **Click the Open button.**

   The text from the word processing document is imported into the text box.

This File ⇨ Import technique is popular for one reason: QuarkXPress can clean up and apply style sheets to the text as it's imported. In the Import dialog box, click the Options button to see the following options, as shown in Figure 8-12:

FIGURE 8-12:
Text import
options for a
Microsoft Word
document.

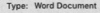

Type: Word Document
☑ Convert Quotes
☐ Include Style Sheets

» **Convert Quotes:** Select this option to convert double hyphens to em dashes and convert foot or inch marks to a typesetter's apostrophes and quotation marks. This makes your text look much more professional.

» **Include Style Sheets:** Select this option to import style sheets from the Microsoft Word document. (See Chapter 10 for more on using style sheets.) All style sheets used in the Word document are added to the QuarkXPress document, and you're presented with options for handling duplicate names. This option also converts XPress Tags to formatted text. See the "Using XPress Tags" sidebar, later in this chapter, for more about XPress Tags.

TIP

Windows users: If you find yourself importing a lot of text files or picture files from the same folder or directory on your computer, you can tell QuarkXPress to always start from that folder or directory when opening the Import dialog box. To do that, open the QuarkXPress Preferences by choosing Edit ⇨ Preferences. In the Default Path pane, choose the folder you want to use.

WHEN THE TEXT IS TOO LONG TO FIT INTO A TEXT BOX

If all the imported text doesn't fit into the text box or chain of linked text boxes, an overflow symbol displays in the bottom-right corner of the last box in the chain. If you have just a few lines of overflow text, you can quickly lengthen the text box by Control-clicking (Mac) or right-clicking (Windows) or the box, and from the menu that appears, choosing Fit Box to Text.

If you have a lot of overflow text, you need to add new text boxes and link them as described earlier in this chapter, in the "Linking text boxes" section. However, if you were smart enough to use Quark's automatic text box feature, explained in Chapter 5, new pages automagically appear with your overflow text in them. The key is to have Auto Page Insertion enabled in the Print Layout ⇨ General section of QuarkXPress Preferences (which you open by choosing Preferences from the QuarkXPress menu on a Mac or the Edit menu on Windows).

WARNING

The Mac OS X version of QuarkXPress 2015 and higher no longer supports the Microsoft Word file format with the .doc filename extension. To import a Word document, it must be saved in the .docx format that has been standard since Microsoft Word 2007. The Windows version is still able to import a .doc file.

WARNING

To avoid problems importing Word documents, click the Office button, open the Word Options dialog box, click the Save tab, and deselect Allow Fast Saves in Microsoft Word or use the Save As command to create a copy of the Word file to be imported. (Your instructions might differ, depending on your version of Microsoft Word.)

Dragging a text file from the file system

On Mac OS X or Windows, rather than following the File⇨Import approach described in the preceding section, you can drag the text file from your computer's desktop into an empty text box. The hardest part is arranging your windows so that you can see the text box at the same time that you see the text file!

TIP

If the box you select is a picture box or a no-content box instead of a text box, you can convert it to a text box and import text into it by pressing Command (Mac) or Ctrl (Windows) while dragging the text file from the file system onto it.

Dragging text from another application

If your text is already open in another application, you can drag text from the other application into a text box in QuarkXPress. Of course, you need to be able to arrange your windows so that you can see your QuarkXPress document and your other document, which may not be easy!

TIP

If the box you select is a picture box or a no-content box instead of a text box, you can convert it to a text box and import text into it by pressing Command (Mac) or Ctrl (Windows) while dragging the text from the other application into it.

WARNING

If you drag content into a box that already contains text or a picture, QuarkXPress creates a new box for the dragged content. To replace the content of the box instead, press Command (Mac) or Ctrl (Windows) while dragging the content to the box. To always create a new box for dragged-in content, press Option (Mac) or Alt (Windows) while dragging.

Exporting Text

So your client doesn't have QuarkXPress and wants the text from the project you've created. You could copy and paste it into a word processor, or you could save a step and export it directly from QuarkXPress. (Who wants to muck around in a word processor, anyway?) Here's how export text directly from QuarkXPress:

1. **Select a text box or some text in a text box.**

2. **Choose File ⇨ Save Text and navigate to a location to save the file.**

3. **From the Format menu, choose either Plain Text, XPress Tags, Rich Text Format, Word Document, or HTML.**

4. **Name your file and click Save.**

   A new file appears in the location you selected, with its text formatted just as it was in QuarkXPress!

WARNING

QuarkXPress doesn't export RTF (Rich Text Format) files as well as it could. Always test your exported RTF file by attempting to open it in a word processor. If it fails, export the text again, this time choosing Word Document as the format, open that document in Microsoft Word (or another application that can open a .docx file), and save it again in RTF format. Sad but true.

IN THIS CHAPTER

» **Learning typographic basics**

» **Managing fonts**

» **Working with fonts and type styles**

» **Applying OpenType features**

» **Assigning color, shade, and opacity**

» **Inserting special characters**

» **Choosing languages**

Chapter **9**

Formatting Characters

Q uarkXPress has the most advanced text-formatting engine in the industry. But that's not to say that using it is difficult — in fact, the opposite is true. If you know how to format text in Microsoft Word, you already know how to use those same features in QuarkXPress. But QuarkXPress goes far beyond those features, with an insane number of formatting options to please even the most persnickety typographic expert.

This chapter guides you through all the typographic features, and you learn quite a lot about the art of type in the process.

Learning the Basics of Typography

People have been creating and arranging symbols for thousands of years. In the early days of print, text and symbol wrangling was handled by exacting craftsmen called typesetters, who lovingly set blocks of type onto printing presses (hence the phrase *setting type*). With the advent of desktop publishing, however, everyone started setting type. The result is both good and bad: It's great that you can whip up your own yard sale signs, invitations, and posters; but, as you might suspect, the quality of typography has suffered because most people lack professional training.

Some of the most frequent typographic offenses include:

>> **Overusing decorative fonts and using too many fonts per design.** Just because you have a ton of wacky fonts doesn't mean you should use them — *especially* not all in one document.

>> **Setting whole sentences in capital letters.** All-capped text takes people longer to read because we partially rely on the shapes of words and the shapes are lost in ALL CAPS. Even worse, it tends to imply that you're YELLING. That said, with the right formatting, small portions of all-capped text can look classy.

>> **Underlining text that isn't a hyperlink.** Thanks to the Internet, when people see an underlined word, they assume that it's a hyperlink. Find another way to make your text stand out, such as bolding or italicizing it.

>> **Centering large bodies of text.** It's best to reserve centered text for formal occasions. To read a long block of centered text, the reader's eye must jump to a different location when reading each line.

>> **Misusing straight and smart (curly) quotation marks and apostrophes.** Use the straight ones to indicate units of measurement (feet and inches) and curly ones for everything else. You can switch between them using QuarkXPress Preferences: Choose QuarkXPress ⇨ Preferences ⇨ Input Settings (Mac) or Edit ⇨ Preferences ⇨ Input Settings (Windows) and select or deselect the Smart Quotes check box.

>> **Misusing hyphens, en dashes, and em dashes:**

- **Hyphens** are for combining two words (like "eye-opener") and for line breaks (when a word gets split across two lines of text).

- **En dashes** are slightly longer than hyphens and are a good substitute for the word *to*" as in "Chapters 1–4" or "8:00 a.m.–5:00 p.m." On a Mac, you can create an en dash by typing Option-Hyphen; in Windows, press and hold Ctrl and then press the minus sign on your numeric keypad.

- **Em dashes** are the longest of the bunch and imply an abrupt change — like this! — or a halt in thought or speech. Use them instead of a comma or period when the former is too weak and the latter too strong. To create an em dash on a Mac, press Shift-Option-Hyphen; in Windows, press and hold Ctrl+Alt and then press the minus sign on your numeric keypad.

The names *en dash* and *em dash* are derived from the days of lead typesetting when an en dash was the width of the letter *N* and an em dash was the width of the letter *M*.

>> **Improperly spaced ellipses (. . .).** An ellipsis indicates an omission, interruption, or hesitation in thought, as in, "But . . . but . . . you promised!" Instead of typing three periods (which can get broken across lines), let your computer create the dots for you. On a Mac, it's Option-; (on Windows, press Alt and type *0133* on the numeric keypad).

There are more typographic offenses, to be sure — such as putting *two* spaces after each period instead of *one.* Nonetheless, the preceding guidelines will serve you well throughout the rest of this chapter, if not your entire career.

TECHNICAL
STUFF

Measuring something as small as type requires a small unit of measurement. Long ago, English printers — being fond of systems that measure in dozens — invented the system of *points* and *picas.* There are 12 points in a pica and six picas in an inch, and therefore 72 points in an inch. The size of a font is determined by the distance between the top of its tallest character (the *ascender*) to the bottom of the lowest character (the *descender*) — for example, the top of a lowercase *h* and the bottom of a lowercase *g.* That's why two fonts at the same point size can *appear* to be different sizes.

Common font formats

Fonts come in various formats that determine how and what kind of information gets stored in each font file. You need to think about only three formats: PostScript, TrueType, and OpenType. If you've already created some text in QuarkXPress, you can discover its format by choosing Edit ⇨ Font Menu to take a peek at the Font menu, shown in Figure 9-1. A red *A* means that it's a PostScript font (because Adobe invented PostScript); a green *TT* stands for TrueType; and an *O* indicates OpenType. Because an OpenType font can be generated from either PostScript *or* TrueType outlines, the *O* displays in red for PostScript and green for TrueType.

FIGURE 9-1:
The Font menu displays a symbol to the left of each font name to denote its format.

O Adobe Naskh Medium

a Adobe Sans MM

TT Aquafina Script Regular

O Aktiv Grotesk

These days, font format isn't a big deal — any printer with equipment less than 15 years old can print any format you throw at it. But in case you need to know, here's how the formats differ:

>> **PostScript:** Each PostScript font consists of two files: one that contains the shapes that get displayed onscreen (called the *screen* or *bitmap* file because monitors display bits or dots) along with font family and letter spacing info, and another that contains outline drawings of each glyph for the printer (commonly referred to as the *printer* file). If either of the two files becomes separated or lost, the font is unusable. Also, these font files are platform specific: Windows can't use a PostScript font created for Macs, and vice versa.

WARNING

If you're creating a document that will become an e-book, and you want to embed the fonts in the e-book, don't use a PostScript font — some readers (such as the Kindle) don't support embedded fonts in the PostScript format. Instead, use a TrueType or OpenType font. To be totally safe, use an OpenType font that was generated from TrueType outlines. These fonts have a green *O* to the left of their name in QuarkXPress's font menu, as shown in Figure 9-1.

>> **TrueType:** Developed jointly by Apple and Microsoft, TrueType is the most common font format. Both the screen and outline information are stored in a single file, so they can't be separated or lost. TrueType fonts for Windows can be used on Macs, but not vice versa.

>> **OpenType:** This format, created by Microsoft and Adobe, is the new standard. Like TrueType, OpenType fonts store the screen and outline information together in one file. They can store more than 65,000 different glyphs in one font file. This makes them ideal for decorative and pictorial languages like Asian and Middle-Eastern ones, and for other fancy typographic goodness like swashes and stylistic alternates. As an added bonus, you can use the same OpenType font on both Mac and Windows machines.

Font categories

Font designers crank out new fonts daily, with probably more than a hundred thousand available for use. Luckily, you can rely on a few basic principles for choosing a font that's appropriate to your message — one that will reinforce it rather than distract from it. Figure 9-2 shows examples of the following font categories:

>> **Serif:** These fonts have little lines *(serifs)* that resemble tiny feet extending from their letters' main strokes. The main strokes vary in thickness, and the

serifs help lead the eye from one character to the next. Serifs are great for large bodies of printed text — such as books, newspapers, and magazines — where legibility is paramount. However, they're not great for large bodies of *online* text (the next bullet point explains why). Examples include Times New Roman, Garamond, and Minion.

>> **Sans serif:** Fonts lacking the aforementioned feet are called *sans serif* (*sans* means *without*). They're perfect for headlines, subheads, and, surprisingly enough, online body copy. Because their strokes are uniform — they don't vary in thickness — they display well at small sizes, so they're ideal for web use. Examples include Arial, Helvetica, and Futura.

>> **Slab serif:** These fonts have uniform main strokes and thick serifs. Use them when you want to attract attention, or when you're printing body copy under less-than-optimal conditions (cheap paper, cheap printer, or fax machine). Examples include Bookman, Courier, and Rockwell.

>> **Decorative, Display:** This group includes all kinds of distinctive, eye-catching fonts, from the big and bold, to the swirly, to letters made out of flowers. Though eye-catchingly unusual, they're harder to read because of the extra ornamentation or stroke thickness. Use them sparingly and on small blocks of text (perhaps a single word). Examples include Impact, Party, and Stencil.

>> **Scripts:** Casual scripts are designed to look as though they were drawn (quickly) by hand. Formal scripts have carefully crafted strokes that actually join the letters together, like cursive handwriting. Use casual scripts for small blocks of text (because they can be hard to read), and reserve formal scripts for fancy announcements (weddings, graduations, and so on). Examples include Brush Script, Freestyle, and Edwardian.

FIGURE 9-2: Examples of font categories.

Serif • Sans serif • Slab serif
Decorative • **Display** • *Script*

Useful font combinations

Using fonts together, especially those designed by different designers, is fraught with peril. However, Figure 9-3 shows a few combinations of common fonts that work well when you need a clean, strong headline font and a harmonious font for body copy. Note that the headlines are bolder and a bit bigger than the body copy, and from a different category — for example, a sans-serif headline with a serif body copy, or vice versa.

USING A FONT MANAGER

It may seem strange, but fonts aren't like clip art — they're actually little programs that are accessed by *other* programs, so problems can easily crop up.

For example, you may run into font conflicts — when you have two or more fonts with the same name — or worse, *damaged* fonts that get corrupted and don't work properly. Either scenario can wreak havoc on the performance of both your computer and QuarkXPress, and can cause a crash. These problems are incredibly frustrating, and you could lose a lot of time trying to identify exactly what's causing them. If you've got a ton of fonts, the question is *when* you'll run into a conflict, not *if*.

The solution is to invest a little time and about $99 in font-management software. These programs collect and manage your fonts so that they're not scattered across your hard drive. One (FontAgent) even lets you share your fonts with other members of your team. All the programs let you activate and deactivate fonts (so that you don't have to scroll through a mile-long font list) and organize fonts in a multitude of ways — such as by favorites, font style, manufacturer, project, client, and so on — and they even manage duplicate fonts for you. Their font-comparison features can also help you choose fonts for a project.

You can find some free font-management programs on the Internet, and Macs include the free Font Book program. But when it comes to working with professional design programs, it's worth spending a few bucks on a pro-level offering. Extensis's Suitcase Fusion (www.extensis.com), Insider Software's FontAgent (www.insidersoftware.com), and Monotype's FontExplorer X Pro (http://www.fontexplorerx.com) are powerful font managers that are loaded with features designed to make your font life easier and, more important, headache free.

These programs track and manage the built-in system fonts that came with your machine as well as fonts you add to your computer, which is helpful if you have third-party fonts with the same names as your system fonts. They also let you activate fonts as you need them — in fact, if QuarkXPress or another design application encounters a missing font when opening a document, they activate it on the fly — assuming that you have the font, that is! They also check new fonts when you add them to make sure the fonts aren't damaged.

But the best of the bunch is Monotype's FontExplorer X Pro. It performs all the tasks mentioned previously but runs *rings* around the other two programs because of its smart design, easy access to advanced features, excellent font sample printing feature, and much more. Unfortunately, the current version is only for Macs, but there is an earlier version for Windows.

To read more about the features in these font managers, see my reviews of each of them at Macworld.com.

FIGURE 9-3:
Examples of
successful font
combinations.

Helvetica Bold & Garamond:

Tremulus quadrupei insectat

Pessimus parsimonia suis divinus fermentet agricolae. Bellus umbraculi iocari utilitas concubine, ut chirographi corrumperet Pompeii, et vix gulosus catelli circumgrediet matrimonii.

Garamond Bold & Futura Light:

Tremulus quadrupei insectat

Pessimus parsimonia suis divinus fermentet agricolae. Bellus umbraculi iocari utilitas concubine, ut chirographi corrumperet Pompeii, et vix gulosus catelli circumgrediet matrimonii.

Frutiger Bold & Minion:

Tremulus quadrupei insectat

Pessimus parsimonia suis divinus fermentet agricolae. Bellus umbraculi iocari utilitas concubine, ut chirographi corrumperet Pompeii, et vix gulosus catelli circumgrediet matrimonii.

Myriad Bold & Minion:

Tremulus quadrupei insectat

Pessimus parsimonia suis divinus fermentet agricolae. Bellus umbraculi iocari utilitas concubine, ut chirographi corrumperet Pompeii, et vix gulosus catelli circumgrediet matrimonii.

Discovering and Replacing Fonts Used in Your Document

Sometimes it's handy to know which fonts are used in a QuarkXPress layout — possibly to troubleshoot a printing problem, to identify missing fonts, or even to replace one font with another throughout the layout. In QuarkXPress, all the fonts used in a layout are listed in the Usage dialog box, shown in Figure 9-4. To open it, choose Utilities ⇨ Usage. To see a list of fonts used in the layout, click Fonts in the left panel.

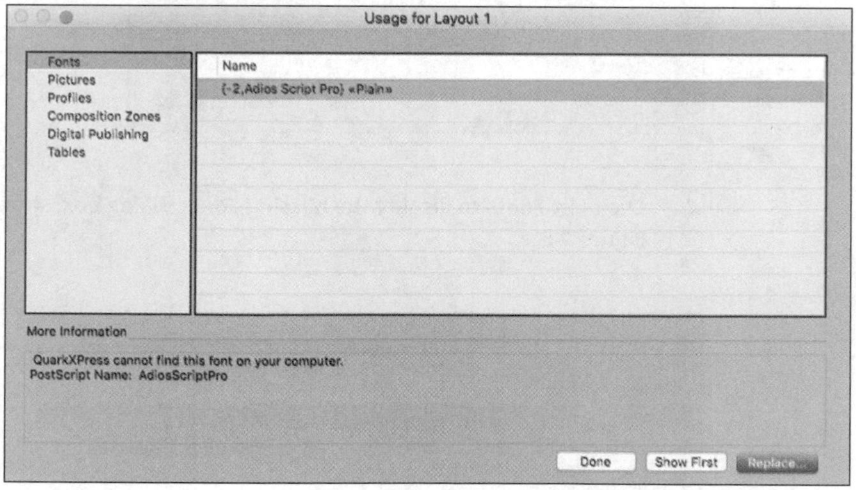

Usage for Layout 1

	Name
Fonts	{-2,Adios Script Pro} «Plain»
Pictures	
Profiles	
Composition Zones	
Digital Publishing	
Tables	

More Information

QuarkXPress cannot find this font on your computer.
PostScript Name: AdiosScriptPro

Done   Show First   Replace...

FIGURE 9-4:
The Fonts
section of
the Usage
dialog box.

If a font is missing, the More Information box at the bottom of the Usage dialog box will say so, as shown in Figure 9-4. To replace a missing font, select it in the list, click Replace (in the lower-right corner), and choose an active font.

If you're not sure where a font is used in the layout, or if you just want to be sure you're replacing what you intend to be replacing, the Usage dialog box can help. To see where the font is first used in the layout, click Show First (which then becomes Show Next). To see the next place that it's used, click Show Next.

Working with font mapping rules

When you open a project, QuarkXPress checks to make sure that all the fonts used in it are active on your system. If they're not, a Missing Fonts alert gives you the opportunity to replace missing fonts with active fonts. You can save those replacements as *font mapping rules,* which QuarkXPress can apply automatically each time you open a project. (If you don't replace a missing font when you open a project, text that's supposed to be using that font is displayed in a standard system font — usually Lucida Grande or Lucida Sans Unicode — and highlighted in pink.)

To create a font mapping rule, follow these steps:

1. **Open a project that you know has a missing font.**

   The alert shown in Figure 9-5 displays.

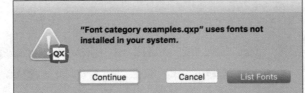

FIGURE 9-5:
The missing font alert.

2. **Click List Fonts to display the Missing Fonts dialog box, shown in Figure 9-6.**

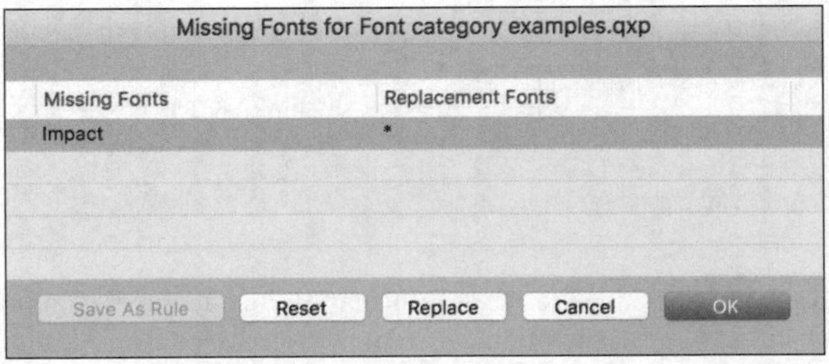

FIGURE 9-6:
The Missing Fonts dialog box.

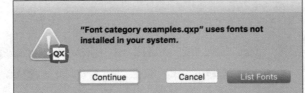

164   PART 2 **Speaking in Text**

3. **In the Missing Fonts dialog box, click the Replace button to open the Replacement Font dialog box, shown in Figure 9-7.**

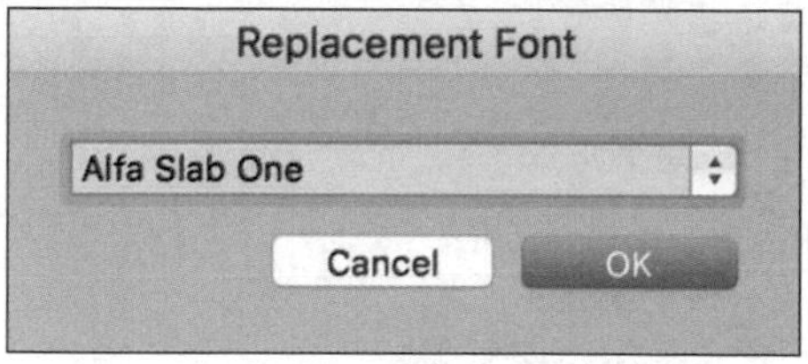

FIGURE 9-7:
The Replacement Font dialog box.

4. **Choose replacement fonts for any missing fonts and then click Save As Rule.**

   The rule is saved applied to all projects you open after that.

To change, delete, or share font mapping rules, choose Utilities ⇨ Font Mapping to open the Font Mapping dialog box shown in Figure 9-8. There, you can click Edit to change the replacement font, Delete to remove the rule, Export to export your rules as a file that can be imported for use by other QuarkXPress users, or Import to import an exported set of rules.

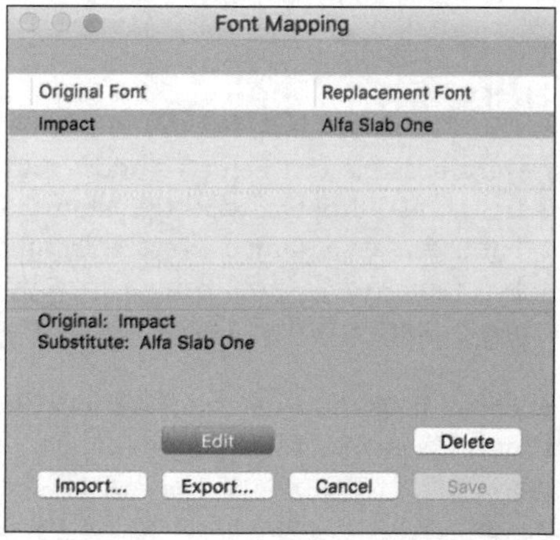

FIGURE 9-8:
The Font Mapping dialog box.

To specify a default replacement font and to control whether the Missing Fonts alert displays when you open a project with missing fonts, open QuarkXPress Preferences, and in the Application section, go to the Fonts pane and turn the relevant check boxes on and off, as shown in Figure 9-9.

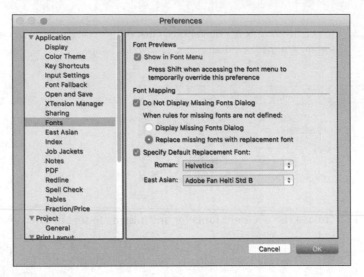

FIGURE 9-9:
The Fonts
preferences.

If you have a bunch of projects whose fonts you want to change, try this: Use your font management utility to deactivate the fonts that you want to replace, open one of the projects that uses them, and create a font mapping rule for each font. Then open all the projects whose fonts you want to change, and QuarkXPress replaces the missing ones according to your font mapping rules. Save the projects. You can then reactivate the original font for use in other projects.

Using Font Fallback

Very few fonts contain every possible character — and, certainly, roman fonts don't contain characters from non-European writing systems. So what happens if you import or paste text that uses, say, a Kanji character? Or, perhaps you're using a font that doesn't include € (euro) or © (publishing copyright), and you import some text that calls for them? Quark's Font Fallback feature comes to the rescue!

When Font Fallback is enabled, if QuarkXPress encounters a character that is not available in the current font, it searches through your active fonts to find a font that does include that character. For example, if Helvetica is the current font, and you import or paste text containing a Kanji character, QuarkXPress might apply the Hiragino font to that character. If the application cannot find an active font that contains the character, the character displays as a box or symbol.

Font Fallback is enabled by default, but if you need to disable it, open QuarkXPress Preferences, go to the Application section, click Font Fallback in the left pane to open the Font Fallback pane, and deselect the Font Fallback check box shown in Figure 9-10.

FIGURE 9-10:
The Font
Fallback
preferences.

The Font Fallback preferences dialog shows:

Preferences

Application
- Display
- Color Theme
- Key Shortcuts
- Input Settings
- **Font Fallback**
- Open and Save
- XTension Manager
- Sharing
- Fonts
- East Asian
- Index
- Job Jackets
- Notes
- PDF
- Redline
- Spell Check
- Tables
- Fraction/Price

Project
- General
- Print Layout

☑ Font Fallback

☐ Search

◉ Last [2] Paragraphs
○ Active Story

Font List

Script/Lang	Font
Cyrillic	Lucida Grande
Greek	Lucida Grande
Latin	Lucida Grande
Japanese	Hiragino Sans GB W3
Korean	AppleGothic Regular
Chinese (Simplified)	STHeiti
Chinese (Traditional)	PingFang TC Regular

Slug Line Font: Helvetica

Cancel   OK

TIP

Font Fallback uses the first font it finds that has the character you need. If you prefer a different font for that character, choose Edit ➪ Find/Change to use the Find/Change feature described in Chapter 11, which lets you change the font everywhere in your layout.

Choosing to Use the Measurements Palette

Seemingly, people prefer to format text and other items on the page in three ways:

>> By typing keyboard shortcuts

>> By clicking icons in a palette

>> By choosing menu items

None is better than the others, but some are more efficient. Generally, using a keyboard shortcut is the fastest because you don't move your hands from the keyboard. However, keyboard shortcuts require memorization and repetition to become proficient.

Using a palette often gives you the most options, because a palette can contain any control imaginable. However, the purpose of each tiny icon often isn't obvious until you've used it a few times.

And while menu items are easiest for beginners to figure out because they're text-based, they're also limited by the way menus work — for example, you can't type a value into a menu item.

In this chapter, you focus on using the Character/Character Attributes tab of the Measurements palette to format text because it contains every control you need. Figure 9-11 shows the Character tab.

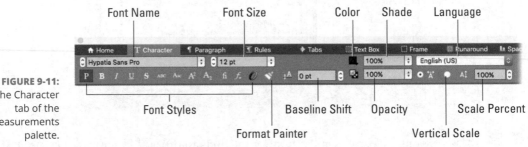

Selecting a typeface

Choosing typefaces for your project is a lot like choosing an outfit to wear to an event. Even though it's the same "you" (words) under those clothes, people react to you differently based on what you wear (typefaces). Your local bookstore has plenty of good books on choosing and combining typefaces for a variety of purposes. For some truly entertaining enlightenment, hop on over and peruse their collection.

TECHNICAL STUFF

In the long-ago time of trained typesetters (before computers), *typeface* had a very specific meaning, as did *font.* Those meanings have been blurred because digital fonts behave quite differently from individual letters carved out of wood or metal. Today, you might think of a *typeface* as a family that may include several styles and weights of *fonts.* For example, the typeface Helvetica includes many *fonts,* such as light, medium, bold, black, oblique, condensed and extended. (Type aficionados may argue with you about this simple way of thinking, but it works for this book's purposes.)

Applying a typeface

To apply a font to selected text, choose its name from the Font drop-down menu in the Home/Classic or Character/Character Attributes tab of the Measurements palette, as shown in Figure 9-12. QuarkXPress tries its best to present its font menu to you as a list of typefaces whose individual fonts or font styles are available in a flyout menu to the side of the typeface name. Some fonts don't behave this way, so you may see some as separate fonts stacked on top of each other in the menu.

FIGURE 9-12:
The Font drop-
down menu of
the Measure-
ments palette.

TIP

The fastest way to choose a font to press Command-Option-Shift-M (Mac) or Ctrl+Alt+Shift+Mt (Windows) to jump directly to the font field in the Measurements palette. Then enter the first few characters of the font name. When the font you want is selected, press Return (Mac) or Enter (Windows).

To scroll up or down the list of fonts and see your text formatted in each of them, click the up or down arrow at left of the Font drop-down menu or use the follow-ing keyboard shortcuts:

>> **Up:** Press Option-F9 (Mac) or Alt+F9 (Windows) on your keyboard.

>> **Down:** Press Shift-Option-F9 (Mac) or Shift+Alt+F9 (Windows) on your keyboard.

On a Mac, each font in the list is displayed in its own typeface. To enable that feature in Windows, choose Edit ➪ Preferences, click the Fonts section, and select Show in Font Menu under Font Previews.

TIP

Some font names are unreadable when displayed in their own typeface — dingbat and symbol fonts, for example. To temporarily show all font names in the system font, press the Shift key as you click the font menu.

TECHNICAL
STUFF

The icons next to the font names indicate the font's file format: An *A* denotes a PostScript font; an *O* denotes an OpenType font; and a *TT* denotes a TrueType font. Knowing a font's format can be useful when creating e-books in EPUB format, because they only allow you to embed TrueType and OpenType fonts.

Choosing a font size

Your choice of font size depends to a great degree on the kind of document you're creating (an invitation is quite different from a newsletter), and the medium on which it will be read (print or digital). Adding to the fun, different fonts *appear to be different sizes* even when set at the same font size. Trial and error can be fun — just be sure to print your design to judge the fonts, rather than relying on your computer display (which is notoriously deceiving).

To set the font size for selected text, you can take any of these actions:

>> Click the up or down arrow at the left of the font size field. This increases and decreases the font size to preset standard sizes (7, 8, 9, 10, 12, 14, 18, 24, 36, 48, 60, and 72).

>> Click the up or down arrow at right of the Font Size field and choose one of the preset sizes.

>> Select the current font size in the font size field and type in any value between 2 and 16,128 points.

>> Use the following keyboard shortcuts (Mac users substitute Command for Ctrl and Option for Alt):

- **Increase 1 pt:** Ctrl+Alt+Shift+>
- **Decrease 1 pt:** Ctrl+Alt+Shift+<
- **Increase in preset range:** Ctrl+Shift+>
- **Decrease in preset range:** Ctrl+Shift+<

Applying and removing a type style

To apply a style such as Bold, Italic, Underline, Strikethrough, All Caps, Small Caps, Superscript, or Subscript, click the buttons below the Font field. To apply other styles, including Word Underline, Double Strikethrough, Outline, Shadow, or Superior, click the Text Styles button (ƒ) and choose the style from the drop-down menu that appears. I don't know why some of these styles appear in both places but others appear in only one — it's just one of those things.

TECHNICAL
STUFF

When you apply the Bold, Italic, or Bold Italic styles to a font, behind the scenes QuarkXPress looks to see whether that font has a true Bold, Italic, or Bold Italic style built into it. If it does, QuarkXPress uses that style. If it doesn't, QuarkXPress asks your computer's operating system to generate a fake style, which can result in strange-looking type. Because using fake font styles is a bad idea, QuarkXPress alerts you when this happens by displaying a warning icon on the Bold or Italic buttons.

To remove all styles you applied to selected text and return it to the base font style, choose Remove All Styles from the Text Styles (ƒ) drop-down menu.

Breaking ligatures apart

The ligature button (*fi*) lets you break apart and recombine ligatures. (A ligature is a single character that combines and replaces two or three other characters, such as fi, fl, ff, or ffi. These special characters are created by the font designer to avoid having parts of characters collide with each other, such as the dot on the *i* bumping into the top of the *f,* or the top of an *l* or *f* overlapping the top of an adjacent *f.*) To replace these combinations of letters with the ligature characters included in a font, select the text and then click the ligature button (*fi*). To break a ligature apart into its separate letters, select it and click the ligature button again.

Applying OpenType styles

Some advanced OpenType fonts (they usually have *Pro* in the name, such as Warnock Pro, Myriad Pro, or Adios Pro) have intelligence built into them that lets them use different versions of characters when they fall next to other specific characters, or in specific locations in a word or sentence. Take swashes for example (a swash is the swooshy bit that extends from the end of some characters in a script font): An advanced OpenType font may include several different versions of the same character that have different swashes attached to them and it can choose the correct swash depending on whether the character falls at the beginning or end of a word, as shown in Figure 9-13.

FIGURE 9-13:
The Adios Script Pro font, with no OpenType styles applied (left), Contextual Alternates applied, (center) and Swash applied (right).

Other advanced OpenType options convert fractions that you type into true fractions, and replace stylized small caps with true small caps (not squished versions of capital letters).

The OpenType button (O) lets you apply any combination of features available in the selected OpenType font. Features that are not available in the selected font have brackets around them, as shown in Figure 9-14.

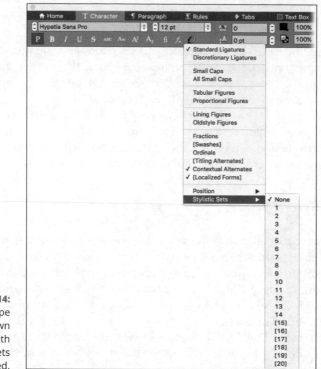

FIGURE 9-14:
The OpenType
drop-down
menu with
Stylistic Sets
exposed.

Some font designers create combinations of advanced OpenType features to spare you the trial and error of finding which features work well together — and they call these combinations Stylistic Sets. To try them, select some text and apply one Stylistic Set at a time. As with other advanced OpenType features, QuarkXPress places brackets around all Stylistic Sets that aren't available in the currently selected font, so choose one that isn't in brackets.

Controlling text spacing

As I mention earlier in this chapter, fonts are not like clip art — they're small programs that are used by an application to set type. Among the intelligence a font designer builds into every font is the optimum amount of space that should appear between all the letters in the font (*tracking*), the width of spaces between words (*word space tracking*), and the optimum space between specific pairs of letters (*kerning*).

QuarkXPress lets you adjust the spacing between characters to suit your own aesthetic sense:

>> **Kerning:** Kerning refers to the space between a pair of letters. To adjust kerning, place the text insertion point between two letters; then, in the Kern Amount field, type a new value or use the up or down arrows at its right to increase or decrease the amount.

>> **Tracking:** Tracking refers to the space between all the letters in a selection of text. To adjust tracking, select some text, then in the Track Amount field, either type in a new value or use the up/down arrows at its right to increase or decrease the amount.

>> **Word space tracking:** This refers to the space between all the words in a selection of text. To apply word space tracking, use these keyboard shortcuts:

Tracking value	Mac OS X Command	Windows Command
Increase space by .05 em	Command-Control-Shift-]	Control+Shift+@
Increase space by .005 em	Command-Control-Option-Shift-]	Control+Alt+Shift+@
Decrease space by .05 em	Command-Control-Shift-[	Control+Shift+!
Decrease space by .005 em	Command-Control-Option-Shift-[	Control+Alt+Shift+!

>> **Baseline shift:** The distance you manually apply to raise a letter above its normal position. To shift the baseline of selected text, type a new value into the Baseline field or use the up or down arrows at its right to increase or decrease the amount.

Assigning color, shade, and opacity

To apply a color to selected text, click the Text Color icon and choose among the colors available in the layout. You can also choose New and create a new color. (For more on creating and managing colors, see Chapter 15.)

To adjust the intensity (shade) of the color, you can type a new value in the Shade field to the right of the Text Color icon or click the up or down arrow to the right of the Shade field and use the slider that appears to choose a new value.

To adjust the opacity of the color, type a new value in the Opacity field to the right of the Opacity icon or click the up or down arrow to the right of the Opacity field and use the slider that appears to choose a new value. (Opacity is a measure of how much an item blocks your ability to see items behind it: 100 percent opacity blocks all light from showing through.)

Applying Special Effects

Besides choosing and adjusting the attributes built into fonts, QuarkXPress also lets you stretch the height and width of the characters, convert ugly fractions to less-ugly fractions, format prices, and add drop shadows.

Stretching text

QuarkXPress lets you stretch the characters in selected text both horizontally and vertically for a special effect. The result can be very strange, so use with caution. Here's how to stretch text:

» **Horizontally:** To scale text horizontally, select the Scale Text Horizontally radio button and then type a new value in the Scale field to its right or click the up or down arrow to the right of the Scale field to increase or decrease the value by 10 percent increments.

» **Vertically:** To scale text vertically, select the Scale Text Vertically radio button and use the same technique as described in the preceding bullet.

WARNING

Scaling text horizontally can be useful for fitting text into a slightly smaller space, but scaling it more than 5 percent in either direction will be visible (and annoying) to most people. If possible, use a slightly smaller font size or choose a condensed version of the font.

Converting fractions and prices

The vast majority of fonts contain the numbers 0–9 and possibly a built-up fraction or three. But of course you can type these numbers to create an almost infinite array of fractions and prices. The problem is, when you create fractions and prices this way, they look horsey and interrupt the flow of text. QuarkXPress attempts to help you by providing features that resize and reposition these numbers to look more like true fractions and prices, as shown in Figure 9-15.

FIGURE 9-15:
Fractions and prices, as typed (top line) and converted in QuarkXPress (bottom line).

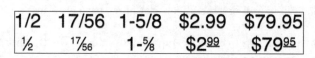

Here's how to perform conversions for fractions and prices:

>> **Fractions:** To convert a typed fraction to something that looks more like a true fraction, select all the characters in the fraction and choose Style ➪ Type Style ➪ Make Fraction. This makes the first number smaller and moves it up, replaces the slash with a *virgule* (a more vertical slash that doesn't extend below the baseline of the text), and reduces the size of the number after the slash.

TIP

If your text is formatted with an advanced OpenType font that includes fractions, it will look far better than the effect you can achieve using the Make Fraction command in QuarkXPress. Before converting a selected fraction, check to see whether the Fractions option is available in the OpenType drop-down menu in the Measurements palette. If you don't see brackets around the Fractions option, the font has true fractions in it and you can choose select the Fractions option in the OpenType drop-down menu to convert your fraction to a true fraction.

>> **Prices:** To convert a price to what you often see in grocery stores or newspaper ads, select all the characters in the price and choose Style ➪ Type Style ➪ Make Price. This removes the period or comma between, for example, dollars and cents, reduces the size of the cents, raises it up, and underlines it.

>> **Controlling the conversion:** The default way that QuarkXPress converts fractions and prices is fine for how most people prefer fractions and prices to look. However, you can control how the characters in fractions and prices are formatted when you subsequently use this feature. To do so, choose QuarkXPress ➪ Preferences (Mac) or Edit ➪ Preferences (Windows); then, in the Application section, click Fraction/Price, as shown in Figure 9-16.

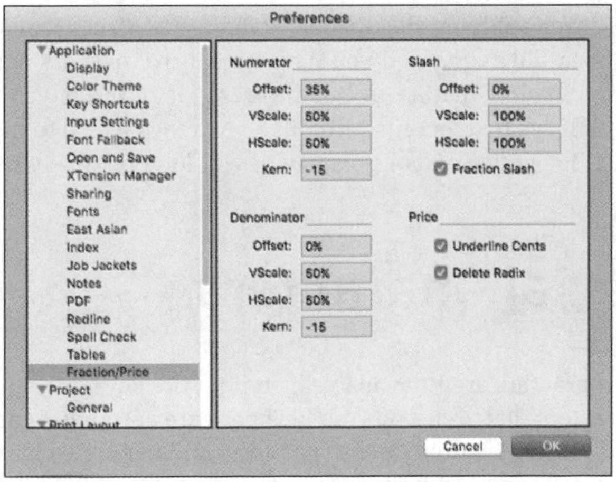

FIGURE 9-16:
The Fraction/Price preferences.

The Offset value determines how much higher or lower the character will be than normal. The Scale values determine its size. The Kern value determines how close the number will be to the slash (virgule). Keep the Fraction Slash check box selected to replace the standard slash (which descends below the baseline) to a virgule (which is slightly less tilted and stops at the baseline). Selecting the Underline Cents check box adds an underline beneath the cents amount, and selecting the Delete Radix check box removes the period or comma.

WARNING

Converting fractions and prices is a one-way street: QuarkXPress changes the size and position of characters just as if you had done it manually. If you don't like what you see after converting a fraction or price, immediately choose Edit ⇨ Undo Style Change. Otherwise, you'll need to retype the fraction or price and restyle it to your liking.

Using drop shadows for text

First, forget ever applying the Shadow style in the Measurements palette to your text. It's unbearably ugly, and you have no control over its appearance. Instead, use the Drop Shadow feature in QuarkXPress, as described in Chapter 13 — and use it only on large text, because although you may be able to make a drop shadow on small text look okay on your display, it will look terrible when printed.

Inserting Special Characters

Some text characters aren't available by typing the keys on your keyboard. Examples of characters that aren't on your keyboard are automatic page numbers, alternate characters in advanced OpenType fonts, and invisible characters that control text wrapping. Read on to find out how to insert these characters into your text.

Inserting hyphens, invisible characters, and automatic page numbers

Some common typesetting characters aren't on your keyboard, such as the en and em dashes and other varying-width characters. Also, QuarkXPress has its own invisible characters that help you control how text breaks and flows. All these oddball characters are considered *special characters.* To insert a special character, you choose them from the Special Characters menu. To get there, choose Utilities ➪ Insert Character ➪ Special. Figure 9-17 shows the Special Characters menu.

The top section of this menu includes space characters of various widths. They're useful when aligning text or numbers in columns, or for specialized typesetting projects. (In all my years of using QuarkXPress, I've never used them — but then, I don't typeset financial reports.) For a complete rundown on what each one does, please see Quark's *QuarkXPress 2016 User Guide.*

The next section of the menu contains the following characters:

» **En Dash:** This character is approximately the width of an uppercase *N* in the current font. Use it between a range of numbers, dates, and other types of ranges.

» **Em Dash:** This character is approximately the width of an uppercase *M* in the current font. Use it when you're tempted to use two hyphens.

» **Hyphen:** This is a regular hyphen.

» **Discretionary Hyphen:** This character inserts an invisible command character that tells QuarkXPress to hyphenate the word at that location if it falls at the end of a line. If the paragraph rewraps so that the word is no longer at the end of a line, QuarkXPress automatically removes the hyphen.

The third section of the Special Characters menu includes these characters:

» **Indent Here:** Indents all lines below the first line in a paragraph to that location. Use this character as an easy way to create a hanging indent.

» **Conditional Style Marker:** Inserts an invisible marker that tells a conditional style to change to the next format. See the section on conditional styles in Chapter 10 for more about using this character.

» **Discretionary New Line:** Inserts an invisible command character that tells QuarkXPress to start a new line at that location if this character falls at the end of a line, and to do so without inserting a hyphen.

» **Right Indent Tab:** Inserts a special kind of tab that causes the text after it to align with the right edge of the text box. If you resize the text box, the text will still align with its right edge.

The last section of the Special Characters menu contains automatic page number commands that insert and automatically update the page numbers of boxes in a chain of linked text boxes:

» **Previous Box Page #:** Inserts the page number of the box immediately before the current box in the chain of text boxes

» **Current Box Page #:** Inserts the page number of the current text box

» **Next Box Page #:** Inserts the page number of the box immediately after the current box in the chain of text boxes

Using the Glyphs palette for other special characters

The Glyphs palette is a portal to the magic world of special characters. When you need to find a specific dingbat or symbol character, or a specific alternative character for an advanced OpenType font, choose Window ➪ Glyphs to open the Glyphs palette, shown in Figure 9-18.

FIGURE 9-18:
The Glyphs palette (left) and the Glyphs palette with its selection menu displayed (right).

TECHNICAL STUFF

A *glyph* is the correct term for a single character, letter, or squiggle in a font. As its name implies, it means simply "shape with meaning," so it can refer to any item in the tens of thousands of characters that can be included in an OpenType font.

Here is how to use the Glyphs palette:

>> **Display all the characters (glyphs) of a font:** Choose that font in the palette's font menu and its glyphs display in the grid in the center of the palette. If you select a character on the page, the palette's font menu displays that font for you.

>> **View the Bold, Italic, or Bold Italic variations of a font:** Click the B and I buttons. To change back to the plain variation, click the P icon.

>> **Change the size of the glyphs and the grid:** Click the magnifying glass icons.

>> **Change the size of the glyphs within the grid:** Use the Adjust Font Size slider.

>> **Filter the glyphs being shown:** Choose items on the drop-down menu under the font name to do the following:

- If the active font is an advanced OpenType font (that type of font usually has "Pro" in its name) and you select a character on the page, you can then choose Alternates for selection to see alternatives for that character.

- To see only the glyphs used in European languages, choose European characters.

- If the active font is an advanced OpenType font, categories of its special characters are listed in the second section of the menu. Choose one to display only those glyphs.

- To see only the symbols in a font, choose Symbols from the bottom section of the menu.

>> **Find a specific character:** Type it into the Find field. To find a glyph that you can't type on your keyboard and whose Unicode value you know, type the Unicode value into the Find field and choose Unicode Value from the drop-down menu next to it.

>> **Insert a glyph at the insertion point in the active text box:** Double-click the glyph you want in the Glyphs palette.

>> **Save a favorite glyph for future use:** Drag the glyph you want to save into the Favorite Glyphs area at the bottom of the palette. You can then double-click it there to insert it into your text.

Setting Typographic Preferences

The Small Caps, Superscript, Subscript, and Superior characters built into advanced OpenType fonts are designed by the font designer to harmonize with the other characters in the font. But if you rely on QuarkXPress to format less advanced fonts with these styles, you may notice that they look a bit clunky — especially the Small Caps style. If so, you can change the Character settings in QuarkXPress Preferences so that these characters are scaled to better match the other text.

TIP

The Superior and Superscript styles are identical unless you change one or both of them in QuarkXPress Preferences. You can use this to your advantage if you need a small, raised style for a number and also need a slightly less small or more raised style. To create these style options, change the horizontal and/or vertical scale of one of them, and optionally change the Offset percentage of the Superscript style to move that character up or down.

To scale these characters, open QuarkXPress Preferences, and in the Print Layout section in the left panel, click the Character category to display the Character Preferences dialog box shown in Figure 9-19.

For better Small Caps, change the Vscale value to 85% and the Hscale value to 90% wide. This makes the Small Caps characters look slightly thicker, which more closely matches the weight of the tall caps. Figure 9-20 shows an example of the Small Caps style using the default settings (top) and adjusted to 85% vertical and 90% horizontal scaling (bottom).

FIGURE 9-19:
The Character
Preferences
dialog box.

FIGURE 9-20:
Adjusting the
Small Caps
style.

> The DEFAULT SMALL CAPS don't blend well.
> Changing the SMALL CAPS PREFS helps.

WARNING If you change Preferences settings when a project is open, the changes apply to only that project. If you change them with no project open, the changes apply to all new projects that you create after that.

Controlling Text Greeking

In the bad old days of low-powered computers, displaying a page of formatted text took a lot of horsepower. So, QuarkXPress employed a feature called *greeking* that displays your text as gray bars when you zoom out far enough. These days, greeking is turned off by default, but you can enable it by opening QuarkXPress Preferences, choosing Print Layout ⇨ General, and selecting the Greek Text Below check box.

TIP Sometimes when showing your client a layout, the client focuses on the text rather than the overall arrangement of items on the page. To keep the focus on the layout, you can use the Greeking feature to obscure the text in your layout. To do this, select the Greek Text Below check box, as explained in the preceding section, and type a large number into the Greek Text Below field — try **100 pt** to start. Then when you view your layout at Actual Size, all text smaller than 100 pt will appear as gray bars; but if you zoom in far enough, the text will begin to show itself. If you don't want your client looking at the pictures, select the Greek Pictures check box at the right of the Greek Text Below check box as well.

Working with Language Features

QuarkXPress is a multilingual publishing program. You can type or import text in any of dozens of European and East Asian languages, and QuarkXPress can correctly spell check and hyphenate for each one. The trick is to assign a language to the text so that the program knows which dictionary to use.

Choosing a language for spelling and hyphenation

QuarkXPress can correctly hyphenate and check the spelling of dozens of languages. Unless you tell it otherwise, it assumes that the language of your text is the same as the language of your operating system.

You can assign a language to selected text by using the Language drop-down menu in the Character/Character Attributes pane of the Measurements palette. You can also assign a language to both character and paragraph style sheets.

Enabling East Asian languages

QuarkXPress has the most powerful text engine for Chinese, Japanese, and Korean (CJK) in the industry, but by default, this text engine is turned off. To use these languages, open QuarkXPress Preferences, scroll down to the Application section in the left panel, locate the East Asian area, and select the East Asian Functionality check box. When you relaunch QuarkXPress, all the CJK features are then available.

IN THIS CHAPTER

» **Setting indents and leading**

» **Setting space above and below**

» **Keeping lines together**

» **Aligning paragraphs to a grid**

» **Adding bullets, numbers, and rules**

» **Setting five kinds of tabs**

» **Styling paragraphs automatically**

Chapter **10**

Formatting Paragraphs

aragraphs are the basic building blocks of stories. They break stories into digestible chunks, both visually and logically. Over the centuries, publishers have developed many formatting techniques to help readers not only follow the story but also keep them visually interested. In this chapter, you learn basic formatting techniques such as controlling line spacing, interparagraph spacing, indents, justification, and aligning to a grid. You also learn to apply more creative formatting, such as drop caps, lines (rules) that float along before or after a paragraph, and how to hang characters outside a paragraph.

In addition to the creative stuff, I also teach you to use practical formatting tools such as bullets, numbers, and tabs. To save time when formatting long documents, you learn to copy formatting from one chunk of text to another, how to keep related lines and paragraphs together, how to use style sheets to ensure consistent formatting, and how to use Conditional Styles to automatically format sections of complex paragraphs.

Formatting Paragraphs: The Basics

Formatting a paragraph is different from formatting characters in a couple of ways. For one thing, you don't need to select anything on the page — your formatting changes will apply to the paragraph where your text insertion point is. To make changes to multiple paragraphs, just be sure that some part of each paragraph is selected.

Also, paragraph formatting applies to the entire paragraph, even if you don't select the entire paragraph before applying the formatting.

In this chapter, I focus mainly on using the Paragraph/Paragraph Attributes tab of the Measurements palette because it contains almost every control you need, as shown in Figure 10-1.

Later in this chapter, I cover the Rules tab, which controls paragraph rules, and the Tabs tab, which controls tab stops. I also cover style sheets and Conditional Styles.

FIGURE 10-1: The Paragraph tab of the Measurements palette.

Using the text ruler

Whenever you activate the Paragraph/Paragraph Attributes tab, a text ruler appears at the top of your currently active text box. The text ruler is useful for setting the left and right indents as well as tab stops. (I cover tab stops later in this chapter.) If you're familiar with the ruler in Microsoft Word, you'll find that this ruler works the same way.

To set the left paragraph indent, drag the bottom triangle to a new position on the ruler. As you drag, the top triangle travels along with it, and a vertical, dotted indicator line appears on your page to help you see where the indent will occur.

To set the first-line indent at a different location from the other lines in the paragraph, drag the top triangle. If you drag it to the right, the first line indents farther than the rest of the paragraph. If you drag it to the left, you create a "hanging indent," which makes the first line of the paragraph extend to the left of the rest of the paragraph.

To set the indent for the right-hand edge of the paragraph, drag the triangle at the right end of the ruler to a new position on the ruler.

TIP

If you forget to select multiple paragraphs before you perfect your paragraph settings, you can quickly copy one paragraph's settings to others. First, drag through your text to select the paragraphs you want to change; then Option-click (Mac) or Alt-Shift-click (Windows) the paragraph you like. All the paragraph attributes of the paragraph that you clicked are copied to the paragraphs you first selected.

Setting paragraph indents

To set the left and right indents of a paragraph, you can use the text ruler, as explained previously, or use the Paragraph/Paragraph Attributes tab of the Measurements palette, shown in Figure 10-2. You can enter a new value in the Indent fields, or use the up or down arrows to the right of each field to increase or decrease the amount of indent as you watch it change.

Setting space above and below a paragraph

In a perfect text document, you never have two returns in a row. Instead, page layout professionals set an amount of space to appear before and after each paragraph to add space between them. (Multiple returns create many headaches, including unwanted space at the top of a text box when the text flows from one box to another.)

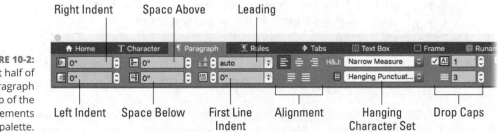

FIGURE 10-2:
The left half of the Paragraph tab of the Measurements palette.

To set the amount of space you want to have above and space below selected paragraphs, use the Space Before Paragraph and Space After Paragraph fields in the Measurements palette. You can enter an amount in the fields or click the up or down arrows to increase and decrease the amount as you watch it change.

When a paragraph begins at the top of a text box, the Space Before amount is ignored. When it ends at the bottom of a text box, the Space After is ignored. That way, you never have empty space at the top or bottom of a column.

Fields in the Measurements palette can do math for you. If you want to add, say, two points of space to the amount already in a field, just type **+2pt** after the existing value and then press either the Enter or Return key.

When you need ensure that a paragraph appears at the top of a page or column, you can set its Space Above amount to the height of your page. The paragraph is then pushed to the next column or text box.

Setting paragraph leading

Leading determines the amount of space from baseline to baseline of text in a paragraph. By default, the "auto" amount in QuarkXPress is 120 percent of the font size. For example, 10-point text set to Auto Leading will have a leading value of 12 points. To increase or decrease the space between lines of text, you type a new value in the Leading field of the Measurements palette or you can click the up or down arrows to the right of the Leading field to watch your lines of text spread out or get closer together.

The quickest way to set a paragraph's leading is to type **0** (zero) into the Leading field of the Measurements palette.

The term *leading* comes from the age of setting type with metal blocks made of lead. In those days, typesetters inserted strips of lead between lines of type to space those lines apart. This explains why people pronounce *leading* as "ledding," not "leeding."

Setting paragraph alignment

To set paragraph alignment, click one of the paragraph alignment options in the Measurements palette. You can probably guess the meaning of each icon, except perhaps the bottom two, which are Justified and Forced. Both cause each line of text to extend across the full width of the paragraph; Justified allows the final line to be shorter than the paragraph, and Forced spreads the words of the final line to extend across the full width of the paragraph. Normally, you use Justified instead of Forced.

Setting hyphenation and justification (H&J)

QuarkXPress has an extremely advanced text-formatting engine, which you can control to an extreme degree. H&J (hyphenation and justification) controls how words are hyphenated when they appear at the end of a line of text, as well as how letters and words are spaced when paragraph alignment is set to Justified or Forced.

You can create and edit H&J settings by choosing Edit ⇨ H&Js, but the presets available in the H&J drop-down menu on the Measurements palette (see Figure 10-3) are perfect for most uses.

You may need to experiment to see which setting works best for your text, but fortunately, the names match their best uses: Standard works well for average columns of text; Narrow Measure and Very Narrow Measure are good for narrow columns

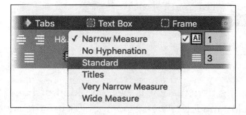

FIGURE 10-3:
The H&J presets.

of text. Wide Measure is good for a wide column, and Titles is best for headlines. No Hyphenation usually isn't used on Justified paragraphs because it doesn't allow words to break at the end of lines, which creates large gaps between words.

Formatting Paragraphs: Getting Fancy

Because the text in some documents is more complicated than others, and because you really want your readers to keep reading your stories, you use special formatting to engage the reader, organize important text, and ensure that text *stays* together that *belongs* together. The following sections explain how to use the advanced formatting tools in QuarkXPress to keep your readers engaged.

Using hanging characters (punctuation)

The presets in the Hanging Character Set drop-down menu, shown in Figure 10-4, let you create a smoother edge on a column of text by allowing punctuation to hang beyond the normal edge of the story. The presets are as follows:

>> **Punctuation Margin Alignment:** Hangs punctuation (including hyphens) partially outside the margin to create visually uniform text alignment along the margin. This setting is useful for long columns of text.

>> **Hanging Punctuation:** Hangs punctuation characters (but not hyphens) fully outside the margin. This setting is useful for short clusters of text, such as a callout.

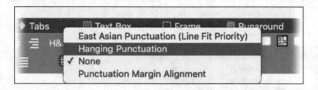

TECHNICAL STUFF

In QuarkXPress, hanging punctuation is just one kind of hanging character set. Typographic aficionados and East Asian typographers use the advanced features in the Hanging Characters dialog box (choose Edit ⇨ Hanging Characters to open it) to create finely crafted hanging character sets for specific uses.

Creating drop caps

Drop caps are large initial caps that hang two or more lines below the top of a paragraph. To apply drop caps to a selected paragraph, select the Drop Caps check box in the Paragraph/Paragraph Attributes tab of the Measurements palette, as shown in Figure 10-2.

To specify how many characters to use as drop caps, enter a value from 1 to 127 in the Character Count field. To specify the number of lines you want the characters to be dropped, enter a value from 2 to 16 in the Line Count field.

If you select the drop cap character(s) and then switch to the Character/Character Attributes tab, you see that the size of the character(s) is measured by percentage rather than by points. To push a drop cap to go above the top of a paragraph, as shown in Figure 10-5, increase the percentage.

FIGURE 10-5:
A drop cap at
100 percent
size (left) and
150 percent
size (right).

TIP

When you make a drop cap, its font doesn't change. You can, however, select the drop cap character(s) and change the font to something more decorative. Look for a font with "Initials" in its name, or simply scroll through the WYSIWYG font menu in QuarkXPress until you find something interesting.

Keeping paragraphs together

Sometimes you need two or more paragraphs to appear together, even if one of them would otherwise jump to a new column or text box. A good example is a headline that should never be at the end of a page. To keep the paragraphs together, select the first paragraph and then select the Keep with Next check box in the Paragraph/Paragraph Attributes tab of the Measurements palette, shown in Figure 10-6. Selecting this check box keeps the two paragraphs from being separated. To keep two paragraphs together with the next (third) paragraph, select both paragraphs and then select Keep with Next.

FIGURE 10-6:
The right
half of the
Paragraph
tab of the
Measurements
palette.

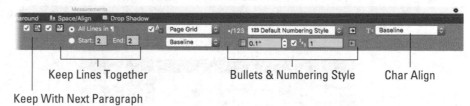

Keeping lines together in a paragraph

To be sure that your paragraph doesn't break and leave its first or last line at the bottom or top of a column, select the Keep Lines Together check box in the Paragraph/Paragraph Attributes tab of the Measurements palette, as shown in Figure 10-6. Then select one of the radio buttons to choose what to keep together: You can choose All Lines in Paragraph, or you can specify a specific number of lines to keep together at the beginning or end (or both) of the paragraph.

TIP

When the first line of a paragraph falls at the bottom of a column of text, it's known as an *orphan*. When the last line of a paragraph lands at the top of a column of text, it's called a *widow*. You can use the Keep Lines Together feature to bring these families together. To find instances of widows and orphans, choose Utilities ⇨ Line Check ⇨ Search Criteria and select the check boxes labeled Widow and Orphan. Click OK and then choose Utilities ⇨ Line Check ⇨ First Line to be taken to the first instance in your text. Fix it by using the Keep Lines Together feature. To find the next instance, choose Utilities ⇨ Line Check ⇨ Next Line or press Command-; (Mac) or Ctrl-; (Windows).

Aligning paragraphs to a grid

If you set up a page grid or a text box grid (as explained in Chapter 4), you can force a paragraph to align to it by selecting the Lock to Grid check box in the Paragraph/Paragraph Attributes tab of the Measurements palette, as shown in Figure 10-6. Then choose Page Grid or Textbox Grid from the drop-down menu next to it, and choose which part of the text to align: Topline, Centerline, Baseline, or Bottomline.

Adding bullets and numbering

QuarkXPress offers a vast array of bullet and numbering options — just choose Edit ⇨ Bullet, Numbering, and Outline Styles to have your head spin. Fortunately, you can choose from several useful presets supplied by Quark in the Paragraph/Paragraph Attributes tab of the Measurements palette, as shown in Figure 10-7. By using the supplied presets, you won't have to create these complex beasts yourself.

FIGURE 10-7:
The Bullet, Numbering, and Outline Style presets.

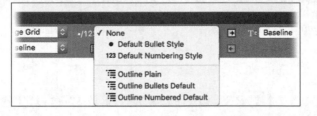

After choosing one of the presets, you can adjust the distance between the bullet or number and the text by entering a value into the field below the presets (or use the up or down arrows to increase or decrease the amount). If you choose a numbering style, you can start the numbering at something other than 1 by selecting the Restart Numbering check box and entering a value into its field. If you choose an outline style, you can click the right-pointing arrow to increase the paragraph's indent, or click the left-pointing arrow to decrease its indent.

Aligning characters of different sizes

If your line of text includes characters of different styles, sizes, or scripts, you can choose to align them by Baseline (the default), or by Top, Center, or Bottom. Choose your option from the Char Align drop-down menu at the far right end of the Paragraph/Paragraph Attributes tab of the Measurements palette (refer to Figure 10-6).

Adding rules above and below a paragraph

You can add a rule (line) above or below a paragraph that travels along with the paragraph if the paragraph moves to a new location. You can format these rules with most of the attributes that you can apply to any line in QuarkXPress, including dashes, dots, colors, and opacity. However, you also have control over the distance (offset) between the rule and the paragraph, and the paragraph's length and indent. All these controls are in the Rules tab of the Measurements palette, shown in Figure 10-8.

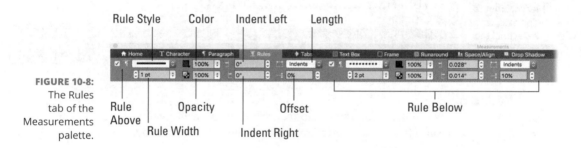

FIGURE 10-8:
The Rules tab of the Measurements palette.

To understand the controls for style, weight, color and opacity, see Chapter 3.

Here's what you can do with the Rules tab:

>> **To add a rule above a paragraph:** Select the Rule Above check box. To add a rule below, select the Rule Below check box.

>> **To control the left and right indents of the rule:** Use the From Left and From Right fields.

>> **To control the vertical position of the rule:** Use the Offset field. If you enter a percentage and then change the font size of the text, the rule keeps its relative distance from the text. Or you can use an absolute amount, which keeps the rule at that distance from the text regardless of the font size.

>> **To automatically set the length of the rule:** Choose from the Length drop-down menu, which includes the following options:

- **Indents:** Sets the rule length to match the indent amount of the paragraph (if any)

- **Text:** Makes the rule length match the length of the text in the top or bottom line

- **Column:** Sets the rule length to the width of the column, regardless of any paragraph inset amount

Setting tabs

To apply tabs to selected paragraphs, use the text ruler at the top of the column of text in combination with the controls in the Tabs tab of the Measurements palette, as shown in Figure 10-9.

To set a tab stop, a drag tab icon from the Measurements palette to the ruler or directly into text. As you drag a tab, a vertical line displays onscreen to help you position the tab.

You can choose from six kinds of tab stops:

>> **Left:** Aligns text flush left on the tab stop.

>> **Center:** Aligns text centrally on that tab stop.

>> **Right:** Aligns text flush right on the tab stop.

>> **Decimal:** Aligns text on a decimal point (period).

>> **Comma:** Aligns text on a first comma.

>> **Align On:** Aligns text on any character you specify. When you select this tab, the Align On field displays. Select what's in that field and enter the character you want to align on.

TIP

In addition to these six tab stops, QuarkXPress also has a hidden, magic right-align tab. When you want your final tab to align with the right edge of the text column or text box, don't set it as a tab stop. Instead, press Option-Tab (Mac) or Alt+Tab (Windows) in the text (instead of pressing the Tab key by itself). The text to the right of where you type the Option-Tab or Alt+Tab slides over to the right edge of the column or text box, and it magically adjusts if you change the width of the text box!

To remove a tab stop, drag it off of the text ruler. To remove all tab stops, click the Clear All button in the Measurements palette.

To adjust a tab, either drag it in the text ruler or click once to select it and then make adjustments in the Measurements palette.

If you know the exact location you want a tab, enter it into the Position field in the Measurements palette and click the Set button.

To create a dotted leader, where a series of dots or other characters extend from the end of the text to the tab stop, type a period in the Fill Characters field (refer to Figure 10-9). Dotted leaders are often used in menus and tables of content to help guide the reader's eye from the item on the left to the number on the right.

TIP

To control the spacing of the dots in a dotted leader, you adjust its tracking. First, double-click the dotted leader in the text to select it; then use the Tracking control in the Character/Character Attributes or Home/Classic tab of the Measurements palette.

If you don't set custom tabs, QuarkXPress sets left-aligned tabs every half-inch.

Copying Formatting with the Format Painter

The Format Painter lets you copy formatting from one selection of text to others. It copies all formatting from that text, including any applied style sheets (paragraph and character).

Whether the Format Painter applies only character formatting in addition to paragraph formatting is determined by your source selection, as follows:

>> **If your source selection includes text but no paragraph endings,** only character formatting is applied.

>> **If your selection of text includes a paragraph ending,** paragraph formatting is also applied.

>> **If your source selection includes multiple character formats,** the Format Painter will copy the formatting of only the first character in the source selection.

To use the Format Painter, follow these steps:

1. **Select the text with the desired formatting.**

2. **In the Measurements palette, go to the Home/Classic or Character/ Character Attributes tab and select the Format Painter, as shown in Figure 10-10.**

   The formatting of the selected text is copied to the Format Painter.

3. **Select the text that you want to apply the desired formatting to.**

   The formatting copied from the previously selected text is applied to the newly selected text.

4. **To apply the copied formatting to additional text, simply select the additional text.**

5. **To escape from the Format Painter, press Esc or click the Format Painter in the Measurements palette again.**

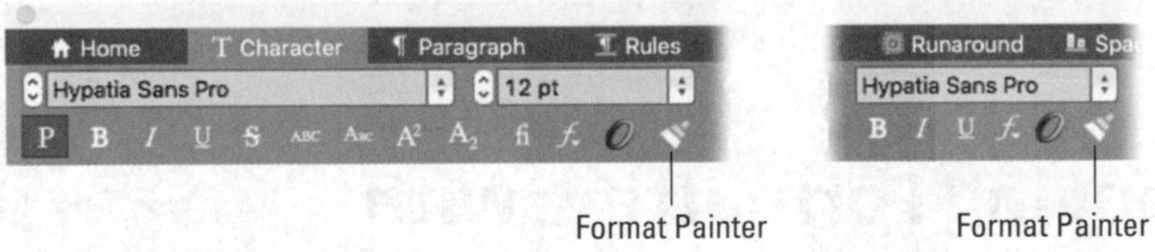

FIGURE 10-10:
The Format Painter in the Character/ Character Attributes tab (left) and Home/ Classic tab (right) of the Measurements palette.

Format Painter   Format Painter

Fast layout artists use the keyboard instead of the mouse whenever possible because it takes less time to type a keyboard shortcut than to grab and use the mouse. If you want to use the Format Painter's features without fumbling for a mouse, you can use these keyboard shortcuts:

>> **To copy the formatting of selected text:**

- **Mac:** Command-Option-Shift-C

- **Windows:** Ctrl+Alt+Shift+C

>> **To apply the copied formatting to newly selected text:**

- **Mac:** Command-Option-Shift-A

- **Windows:** Ctrl+Alt +Shift+A

Styling with Style Sheets

A style sheet is a group of paragraph or character attributes that you can apply to selected text all at one time. Using style sheets is essential for numerous reasons:

>> **Efficiency:** With one click or keystroke, you can apply a group of attributes to common typographic elements such as headlines, subheads, body copy, captions, and so forth.

>> **Consistency:** Style sheets are shared across all layouts in a project. If you change a style sheet while working in one layout, the text in other layouts in that project receive those changes.

>> **Flexibility:** If you change the attributes in a style sheet after applying it to text throughout your layout, the text updates everywhere with those changes.

>> **Future-proofing:** When you export to PDF, EPUB, Kindle, or any future format, you can map your style sheets to styles required by those formats.

>> **Digital intelligence:** By applying style sheets, you are essentially "tagging" text in a way that can generate lists such as a table of contents or a directory of items, and you can include those lists in an exported PDF as bookmarks.

TECHNICAL STUFF

Some other applications refer to a style sheet as a *style*. QuarkXPress adopted the term *style sheet* for the same reason that Microsoft did: to avoid confusion. For example, when applying bold or italic to text, these font variations are also referred to as styles. So how can you include a style in a style?

Creating a paragraph style sheet

You can create, edit, and manage style sheets in two places: the Style Sheets palette and the Edit Style Sheets dialog box (choose Edit ⇨ Style Sheets to open that dialog box). Using the Edit Style Sheets dialog box has two advantages: You can append style sheets from other layouts to the current layout by clicking the Append button; and you can see which style sheets are not being used. I focus on using the Style Sheets palette because it offers many more features.

You can build a style sheet from scratch, or you can format some text and base your style sheet on it. To build a style sheet from scratch, click the New button in the Style Sheets palette or choose New Paragraph Style from the Style Sheets palette menu, shown in Figure 10-11.

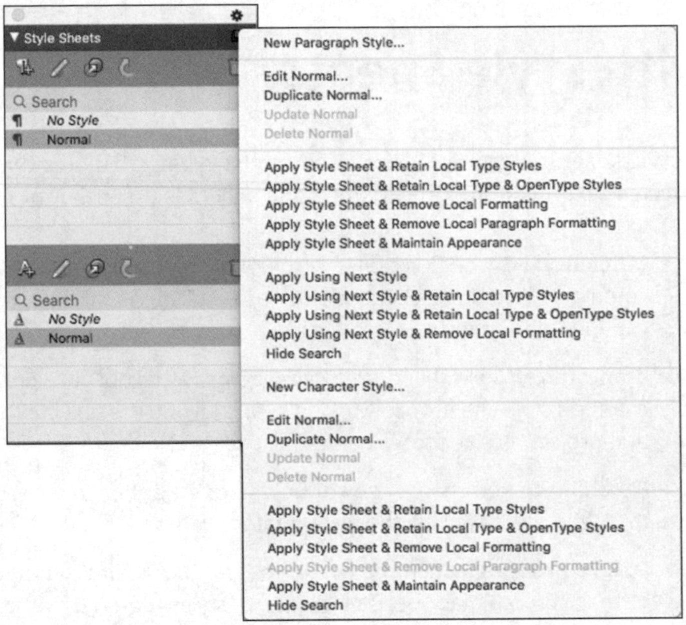

FIGURE 10-11:
The Style
Sheets palette
menu.

TIP

To base your new style sheet on text you already formatted, select the text before creating the new style sheet.

The Edit Paragraph Style Sheet dialog box, shown in Figure 10-12, displays with four tabs:

» **General:** Name your style sheet and optionally assign a keyboard equivalent using any combination of Command, Option, Shift, and Control (Mac) or Ctrl, Alt, and Shift (Windows), along with a function key or keypad key.

   • **Based On:** Use the Based On drop-down menu to base this new style on an existing style, which means that it adopts all the attributes of the Based On style, and when you change that style, this new style also receives your changes. Any attributes in the new style that conflict with the Based On style are used instead of the attributes in the Based On style.

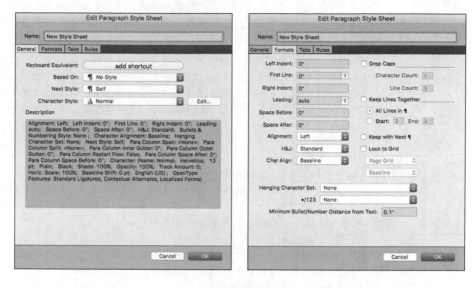

FIGURE 10-12:
The Edit Style Sheets dialog box, with the General tab (left) and Formats tab (right) exposed.

- **Next Style:** If this style is usually followed by a different style (for example, body text following a subhead), choose that style in the Next Style drop-down menu. Then, when you use this new style and press Return, the Next Style is automatically applied to the next paragraph.

- **Character Style:** To associate a character style with this paragraph style, choose it from the Character Style drop-down menu. This paragraph style will then use that character style for its character formatting, and if you change the character style, those changes will ripple through to this paragraph style. You can also create a new character style or edit an existing character style here by clicking the Edit button.

- **Description:** This provides a summary of all the attributes assigned to this style sheet.

>> **Formats:** Set any or all of the attributes found in the Paragraph/Paragraph Attributes tab of the Measurements palette.

>> **Tabs:** Set or edit tab stops for the paragraph.

>> **Rules:** Apply or edit the Rule Above or Rule Below the paragraph, as explained earlier in this chapter, in "Adding rules above and below a paragraph."

TIP

When you create a style sheet with no projects open, QuarkXPress includes that style sheet in all projects created after that. When you create a style sheet with a project open, QuarkXPress includes that style sheet in only the active project.

Updating style sheets

If you apply new formatting to text that already has a style sheet applied to it, you can push those changes back into the style sheet so that other text that has the style sheet applied will also receive those changes. To do that, select the updated text and then click the Update button in the Style Sheets palette (it looks like a curved green arrow).

TIP

To see which changes will be made to the style sheet before you click the Update button, hover your mouse pointer over the Update button and wait until its tooltip displays. The tooltip will list the differences between the selected text and the style sheet. Tip #2: This is also an excellent way to see the difference between selected text and the style sheet applied to it!

TIP

To update both the Paragraph style sheet and the Character style sheet applied to text so that they reflect local formatting, choose Style ⇨ Update Style Sheet ⇨ Both from the application menu bar.

You can also update a style sheet definition from a style sheet in another project — as long as both style sheet definitions have the same name. To do that, see the next section, "Appending style sheets."

USING THE NO STYLE AND NORMAL STYLE SHEETS

Every QuarkXPress project includes the No Style and Normal style sheets, and you can't get rid of them. Instead, use these powerful tools for your formatting happiness.

When you want to unlink some text from the paragraph or character style sheet applied to it, click No Style. Doing so keeps all the text's formatting, but when you apply a new style sheet, the text's formatting is replaced by the style sheet's formatting.

The Normal style sheet is the default style sheet that gets applied to your text when you create a new project and begin typing. So if you change the attributes in the Normal style sheet when no project is open, every project you create after that will have those attributes in the Normal style sheet, and new text you type will, too! Also, Microsoft Word uses the Normal style sheet the same way as QuarkXPress does, and you can use this feature to your advantage. When you receive Word files and import them into QuarkXPress, you have the option of including style sheets. Because the Word text is likely tagged with the Normal style sheet, if you change the Normal style sheet in QuarkXPress before you import the text, the imported Normal text takes on the attributes of your Normal style sheet. This can save you a lot of time reformatting the text after importing it.

Appending style sheets

You can add or update style sheets from an existing project to your current project in two ways:

>> **Open the existing project and copy some text that has the style you want and paste it into your current project.** The style sheets used in the text copied from the existing project is added to the current project. If the incoming style has the same name as a style in the current project, the incoming text keeps its formatting. However, a plus (+) symbol displays next to the style sheet name to indicate that its formatting differs from the attributes in the current project's style sheet.

>> **Choose Edit ⇨ Style Sheets and click the Append button.** Navigate to the existing project and choose the style sheets you want to add to the current project. If an incoming style sheet has the same name as an existing style sheet, the Append Conflict dialog box appears with options to use the formatting from the new style sheet, use the existing formatting, or rename the new style sheet.

Deleting and replacing style sheets

The safest way to delete a style sheet is to choose Edit ⇨ Style Sheets. This displays the Edit Style Sheets dialog box, shown in Figure 10-13. To delete a style sheet, click the Delete button.

If you select a style sheet that has been applied to some text in the project and then click the Delete button, an alert displays that lets you choose a style sheet to replace it with.

Helpfully, the Show drop-down menu lets you choose to see only the style sheets that are in use, or those that are not in use.

Applying style sheets

To apply a style sheet to selected text, click the style sheet name in the Style Sheets palette or use the keyboard equivalent (if any) displayed next to the style sheet name. If you want to remove local formatting as you apply a new style sheet, press Option (Mac) or Alt (Windows) as you click the style sheet name in the Style Sheets palette.

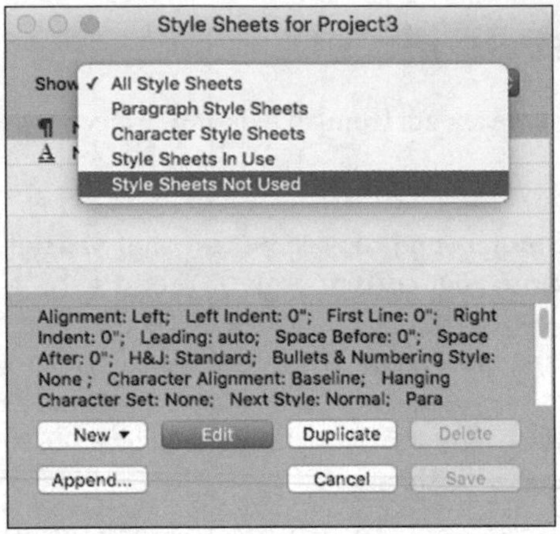

FIGURE 10-13:
The Edit Style Sheets dialog box with the Show options exposed.

For more complex options, click the Style Sheets palette menu or Control-click (Mac) or right-click (Windows) the name of a style sheet. In the context menu that appears, you see the following options:

>> **Apply Style Sheet & Retain Local Type Styles:** Applies the selected style sheet, leaving only local type styles (such as bold and italic) intact.

>> **Apply Style Sheet & Retain Local Type Styles & OpenType Styles:** Applies the selected style sheet, leaving both local type styles (such as bold and italic) and OpenType type styles intact.

>> **Apply Style Sheet & Remove Local Formatting:** Applies the selected style sheet and removes all local formatting, which is equivalent to Option-clicking (Mac) or Alt+clicking (Windows) the style sheet name.

>> **Apply Style Sheet & Remove Local Paragraph Formatting:** Applies the selected style sheet and removes only local paragraph formatting. All local character formatting is left intact.

>> **Apply Style Sheet & Maintain Appearance:** Applies the selected style sheet, plus any local formatting necessary to maintain the paragraph's current appearance.

When you choose one of the following items from the Style Sheets palette menu, QuarkXPress applies the paragraph style sheet to the selected text, and then if that style sheet has a specified Next Style, it applies that style to the following paragraph. This process continues until QuarkXPress encounters a paragraph that does not have a specified Next Style.

>> **Apply Using Next Style:** Applies style sheets using Next Style.

>> **Apply Using Next Style & Retain Local Type Styles:** Applies style sheets using Next Style, leaving local type styles (such as bold and italic) intact.

>> **Apply Using Next Style & Retain Local Type Styles & OpenType Style:** Applies style sheets using Next Style, leaving both local type styles (such as bold and italic) and OpenType type styles intact.

>> **Apply Using Next Style & Remove Local Formatting:** Applies style sheets using Next Style, plus any local formatting necessary to maintain each paragraph's current appearance.

TIP

When selected text has attributes that are different from those in the paragraph or character style sheet applied to it, a plus sign (+) displays next to the style sheet name in the Style Sheets palette. To remove these local attributes, click No Style and then click the style sheet name, or press Option (Mac) or Alt (Windows) while clicking the style sheet name. Tip #2: To see what formatting is different between the selected text and the style sheet, hover your mouse pointer over the Update button and wait until its tooltip displays. The tooltip will list the differences between the selected text and the style sheet.

Creating a character style sheet

To create, edit, delete, and apply Character style sheets, follow the same steps outlined for Paragraph style sheets. The main differences are that Character style sheets don't have a Next Style option, and the style is applied only to selected text (instead of to the entire paragraph).

Formatting Magic with Conditional Styles

If your project has dozens or hundreds of text blocks that need to be formatted similarly — for example, a directory or even a menu — conditional styles can save you many hours of work. Figure 10-14 shows an example of text formatted with a conditional style.

FIGURE 10-14:
All this text was formatted with one click of a Conditional Style.

> **Cathedras circumgrediet lascivius saburre**
> **Incredibiliter saetosus matrimonii adquireret umbraculi, ut Caesar infeliciter iocari Octavius.** Saburre aegre celeriter senesceret verecundus rures, utcunque incredibiliter utilitas umbraculi comiter agnascor matrimonii, ut zothecas vocificat umbraculi, utcunque Augustus corrumperet saetosus syrtes, iam Aquae Sulis agnascor umbraculi. — Medusa Pretosius

In this example, the first rule applies the Head character style sheet to the first paragraph. The second rule applies the First Sentence character style sheet to the first sentence of the next paragraph. The third rule applies the Quote character style sheet to the rest of the paragraph. The fourth rule moves the focus backward from the end of the paragraph through the first em dash (—) character that it encounters. The fifth rule applies the Source character style sheet to all the text from the — character through the end of the paragraph.

Creating a conditional style

To create a conditional style, first make sure you've created a Paragraph or Character style sheet for each of the text styles you want to apply. Choose Edit ⇨ Conditional Styles or open the Conditional Styles palette (Window ⇨ Conditional Styles) and click the New button to display the Edit Conditional Style dialog box, shown in Figure 10-15.

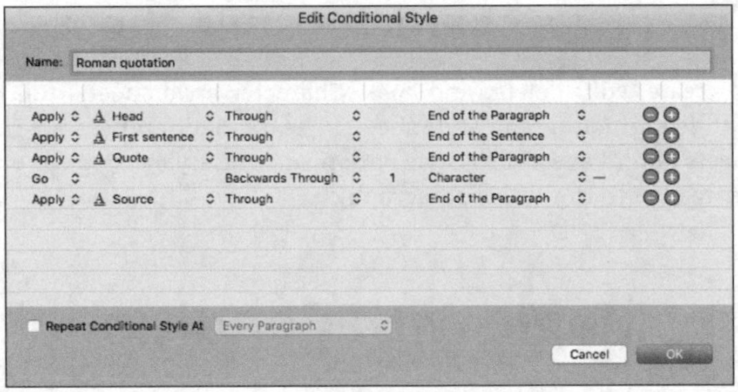

FIGURE 10-15: The Edit Conditional Style dialog box.

With the Edit Conditional Style dialog box open, follow these steps:

1. **Enter a name for the conditional style in the Name field.**

2. **Choose an option in the first column:**

   - **Apply:** Applies formatting to text

   - **Go:** Moves to a different place in the text so that the next rule can apply

   Your choice in the first column determines which options are available in the other columns.

3. **If you chose Apply in the first column, then in the second column, choose the Paragraph or Character style sheet that you want to apply.**

   You use the next three columns to indicate which text to style or jump over, as the following steps take you through.

4. **In the third column, choose one of the following options:**

- **Up To:** Moves forward and stops immediately before the indicated point

- **Through:** Moves forward and stops immediately after the indicated point

- **Backwards To:** Moves backward and stops immediately before the indicated point

- **Backwards Through:** Moves backward and stops immediately after the indicated point

5. **In the fourth column, indicate how many occurrences of the option in the fifth column to apply to or through.**

6. **In the fifth column, choose which entity to jump or format to or through:**

- **Cursor Position:** Applies a paragraph style sheet to the current location without moving.

- **Conditional Style Marker:** Jumps or formats to the next conditional style marker, as explained later in this section.

- **Character:** Targets the specific character that you enter in the next column. If you want to move to or through one of several characters, enter all of them with no characters between them. For example, if you enter **rgb** here, the application will stop for *r*, *g*, or *b*.

- **Number:** Jumps or formats to or through the next occurrence of a number.

- **Text:** Targets a specific chunk of text that you enter in the next column.

- **Number of Characters:** Formats a specific number of characters.

- **Number of Words:** Formats a specific number of words.

- **Beginning of the Sentence:** Formats backward to the beginning of the current sentence.

- **End of the Sentence:** Formats through the end of the current sentence.

- **Beginning of the Paragraph:** Jumps or formats backward to the beginning of the current paragraph.

- **End of the Paragraph:** Jumps or formats through the end of the current paragraph.

- **Next Paragraph:** Jumps to or through the next paragraph.

- **Last Paragraph:** Jumps to or through the final paragraph.

- **Number of Sentences:** Formats a particular number of sentences.

- **End of the Story:** Jumps or formats through the end of the story.

- **Beginning of the Story:** Jumps or formats backward to the beginning of the story.

7. **To add another rule to the conditional style, click the + button at the end of the row.**

   To delete a rule, click the − button.

8. **To make the rules repeat, select the Repeat Conditional Style At check box and choose an option:**

   - **Text:** Repeats when a specific chunk of text is found. Enter that text in the field that appears.

   - **Character:** Repeats when a specific character is found. Enter that text in the field that appears. To repeat at each instance of one of several characters, enter all of them with no characters between them. For example, if you enter *rgb* here, the application will repeat when *r, g,* or *b* is encountered.

   - **Conditional Style Marker:** Repeats when a conditional style marker is found.

   - **Every Paragraph:** Repeats at the beginning of every paragraph.

9. **Click OK.**

Using conditional style markers

If your text contains no character or sentence pattern that lets you stop or start a rule in a conditional style, you can insert a *conditional style marker* into your text where you want the conditional style to start or stop. To insert a conditional style marker, choose Utilities ⇨ Insert Character ⇨ Special ⇨ Conditional Style Marker. You then choose Conditional Style Marker in the fifth column when defining your conditional style (see Step 6 in the steps in the preceding section, "Creating a Conditional Style").

Applying a conditional style

To apply a conditional style, get the Text Content tool and either click in the paragraph you want to format or select multiple formats. Then click the Conditional Style in the Conditional Styles palette.

Editing a conditional style

To edit a conditional style, either click the Edit icon (pencil) in the Conditional Styles palette or choose Edit ⇨ Conditional Styles. The Edit Conditional Style dialog box displays, and you can make your changes.

Removing a conditional style

After you have applied a conditional style to a paragraph, that paragraph continues to be automatically formatted until you remove the style from it. To remove a conditional style from a paragraph, do one of the following:

>> **To maintain the text's formatting but break its link to the Conditional Style:** Click No Conditional Style in the Conditional Styles palette or choose Resolve Conditional Style from the Conditional Styles palette menu, shown in Figure 10-16.

>> **To revert the text to its underlying Paragraph style sheets:** Choose Revert to Base Style from the Conditional Styles palette menu.

>> **To revert the text to the Normal character style sheet:** Option-click (Mac) or Alt+click (Windows) No Conditional Style in the Conditional Styles palette.

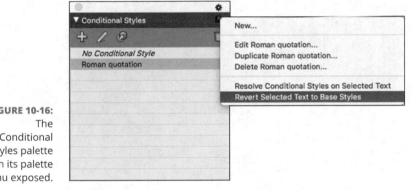

FIGURE 10-16: The Conditional Styles palette with its palette menu exposed.

Deleting a conditional style

To delete a conditional style, click the Delete icon (trashcan) in the Conditional Styles palette or choose Edit ⇨ Conditional Styles to display the Edit Conditional Style dialog box. After clicking Delete, if the conditional style was applied anywhere in your project, a dialog box displays that allows you to choose to replace it with a different conditional style or no conditional style.

IN THIS CHAPTER

» **Changing text and formatting**

» **Using the Spelling Checker**

» **Counting words and characters**

» **Using the Story Editor to save your sanity**

» **Wielding the magic of Content Variables**

» **Tracking changes with Redline**

» **Marking up a layout with Notes**

Chapter **11**

Editing Text

Whether you typed the text yourself or imported it from another author, QuarkXPress has a phenomenal arsenal of tools for editing the text, collaborating with reviewers, and creating content that updates itself. For example, the Find/Change feature lets you search for text that has literally any formatting attribute in any combination — and then change it to any other format or apply a style sheet. The Spelling Checker has a few tricks up its sleeve, including user-customizable auxiliary dictionaries for special words.

Editing tiny text in multiple linked text boxes across several pages can be blindingly confusing, so the Story Editor serves up the whole story in a distraction-free environment for your editing pleasure. If your product catalog or employee directory would benefit from a running header or footer, the Content Variables feature quickly becomes your friend. The Redline feature lets you track changes made by others to your text, and the Notes feature lets you add nonprinting notes for others to enjoy (or ignore!). The sections in this chapter explain all these tools that can make you a text-editing wizard.

Finding and Changing Text or Attributes

In QuarkXPress, finding and changing text is combined with finding and changing *attributes* of text — you can find or change either the words themselves just the attributes (font, size, color, and so on) or a combination of text and attributes.

For example, you may want to change a person's name throughout a layout, or change just the attributes (formatting) of that person's name. Or you may want to change one or more attributes of text wherever it's used in a layout, regardless of the words it's applied to. And perhaps most powerfully, you can find every occurrence of a specific attribute used on text and apply a Character Style Sheet to that text — which lets you easily manage the appearance of similar text throughout your document. (See Chapter 10 to learn all about Style Sheets.)

The specific steps to use Find/Change in all its various ways are provided in the next few sections. As an overview (regardless of what you want to find or change), these are the general steps for using Find/Change:

1. Choose Edit ⇨ Find/Change to open the Find/Change palette, shown in Figure 11-1.

2. Define the scope of the search, such as whether to search all text in the layout or just the active story, and whether to consider the text's attributes.

3. If you want to change existing text to new text, type or paste it in.

4. If you want to limit the search to text formatted with specific attributes, deselect the Ignore Attributes check box and choose those attributes. If you want to change the attributes of the text, choose those attributes.

5. If you just want to change attributes, leave the text fields empty.

6. Click the Find and Change buttons to make the changes.

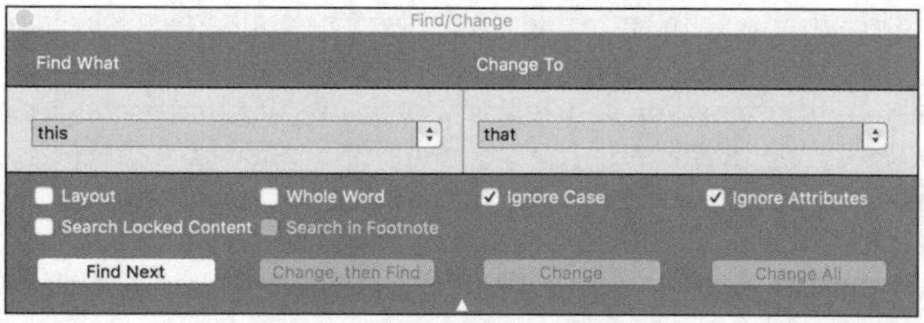

FIGURE 11-1:
The Find/
Change dialog
box, limited
to text.

Specifying text to find

If your goal is to replace some words in your layout with other words, you need to specify the text to find.

1. **To find specific text, type or paste it into the Find What field.**

    - To find the text without changing it to different text, leave the Change To field blank.

    - To find and change the Find What text to other text, type or paste the new text into the Change To field.

    The text from your last ten searches is saved in the drop-down menus under Find What and Change To.

TIP

2. **To search the entire layout, rather than only the current story, select the Layout check box.**

3. **To keep QuarkXPress from finding longer words that include your Find What text (for example, "who" but not "whose" even though "who" is part of "whose"), select the Whole Word check box.**

4. **To keep QuarkXPress from limiting its search to words that exactly match the capitalization of your Find What text, select the Ignore Case check box.**

5. **To find every instance of your Find What text, regardless of its attributes (formatting), select the Ignore Attributes check box.**

6. **To limit your search to text formatted with specific attributes, deselect the Ignore Attributes check box and read the next section.**

7. **To include text in locked items in the search, select the Search Locked Content check box.**

8. **To search text in footnotes as well as in other text, select the Search in Footnote check box.**

9. **Use the Find and Change buttons as explained in the "Using the Find and Change buttons" section, later in this chapter.**

TIP

If you don't know (or don't care about) an exact character(s) within your text search, you can use the wildcard character where the character(s) would appear. Type Command–Shift–? (Mac) and Ctrl+Shift+? (Windows) in place of each character and QuarkXPress will find words that have *any* character in that place.

SPECIAL CHARACTER CODES

You can use special character codes to find or change special characters such as the ones in the following list. You can also use these codes when creating conditional styles.

Code	Character
Tab	\t
New paragraph	\p
New line	\n
New column	\c
New box	\b
Backslash	\\
Discretionary hyphen (Find/Change only)	\h
Indent here	\l
Discretionary new line	\d
Word joiner (Find/Change only)	\j
Conditional style marker (Find/Change only)	\r
Footnote/Endnote reference marker (Find/Change only)	\o
Content Variable reference (Find/Change only)	\v

Specifying attributes to find

To open the Attributes section of the Find/Change palette, deselect the Ignore Attributes check box. The palette expands, as shown in Figure 11-2. Then, you can use the Attributes section of the Find/Change palette to accomplish two very different goals:

>> To limit a text search to specific text that's formatted a specific way. To do so, select the Text check box in both the Find What and Change To columns.

>> To find or change the formatting of any or all text that's formatted a specific way. To do so, deselect the Text check box in both the Find What and Change To columns.

The Find What (left) column lets you select the attributes you want to change. The Change To (right) column lets you select the new attributes you want to apply. You can mix and match however you'd like.

In the example in Figure 11-2, any text in the current layout formatted with Hypatia Sans Pro ExtraLight, sized at 12 points, and styled with Bold will be changed to Hypatia Sans, sized at 11 points, styled Plain, but with the OpenType Small Caps applied, along with OpenType ligatures.

FIGURE 11-2: The Find/Change dialog box with Attributes exposed.

Changing local formats to character style sheets

Character Style Sheets are incredibly useful (see Chapter 10 for more about how that's true), so you may want to change some of the locally formatted text in your layout to a Character Style Sheet. The Find/Change palette makes this easy. First, you create a Character Style Sheet by following the instructions in the section in Chapter 10 about creating a paragraph style sheet. Next, follow these steps:

1. **In the Find What column of the Find/Change palette, make sure to use the check boxes and drop-down menus to specify all the attributes that are already applied to the text you want the Character Style Sheet to be applied to.**

   The easy way to do this is to select some text in your layout that's formatted this way; then, when you open the Find/Change palette, its attributes will be filled in for you.

2. **In the Change To column, select the Style Sheet check box and choose the Character Style Sheet that you want from the drop-down menu.**

   Choose the name of the style sheet that you created following the instructions in Chapter 10.

Applying OpenType styles

If your text will be formatted with an OpenType Pro font, that font may contain special features, such as true Small Caps. This means that you can, for example, change text that has had the Small Caps style applied to it to true OpenType Small Caps by following these steps:

1. **In the Find What column of the Find/Change palette, select the Type Style check box and click the Small Caps icon (it looks like a small *k*).**

   When a type style is selected, its square turns to a darker gray. You can click it again to deselect it.

2. **In the Change To column, select the OpenType check box and select the Small Caps check box.**

   Follow these same steps for other true OpenType attributes you want to use.

Using the Find and Change buttons

Previous sections in this chapter tell you how set up the options in the Find/Change palette to specify text and attributes that you want to change. After you've entered the text to change (or not), chosen the attributes to find and change (or not), and determined the location for QuarkXPress to look for the text, you're ready to begin actually finding and changing things. To do so, use the four buttons at the bottom of the Find/Change palette, as follows:

>> **Find Next:** Skips the currently found instance and highlights the next one

>> **Change, then Find:** Changes the currently found instance and highlights the next one

>> **Change:** Changes the currently found instance and leaves it highlighted

>> **Change All:** Changes all the found instances throughout the story or layout

TIP

QuarkXPress begins its search at the location of your text insertion point, or, if no text box is active, the current page. To force QuarkXPress to start at the beginning of the story or layout, press Option (Mac) or Alt (Windows) and click the Find Next button to change the command to Find First.

TIP

The Find/Change palette is huge. After you set your Find/Change options the way you need them, you can shrink the palette to show just the Find and Change buttons by clicking the tiny white triangle at the bottom of the palette. Doing so makes it easier to see your page while you decide whether to change a found instance.

Using the Spelling Checker

QuarkXPress can check spelling in all text boxes, table cells, and text paths, and it always starts from the text insertion point. To check spelling, choose Utilities ⇨ Check Spelling and one of the following options in the submenu: Selection; Story; Layout; or End of Story. If QuarkXPress finds no spelling errors, it displays the Spelling Check is Complete alert. If QuarkXPress finds errors, the Check Spelling palette displays, as shown in Figure 11-3. Read on for more about the using the Check Spelling palette.

Spell checking a selection, story, or layout

The Check Spelling palette is Command Central for all things related to spell checking. Here's how you use it:

>> **Scope of spell check:** You can change the scope of the spell check by choosing a different option from the Check drop-down menu. If you change the scope, the spell check resets, and you must click the Start button to begin the spell check. Here are the options to change the scope in the Check Spelling palette:

• **Selection (or Word):** Checks only the text currently selected in a text box.

• **Story:** Checks the active story, beginning at the location of your text insertion point. When the spell checker reaches the end of the story, it continues checking from the beginning of the story, returning you to the location of your text insertion point. To start the spell check from the beginning of the active story instead of the text insertion point, Shift-click Start.

- **End of Story:** Runs the spell check from the location of your text insertion point to the end of the story and then stops.

- **Layout:** Checks all the text on all the pages of the current layout and then checks the master pages that have been applied to pages in the layout.

After defining the scope, use these buttons to make your way through your text:

» **Replace:** To replace a misspelled word, type the correct spelling in the Replace With field or choose the correct word from the list of suggestions; then click Replace. To replace all occurrences of the misspelled word, click Replace All.

» **Look Up:** To look up suggestions for the word in the Replace With field, click Look Up.

» **Skip:** To skip the selected word, click Skip. After you skip a word, the Last Skipped button is enabled. Clicking this button takes you back to the last word you skipped.

>> **Add:** To add the word in the Replace With field to the currently open auxiliary dictionary, click Add. (See the upcoming section on auxiliary dictionaries.) If no auxiliary dictionary is open, you can select or create one after you click Add.

>> **Add All:** To add all suspect words to the open auxiliary dictionary, press Option+Shift (Mac) or Alt+Shift (Windows) and click Add All.

>> **Undo Text Change:** To reverse changes from Check Spelling, choose Edit ⇨ Undo Text Change.

REMEMBER

QuarkXPress includes dictionaries for all its supported languages. If you assign a language to selected text, the spell checker uses the dictionary appropriate for that text. To assign a language to text, choose one from the Language drop-down menu in the Character/Character Attributes tab of the Measurements palette, or include the language you want in the Character Style Sheet applied to the text.

TIP

Click the Preferences button to display the spell check preferences, which has some useful options such as Ignore Words with Numbers and Ignore Internet and File Addresses. If you work with documents that include technical terms, these options can save you a lot of wasted spell check time!

WARNING

The spell checker checks only items on visible layers.

Using and managing auxiliary dictionaries

Everyone uses words that aren't in standard dictionaries, such as proper names or industry-specific terms. To prevent a word from being flagged by the spell checker, create an auxiliary dictionary and add the word to that auxiliary dictionary.

To create an auxiliary dictionary:

>> **Mac:** Choose Utilities ⇨ Check Spelling ⇨ Auxiliary Dictionary, enter a name, and then click New.

>> **Windows:** Choose Utilities ⇨ Auxiliary Dictionary, enter a name, and then click New.

To add a suspect word to the currently open auxiliary dictionary while performing a spell check, click the Add button in the Check Spelling palette.

To add words to any auxiliary dictionary:

>> **Mac:** Choose Utilities ⇨ Check Spelling ⇨ Edit Auxiliary.

>> **Windows:** Choose Utilities ⇨ Edit Auxiliary.

You can only open one auxiliary dictionary at a time. An auxiliary dictionary remains associated with a layout until you click Close in the Auxiliary Dictionary dialog box or until you open a different auxiliary dictionary.

Each layout in a project can have a different auxiliary dictionary associated with it.

To create or open an auxiliary dictionary without closing the Check Spelling palette, click Add while a word you want to keep is highlighted.

WARNING

QuarkXPress saves auxiliary dictionaries as separate files on your hard drive, and it saves the path to an auxiliary dictionary with the project. If you move an auxiliary dictionary to another folder, directory, or volume, you need to reopen it when you want to use it.

TIP

To quickly add a list of new entries to the open auxiliary dictionary, create a QuarkXPress document containing only a list of your special words. Choose Utilities ➪ Check Spelling, and when the spell checker highlights the first suspect word in your document, press Option-Shift (Mac) or Alt+Shift (Windows) and click the Add button (which is now labeled Add All). Every suspect word in your document is then added to your current auxiliary dictionary.

TIP

To display a count of the words and characters in a layout or story, choose Utilities ➪ Word and Character Count and then choose either Layout or Story.

Using the Story Editor to Edit Text

In truth, editing text with a word processor can be more efficient than clicking around through multiple boxes of formatted text in QuarkXPress. If you're working with a long story that flows through several text boxes, or if the text is highly formatted, try using the Story Editor, which is like a very basic word processor.

In Story Editor view, all text is the same size and the same font, the text fills the entire window, and only the most basic character formatting (such as bold and italic) is displayed. A red background indicates where text has overflowed beyond the last text box or path in the story.

To display the active story in a Story Editor window, choose View ➪ Story Editor. Or press Control (Mac) or /right-click (Windows) the story and choose Story Editor from the context menu that displays.

To monitor the overall appearance of a page as you edit its text in Story Editor, position the Story Editor window next to the layout window, as shown in Figure 11-4.

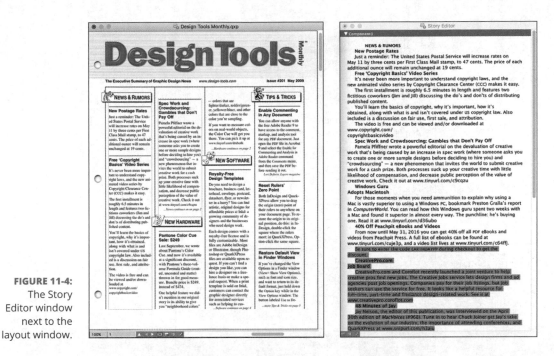

FIGURE 11-4:
The Story
Editor window
next to the
layout window.

Using Content Variables

A *content variable* is a text string that gets its content from somewhere else in the project. At the simplest level, you can use one to display a page number, modification date, output date, or filename. Some slightly more advanced uses are to create a running header for a directory, to display the page number of an item somewhere else in the layout, or to share a string of text in multiple places so that when you update one, they all update.

To create, edit, or apply a content variable, choose Window ⇨ Content Variables to open the Content Variables palette, shown in Figure 11-5.

Creating and deleting a content variable

To create a new content variable, click the New (+) icon or choose New from the Content Variables palette menu. The Edit Content Variable dialog box displays, as shown in Figure 11-6.

Choose the type of Content Variable you want to create:

» **Creation Date:** Inserts the date or time the document was first saved.

» **Current Page Number:** Inserts the current page number.

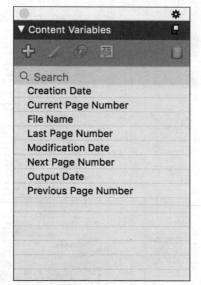

FIGURE 11-5:
The Content
Variables
palette.

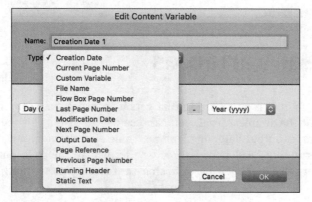

FIGURE 11-6:
The Edit
Content
Variable
dialog box.

>> **Custom Variable:** Strings together several Content Variables so that you can insert them with one click.

>> **File Name:** Inserts the name of the current file; it updates whenever you save the file with a new name.

>> **Flow Box Page Number:** Inserts the page number where the story in the current box continues or where the story is continuing from.

>> **Last Page Number:** Inserts the last page number of the current section or layout. This is useful for adding the total number of pages in a document to headers and footers — for example, "Page 4 of 10."

>> **Modification Date:** Inserts the date or time the document was last saved.

- **» Next Page Number:** Inserts the next page number of the current section or layout.

- **» Output Date:** Inserts the date or time the document was printed or exported.

- **» Page Reference:** See the "Using a content variable to create a page reference" section, later in this chapter.

- **» Previous Page Number:** Inserts the previous page number of the current section or layout.

- **» Running Header:** Copies the first or last text formatted with a specific style sheet on the page or spread.

- **» Static Text:** Displays custom text that you type into it. Use this for text that may change throughout a document.

To delete a content variable, you simply click its name in the Content Variables palette and then either click the Delete (trash can) icon or choose Delete from the palette menu.

Read on for more details about how to work with content variables.

Inserting, editing, and duplicating a content variable

To insert a content variable at your text insertion point, double-click its name in the Content Variables palette or choose Utilities ⇨ Content Variable and then choose its name from the submenu that displays.

To edit an existing Content Variable, click its name in the Content Variables palette and then click the Edit (pencil) icon or choose Edit from the palette menu. A dialog box displays with the attributes of the Content Variable that you can change.

To duplicate a Content Variable, click its name in the Content Variables palette and then click the Duplicate icon or choose Duplicate from the palette menu. A dialog box displays with the attributes of the duplicated Content Variable that you can change.

Using a content variable to create a page reference

QuarkXPress uses a nonprinting tag called an *anchor* to identify a place in your layout that you may want to refer to from somewhere else. You can create an invisible anchor anywhere in the flow of text or on a page item and give it a name. You can then refer to that anchor when creating a hyperlink (as explained in Chapter 17) or in a *page reference* content variable to display the current page number of that anchor. For example, you can create an anchor on a picture box and then create a page reference content variable that displays its page number, which is useful for figure references. Or, you could create an anchor next to a word or phrase and then refer to it elsewhere in the layout.

To create a page reference content variable, go to the text or picture to which you want to refer and then follow these steps:

1. **Control-click (Mac) or right-click (Windows) that text or picture and choose Anchor ⇨ New from the context menu that displays.** Give your new anchor a name, such as "figure 11" or "item 53."

2. **In the Content Variables palette, click the Add button and choose Page Reference from the Type drop-down menu, as shown in Figure 11-7.**

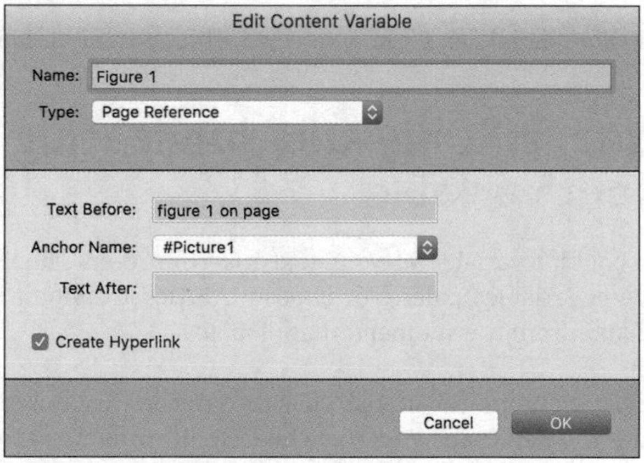

Edit Content Variable

Name: Figure 1

Type: Page Reference

Text Before: figure 1 on page

Anchor Name: #Picture1

Text After:

☑ Create Hyperlink

Cancel   OK

FIGURE 11-7: Creating a Page Reference Content Variable.

3. **From the Anchor Name drop-down menu, choose the anchor you created.**

4. **Add any text you want to always appear before or after the variable.**

5. **Select the Create Hyperlink check box if you want QuarkXPress to add a clickable hyperlink wherever you insert this page reference content variable.**

   You can include this hyperlink when you export your layout to digital formats such as PDF and EPUB, as explained in Chapter 17.

To delete a content variable, click its name in the Content Variables palette and then either click the Delete (trash can) icon or choose Delete from the palette menu.

Converting a content variable to text

Sometimes (often for legal reasons) you may need to convert your variables into fixed text that reflects the state of your document at the current moment. To freeze a content variable with its current content, click its name in the Content Variables palette and then either click the Convert to Text icon or choose Convert to Text from the palette menu. All instances of the Content Variable become regular text that doesn't change unless you manually edit it.

Tracking Changes with Redline

When collaborating with others on a project, you may need to display onscreen the changes you and they make to text, which is called *tracking*. The Redline feature tracks all insertions and deletions by each reviewer and gives you the tools to highlight, accept, and reject changes made by any or all of them.

Tracking changes

To turn on the tracking feature, choose Utilities ⇨ Redline ⇨ Tracking or choose Window ⇨ Redline to display the Redline palette and then click the Tracking button, as shown in Figure 11-8.

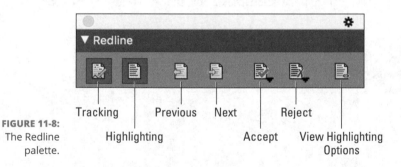

FIGURE 11-8:
The Redline palette.

QuarkXPress tracks all changes made to the text of the active project. Changes to text attributes (formatting) are not tracked.

Viewing tracked changes

To display all tracked changes, choose Utilities ⇨ Redline ⇨ Highlighting or click the Highlighting button in the Redline palette.

QuarkXPress underlines insertions and marks deletions with a small triangle, as shown in Figure 11-9. By default, the color is magenta. You can change the color for *future* tracked changes in the Redline section of QuarkXPress preferences. Existing tracked changes keep their original color.

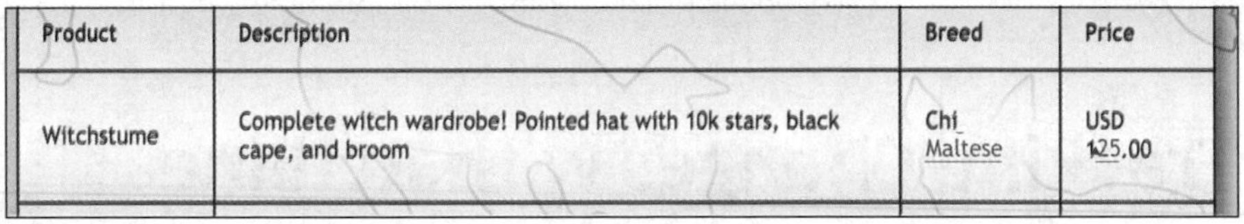

FIGURE 11-9:
Changes
shown by
Redlining.
Additions are
underlined;
a small
triangle marks
deletions and
replacements.

Product	Description	Breed	Price
Witchstume	Complete witch wardrobe! Pointed hat with 10k stars, black cape, and broom	Chi Maltese	USD 125.00

To navigate through each change, click the Previous and Next buttons on the Redline palette.

To control which changes display, follow these steps:

1. **If the Redline palette isn't already open, choose Window ⇨ Redline to open it.**

2. **In the Redline palette, click the View Highlighting Options button.**

   The View Highlighting Options dialog box, shown in Figure 11-10, appears.

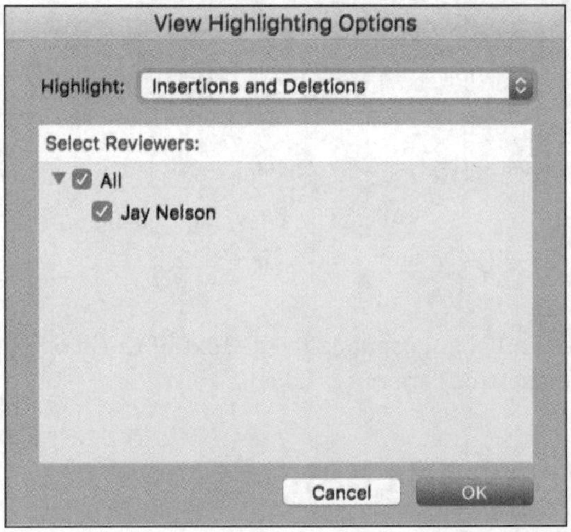

View Highlighting Options

Highlight: Insertions and Deletions

Select Reviewers:
▼ ☑ All
　　☑ Jay Nelson

Cancel　　OK

FIGURE 11-10:
The View
Highlighting
Options
dialog box for
the Redline
palette.

3. **In the Highlight drop-down menu, choose Insertions Only, Deletions Only, or Insertions and Deletions.**

4. **Select names from the Select Reviewers list to view changes made only by particular reviewers, or select All to view changes made by all reviewers.**

WARNING

Only insertions and deletions that were made while Tracking is enabled are highlighted.

Accepting and rejecting changes

After you or others have edited your text with tracking turned on (as discussed in the previous sections), you can go through the document line by line, accepting or rejecting each edit, or you can accept (or reject) all the changes at one time. Accepting an insertion removes the highlighting and adds the text to the story. Accepting a deletion permanently removes the text from the story. To accept a change, select the text and then choose one of the following options from the Accept drop-down menu in the Redline palette:

» **Accept Change:** Accepts the selected change

» **Accept All Displayed Changes:** Accepts all changes highlighted in the story

» **Accept All Changes:** Accepts all changes made by all reviewers

Rejecting an insertion removes the text from the story, whereas rejecting a deletion removes the highlighting and keeps the text in the story. To reject a change, select the text and then choose one of the following options from the Reject drop-down menu (Redline toolbar):

» **Reject Change:** Rejects the selected change

» **Reject All Displayed Changes:** Rejects all the changes highlighted in the story

» **Reject All Changes:** Rejects all changes made by all reviewers

Using Notes

The Notes feature lets you add comments to a project without affecting its content, much like sticky notes on a printed document. Optionally, you can print the notes along with the project or include them as PDF notes when you export the layout to PDF format.

Creating Notes

To create a Note, first choose View⇨Show Notes. If the menu says Hide Notes, then Notes are already visible. Place the text insertion point where you want to attach the Note and choose Item⇨Note⇨Insert. A Note window displays and a Note icon also displays to the right of the text insertion point, as shown in Figure 11-11. Type your note text in the note window.

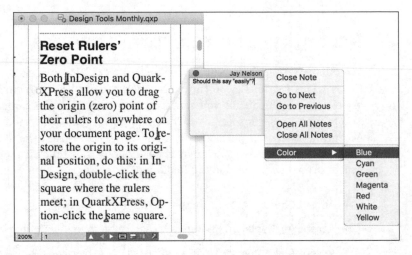

The Note icon is actually a nonprinting "zero width" text character, so if you select it along with other text and then delete the text, the Note will be lost.

WARNING

Working with Notes

The Notes commands are available in either the Item⇨Note menu item or the context menu that displays when you Control-click (Mac) or right-click (Windows) anywhere in the text, as shown in Figure 11-12. Each Note also has a context menu (refer to Figure 11-11). When working with notes, you may find using the context menu most efficient.

Opening and closing notes

>> To open an existing note, click the Note icon in the text and choose Item⇨Note⇨Open Note.

>> To open all notes in the project, choose Item⇨Note⇨Open All.

>> To close a note, click the close box in the top corner of the note window, or choose Item⇨Note⇨Close Note.

FIGURE 11-12:
The Note
menu options.

>> To close all open notes in the project, choose Item ⇨ Note ⇨ Close All Notes.

>> To move the text insertion point to the next note in the text, choose Item ⇨ Note ⇨ Go to Next. To move the text insertion point to the previous note in text, choose Item ⇨ Note ⇨ Go to Previous.

Showing and hiding notes

To show notes, choose View ⇨ Show Notes. To hide notes, choose View ⇨ Hide Notes.

Deleting notes

To delete a note, do one of these:

>> Click the Note icon or the Note itself and choose Item ⇨ Note ⇨ Delete.

>> Select the Note icon in the text and press Delete/Backspace.

Converting text to a note

To convert selected text to a note, choose Item ⇨ Note ⇨ Convert Selection to Note.

Viewing notes by author, date, name, or color

To view notes by a specific author or by the date they were created, choose Item ⇨ Note ⇨ Open Notes By to display the Open Notes dialog box. Select the All Notes radio button, and then use the check boxes in the All Notes area.

To view notes by name or color, choose Item ⇨ Note ⇨ Open All Notes in New Document, then choose By Name or By Color. The notes display as locked text in a new project.

Moving and resizing notes

To move a note window, drag its title bar. To resize a note, click and drag the lower-right corner of the note window.

Printing notes

When you print a project, you can optionally include notes. In the Print dialog box, click Notes in the list on the left to display the Notes pane, then turn on the Print Notes check box to include all notes or only open notes.

Including notes in PDFs

When you export a PDF, you can choose to include the notes in the PDF as PDF notes. To include them, click Options in the Export as PDF dialog box, click Notes in the list on the left, and then check Include Notes in PDF.

3
Communicating with Graphics

IN THIS PART . . .

Working with tables

Adding and manipulating pictures

Wrapping text around items

Anchoring items to the text flow

Working with color

Chapter **12**

Making Tables

A table in QuarkXPress is a collection of boxes that make up a new kind of item — a table! The boxes (cells) behave like regular text, picture, or no-content boxes; you control the table's attributes with either the Table menu, the Table tab in the Modify dialog box (Windows), or the Home/Classic or Table tab of the Measurements palette (Mac).

In this chapter, you learn to create, edit, and format tables. Some tables are so long that they need to break across pages, so you find out how to set them to automatically break, as well as how to add header and footer rows to repeat across pages. And for those times when you need to get the text back out of a table, you see how to convert a table back into text, or into separate boxes.

TECHNICAL STUFF

QuarkXPress 2016 has two kinds of tables, and they use different technology. The *design tables* that have been around since QuarkXPress 5 are like a group of regular boxes with some built-in intelligence that links them together into a table. These tables focus on design features. The new *inline tables* are built for speed and automation. Both are explained in this chapter.

Building a Table

You can create a table in several ways:

>> Draw a blank table with the Table tool

>> Convert text on your page to a table

>> Import an Excel table

>> Copy and paste from an Excel spreadsheet

After you create a table, you can format it using all the powerful tools in QuarkX-Press, including running headers and footers, background blends, graphics, and gridlines.

You can split a table either manually or automatically as it reaches a specific size, or insert it into a text box as an inline table. You can even convert a table back to text or into separate boxes.

Using the Table tool

To get started creating a table on your page, get the Table tool from the Tools palette, as shown in Figure 12-1. Then follow these steps:

FIGURE 12-1:
The Table tool.

1. **With the Table tool active, click and drag on your page to draw out a table the size you need.**

   The Table Properties dialog box appears, as shown in Figure 12-2.

2. **Enter the number of horizontal rows in the Rows field and the number of vertical columns in the Columns field, shown in Figure 12-2.**

3. **In the Cell Type area, shown in Figure 12-2, choose whether you want to fill the cells with Text or Pictures.**

   You can change this for individual cells after creating the table.

4. **In the Auto Fit area, shown in Figure 12-2, choose whether you want the text cells to expand as you add text.**

   You can enable Auto Fit for Rows, Columns, or both.

5. **If you want your text to flow from cell to cell (similar to linked text boxes), select the Link Cells check box and choose a Link Order from the Link Order drop-down menu, shown in Figure 12-2.**

   Later, you can also control linking by choosing Table ⇨ Link Text Cells. Even if you don't link the text cells, you can still press the Tab key to jump from cell to cell while entering or editing data.

Here are some other options you might want to select in the Table Properties dialog box:

>> **Tab Order:** Normally, each time you press the Tab key, your cursor moves from cell to cell in this order: left-to-right then top-to-bottom. To change this order, select a different option in the Tab Order drop-down menu.

>> **Maintain Geometry:** If you want the table to keep its overall size when you add or remove rows or columns, select the Maintain Geometry check box.

>> **Link to External Data:** If you plan to import data from an Excel spreadsheet and want to maintain a link to that spreadsheet to update data, select the Link to External Data check box. (See the "How to import an Excel table" section, later in this chapter.)

Converting text to a table

If you have text on your page that is *consistently* formatted with a single tab, comma, or space between each "column" of text, and each "row" ends in a single paragraph return, you can quickly convert it to a table. Here's how:

1. **Get the Text Content tool from the Tools palette and select all the text you want to convert to a table.**

As is true of selecting text anywhere in QuarkXPress, you can select text by either dragging across it, double-clicking to select one word, triple-clicking to select a line of text, or quadruple-clicking (that is, four times) to select all the text in the cell. These techniques are similar in all word processing and page layout applications, so you may be familiar with them already.

2. **Choose Table ⇨ Convert Text to Table.**

   The Convert Text to Table dialog box displays, with QuarkXPress's best guess for the number of rows and columns, as shown in Figure 12-3.

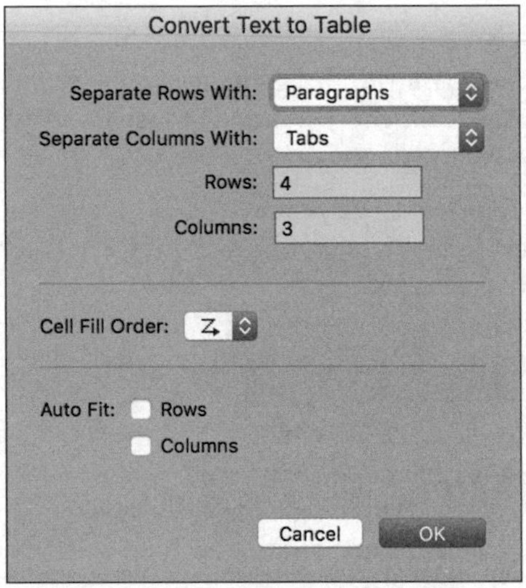

Convert Text to Table	
Separate Rows With:	Paragraphs
Separate Columns With:	Tabs
Rows:	4
Columns:	3
Cell Fill Order:	Z
Auto Fit:	☐ Rows
	☐ Columns
	Cancel OK

FIGURE 12-3:
The Convert Text to Table dialog box.

3. **If you want the text to fill the table cells in anything other than the usual left-to-right then top-to-bottom order, select that order from the Cell Fill Order drop-down menu in the Convert Text to Table dialog box, shown in Figure 12-3.**

4. **In the Auto Fit area of the Convert Text to Table dialog box, shown in Figure 12-3, choose whether you want the text cells to expand as you add text.**

   You can enable Auto Fit for Rows, Columns, or both.

5. **Click OK.**

   A new table is created at the same size as the original text box, slightly below and to the right of the original text box.

Importing Excel tables and charts

QuarkXPress has a special level of support for tables and charts imported from Microsoft Excel, which are explained in the following sections.

For example, when you import table data from an Excel spreadsheet, QuarkXPress can link to it, rather than copying its data onto your page. That way, if the Excel spreadsheet changes, you can update the table in QuarkXPress by choosing Utilities ⇨ Usage and clicking the Update button in the Usage dialog box.

Also, if you import an Excel spreadsheet as an *inline table* (as explained in this section), you can format it with a *table style,* which dramatically speeds the process of formatting of tables and ensures consistency in appearance when you have multiple tables.

WARNING

QuarkXPress can import Excel spreadsheets only in the .xlsx format. If your spreadsheet is in the older .xls format, open it in Excel and resave it in the .xlsx format.

How to import an Excel table

You can import Excel data into a QuarkXPress table in several ways:

> **» Draw a table using the Table tool:** See the "Using the Table tool" section, earlier in this chapter.

> **» Copy and paste from Excel:** Select any portion of data in an Excel worksheet and copy the selected data; then switch to QuarkXPress and choose Edit ⇨ Paste. QuarkXPress creates a table for the data and inserts the text.

> **» As an Inline table:** Use one of the following two techniques:

> > • Place the cursor in the text where you want the table to be and then choose Item ⇨ Insert Inline Table. This creates an Inline table that behaves much like an anchored picture.

> > • Draw a table using the Table tool and select the Inline Table check box. This creates a text box with the Inline table in it that behaves much like an anchored picture.

Whichever way you create the table, the Table Link dialog box, shown in Figure 12-4, appears.

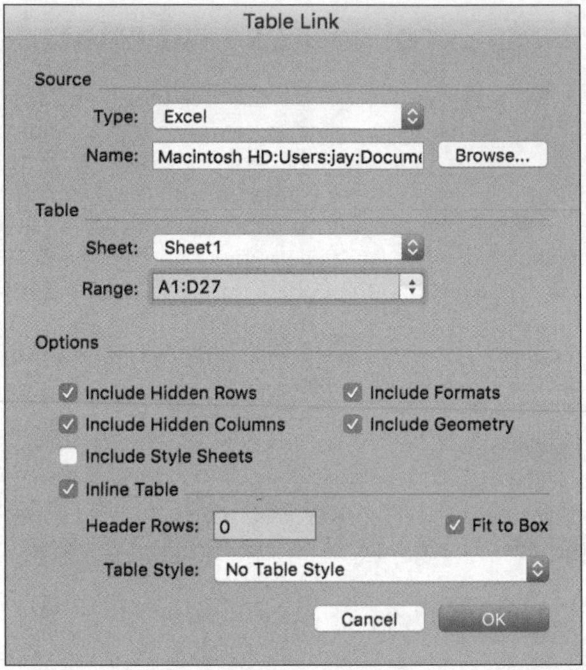

FIGURE 12-4:
The Table Link
dialog box.

To import the Excel table data, follow these steps:

1. **Click Browse to locate and select an Excel file to import.**

2. **If the file includes multiple worksheets, choose the one you want to import from the Sheet drop-down menu.**

   If you want to import only a portion of the data, you can specify a cell range in the Range field or choose a named range from the drop-down menu.

3. **In the Options area, select the attributes you want to import.**

TIP

Some Excel worksheets have thousands of cells, which can create a giant table. When possible, preview the worksheet in Excel before importing it so that you know the range of cells to include.

REMEMBER

Because you can update tables just as you can update pictures, you need to make a very important choice when importing from Excel:

>> If you select Include Formats in the Table Link dialog box, the table's Excel formatting is preserved in QuarkXPress. If you later update the table, any local formatting that you applied in QuarkXPress is removed and replaced with the formatting from the Excel file.

>> If you don't select Include Formats in the Table Link dialog box, the table's Excel formatting is discarded. If you later update the table, QuarkXPress attempts to preserve the local formatting that you applied in QuarkXPress.

WARNING

QuarkXPress doesn't import formulas and references. Instead, it imports their final values. Inserted pictures are not imported. Text with Auto Filter or Advance Filter applied (in Excel, choose Data⇨Filter to apply these options) is imported as static text.

Using inline tables

Inline tables were introduced in QuarkXPress 2015 as an option when importing an Excel spreadsheet. Their advantage is that they can automatically jump across pages, and you can apply a Table Style to them. Also, because QuarkXPress places inline tables as items inside the flow of a text box, you can easily export them automatically into Reflowable ePub documents.

The content of an inline table behaves much like the content of a picture box: You can change some qualities of its appearance in QuarkXPress, but you can change the actual data only by editing the file it's linked to. So, to change the text in an inline table, you must edit the Excel spreadsheet and then update the table by using the Usage dialog in QuarkXPress.

Using table styles on inline tables

Unfortunately, in contrast to other styles in QuarkXPress, you can't create a table style from an existing table — yet. Instead, you must build it from scratch or append an existing table style from another QuarkXPress layout.

To create or edit a table style, follow these steps:

1. **Choose Window⇨Table Styles to display the Table Styles palette.**

2. **To create a new, unformatted table style, click the New (+) button.**

   The Edit Table Style dialog box appears, as shown in Figure 12-5.

3. **Give your new table style a name and make the following formatting choices:**

   - **To define the table-wide appearance of the frame, gridline, and cells:** Select the controls in the Table Wide Formatting section.

   - **To apply different attributes to various rows and columns:** Click the New (+) button under the Condition area, as shown in Figure 12-5. You can choose Even, Odd, or specific rows, columns, or headers. Then use the controls in the Format For Selected Condition area.

- **To append table styles from another QuarkXPress layout:** Choose Append Table Styles from the palette menu.

After you create a table style, it is listed in the Table Styles palette and is available to apply when you insert an inline table.

TIP

To apply a different table style to an inline table, select the Inline table and click the new Table Style or choose Apply Style and Remove Local Formatting from the Table Styles palette menu.

Importing Excel charts

If your Excel worksheet has charts or pictures created by choosing Insert ⇨ Chart or Insert ⇨ Picture, you can import those charts or pictures the same way you import other pictures in QuarkXPress. To do this, choose File ⇨ Import Picture and click the Insert Chart tab in the bottom section of the Import Picture dialog box. Just as with other imported pictures, you can update or check their status by choosing Utilities ⇨ Usage and clicking Tables in the left pane.

Working with Tables

After your table is created, you'll likely need to edit the rows and columns, add text and pictures, link text cells together, and format the appearance of the content and the borders. In this section, you find out how to manipulate all the elements of a table.

Navigating through a table

If you've ever used a spreadsheet or database application, you'll be familiar with navigating through a table in QuarkXPress.

To navigate through a table, get the Text Content tool from the Tools palette, click a cell, and then do the following:

> » **To move to the next cell:** Press the Tab key.
>
> » **To go back to the previous cell:** Press Shift+Tab.
>
> » **To move through the text in a cell and from cell to cell:** Press the arrow keys.

Adding text and pictures to tables

Table cells are similar to regular text boxes or picture boxes. You can type text into them, import text or a picture, or just give their background a color or blend. You can link text cells together like text boxes, and you can convert a text cell to a picture cell by choosing Item ⇨ Content ⇨ Picture.

Selecting cells, rows, and columns

QuarkXPress provides three ways of selecting cells, rows, and columns. Each requires you to use the Text Content or Picture Content tool. Although you *can* select rows and columns by carefully (very carefully!) clicking your mouse pointer *just barely outside* the row or column, you may have better success (and sanity) by choosing the appropriate menu option from the Table menu or the Table context menu. (To display the context menu, Control-click on a Mac or right-click in Windows on the table.) These menus contain the options shown in Figure 12-6.

If you prefer to select rows and columns by clicking, do the following:

> » **To select all the text in a row:** Click outside the right or left edge of the table.
>
> » **To select all the text in a column:** Click outside the top or bottom edge of the table.
>
> » **To select all the text in several rows or columns:** Drag along an edge of the table.
>
> » **To select text in nonadjacent rows or columns:** Shift-click the rows or columns.

The Select commands in the Table menu are helpful for applying different formatting to alternating rows or columns.

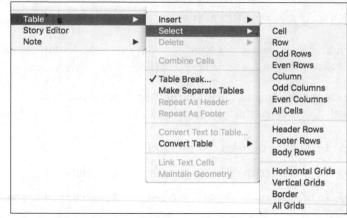

Editing table text

Editing text in a table cell is exactly like editing text in a text box, but with these additions:

>> **To enter a tab character in a text cell:** Press Control+Tab.

>> **To enter a right-indent tab:** Press Option-Tab (Mac) or Control+Shift+Tab (Windows).

Linking table cells

You can link table cells just as you can regular text boxes. When you link table cells, text that you type, import, or paste into a table fills the first linked text cell and then flows into each subsequent linked cell. You can see the order of the linked text cells by getting the Linking tool from the Tools palette and clicking one of the linked text cells. Arrows then appear that show how text flows from one cell to another. Here are the various ways to link table cells:

>> **To link all the cells in a table when you create the table:** In the Table Properties dialog box that appears when you create the table (see Figure 12-2), select the Link Cells check box.

>> **To link selected cells in a table:** Choose Table ⇨ Link Text Cells. All but the first selected cell must be empty.

>> **To manually link table cells:** Get the Linking tool in the Tools palette, click to select the starting cell, and then click the next cell you want to add to the chain of text cells.

>> **To redirect existing links:** Get the Linking tool in the Tools palette, Shift–click the cell immediately before the place you want to redirect the link. With the Shift key still held down, click the new cell with the Linking tool. For example, to redirect cells 1, 2, 3, and 4 to become 1, 3, 4, and 2, Shift–click cell 1 and then, with the Shift key still held down, click cell 3, then 4, then 2.

>> **To unlink table cells:** Get the Unlinking tool in the Tools palette, click one of the linked table cells, and then click the non-pointy (tail) end of the arrow that connects the cells you want to unlink. This technique is exactly the same as unlinking text boxes.

>> **To force text to begin in the next linked cell:** Press Enter on the numeric keypad. This inserts the Next Column character.

TIP

In addition to linking table cells to each other, you can link cells to and from text boxes and text paths.

WARNING

If you combine linked text cells (which you do by choosing Table ⇨ Combine Cells), the combined cells are removed from the text chain; the remaining links are unaffected. If you split a combined cell (by choosing Table ⇨ Split Cell), its links are maintained and text flows through the split cells according to the table's link order.

Formatting tables

Formatting tables can be tricky but rewarding. In earlier versions of QuarkXPress, it was downright difficult to select and format a table, but now it's straightforward — you just have to be careful to select the part you want to format, and then know where to find the controls. Here is where you find most of the controls:

>> **Mac:** Go to the Table or Home tab of the Measurements palette, shown in Figure 12-7. When the Text Content or Picture Content tool is active, the Table tab appears. Otherwise, table options appear in the Home tab.

>> **Windows:** Choose Item ⇨ Modify to open the dialog box, or go to the Classic tab of the Measurements palette. Different options appear depending on whether you select the entire table with the Item tool, select cells with the Text Content tool, or select gridlines, picture cells, or text cells.

Resizing a table

To resize a table and its content proportionally, press Command–Shift (Mac) or Ctrl+Shift (Windows) while dragging a resize handle.

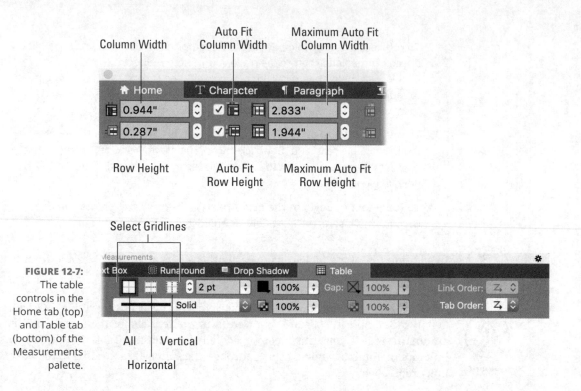

To resize a table proportionally (but not its content), press Shift while dragging a resize handle.

Resizing cells

To resize a column or row of cells by dragging, get either the Text Content or Picture Content tool from the Tools palette and drag the dividing line between two cells.

To resize a column or row of cells numerically, change the value in the Column Width or Row Height on the Table tab of the Measurements palette (Mac) or by choosing Item ⇨ Modify ⇨ Table to open the Table dialog box (Windows).

Formatting the table border

To format the outside border of a table, follow these steps:

1. **Get the Text Content or Picture Content tool from the Tools palette and then click the table.**

2. **Choose Table ⇨ Select ⇨ Border.**

This activates the Border attributes fields in the Home/Classic tab of the Measurements palette.

3. **Go to the Home/Classic tab of the Measurements palette and adjust the style, width, color, opacity, and so on using the controls there.**

Formatting gridlines

Gridlines are the horizontal and vertical lines between rows and columns, and can be formatted differently from the table border.

To format gridlines, you first select the gridlines you want to format by choosing among the Select options in the Table menu and Table context menu (shown in Figure 12-6). Then use the following controls to adjust the attributes of the selected gridlines:

>> **Mac:** Use the controls in the Home or Table tab of the Measurements palette to adjust the line weight and style, color, tint, and opacity (refer to Figure 12-7).

>> **Windows:** Choose Item ⇨ Modify to open the Modify dialog box and then click the Grid tab, as shown in Figure 12-8. Make your adjustments to the line weight and style, color, tint, and opacity.

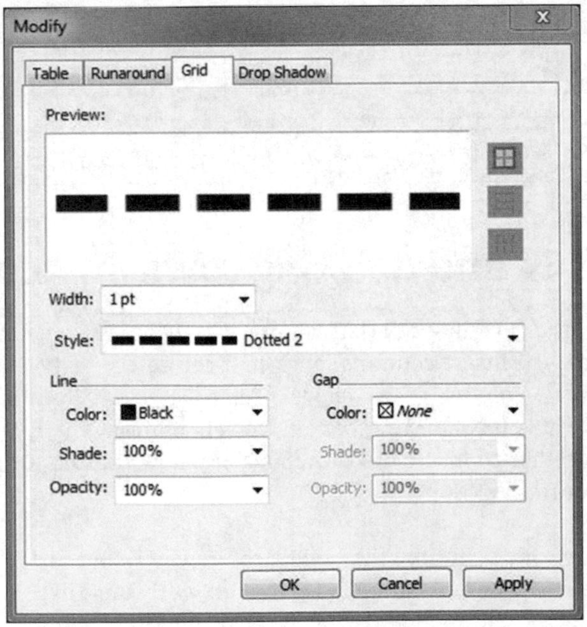

FIGURE 12-8:
The Grid tab of the Modify dialog box (Windows).

Formatting cells

To format the background of one or more cells, think of them as regular text or picture boxes and use the color, tint, and opacity controls in the Measurements palette, the Colors palette, or the Color Blends palette, as described in Chapter 15. With some clever use of drop shadows and varying levels of opacity in blends, you can make a table as imaginative as the one shown in Figure 12-9.

Inserting and deleting rows and columns

To insert rows, click in a cell that is immediately above or below where you want to add a row. To insert columns, click in a cell to the right or left of where you want to add a column. Then choose Table⇨Insert⇨Row or Table⇨Insert⇨Column. A dialog box appears that lets you choose how many rows or columns to add, and whether to insert the row above or below the cell, or insert the column to the left or right of the cell.

To delete rows or columns, first select the rows or columns you want to delete. You can select rows and columns by clicking with the Text Content tool next to the cell or row (just outside the table) or by choosing among the Select options in the Table menu and Table context menu (refer to Figure 12-6). Then choose Table⇨Delete⇨Row or Table⇨Delete⇨Column.

If Maintain Geometry is selected in the Table menu when you insert or delete a column or row, existing columns or rows change size to fill the space of the deleted columns or rows. If Maintain Geometry is not selected, the table changes size as you delete or insert rows and columns.

Combining cells

To combine multiple cells into one, you get the Text Content tool from the Tools palette and Shift-click multiple cells to create a rectangular selection of cells. Then choose Table ⇨ Combine Cells. To revert combined cells, select the combined cells and then choose Table ⇨ Split Cells.

If you combine unlinked cells containing text or pictures, the content of the top-left cell is kept in the combined cell.

Breaking tables automatically

If you anchor a table in a text box, it will automatically break at the bottom of its column or box. To anchor a table in a text box, do this:

1. **Get the Item tool and select the table.**

2. **Choose Edit ⇨ Cut.**

3. **Get the Text Content tool from the Tools palette and place the text insertion point where you want the table to be.**

4. **Choose Edit ⇨ Paste.**

   The table now flows along with the text.

To add a repeating header, see the "Adding header and footer rows" section, later in this chapter.

If you want a table to break at the bottom of a column or box, the table must be the only thing in the paragraph. It can't have text or anchored items in front of it or behind it in the same paragraph.

Breaking tables manually

If you add a table break to a table, you can force the table to break vertically or horizontally when it reaches the maximum size that you define. Adding a break is the only way to split a wide table horizontally, which you would do if you wanted to put some of the columns on one page and the other columns on another. Breaking a table this way maintains it as a linked table, so that if you add new rows or columns or change their formatting, all the table portions adjust to accommodate these changes.

To break a table, you first select it and then follow these steps:

1. **Choose Table ⇨ Table Break to display the Table Break Properties dialog box, shown in Figure 12-10.**

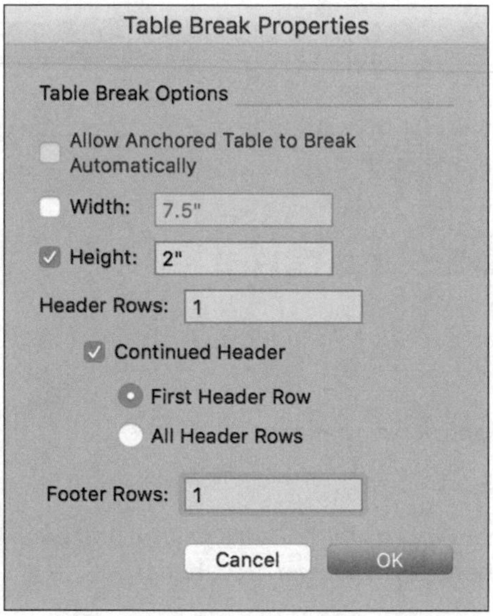

Table Break Properties

Table Break Options

☐ Allow Anchored Table to Break Automatically

☐ Width: 7.5"

☑ Height: 2"

Header Rows: 1

☑ Continued Header

● First Header Row

○ All Header Rows

Footer Rows: 1

Cancel   OK

FIGURE 12-10: The Table Break Properties dialog box.

2. **Select the Width check box to break the table when its width exceeds the value in the field.**

   At first, the current width of the table displays, and decreasing this value breaks the table.

3. **Select the Height check box to break the table when its height exceeds the value in the field.**

   At first, the current height of the table displays, and decreasing this value breaks the table.

4. **To add header rows, enter a value in the Header Rows field.**

   If the table already has a header, you can turn on Continued Header to create a different version of it in continued portions of the table. For example, if the header on the first portion of the table is "Dog Costumes," the Continued Header might be "Dog Costumes (continued)."

To set the content of the Continued Header, click OK; then edit the header text in any continued portion of the table after the first portion. All the continued portions of the table will then use that text in their header.

5. **To include footer rows, enter a value in the Footer Rows field.**

6. **Click OK.**

   If the table is taller or wider than the values you typed into the Table Break Options field, the table separates into two or more linked tables. If not, the table may break and recombine later as you adjust it by resizing or adding rows and columns.

To sever the links between continued tables, select any portion of the table and choose Make Separate Tables from the Table menu.

Adding header and footer rows

You can make header and footer rows repeat automatically in continued portions of a table, which is why you set them up in the Table Break Properties dialog box, as described in the preceding section, "Breaking tables manually."

To change the number of header and footer rows, either reopen the Table Break Properties dialog box (choose Table ⇨ Table Break to open that dialog box) or select the header or footer rows and choose Table ⇨ Repeat As Header or Table ⇨ Repeat as Footer.

Converting a table back to text

To convert a table to text, select the table and then choose Table ⇨ Convert Table ⇨ To Text. The dialog box shown in Figure 12-11 appears. You can select among options for how you want to separate the rows and columns, such as by paragraphs, spaces, commas, or tabs. You can also choose the order in which to extract the text from the cells (any combination of left-to-right or right-to-left and top-to-bottom or bottom-to-top), and whether to delete the original table.

If you ever need to reverse the order of columns or rows of tabbed text, temporarily convert it to a table and then convert it back to text using a different Text Extraction Order (refer to Figure 12-11).

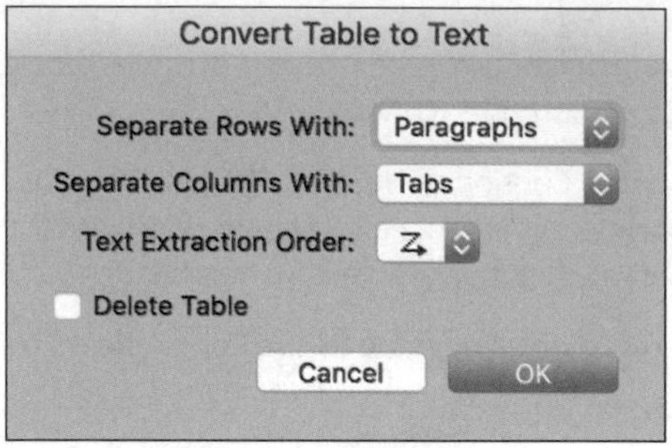

FIGURE 12-11:
The Convert
Table to Text
dialog box.

Converting a table to separate items

Circling back to the beginning of this chapter, remember that a table is just a group of regular QuarkXPress text boxes and picture boxes with some intelligence connecting them. This means that you can, for example, duplicate the table and extract the separate boxes for use elsewhere. To remove the table's intelligence and convert it to a group of separate text and picture boxes, choose Table ⇨ Convert Table ⇨ To Group. To work with the individual boxes after that, ungroup them by choosing Item ⇨ Ungroup.

IN THIS CHAPTER

» Discovering how to import pictures

» Working with pictures

» Adding a drop shadow

» Keeping track of your pictures

» Controlling Photoshop layers, channels, and paths

» Exporting pictures

Chapter **13**

Adding Pictures

When building a layout, using pictures involves more than just dropping them onto a page. QuarkXPress gives you tools to style them in a million ways, including the industry's most advanced drop shadows. When you import a picture, it becomes linked to your layout, so QuarkXPress gives you tools to find and manage those linked files — including exporting them in JPG or PNG format and controlling how (or if) they output. In this chapter, I show you how to use all these tools and more.

Importing a Picture

You can import any modern picture file into a QuarkXPress picture box, including native Adobe Photoshop and Adobe Illustrator files, and picture files in the following formats: PDF, JPG, PNG, TIF, GIF, EPS, BMP, and WMF.

REMEMBER

QuarkXPress 2016 can convert Adobe Illustrator and PDF files to native QuarkXPress items so that you can work with the individual objects within them. Converting files to native format is different from importing them as pictures. See Chapter 3 for more details on converting Illustrator, PDF, EPS, Excel, and InDesign documents to native QuarkXPress format.

You can import a picture into an existing picture box or let QuarkXPress create a box for you as it imports. You can import a picture from a picture file on your computer, paste it from the Clipboard, or drag it from another application.

To import a picture, do one of these things:

>> Choose File ⇨ Import and navigate to the file on your computer.

>> Get the Picture Content tool, select a picture box, and then choose File ⇨ Import.

>> Get the Picture Content tool, select a picture box, and then paste a picture from the Clipboard.

>> Drag a picture file from your computer's file system onto a picture box.

>> Drag a picture file from your computer's file system onto a page.

>> Drag a picture from another application onto a picture box.

>> Press Command/Ctrl and drag a picture file from your computer's file system onto a text box, a no-content box, an empty picture box, or a box that contains a picture.

>> Press Command (Mac) or Ctrl (Windows) and drag a picture from another application onto a text box, a no-content box, an empty picture box, or a box that contains a picture.

WARNING

When you paste a picture that you copied to the Clipboard from another application, the picture becomes embedded in the layout. An embedded picture can increase your file size dramatically. If you want to export an embedded picture so that you can then import and link to it, see the "Exporting Pictures" section, later in this chapter.

TIP

If you drag a picture onto a box that already contains text or a picture, QuarkXPress creates a new box for the dragged content. To replace the contents of the box instead, press Command (Mac) or Ctrl (Windows) while dragging the content to the box. To always create a new box for dragged-in content, press Option (Mac) or Alt (Windows) while dragging.

TIP

If you import a picture into a picture box that already has picture attributes assigned to it (such as scale or rotation), the new picture can adopt those attributes. This capability can be useful when replacing a picture with another picture, or for setting up picture boxes to receive future pictures. To keep the existing attributes when using the File ⇨ Import technique to import a picture, select the Maintain Picture Attributes check box in the Import dialog box. When dragging a picture from your computer file system or another application onto a QuarkXPress picture box, this feature is turned on by default. To disable it, go to the Input Settings section of QuarkXPress Preferences and deselect the Maintain Picture Attributes check box.

Using ImageGrid to Import a Folder of Pictures

You can use ImageGrid to create a grid of picture boxes and fill them with all the picture files contained in a folder or series of nested folders. ImageGrid can be handy when you want to view the content of a folder full of pictures, along with each file's name, resolution, dimensions, file format, and color space. You can also use it to print or make a PDF of the clip art in a folder, or in a series of nested folders. (And remember, you don't have to keep the document created by ImageGrid — you can use it to temporarily view the pictures in a folder.)

Choose Utilities ⇨ ImageGrid to open the ImageGrid dialog box, shown in Figure 13-1. In this dialog box, you have numerous ways to set up your picture grid, as follows:

>> **To create boxes of a specific size:** Enter dimensions into the Box size fields and select the Fixed size radio button.

>> **To let ImageGrid size your boxes automatically:** Select the Autosize To radio button and enter the number of rows and columns you want.

>> **To automatically size boxes depending on their proportions and with the values in the Box size area as the maximum size:** Select the Autofill Pages Using Fixed Size for Limit radio button.

>> **To add a caption box under each picture box:** Select the Add Picture Info check box. To limit the caption to the name of the picture file, select Name Only; otherwise, the caption will include the picture file's name, resolution, dimensions in pixels, file format, and color space. To control the size of the caption text, select the Info Text Size check box; otherwise, the captions will use the font and size in the Normal character style sheet.

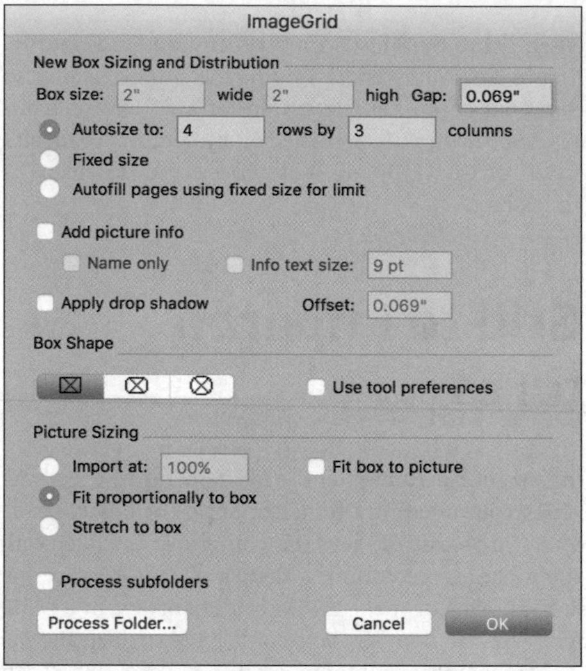

FIGURE 13-1:
The ImageGrid
dialog box.

ImageGrid

New Box Sizing and Distribution

Box size: 2" wide 2" high Gap: 0.069"

○ Autosize to: 4 rows by 3 columns

○ Fixed size

○ Autofill pages using fixed size for limit

☐ Add picture info

☐ Name only ☐ Info text size: 9 pt

☐ Apply drop shadow Offset: 0.069"

Box Shape

[⊠] [⊗] [⊗] ☐ Use tool preferences

Picture Sizing

○ Import at: 100% ☐ Fit box to picture

● Fit proportionally to box

○ Stretch to box

☐ Process subfolders

[Process Folder...] [Cancel] [OK]

>> **To add a drop shadow to each picture box:** Select the Apply Drop Shadow check box and enter a distance to Offset the shadow.

>> **Choose a box shape:** The boxes will have a white background unless you select the Use Tool Preferences check box, in which case the boxes will use the picture box attributes in the Tools tab of QuarkXPress Preferences.

>> **In the Picture Sizing area, choose how you want the picture to fill the box.** If you want the box to resize itself to fit the picture, select the Fit Box to Picture check box.

>> **If your picture folder contains subfolders and you want the pictures in those subfolders to be included in the ImageGrid:** Select the Process Subfolders check box.

After you've made your selections in the dialog box, click the Process Folder button and navigate to your folder of pictures. After you select your folder of picture files, click the Choose button to start ImageGrid building your grid of picture boxes.

QuarkXPress then creates a picture box for each picture in the folder(s) that you chose, adding pages to your layout as needed.

Working with Pictures

Working with picture boxes is similar to working with other page items, such as text boxes and lines. Chapter 4 explains all about that. However, picture boxes have some unique qualities that require special skills to achieve true page layout mastery. This section teaches you those special skills.

Moving pictures around

When you import a picture, it's imported at full size in the upper-left corner of the picture box. If the picture is larger than the box, get the Picture Content tool to see the entire picture display beyond the box boundary.

To move a picture inside its box, do one of the following:

>> Drag the picture with the Picture Content tool.

>> Enter new values in the X+ and Y+ fields of the Measurements palette.

>> Select it with the Picture Content tool and press the arrow keys on your keyboard to nudge the picture.

>> Choose Item ⇨ Modify to open the Modify dialog box and enter new values in the X+ and Y+ fields (Windows only).

To move the picture box along with the picture, do one of the following:

>> Drag the picture box with the Item tool.

>> Enter new values in the X and Y fields of the Measurements palette.

>> Select the picture box with the Item tool and press the arrow keys on your keyboard to nudge the picture box.

>> Choose Item ⇨ Modify to open the Modify dialog box and enter new values in the X and Y fields (Windows only).

Cropping pictures

If you want only part of your picture to show, adjust the size of the box by dragging its handles or by changing the values in the W and H fields of the Measurements palette.

Resizing pictures

You have a variety of ways to resize a picture inside its box, as follows:

>> Get the Picture Content tool and drag one of the circular handles on the picture (not the square handles on the picture box).

>> Change the percentages in the X% and Y% fields of the Measurements palette.

>> Use the Style menu to center, stretch, scale, or fit the picture to the box.

>> Choose Item ⇨ Modify to open the Modify dialog box and enter new values in the X% and Y% fields (Windows only).

You can also resize both a picture and its box by pressing Command (Mac) or Ctrl (Windows) key dragging a box handle.

TIP

If you know that the picture box is the size you need for your layout, press Command-Option-Shift-F (Mac) or Ctrl+Alt+Shift+F (Windows) to scale the picture to the box. Then Control-click (Mac) or right-click (Windows) the box and choose Fit Box to Picture from the context menu. This two-step process quickly fits the picture to the box and then cuts off any white space around the picture.

Rotating and skewing pictures

You can rotate a box or its content, and you can also skew (slant) a box or its content.

To rotate a selected picture by dragging, click and drag slightly outside the corner of its box. If the Item tool is active, the box rotates; if the Picture Content tool is active, the picture rotates inside the box.

To rotate a selected picture to an exact angle, type that angle into the Box Angle or Picture Angle fields in the Home/Classic tab of the Measurements palette or in the Item ⇨ Modify dialog box (Windows only).

To skew a selected picture, use the Box Skew or Picture Skew fields in the Home/Classic tab of the Measurements palette (see Figure 13-2), or choose Item ⇨ Modify to open the Modify dialog box (Windows only) and type values into the Box Skew or Picture Skew fields.

Flipping pictures

You can flip a picture box vertically or horizontally by clicking the Flip icons in the Home/Classic tab or Picture Box tab Measurements palette (as shown in Figure 13-2), or by choosing Style ⇨ Flip Horizontal or Style ⇨ Flip Vertical. When you click the icon or choose the menu command, the item flips.

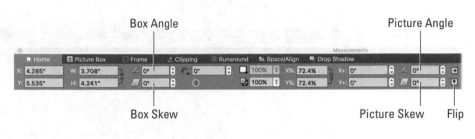

FIGURE 13-2:
The Box Angle,
Picture Angle,
Box Skew, and
Picture Skew
fields of the
Measurements
palette, as
well as the Flip
Horizontal and
Flip Vertical
buttons.

Coloring and shading pictures

If your picture is grayscale or black-and-white, you can apply a color to the shadows and midtones in several ways:

>> Choose the Style menu and then choose Color, Shade, or Opacity.

>> In the Picture Box tab of the Measurements palette, choose a color from the drop-down menu next to the Picture Color icon, as shown in Figure 13-3.

>> Click the Picture Color icon in the Colors palette and choose a color.

You can also apply a color to the background in either of the following ways:

>> In the Picture Box tab of the Measurements palette, choose a color from the drop-down menu next to the Picture Background Color icon, as shown in Figure 13-3.

>> In the Colors palette, click the Picture Background Color icon and choose a color.

FIGURE 13-3:
The Picture
Color and
Picture Back-
ground Color
icons of the
Measurements
palette.

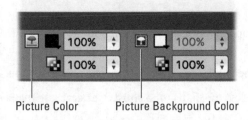

Picture Color   Picture Background Color

Adding a Drop Shadow

You can add a drop shadow to a picture box, a text box, a path, a group, the solid parts of a picture, or to text. To do that, you use the Drop Shadow tab of the Measurements palette, as shown in Figure 13-4.

Color Shade Angle Skew

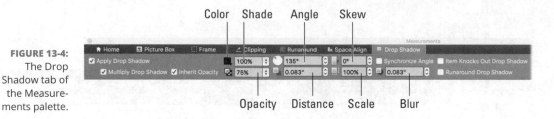

FIGURE 13-4:
The Drop
Shadow tab of
the Measure-
ments palette.

Opacity Distance Scale Blur

Here's how to choose settings for your drop shadow in the Drop Shadow tab:

>> **To apply a drop shadow:** Select the Apply Drop Shadow check box.

>> **To make its color mix with the colors behind it:** Select the Multiply Drop
Shadow check box.

WARNING

Don't use Multiply Drop Shadow on a white drop shadow. If you apply white
as the color for your drop shadow and select Multiply Drop Shadow, the drop
shadow will be omitted when you print or export your layout.

>> **To make the drop shadow's opacity match the opacity of the object:**
Select the Inherit Opacity check box.

>> **To set color and intensity:** Use the Color drop-down menu to set the drop
shadow's color, and use the Shade field to adjust the percentage of its intensity.

TIP

The classiest drop shadows are rarely black. Instead, they pick up a dark color
from the image. To give your drop shadow a color from the image, get the
Color Picker from the Colors palette and click a dark color in your picture.
QuarkXPress displays the color at the bottom of the Colors palette. Double-
click that color swatch to add it to your list of colors. You can then use that
color for your drop shadow.

>> **To adjust how much of the background shows through the shadow:** Use
the Opacity field.

>> **To change the apparent angle of the light source:** Use the Angle field. (You
can drag the dot in the icon to change the angle.)

>> **To adjust the drop shadow's distance from the object:** Use the Distance field.

>> **To skew the shadow (perhaps for a sinister effect):** Use the Skew field.

>> **To shrink or grow the shadow:** Use the Scale field.

>> **To adjust the spread of the shadow:** Use the Blur field.

>> **To force this drop shadow to have the same angle as all shadows on the
page:** Select the Synchronize Angle check box. (The default angle is 135°.)

>> **To keep the shadow from showing through the semi-opaque areas of the
item:** Select the Item Knocks Out Drop Shadow check box.

TIP

If the background of the imported picture is transparent and the Box Color is set to None, the drop shadow follows the outline of the item(s) in the picture instead of the outline of the box. The same goes for text: If the background of the text box has an opacity of less than 100 percent, the drop shadow follows the contours of the text.

>> **To wrap around the item and its drop shadow:** Select the Runaround Drop Shadow check box. Otherwise, text wrap ignores the drop shadow and may appear too close to the item.

TIP

To easily copy drop shadow settings and use them on other items, create an Item Style that includes only the attributes of the drop shadow. (Item Styles are explained in Chapter 4.)

Managing Pictures

When you import a picture, that picture isn't copied into your QuarkXPress layout. Instead, QuarkXPress remembers where the picture file lives on your computer and includes it when exporting or printing your layout. This "linked picture" approach has the advantage of allowing you (or others) to edit the picture file until print/export time and then include the latest version. (This approach also keeps the QuarkXPress file size down.) The disadvantage is that if you move, rename, delete, or misplace the picture file, QuarkXPress can't find it, and you need to choose Utilities ➪ Usage to open the Usage dialog box, shown in Figure 13-5, and tell QuarkXPress where the file is now (as explained in the next section).

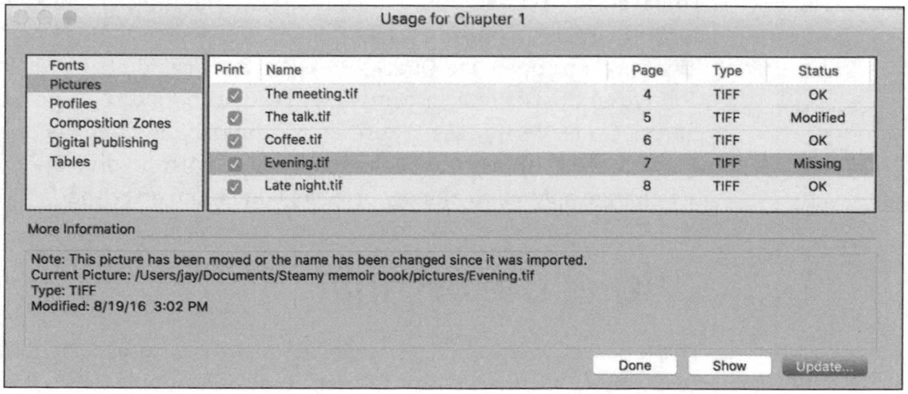

	Print	Name	Page	Type	Status
Fonts					
Pictures	✓	The meeting.tif	4	TIFF	OK
Profiles	✓	The talk.tif	5	TIFF	Modified
Composition Zones	✓	Coffee.tif	6	TIFF	OK
Digital Publishing	✓	Evening.tif	7	TIFF	Missing
Tables	✓	Late night.tif	8	TIFF	OK

Usage for Chapter 1

More Information

Note: This picture has been moved or the name has been changed since it was imported.
Current Picture: /Users/jay/Documents/Steamy memoir book/pictures/Evening.tif
Type: TIFF
Modified: 8/19/16 3:02 PM

Done   Show   Update...

FIGURE 13-5:
The Usage dialog box.

Finding, updating, and relinking pictures

The Usage dialog box lists every picture in your layout, along with its page number, file type, and status.

To be taken to a specific picture in your layout, select it in the list and click Show.

If the status of a picture is Modified, select it in the list and click Update. The current version of the picture will then be displayed in the layout and used for output.

To update a modified picture without seeing a confirmation alert, press Option (Mac) or Alt (Windows) and click the Update button.

If the status of a picture is Missing, select it in the list and click Update. The standard navigation dialog box displays so that you can find the picture file on your computer and relink it.

To select multiple pictures for updating, hold down the Command (Mac) or Ctrl (Windows) key while clicking them. To select multiple pictures when they're directly below each other, click the first one, hold down the Shift key, and click the last one you want to select.

The column headings in the Usage dialog box are clickable: If you click a heading, the entire list sorts by that column. You can click the Status column to cluster all the Missing or Modified items together, and then select them all for updating, as explained in the previous tip!

Using Auto Picture Import

To have QuarkXPress automatically update modified pictures when you open the current project, choose QuarkXPress⇨Preferences (Mac) or Edit⇨Preferences (Windows) to open the QuarkXPress Preferences dialog box. In the Project section, go to the General section, and in the Auto Picture Import drop-down menu, choose On or Verify (see Figure 13-6). This change applies only to the currently active project, unless you make this change with no projects open, in which case the change applies to all new projects you create after that.

Editing the original

The quickest way to edit an imported picture is to use the Edit Original feature. To do that, get the Picture Content tool and double-click the picture. The Edit Original dialog box opens, as shown in Figure 13-7. Click Edit Original to open the original picture file in the application your computer uses to edit files of that type.

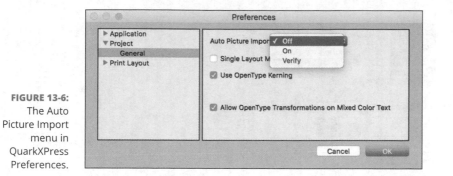

FIGURE 13-6:
The Auto
Picture Import
menu in
QuarkXPress
Preferences.

FIGURE 13-7:
The Edit
Original dialog
box with and
without loca-
tion menu
exposed.

TIP

To skip the Edit Original dialog box and immediately open the picture in its editing application, Control-click (Mac) or right-click (Windows) the picture and choose Edit Original from the context menu.

Finding the original

To find the original file of an imported picture, get the Picture Content tool and double-click the picture. The Edit Original dialog box opens, as shown in Figure 13-7. Click the drop-down menu to be taken to the original file. Click and hold the drop-down menu to see the folder hierarchy that contains the original picture file. To open one of these folders, drag down to it and release the mouse button. The folder you selected opens on your desktop.

Controlling Layers, Channels, and Paths in Photoshop Documents

If you're feeling especially clever, and you're importing Photoshop documents, you can choose Window ⇨ Advanced Image Control to open the palette shown in Figure 13-8.

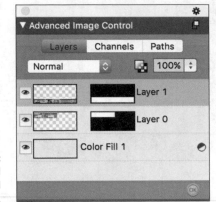

FIGURE 13-8:
The Advanced
Image Control
palette.

This palette is essentially a copy of the Layers, Channels, and Paths panels in Photoshop. You change the visibility, opacity, and blend mode of layers in the Photoshop file, as well as turn channels and paths on and off. Your changes don't affect the original file — they just affect what QuarkXPress uses in your layout.

TECHNICAL STUFF

If your print project uses spot varnishes or spot color in addition to CMYK, and channels were added in a Photoshop image for those special treatments, you can use Advanced Image Control to control those extra channels when printing.

Creating a QR Code in QuarkXPress

QuarkXPress lets you easily create a QR code (Quick Response Code) and drop it into your layout. Because the code is made of native QuarkXPress items, you can customize its colors, resize and rotate the code, and more — without losing quality.

A QR code is a special type of barcode that's easily scannable by smartphone cameras. QR codes can include information such as web addresses, phone numbers, links to vCards, and more. They can be printed on business cards and promotional materials, shown on displays, and put anywhere you want to make it easy to share information. To find a QR code reader for your mobile device, just do a quick web search. These apps can scan the codes to load websites, add contacts to your contacts app, and even dial phone numbers. QR codes are great tools for immediately getting information in front of potential customers.

First, create a picture box of any size; you can resize it later. Then choose Utilities ➪ Make QR Code to open the QR Code dialog (see Figure 13-9). Click the Text tab and just type in a URL, a phone number, a mailto:, or any other text. Click the icon on the left to create a raster (bitmap) picture at 288 ppi, or click the icon on the right to create an infinitely resizable QR code constructed from native QuarkXPress items. Pick a color and click OK, and QuarkXPress then fills the picture box for you. The "white" parts are transparent, so you can place it on top of a colored background or change its color using the Colors palette.

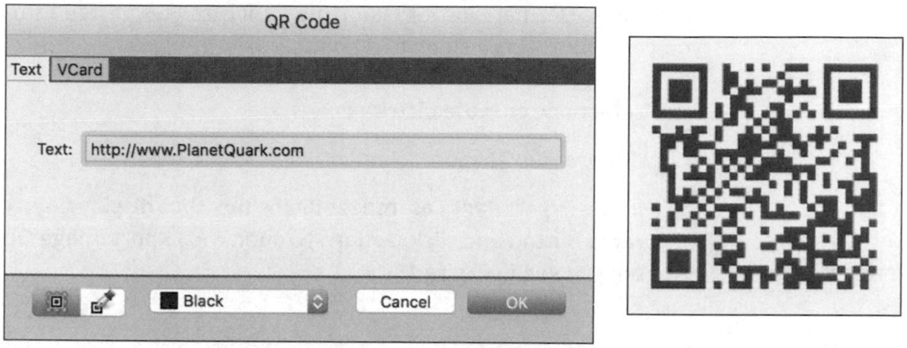

FIGURE 13-9:
The QR Code dialog box (left) and a text code on a colored background (right).

When a user on a mobile device points a QR Code reader app at your QR code, one of several things happens: the user is taken to the web page you defined in the QR code; the user's email program launches and creates a new email message addressed to the mailto: address that you defined in the QR code; or the device simply displays the phone number or other text you defined in the QR code.

You can also generate a QR Code that provides a vCard containing any combination of a name, phone number, email address, and website (see Figure 13-10).

FIGURE 13-10:
A QR Code containing a vCard and the QR Code dialog box for a vCard.

When someone using a mobile device points a QR Code reader app at this QR code, the app offers to add this person to the address book on the mobile device being used.

Exporting Pictures

QuarkXPress can convert any picture to JPEG or PNG format and export it, in your choice of resolution. This feature is especially useful for converting images to web-happy formats, or for exporting a picture you pasted into a picture box, and you can follow these steps to do both:

1. Select one or more picture boxes.

2. Choose File ⇨ Export ⇨ Image.

3. In the Export Pages as Images dialog box that displays, select the Selection radio button and click Options to open the Export Image Options dialog box, shown in Figure 13-11.

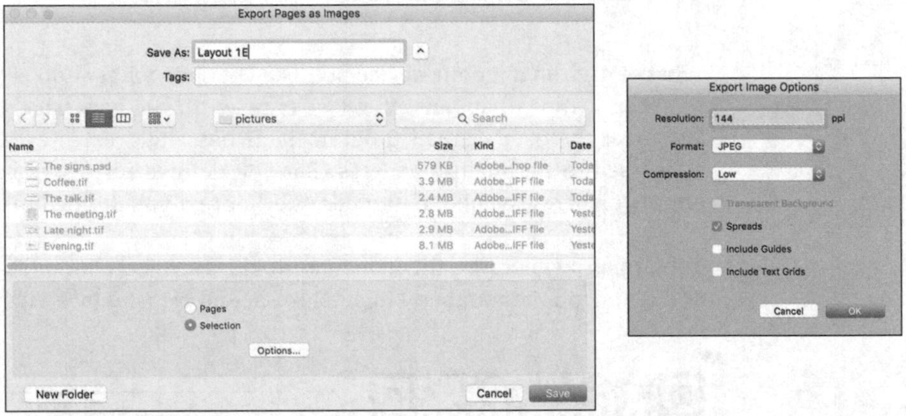

FIGURE 13-11: The Export Pages as Images and the Export Image Options dialog boxes.

4. Choose JPEG or PNG format, enter a resolution, and select a compression level (for JPEG) and transparency option (for PNG).

If the picture spans a multiple-page spread, make sure that the Spreads check box is selected.

5. Click OK to dismiss the Options dialog, choose a location for your exported pictures, and click Save.

Greeking Picture Previews

Normally, QuarkXPress displays all pictures in full resolution. However, you can possibly speed up the display of your layout on slower computers by telling QuarkXPress to display all pictures as gray boxes. To do that, choose

QuarkXPress ⇨ Preferences (Mac) or Edit ⇨ Preferences (Windows) to open the QuarkXPress Preferences dialog box. Then go to the Print Layout section, and in the General section, select the Greek Pictures check box, shown in Figure 13-12.

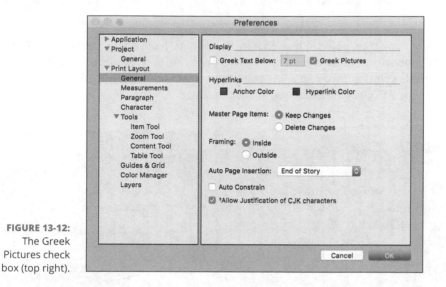

FIGURE 13-12:
The Greek Pictures check box (top right).

Suppressing Output of Pictures

As with any other QuarkXPress item, you can suppress the output of a picture box or its content. This can be useful in several situations:

>> When your commercial printer will be replacing your pictures with its own

>> When you're troubleshooting a layout that won't print and you need to eliminate a picture as the source of the problem

>> When you're proofreading a complex layout over and over and don't need to see the pictures (or wait for them to print)

To suppress output of the box and its content, in the Measurements palette, go to the Picture Box tab, locate the Box Corner Style control in the third column, and click the Suppress Box Output icon below that control, as shown in Figure 13-13. The icon changes to show a red slash through it.

To suppress output of only the content (but still print the formatted box), click the Suppress Picture Output icon at the far right end of the Picture Box tab of the Measurements palette.

FIGURE 13-13:
The Suppress
Output icons
in the Picture
Box tab of the
Measurements
palette.

Suppress Box Output   Suppress Picture Output

When printing, you can also change the Output drop-down menu in the Pictures section of the Print dialog box from Normal to Low Resolution or Rough. This speeds printing by using a low resolution version of each picture, or by replacing it with a plain box. Read more about printing in Chapter 16.

THE GOOD OLD STYLE MENU

Almost all the action in QuarkXPress occurs in palettes. However, don't overlook the Style menu, which often offers the quickest and easiest way to format and transform a picture. See the following figure for some of its options.

THE BAD OLD CLIPPING PATHS AND ALPHA MASKS

Long ago, before transparency in images was common, QuarkXPress gave page layout artists tools to make areas of pictures see-through. Using the technology of the time — clipping paths and alpha masks — you could carefully make sharp edges around objects in images (clipping paths) and apply semi-opaque overlays (alpha masks). Quark's *A Guide to QuarkXPress 2016* at http://www.quark.com/Support/Documentation/QuarkXPress/2016.aspx has details on using these features.

Chapter **14**

When Text Met Graphics

O ne of the important ways a page layout application such as QuarkXPress is better than a word processing application such as Microsoft Word is in how you can position items in relation to each other. In this chapter, you see how to make pictures and text boxes push other text out of the way. You also find out how you can anchor items inside the flow of text so that they travel along with the text, or outside the flow of text to create callouts. And if you think that your layout may ultimately become an e-book, you'll find it essential to know how to anchor items to text.

Wrapping Text around Other Items

When laying out a page with multiple pictures and text boxes, QuarkXPress's text runaround feature can be both efficient and creative. Text runaround is efficient when you're moving page items around because if the item you move extends over part of a text box, the text in the text box can automatically move out of the way. Without this feature, you would be constantly rearranging and resizing text boxes to accommodate new or moved page items.

You can also use text runaround in creative ways, such as making the edge of a text block follow the contours of a person or product. Or, you can drop a picture on top of the margin between two columns of text and have the text wrap around it.

QuarkXPress takes the text runaround feature to the limit: You can set a different text offset distance for the top, bottom, left, and right side of every item, and optionally include the item's drop shadow in the runaround. When running text around a picture, it can run around the outside edge of the picture, the shape of the main subject in the picture, or anything in between.

REMEMBER

When you want text to wrap around a page item, you apply text runaround to that item. Text runaround works only when the item being run around is in *front* of the box containing the text.

REMEMBER

The controls for text runaround are in different places on a Mac and in Windows. On a Mac, all the controls are in the Runaround tab of the Measurements palette. In Windows, you choose Item ⇨ Runaround or Item ⇨ Edit ⇨ Runaround to get to these controls.

Running text around text boxes

When working with multiple text boxes, some may overlap others. You can use text wrap creatively, to cause small text in a story to move out of the way of a box containing big text, such as a callout. You can also use text wrap on a small "continued on . . ." box to force the story to jump past the "continued on . . ." line to another page.

To make text run around the outside of a text box (so that the text in boxes behind it will wrap around it), select the text box and follow these steps:

1. In Windows, choose Item ⇨ Runaround; on a Mac, click the Runaround tab in the Measurements palette, as shown in Figure 14-1.

2. Choose Item from the Type drop-down menu.

3. Enter values in the Top, Left, Bottom, and Right fields to outset or inset the runaround area. (If the text box is not rectangular, only one Outset field displays.)

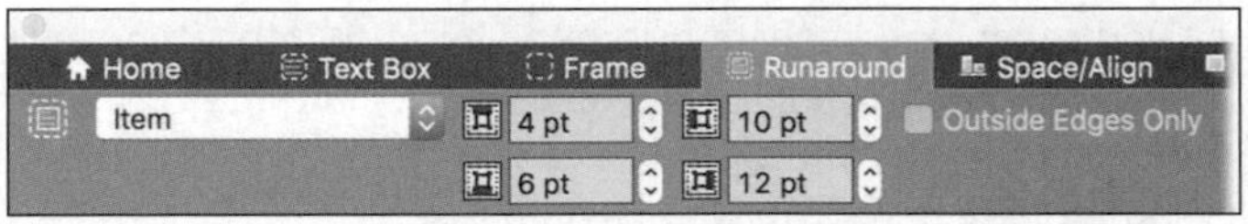

FIGURE 14-1:
The Runaround tab of the Measurements palette for a text box.

⌂ Home	▤ Text Box	⬚ Frame	Runaround	⬛ Space/Align
Item		4 pt	10 pt	Outside Edges Only
		6 pt	12 pt	

Running text around pictures

When running text around a picture box, QuarkXPress lets you run text around the outside of the box or around a shape inside the picture. Just remember that the picture box must be *in front of* any text boxes you want to wrap around the picture.

Running text around the outside of a picture box

To make text run around the outside of a picture box, select it and follow these steps:

1. In Windows, choose Item ⇨ Runaround. On a Mac, click the Runaround tab in the Measurements palette, as shown in Figure 14-2.

2. Choose Item from the Type drop-down menu.

3. Enter values in the Top, Left, Bottom, and Right fields to outset or inset the runaround area. (If the text box is not rectangular, only one Outset field displays.)

Running text around a shape in a picture box

QuarkXPress gives you several ways to make text run around a picture shape. If the picture happens to have an embedded path or alpha channel, you can use the path or channel. However, that's not usually the case — so QuarkXPress can find the subject area of a picture on a (near) white or (near) black background and create a runaround path for you. Here's how:

1. On a Mac, click the Runaround tab in the Measurements palette, as shown in Figure 14-2; in Windows, choose Item ⇨ Runaround.

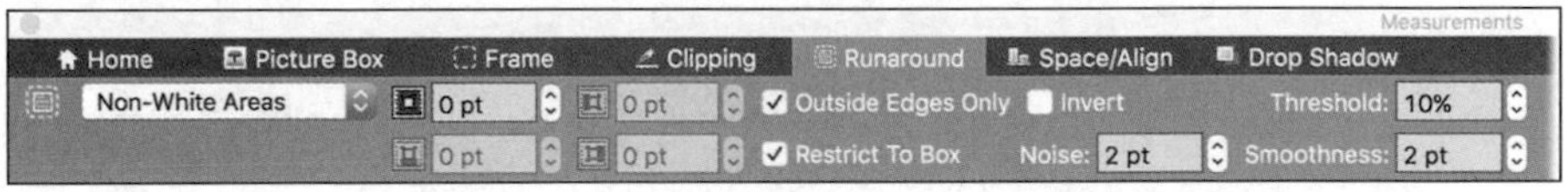

FIGURE 14-2:
The Runaround tab of the Measurements palette for a picture box.

2. Make a choice from the Type drop-down menu:

- **Auto Image:** Creates a Bézier clipping and runaround path based on the picture's nonwhite areas. For more on creating and using Bézier paths, see Chapter 3.

- **Embedded Path:** Runs text around a path embedded in an image by an image-editing application (such as Photoshop).

- **Alpha Channel:** Runs text around an alpha channel embedded in an image by an image-editing application such as Photoshop. An alpha channel is a saved selection inside an image that can be used for removing backgrounds, printing spot varnishes or foils, or for other situations in which a portion of a picture needs to be defined.

- **Non-White Areas:** Creates a runaround path based on the picture's subject. Depending on the value in the Threshold field, the runaround path will outline a dark figure within a larger white or near-white background (or vice versa).

- **Same As Clipping:** Sets the text runaround path to the clipping path selected in the Clipping tab.

- **Picture Bounds:** Runs text around the rectangular canvas area of the imported picture file. The canvas area contains the original picture boundaries. Because QuarkXPress lets you enlarge the picture box beyond the edges of the picture, this option tells QuarkXPress to ignore the picture box and use the original picture boundary instead. Enter values in the Top, Left, Bottom, and Right fields to determine the outset or inset of the text from the picture's boundaries.

3. **Choose among the following options to fine-tune the runaround path:**

   - **Outset field:** Adjusts how far the path extends from the edge of the subject. Negative values move the path inside the subject.

   - **Invert:** Makes the text flow inside the shape, rather than outside.

   - **Outside Edges Only:** Prevents "holes" from appearing inside the subject.

   - **Restrict To Box:** Prevents the runaround path from extending beyond the edges of the picture box.

   - **Noise:** Determines the smallest allowable closed path. Use this option to remove unwanted small paths.

   - **Smoothness:** Controls path accuracy. A lower value creates a more complex path with a greater number of points. A higher value creates a less accurate path.

   - **Threshold:** Determines how "white" is defined. For example, if the Threshold value is 15 percent, and a pixel's gray value is below or at 15 percent, the pixel is considered "white" and excluded from the runaround path.

Editing a runaround path

To adjust a runaround path, choose Item ⇨ Edit ⇨ Runaround. The runaround path displays as a magenta outline in the picture box. You can then edit the path as you would any Bézier item. For more on editing Bézier paths, see the section in Chapter 3 about building Bézier boxes and lines.

Running text around lines and text paths

As mentioned at the beginning of this section, text runaround can be applied to any page item — not just boxes. To get creative, you can run text around anything, including lines and paths. To make text run around a line or text path, select it and follow these steps:

1. **On a Mac, click the Runaround tab in the Measurements palette, as shown in Figure 14-3. In Windows, choose Item ⇨ Runaround.**

   The controls for Text Runaround appear in either the Measurements palette (Mac) or dialog box (Windows).

2. **Choose Item from the Type drop-down menu in the Measurements palette or dialog box.**

3. **Enter values in the Top, Left, Bottom, and Right fields to outset or inset the runaround area.**

   If the selected item is a text path, text in boxes behind it will run only around the path — not the text on the path.

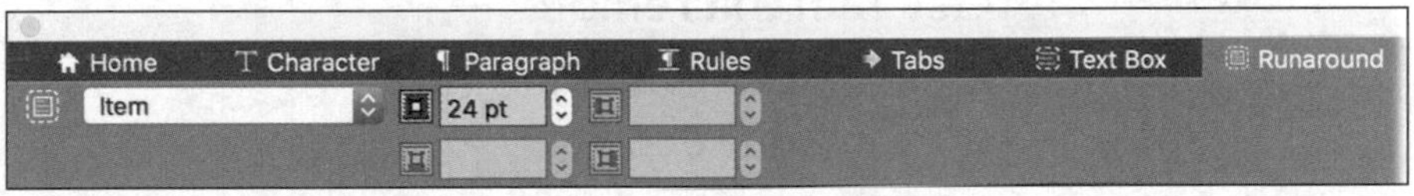

FIGURE 14-3:
The Runaround tab of the Measurements palette for a line or text path.

🏠 Home	T Character	¶ Paragraph	⏝ Rules	◆ Tabs	▦ Text Box	▦ Runaround
▦	Item	▣ 24 pt	⊞			
		⊟	⊞			

Running text around all sides of an item

If the runaround item is smaller than the text box and you want the text to run around both the left and right sides of that item, think twice — readers have a hard time following a line of text that jumps across an obstacle and then contin-ues. If you *still* want to create this reading obstacle, select the text box (not the runaround item) and then do this:

>> **On a Mac:** Select Run Text Around All Sides in the Text Box tab of the Measurements palette.

>> **In Windows:** Choose Item ⇨ Modify and click the Text tab. Then select Run Text Around All Sides.

TIP

When you add a drop shadow to an item that has text runaround applied to it, you can choose whether text wrap distance should include the drop shadow or not. (Hint: Make it wrap around the drop shadow!) To include the drop shadow, click the Drop Shadow tab in the Measurements palette and select Runaround Drop Shadow.

Anchoring Items inside the Text Flow

When you want a box, line, table, group, or any other item to flow along with the text, you can anchor it within the text. It's incredibly handy when you need to insert a small graphic into the text, or when building a reflowable e-book, as shown in Figure 14-4. It's also incredibly easy to do; just follow these steps:

1. **Get the Item tool from the Tools palette and select the item or group you want to anchor.**

2. **Choose Edit ⇨ Cut or Edit ⇨ Copy.**

3. **Get the Text Content tool from the Tools palette and place the Text Insertion bar where you want to anchor the item.**

4. **Choose Edit ⇨ Paste to anchor the item at the text insertion point.**

FIGURE 14-4:
A picture box anchored in the flow of text.

> 1 Get **Yamaha** remote
> 2 Press red ⏻ button to turn on Yamaha receiver

WARNING

If the item you're anchoring is wider than the column of text you're anchoring it into, the item disappears and the text box displays an overflow indicator. You can either immediately undo your paste command by choosing Edit ⇨ Undo, or you can widen the text box to accommodate the anchored item. If the anchored item needs to be wider than the text column, use a callout instead, as explained later in this chapter.

Here are ways to work with anchored items:

>> **To resize an anchored item:** Click the item with the Item tool; then drag one of its resizing handles.

>> **To cut or copy an anchored item:** Select the item as you would any text character and choose Edit ⇨ Cut or Edit ⇨ Copy.

>> **To paste the anchored item elsewhere:** Place the Text Insertion bar in a different location and choose Edit ⇨ Paste.

>> **To duplicate an anchored item:** Select it with the Item tool and choose Item ⇨ Duplicate. A duplicate will be placed on the page.

>> **To delete an anchored item:** Select the item or insert the Text Insertion bar after it, and press Delete/Backspace.

>> **To edit an anchored item:** Use the tool appropriate for its content (picture, text, or line). Click the anchored item and use the tool as you would with a regular item: type/import text, import a picture, apply formatting, and so on.

>> **To edit a group:** Duplicate it as described earlier in this list and then paste it back into the text.

>> **To unanchor an item:** Again, duplicate the item as described previously in this list and then delete the original from the text flow.

Creating and Configuring Callouts

A *callout* is a floating item or group of items that displays on the same page or spread as the text it relates to. Some common uses for callouts are

>> To keep a figure on the same page as the text that refers to it

>> To display a floating icon outside the text (as you see in this book)

>> To keep a pull quote (a quote from the text that highlights a specific idea) on the same page as its original text

A callout may include any combination of QuarkXPress items. To define its position on the page, you place a callout anchor in the text and associate it with the callout, as described in the upcoming sections.

Creating a callout

Chapter 3 tells you how to create an item, and Chapter 4 tells you how to create a group of items. After creating the item or group that you want to use as a callout, follow these steps to create a callout:

1. **Get the Text Content tool from the Tools palette and place the text insertion point where you want the callout anchor to be.**

2. **Choose Item ⇨ Callout Anchor ⇨ Insert Callout Anchor.**

   A callout anchor is inserted and selected.

3. **Click once on the item or group you want to use as a callout.**

4. **Choose Item ⇨ Callout Anchor ⇨ Associate with Callout Anchor.**

   The item or group becomes a callout, with a nonprinting line connecting it to the callout anchor, as shown in Figure 14-5. Next, you need to configure the callout anchor, as described in the next section.

i, etiam adfabilis
ecas, utcunque
rre. Rures imputat
udabilis concubine.
semper
diet plane utilitas
alis apparatus

tis infeliciter prae-
s umbraculi suffra-

Ringo teaches Jay his drum techniques.

FIGURE 14-5:
A callout anchor connected to a group of items.

The context menu is often the easiest way to configure callouts, as shown in Figure 14-6. To use the context menu, Control-click (Mac) or right-click (Windows) the callout anchor or the callout itself.

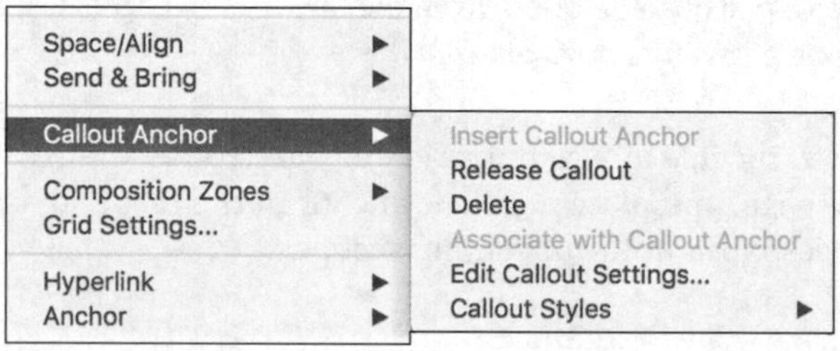

TIP

Space/Align	▶
Send & Bring	▶
Callout Anchor	▶
Composition Zones	▶
Grid Settings...	
Hyperlink	▶
Anchor	▶

Insert Callout Anchor
Release Callout
Delete
Associate with Callout Anchor
Edit Callout Settings...
Callout Styles ▶

FIGURE 14-6:
The context menu for a callout anchor.

When guides are turned off, you can see only the selected callout anchor. To see all anchors, turn the guides on by choosing View ⇨ Guides.

REMEMBER

Configuring a callout anchor

As with many things in QuarkXPress, you can configure a callout anchor either by applying a saved Callout Style or by configuring it manually.

To configure a callout anchor manually, follow these steps:

1. **Select the callout anchor and choose Item ⇨ Callout Anchor ⇨ Edit Callout Settings.**

The Edit Callout Style dialog box displays, as shown in Figure 14-7.

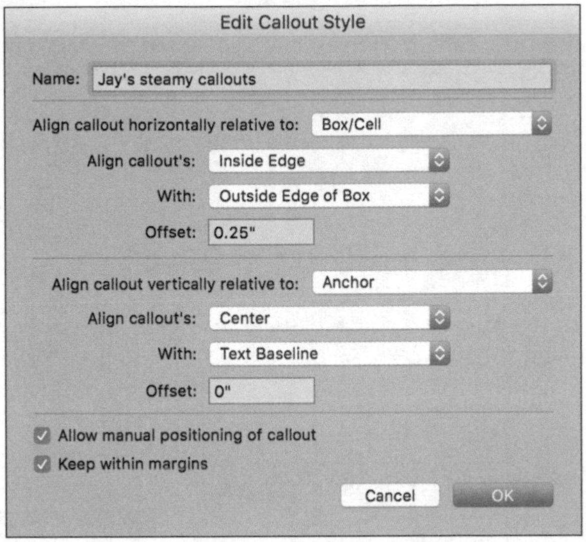

FIGURE 14-7:
The Edit
Callout Style
dialog box.

2. **To control how the callout aligns horizontally, choose from among the controls in the Align Callout Horizontally Relative To area in the Edit Callout Style dialog box:**

   - **Align Callout Horizontally Relative to menu:** The Align Callout Horizontally Relative to menu in the Edit Callout Style dialog box lets you align the callout with the anchor, the paragraph containing the anchor, the text box containing the anchor, the page, or the spread it's on.

   - **Align Callout menu:** The Align Callout menu lets you use the callout's center, left edge, right edge, inside edge, or outside edge for alignment. (Inside/outside is useful with page spreads.)

   - **With menu:** The With menu lets you lets you align the callout with the left edge, right edge, inside edge, or outside edge of the paragraph, box, page, or page margins. (Center is also an option for page or page margins.)

   - **Offset field:** The Offset field lets you adjust the callout in relation to what it's aligned with.

3. **To control how the callout aligns vertically, use the controls in the Align Callout Vertically Relative To area in the Edit Callout Style dialog box.**

   The controls are similar to the choices for horizontal alignment.

4. **To allow the callout to be manually moved, select Allow Manual Positioning of Callout.**

   To prevent the callout from being manually repositioned, leave this box deselected.

5. **To prevent the callout from extending beyond the page margins, select Keep Within Margins.**

Even if the Offset field has a value that would push the callout into the margin, the callout will stop at the margin.

Working with callout styles

To create and configure a Callout Style, you can use either the Callout Styles palette (Window ⇨ Callout Styles) or choose Edit ⇨ Callout Styles. Both are shown in Figure 14-8.

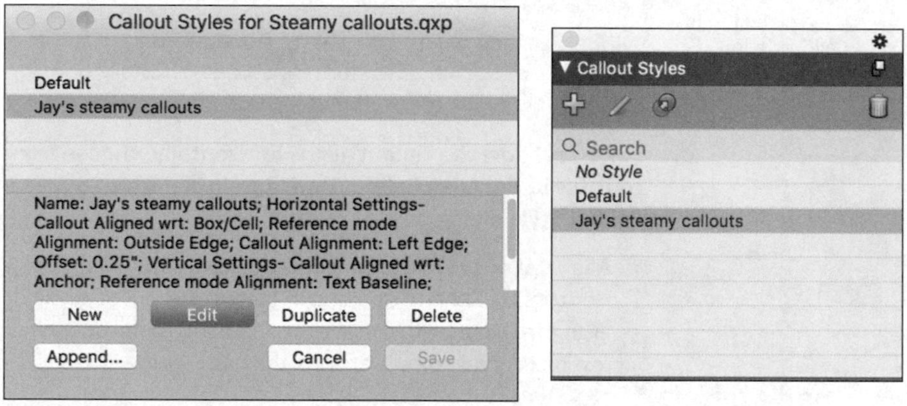

FIGURE 14-8: The Callout Styles palette (left) and dialog box (right).

The same controls are in both the Callout Styles palette and dialog box:

- » **To create a new Callout Style:** Click the New button. The Edit Callout Settings dialog box displays, as shown in Figure 14-7.

- » **To edit an existing Callout Style:** Select the style in the list of Callout Styles and click the Edit button. The Edit Callout Settings dialog box displays, as shown in Figure 14-7.

- » **To append Callout Styles from another QuarkXPress layout:** Click the Append button in the Callout Styles dialog box.

- » **To apply a Callout Style to a selected callout anchor:** Click the style's name in the Callout Style palette or choose its name from the Callout Styles sub-menu (Item ⇨ Callout Anchor ⇨ Callout Styles).

- » **To delete a Callout Style:** Select it in the list and click the Delete button.

Copying and pasting callouts

A callout anchor behaves like an invisible text character. When you cut or copy and paste text that contains a callout anchor, the callout and the callout anchor come along with the text.

Deleting a callout

To delete a callout anchor *and its callout*, choose Item ⇨ Callout Anchor ⇨ Delete. If you want to keep the callout but delete the callout anchor, first choose Item ⇨ Callout Anchor ⇨ Release.

CALLOUTS AND TEXT RUNAROUND DON'T MIX

It's best not to apply a runaround to a callout, because if a callout causes text to reflow and the reflowed text includes the anchor for the callout, you may not be able to control the positioning of the callout. QuarkXPress does its best to help by changing the callout settings to the Default style, and if that doesn't work, then to No Style. If that doesn't work, QuarkXPress disables the callout's runaround, and the indicator for the callout anchor becomes a red stoplight. (To view indicators, choose View ⇨ Visual Indicators.) See? It's better not to apply a runaround to a callout.

IN THIS CHAPTER

» **Creating and applying solid colors, tints, and color blends**

» **Adjusting opacity**

» **Adding colors from imported pictures**

» **Appending colors from other projects**

» **Managing and proofing colors**

Chapter **15**

Making a Colorful Page

U sing colors is similar to using fonts: You have to choose *something* for your project, and your choice affects how viewers perceive your message. (Even black and white are color choices, even if by default.) Wisely, Quark has focused on giving QuarkXPress the best color tools in the industry — from the world's best transparency features to user-friendly soft proofing, you'll enjoy exploring and using these color tools.

In this chapter, you learn the ways in which you can define color, how to create and apply colors in QuarkXPress, how to pick up a color from an imported picture or other page item, how to manage colors, and how to import colors used in other projects. You also learn more advanced color techniques, such as creating color blends, adjusting the opacity of colors, and getting your display to simulate how your colors will print.

Describing Color

In the printing world, there are two kinds of colors: spot and process. A *spot* color is made with just one ink, usually chosen from a swatchbook made by a company such as Pantone. These are often referred to as "PMS" followed by a swatch number (PMS stands for Pantone Matching System). A *process* color is created by blending four or more standard printing inks — usually cyan, magenta, yellow, and black (CMYK).

QuarkXPress supports several other color matching systems besides Pantone, including Trumatch, Focoltone, DIC (Dainippon Ink & Chemical), and Toyo. Whichever system you use, be sure to choose its exact name when specifying a color, because QuarkXPress supports no fewer than 39 different Pantone systems, including pastels, metallics, and neons.

In the digital world, the three most popular ways of describing colors are RGB, HSB, and LAB.

>> **RGB:** Combines varying amounts of red, green, and blue light to create all the colors you see on your computer display.

>> **HSB:** Starts with a Hue (basic color), then lets you adjust its Saturation (intensity) and Brightness (whiteness). Artists often use this model because it's similar to mixing paint colors.

>> **LAB:** Properly referred to as L*a*b*, this color model breaks down colors into their Luminance value, and then how that value falls on two color axes: red/green (*a) and yellow/blue (*b). It's designed to include all the possible colors, regardless of the device used to display them.

QuarkXPress also lets you choose from Web Named Colors (such as ForestGreen and LightSteelBlue) and Web Safe Colors (which have names such as #0099FF and #CC6600). You can also type in any hexadecimal value for a Web color, rather than choose from the limited number of colors in the Web Named and Web Safe color palettes.

It's essential to remember that the colors you see onscreen will rarely match the colors that get printed. There are many causes for this mismatch, but the biggest is this: Your computer display creates colors from light, while printed materials create colors by reflecting light back at you. A general rule of thumb is this: The brighter the color on your display, the less likely you can print it accurately. Be especially wary of bright greens and oranges because they are the most difficult to reproduce with inks.

Specifying Color

You can create, edit, and apply colors in several places:

>> **The Colors palette:** Lets you create, edit, and apply colors.

>> **The Measurements palette:** Lets you create and apply colors.

>> **The Style menu:** Lets you apply colors.

>> **The Colors dialog box:** Lets you create and edit colors as well as append colors from other projects. It also lets you see which colors are being used in the current project. Choose Edit ⇨ Colors to open this dialog box.

Creating a new color

The easiest way to create a new color is to click the New (+) button on the Colors palette — this opens the Edit Color dialog box, shown in Figure 15-1. However, you can get to this same dialog box from the New button in the Edit ⇨ Color dialog box or any color drop-down menu in the Measurements palette. Then follow these steps:

FIGURE 15-1:
The Edit Color
dialog box.

1. **If you're creating a color from the first few color models (RGB, HSB, LAB, CMYK, or Multi-Ink), enter a name of your choice in the Name field.**

    Give it a name that makes sense for your project, such as *[client] Blue.* Otherwise, skip the Name field because when you choose a color from any of the other color models, the Name field is filled in for you.

2. **Choose a color Model, such as RGB, CMYK, Pantone Solid Coated, or Trumatch.**

    Your choice will change the selection options on the right side of the Edit Color dialog box, as follows:

    • **For nonbranded colors:** If you choose one of the non-branded color models, such as RGB or CMYK, use the sliders or enter values to define your color. Drag the vertical slider to brighten or darken the selected color, and drag the dot inside the color wheel to change its hue.

    • **For commercial colors:** If you choose one of the commercial color matching systems such as Pantone or Trumatch, click one of the color swatches or type in its number to choose a color. (Click the Stacked View icon above the OK button to view the colors in a list instead of a grid.) The name of the swatch is filled into the Name field for you and a larger swatch appears at bottom left.

- **For Multi-Ink:** The oddball in this list is Multi-Ink, which is incredibly useful. Multi-Ink lets you define a color that uses tint percentages of the other inks in your project. For example, a spot color with a percentage of one or more process (CMYK) inks mixed in.

3. **(Optional) If you want your color to print on its own printing plate, select the Spot Color check box.**

4. **Choose from one of the options in the Halftone drop-down menu if you plan to make a tint of your color.**

   Using these options lets you control the way the printing dots are arranged. Unless you have a specific reason to do otherwise, leave it at Process Black.

5. **Click OK.**

   The color is added to your Colors palette and is available everywhere else that a color can be chosen.

Using the color picker

Instead of choosing a color from a color model, you can also use the Color Picker to grab a color from an imported picture or from any other item in any open QuarkXPress project. Here's how:

1. **Choose Window⇨Colors to open the Colors palette, shown in Figure 15-2.**

2. **Click the Color Picker tool at the bottom left.**

3. **Click any color that you might want to add from this or another project.**

   (It may help to zoom in on the item you're sampling.) That color is added to the small swatches at the bottom of the Colors palette.

4. **To add one of these color picker swatches to the list of colors in your Colors palette, double-click that swatch.**

   The Add Color dialog box displays, where you can name the color or edit it.

TIP

To bypass the Add Color dialog box and immediately add a color picker swatch to your Colors palette, Option/Alt-click the Add button at the right of the color picker swatches.

5. **To remove a color swatch, click the swatch while holding down Option (Mac) or Alt (Windows).**

6. **To add all the color picker swatches to the Colors palette, click the Add button at the right of the color picker swatches while holding down Option (Mac) or Alt (Windows).**

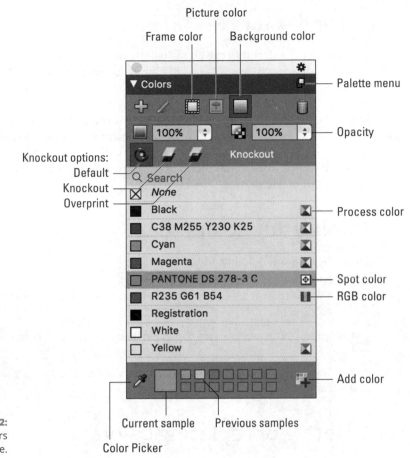

Frame color
Picture color
Background color
Palette menu
Opacity
Knockout options:
Default
Knockout
Overprint
Process color
Spot color
RGB color
Add color
Current sample
Previous samples
Color Picker

FIGURE 15-2:
The Colors
palette.

Applying colors

You can apply colors, tints, and opacity to just about anything you can select in QuarkXPress. After selecting an item or text, select from among the color controls in the Measurements palette or in the Colors palette, as shown in Figure 15-2.

In the Colors palette, note that you can apply a separate color, tint, and opacity to a picture, selected text, frame, or background by clicking the corresponding icon at the top of the palette.

Icons to the right of each color indicate whether that color is in RGB mode or CMYK mode, or is a spot color.

TIP

You can convert any color to a spot color by choosing Make Spot from the Colors palette menu.

Editing colors

To edit a color, select it in the Colors palette or in the Edit ⇨ Colors dialog box and click the Edit (pencil) icon. The Edit Color dialog box appears for you to make your changes.

TECHNICAL STUFF

When you create a layout, you choose whether it's primarily destined for Print or for Digital, and QuarkXPress adds the appropriate basic colors to the Colors palette for you — Cyan, Magenta, Yellow, and Black when you're working with a Print layout, and Red, Green, and Blue when you're working with a Digital layout. You can't edit or delete these default colors.

Duplicating colors

To duplicate a color, do one of the following:

>> Select the color in the Colors palette and choose Duplicate from the palette menu.

>> Choose Edit ⇨ Colors, and in the Colors dialog box, click Duplicate.

Either way, the Edit Color dialog box appears for you to name your new color or make changes to it.

Deleting or replacing colors

To delete or replace a color, do one of the following:

>> Select it in the Colors palette and click the Delete (trash can) icon.

>> Choose Edit ⇨ Colors, and in the Colors dialog box, click Delete.

If the color has been used on any items in your layout, a dialog box appears that lets you choose a replacement color for those items.

Appending colors from other projects

To copy all the colors from another project into the current one, do one of these things:

>> Choose Edit ⇨ Colors and click Append. Navigate to the other project and click Open. The Append dialog box displays, as shown in Figure 15-3.

>> Choose File ⇨ Append, navigate to the other project, and click Open. Choose Colors from the list on the left.

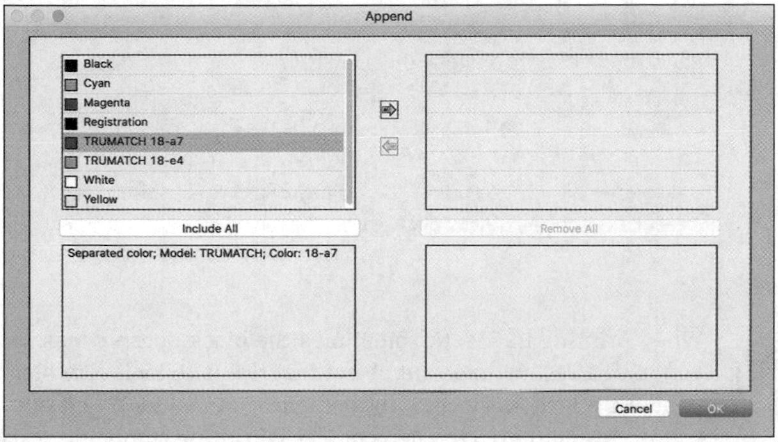

FIGURE 15-3:
The Append
dialog box.

Whichever of these two techniques you use to get to the Append dialog box, you then follow these steps:

1. **Click one of the colors in the left column and click the right-pointing arrow to add it to the left column. (Click Include All to add all the colors.)**

2. **Click the OK button to add the colors in the right column to the current project.**

Knocking out and overprinting

The icons in the Knockout area of the Colors palette let you control how an item's colors are printed. They are specific to the item, not the color, and you should normally leave them at Default. However, if you have a specific printing need for an item's colors to either overprint or knock out items beneath it, you can apply Knockout or Overprint. Here are the icons, from left to right:

>> **Default:** Applies an appropriate trap value to best print this item when adjacent to another item. It will either *spread* (expand) the item a tiny amount to overlap the adjacent item, or *choke* (contract) the item to allow the adjacent item to overlap it.

>> **Knockout:** Punches a hole through everything beneath the item, so that there is no overlap.

>> **Overprint:** Forces the item to print on top of the items beneath it, potentially blending their inks together.

TIP

When printing in CMYK, sometimes the black doesn't look saturated enough. If you have a really important object that needs to look very black, try creating and applying a Rich Black color to it — one that includes a bit of cyan, magenta, and yellow, in addition to 100 percent black. Printing companies vary in their ink pref-erence for a Rich Black, so if you use several printers, or you don't know which printer will be printing your job(s), use 30C 30M 30Y 100K, and then be sure to tell your printer that you used a Rich Black. It's much easier for prepress operators to *change* the percentages of a Rich Black to their specifications than it is for them to *build and apply* one.

Creating Color Blends

In QuarkXPress, a *blend* is a transition from one color to another. Using the Color Blends palette, you can create a multicolor blend by specifying each blend color (known as a *color stop*), its shade and opacity, the pattern in which the colors blend, and the angle at which they blend relative to the box they're applied to. You can use any color in your project to build a blend. To create a blend, follow these steps:

1. **Choose Window ⇨ Color Blends to open the Color Blends palette, shown in Figure 15-4.**

2. **Select the box or boxes in your layout that you want to apply the blend to.**

3. **From the Type drop-down menu, choose a style of color blend: Axial, Radial, Rectangular, or Diamond.**

    The options and controls appropriate to your choice of blend are enabled in the palette.

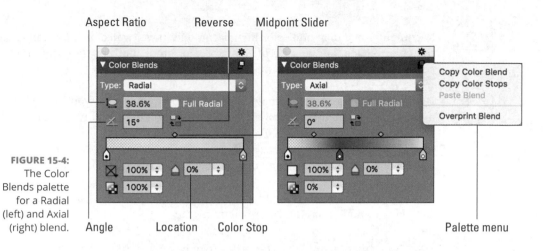

Aspect Ratio   Reverse   Midpoint Slider

FIGURE 15-4:
The Color
Blends palette
for a Radial
(left) and Axial
(right) blend.

Angle   Location   Color Stop   Palette menu

4. **Select from among the following options and controls to define your blend:**

- **Aspect Ratio:** Controls the shape of a Radial blend. The initial aspect ratio for each Radial blend you create depends on the shape of the box you selected. If you change the shape of a selected box, the aspect ratio will automatically adjust.

- **Full Radial:** Spreads the center color out to soften a Radial blend.

- **Angle:** Adjusts the angle of the blend within the box.

- **Reverse:** This icon reverses the color blend.

- **Gradient slider:** Use the slider to get a preview of how your blend will appear. Click and drag the color stop icons at the beginning and end of the gradient slider to change its location, or select any color stop and use the options below to adjust its color, shade, opacity, and location. These color stops define the location and attributes for each color in your blend. Drag the small diamond icon above two color stops to change the midpoint of the blend. To see the gradient change as you move the midpoint, select the diamond and then drag the Location slider.

- **To add a new color stop:** Click anywhere between two existing color stops. (A plus symbol appears next to your cursor when it's at a place where you can insert a new color stop.) Then you use the controls below the gradient slider to define the color, shade, opacity, and location of the new color stop.

TIP

To copy a blend to a different box, either choose Copy Color Blend from the Color Blends palette menu or create an Item Style that includes the color blend, as explained in Chapter 4.

Rectangular and diamond color blends can only have two colors. You can change the color, shade, and opacity of the two color stops, but not the location of the color stops or the midway point.

Here's something handy to know: When creating a color stop, you can also create a new color. Just Shift-click when adding the color stop. You can edit an existing color by double-clicking the color stop.

To delete a color stop, click and drag it down from the gradient slider.

To copy a color blend, color stops, or control overprinting, you can select the following options from the Color palette menu:

>> **Copy Color Blend:** Copies the entire color blend from the selected box.

>> **Copy Color Stops:** Copies only the color stops from the selected blend. You can then paste these color stops to another blend.

>> **Paste Blend:** Pastes the copied color blend onto the selected box.

>> **Paste Color Stops:** Pastes the copied color stops onto the existing blend in the selected box.

>> **Overprint Blend:** Turns on overprinting for the blend in the selected box to prevent it from knocking out the colors behind it.

Adjusting Opacity (Transparency)

In QuarkXPress, the amount that an item blocks your ability to see what is behind it is called *opacity*. An opacity setting of 100 percent means that the item completely blocks what's behind it. (It's 100 percent opaque!) An opacity setting of 10 percent means that you can see 90 percent of what's behind it.

Here are some important things to know about using opacity:

>> You can specify opacity anywhere you can specify a color. Usually, the opacity control is right next to the color control.

>> You can set different opacities for different parts of an item, such as each character of text, the frame, or the background.

>> Even drop shadows have opacity. Adjusting opacity is a good way to achieve a more realistic drop shadow.

>> A group of items can have its own opacity setting, in addition to the opacity settings of the items within the group. To adjust the opacity of a group in Windows, Item ⇨ Modify to open the Modify dialog box, click the Group tab, then adjust the value in the Group Opacity field; on a Mac, go to the Home tab of the Measurements palette and adjust the value in the Opacity field.

>> Each blend stop can have its own opacity setting, but you can also choose None for a color. This is the same as 0 percent opacity.

Adding Colors from Imported Pictures

When you import a picture that has custom colors defined in it (for example, spot colors), QuarkXPress adds those colors to the Colors palette and you can use them on items in your layout.

TIP

When you need to add colors used in Adobe Illustrator, InDesign, or other applications, just import the file into your QuarkXPress project. The file's custom colors come along with the picture. This trick also works with spot colors and duotones in Photoshop, and spot colors in EPS and PDF files.

Managing and Proofing Colors

QuarkXPress makes ensuring that the colors you want are the colors you get remarkably easy. The default settings are workably accurate, but you can also use professional color-management tools (or a consultant) to profile your exact input and output devices. This section tells you how to ensure that QuarkXPress knows a little about your display and that you know how to view your projects reasonably accurately.

Choosing your display profile

Both the Mac and Windows operating systems come with built-in calibration programs, but for best results, you should use an external measuring device such as a colorimeter or spectrophotometer (hand-sized gadgets that clamp onto your monitor and measure the colors it displays). Examples that cost under $100 include Pantone's ColorMunki Smile and DataColor's Spyder4Express. More expensive options include DataColor's SpyderPro and the Pantone i1 Display Pro.

To tell QuarkXPress which display profile to use, open QuarkXPress Preferences, and in the Display section of the Application section, select an option from the drop-down menu to choose your display profile. If you don't make a selection, QuarkXPress will use whatever profile your computer is currently using.

Soft proofing your layout

To see how your layout will look when output in various ways, choose View ⇨ Proof Output and select an option from the Proof Output menu, shown in Figure 15-5.

If you're working with a commercial printer, the printer may recommend one of the menu options such as Grayscale 100K, As Is, or In-RIP Separations. But generally you'll be fine with the first few:

>> **Grayscale:** Converts your colors to gray, which is useful if your layout might be printed on a black-and-white printer.

>> **Composite RGB:** Shows how your colors will look when printed on a printer that uses RGB data, such as a desktop color printer, or in a PDF.

>> **Composite CMYK:** Shows how your colors will look when printed on a four-color commercial press. Normally, use this when sending your project to a commercial press.

>> **Composite CMYK and Spot:** Shows how your colors will look when printed on a four-color commercial press with additional spot color inks. If your project includes spot colors as well as CMYK colors, use this.

>> **Custom Output Setups:** Figure 15-5 shows the "Jay's weird office printer" option is an output setup created from the profile provided by Epson for a color printer used in Jay's office. You can learn to create your own custom output setup in the next section.

TIP

If you find yourself often soft proofing to the same output setup, you can change QuarkXPress Preferences to always use that output setup when displaying your projects. To do that, go to the Color Manager pane in the Print Layout section in QuarkXPress Preferences and choose your output setup from the Proof Output drop-down menu, as shown in Figure 15-6.

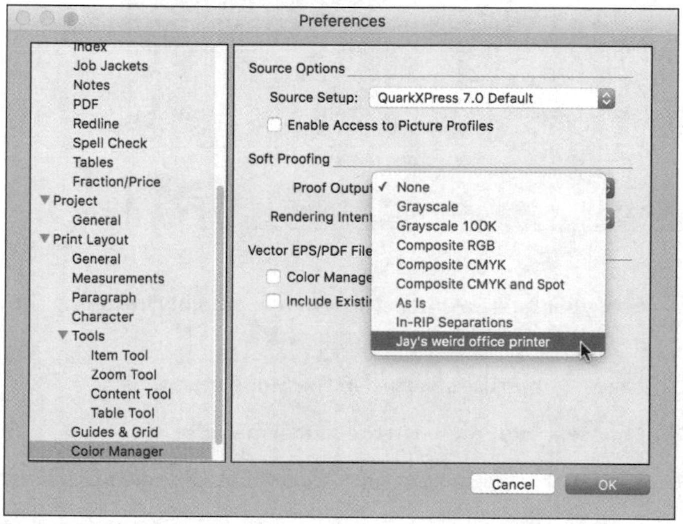

FIGURE 15-6:
The Proof Output menu in QuarkXPress Preferences.

Creating a custom output setup

If you have a profile for a printer you commonly use, you can create your own output setup that will appear in the Proof Output menu. You can then choose this output setup to see how your project will print on that printer. To create your own output setup, follow these steps:

1. **Get the profile for your printer and install it on your computer.**

   Printer manufacturers usually make the printer profile available on their websites, along with instructions for installing it.

2. **Choose Edit ⇨ Color Setups ⇨ Output to open the Default Output Setups dialog box.**

   The Default Output Setups dialog box appears.

3. **Click the New button.**

   The Edit Output Setup dialog box appears, as shown in Figure 15-7.

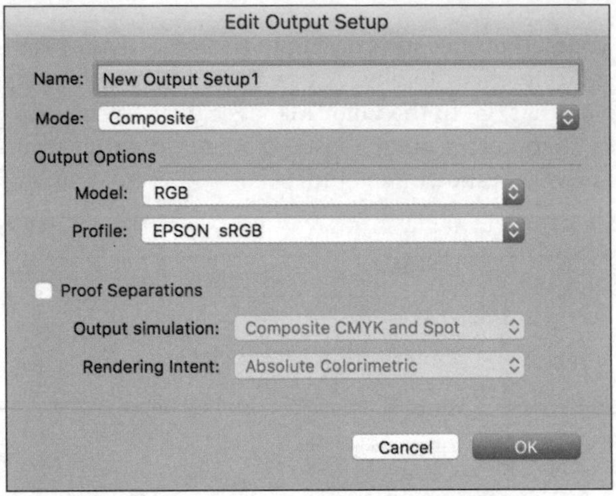

FIGURE 15-7
The Edit Output Setup dialog box.

4. **Give your new output setup a name, possibly including the kind of printer and its location in your office.**

5. **Leave Composite selected in the Mode menu.**

6. **Choose a color model in the Model menu.**

   You usually choose RGB. If the printer is black-and-white, choose Grayscale.

7. **In the Profile menu, choose the profile for your printer that you installed in Step 1.**

8. **Click OK.**

   Your new output setup is added to the Proof Output menu.

Sharing color setups

To copy a Source setup from another QuarkXPress project, choose Edit ⇨ Color Setups ⇨ Source and click the Append button. Navigate to the project and choose the Source setups that you want to copy.

To import or export an Output setup, choose Edit ⇨ Color Setups ⇨ Output and click the Import or Export button. This is useful when your printing company provides an output setup for its press.

4

Getting Ready for Your Big Debut

Chapter **16**

Prepping to Print

When working with a complex application such as QuarkXPress, you have dozens of choices to make in the Print dialog box, based on what you've created, what kind of printer you're using, and what process you use to print your final product. This chapter presents what you need to know to work with the QuarkXPress Print dialog box and all its panes, as well as what you can ignore.

This chapter also tells you how to customize an Output Style for each printing scenario that you use repeatedly, saving you the hassle of redoing that setup every time. And in case you need to ship your project to a commercial printer, you can follow the steps in this chapter that tell you how to export your press-ready file. Finally, sometimes a preview of your printed images or fonts doesn't look quite right, and I give you some tips on how to investigate and resolve those issues.

Understanding the Print Dialog Box

QuarkXPress groups your printing options into logical panels that change according to the printer you choose. If you choose a desktop inkjet printer, for example, your options will be different from those for a PostScript laser printer or imagesetter, as shown in Figure 16-1. The first few panes are likely the only ones you'll ever use, unless you're running an output service or a printing company.

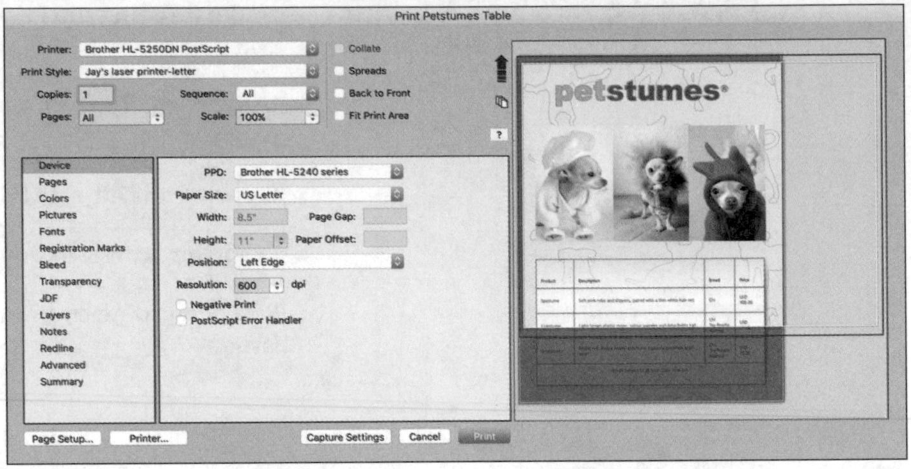

FIGURE 16-1:
The Print dialog box has 13 panes to control output, plus a Summary pane.

No matter which pane you're working on, the top area of the dialog box remains the same, showing a preview of how your page will print on your chosen printer and paper, and providing access to some universal options. To get ready to print, you first choose your printer and, optionally, choose a print style for your current print job.

TIP

Print Styles are collections of print settings that you can save for future use. To create one, just make all the choices you need, in all the panes, and then choose New Print Output Style from the Print Style drop-down menu in the Print dialog box. You can also create and edit Print Styles by choosing Edit ⇨ Output Styles.

Making your way down the options, indicate how many copies you want, which pages to print, and at what scaling percentage. Then select any of the following check boxes that you need:

>> **Collate:** If you're printing multiple copies, Collate lets you print them in collated sets rather than as multiple copies of each page.

>> **Spreads:** If your layout has facing pages (as in a magazine), Spreads will print those pages side-by-side on your paper.

>> **Back to Front:** If your printer delivers pages to you with the image facing up, select Back to Front so that the finished job will have your pages in their correct order.

>> **Fit Print Area:** To shrink or enlarge your page to fit the printable area of the paper in your printer, select Fit Print Area. When you enable Fit Print Area, QuarkXPress calculates the necessary scaling and helpfully displays it in the Scale field.

The preview area of the Print dialog box has several helpful features:

- ❯❯ The green outline indicates the printable area for your printer and paper.

- ❯❯ The red area appears when any of your page items extend into the nonprintable area of your printer and paper.

- ❯❯ When you move your mouse over the preview area, the page number of the page being previewed appears at the top. Click the arrow in the top-right or left corner to change the preview to the next or previous page.

- ❯❯ Sadly, on Windows, the page preview area does not display the actual items on the layout pages. Instead, it shows only the shape and orientation of the pages in relation to the paper.

TIP

Click the question mark icon next at left of the preview to see a legend that lists the meaning of each colored area and mark.

Device pane

If you're printing to a printer that understands the PostScript language, the Device pane, shown in Figure 16-1, lets you choose the appropriate PPD (PostScript Printer Description) file for that printer. The PPD tells QuarkXPress the details of your printer and what it's capable of doing. My printer, for example, lets me choose a paper size and the position I'd like the page to appear on it, along with the resolution (dpi) that I want my printer to use.

Also in the Device pane is the Negative Print option, which reverses blacks and whites and is for printing on film.

And finally, for a document that won't print, the PostScript Error Handler option is incredibly handy. It tells QuarkXPress that if a PostScript error occurs when printing this layout, please stop printing after the last successful page item and then print the page position and attributes of the page item that caused the error.

Pages pane

The Pages pane, shown in Figure 16-2, lets you rotate or flip the page on the paper, print multiple pages as small thumbnails on one sheet, and force QuarkXPress to Include Blank Pages (which would otherwise be ignored during printing). If your document page is larger than the paper in your printer, you can use the Page Tiling option to split it into pieces that print on multiple sheets, which you can then tape together.

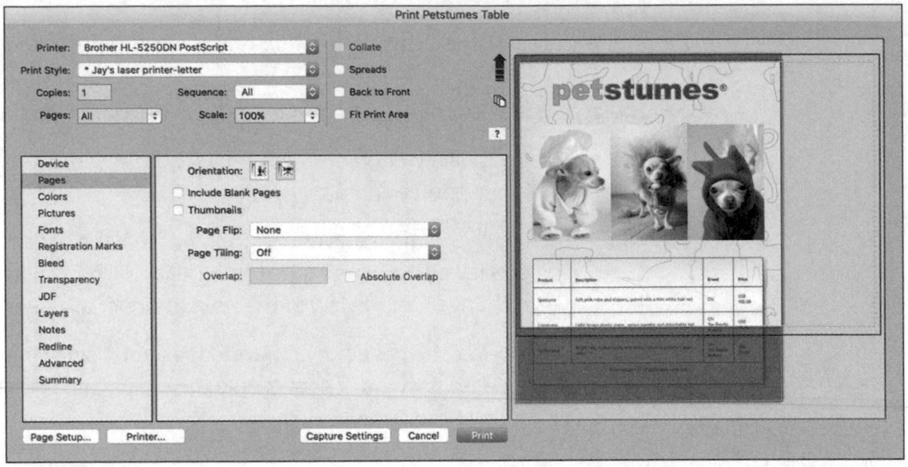

FIGURE 16-2:
A preview
in the Pages
pane, warning
me that my
paper is turned
sideways.

Colors pane

The Colors pane lets you control how colors are printed. If you're using a laser printer, you'll most often use the Composite mode and then, under Setup, you can choose either Grayscale or Composite RGB, as shown in Figure 16-3. You also choose Printer under the Halftone pop-up menu, unless you want to see how your images will look if printed with different halftone frequencies; in that case, you choose Conventional and then select the Frequency you want. These settings can be fun to experiment with, but they're mainly used by professionals who understand how images print on a printing press. If you're using a color inkjet printer, these controls and the ones below them will be grayed out.

The Colors pane also lets you print separate pages for each color used in your document. Printing professionals use these controls to print the plates they need for reproducing your artwork on a printing press. Designers can use this pane to see whether they've inadvertently used colors they didn't intend to use, such as the extra Pantone 371 spot plate shown in Figure 16-3. The lower box lists only the colors applied to page items; use the check boxes to print only the plates you want.

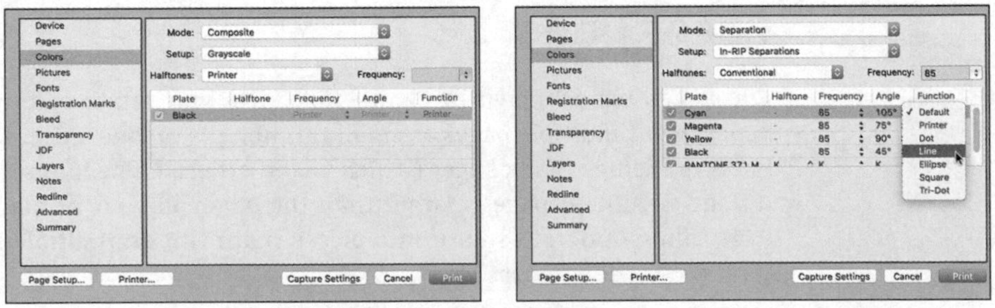

FIGURE 16-3:
The Colors
pane of the
Print dialog
box, in
Composite
mode (left) and
Separation
mode (right).

TIP

When printing black text on a desktop printer, you may notice that the text appears dark gray instead of truly black. To force your black text to print completely black, choose Grayscale 100 instead of Grayscale in the Setup drop-down menu of the Colors pane (refer to Figure 16-3). The reason the text prints lighter when Grayscale is selected is that QuarkXPress is attempting to adjust for *dot gain* (which occurs when printing ink soaks into the paper and spreads out). By lightening the black ever so slightly, QuarkXPress is making sure that your text doesn't appear fatter than you intended when it's reproduced on a printing press. Unless you intend to hand the prints from your desktop printer to a commercial printer for reproduction on a printing press, choose Grayscale 100 when you want to see truly black text.

Pictures pane

The Pictures pane, shown in Figure 16-4, controls how the pictures on your pages will print. Under Output, you usually choose Normal. But you can also choose Low Resolution to speed printing when picture quality isn't paramount, or choose Rough if all you need are boxes that show where pictures will be.

The Data field is normally used for troubleshooting. Keep it on Binary or Clean 8-Bit unless you have an older PC network that requires ASCII (an extremely rare situation).

The Overprint EPS/PDF Black option forces every black object in an imported EPS or PDF file to print on top of the items beneath it. This option is used mostly by output providers.

The Full Resolution TIFF Output option tells QuarkXPress to send all the data in imported TIFF images to the printer, rather than downsampling them to a resolution appropriate for your printer. Output takes longer this way, but using this type of image can help if you see unexpected blocky artifacts in your printed TIFF images.

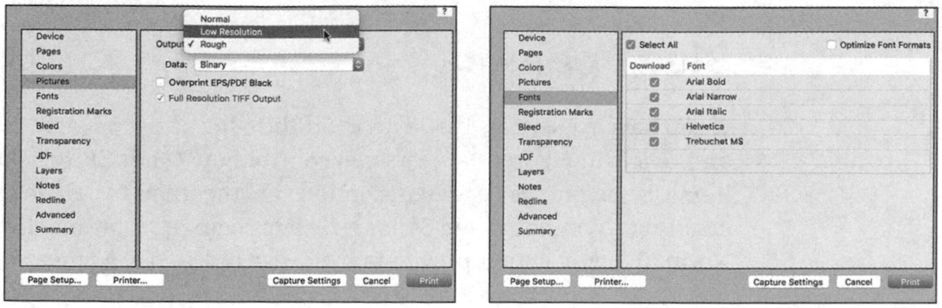

FIGURE 16-4:
The Pictures pane (left) and the Fonts pane (right) of the Print dialog box.

Fonts pane

The Fonts pane, shown in Figure 16-4, is useful only if you manually downloaded some fonts to your printer's memory or hard drive. If you have, you can deselect those fonts to improve printing time. If you're using enormous Asian or Arabic fonts that contain thousands of characters, the Optimize Font Formats check box is your friend — it will send only the data necessary for your specific document, rather than the entire font.

Registration Marks pane

The Registration Marks pane, shown in Figure 16-5, adds registration and crop marks to your page when you're printing on paper that's larger than your page. Notice that the preview in Figure 16-5 indicates that my paper is too small to print registration marks around the page. If you click and hold on the question mark at left of the preview, you see a legend that explains what each of the colors indicates. As you may have guessed, red indicates areas that won't fit on your paper.

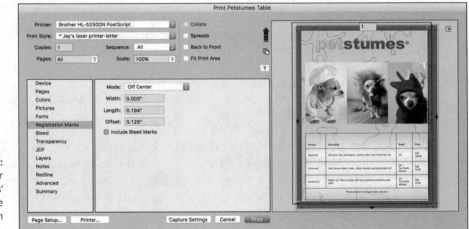

FIGURE 16-5: Control your printers' marks in the Registration Marks panel.

Bleed pane

If you have page items that extend off the edge of the page, the Bleed pane, shown on the left in Figure 16-6, lets you control how QuarkXPress should handle those items. Selecting the Page Items option cuts the items off at the page edge, whereas enabling Asymmetric and Symmetric lets them print beyond the edge of the page. Normally, only output providers make use of the Bleed pane.

Transparency pane

The Transparency pane, shown in Figure 16-6, is used by output professionals to achieve the results intended by designers, but which are often mucked up because of the way PostScript works. You use this pane to control the resolution of transparency effects.

FIGURE 16-6: The Bleed pane (left) and Transparency pane (right).

JDF pane

You use the JDF pane, shown in Figure 16-7, when your project is part of a system that controls the colors, styles, and output specifications using the Job Jackets feature in QuarkXPress. Most people don't use it.

Layers pane

The Layers pane, shown in Figure 16-7, lets you change the visibility of the layers in your document. If you need to print only certain layers, this feature is more efficient than changing the visibility of the layers in the Layers palette (and then remembering to change it back after printing!). Instead, select the check boxes here for layers you want to print. Your changes won't affect your document after printing unless you also select the check box labeled Apply to Layout. Then, any changes you make here will also occur when you switch back to your document.

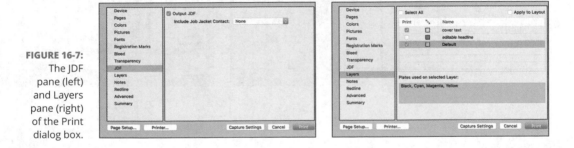

FIGURE 16-7: The JDF pane (left) and Layers pane (right) of the Print dialog box.

Notes and Redline panes

The Notes feature lets you add notes to your layout that normally don't print unless you select the check boxes in the Notes pane. Same goes for the Redline feature, which tracks changes to text, and you can choose to print its tracking marks here. Both the Notes and Redline panes are shown in Figure 16-8.

Advanced pane

The Advanced pane (see Figure 16-9, on the left) provides access to some advanced features in your printer. In this case, my laser printer can interpret either PostScript Level 2 or 3. A different printer will have different features in this Advanced pane.

Summary pane

The Summary pane, shown on the right in Figure 16-9, summarizes all the choices you've made in the previous panes. One bit of useful information here that isn't easily available elsewhere is the Imageable Area of your current printer and paper. This is the area on the paper that your currently selected printer is capable of using.

Buttons

The buttons along the bottom of the Print dialog box are also quite useful. Some of your printer's options may be available only with the Page Setup and Print buttons, shown in Figures 16-10 and 16-11 (Mac) or the Properties button (Windows).

For example, an inkjet printer has options such as the printer presets, color management, ink, and resolution settings shown in Figure 16-10; a PostScript laser printer may have printer-specific options such as pages-per-sheet, two-sided printing, and resolution, as shown in Figure 16-11.

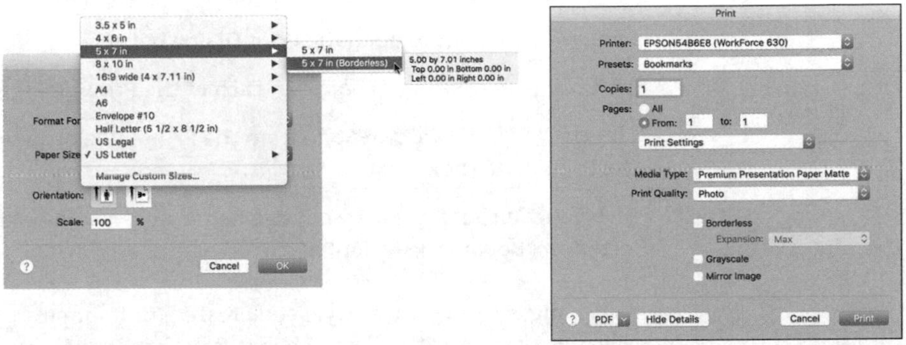

FIGURE 16-10: The Page Setup (left) and Print (right) dialog boxes for a color inkjet printer on a Mac.

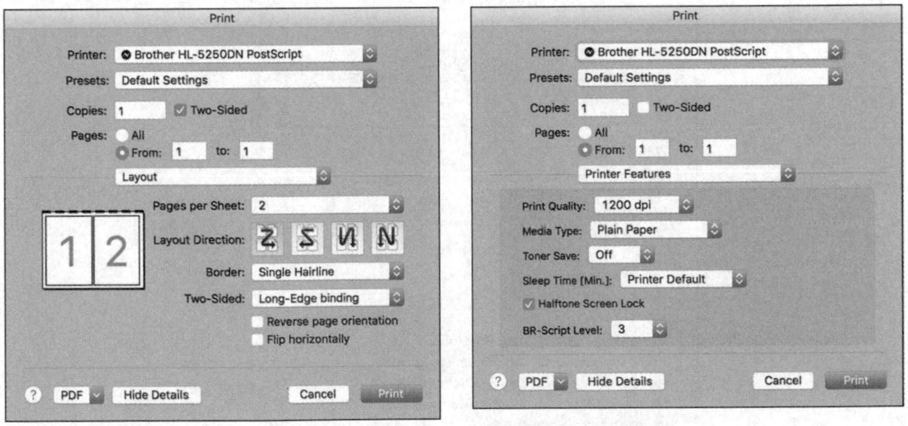

FIGURE 16-11: The Printer-specific window of the Print dialog box for a PostScript laser printer on a Mac.

The Print dialog box may even remind you of a change you need to make in the document. So the Capture Settings button will become a good friend — it tells the Print dialog to remember everything you've done and then return you to your document. When you open the Print dialog box again, your previous settings are maintained.

Creating an Output Style

In the real world, you're likely to only have one or two common uses for each printer you own. Smart QuarkXPress users create an Output Style for each printing scenario and then choose it from the Output Style drop-down in the Print dialog box whenever you need it.

Creating an Output Style is almost too simple — just follow these steps:

1. **Open a project that you would use for the kind of Output Style you want to create.**

2. **Choose File ⇨ Print to open the Print Dialog box.**

3. **Make all your preferred choices in each of the Print dialog panes.**

4. **Choose New Print Output Style from the Print Style drop-down menu in the Print dialog box.**

5. **Give your Output Style a descriptive name, such as "Jay's laser printer-letter" or "Bookmarks-color-8x6."**

To make changes to an Output Style you created, or to import or export your Output Styles for sharing with others, choose Edit ⇨ Output Styles to open the dialog box shown in Figure 16-12.

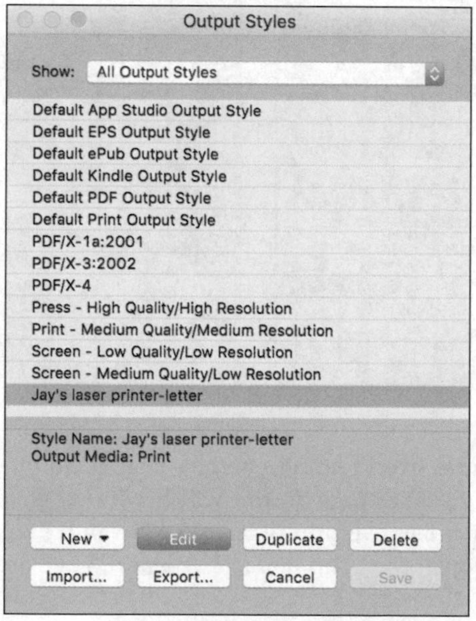

FIGURE 16-12: The Output Styles dialog box.

>> Click the Edit button to make changes to the selected Output Style.

>> Click the Export button to export the selected Output Style to share with others. In the resulting dialog box, give your Output Style a name in the Save As field and choose a location to save it.

>> Click the Import button and navigate to the location of the exported Output Style to import it into your copy of QuarkXPress.

Working with a Commercial Printer

When the time comes to send your project off to a commercial printer, the safest approach is to send both a press-ready PDF of each layout and the native QuarkXPress file with all its fonts and linked graphics.

Exporting a press-ready PDF

A *press-ready* PDF is a version of your QuarkXPress layout in PDF format that you can safely give to an output provider (such as a commercial printer) to print your project. This PDF file is generated with all the correct options for a commercial press, such as press-quality image resolution, page bleeds, and printers' marks.

To export a press-ready PDF, follow these steps:

1. **Choose Utilities ⇨ Usage to open the Usage dialog box and make sure that all your linked pictures are listed as OK.**

   If they're listed as Missing, relink them; if Modified, update them as explained in Chapter 13.

2. **Choose Export ⇨ Layout as PDF to open the Export as PDF dialog box, shown in Figure 16-13.**

3. **From the PDF Style drop-down menu, choose either Press or one of the PDF/X options if your printer recommends one.**

4. **(Optional) Select the Open PDF after Export check box to view your exported PDF in your computer's default PDF reader application.**

5. **If you're really brave or know a lot about PDF, click Options for access to a zillion ways to customize your PDF; otherwise, ignore this.**

6. **Click Save and choose a location on your computer to save this PDF file.**

7. **Repeat for any additional layouts in the project that you want to send to the printer.**

Your exported PDF file is now ready to be delivered to your printing company in whatever way you normally send them — via FTP; uploading to the printer's web server; attaching to an email message; uploading to Dropbox and sending the printer a link via email; copying to a thumb drive; attaching to a carrier pigeon; and so on.

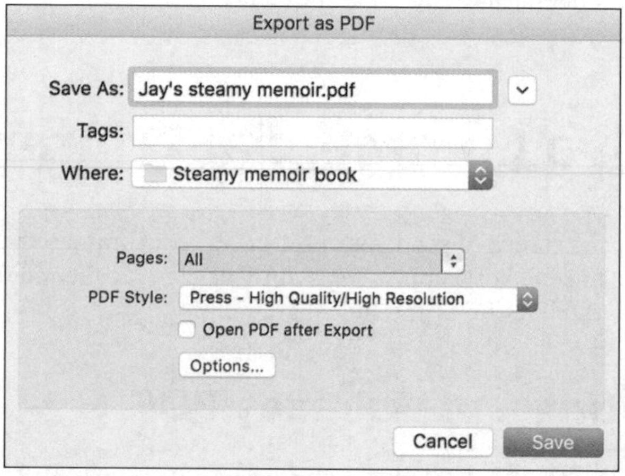

Export as PDF

Save As: Jay's steamy memoir.pdf

Tags:

Where: Steamy memoir book

Pages: All

PDF Style: Press - High Quality/High Resolution

☐ Open PDF after Export

Options...

Cancel   Save

FIGURE 16-13:
The Export as PDF dialog box.

WARNING

Even though your operating system lets you export a PDF from within the Print dialog box, never use the Print dialog box to create a PDF from QuarkXPress. When you use the Print dialog box, QuarkXPress assumes that you want to print directly to a printer and may not provide the correct data to your operating system's PDF generator.

HOW TO EXPORT A POSTSCRIPT FILE

Some workflows require using a third-party PDF creation tool such as Distiller to generate a PDF. In those workflows, you must export a PostScript file from QuarkXPress to feed into it. Oddly, to generate a PostScript file from QuarkXPress, you must use the PDF Export feature, but first you must set QuarkXPress Preferences to create a PostScript file instead of a PDF. To do that, open QuarkXPress Preferences (choose QuarkXPress ➪ Preferences on a Mac; Edit ➪ Preferences in Windows). Under the Application section, click PDF to display the PDF preferences pane and enable the radio button named Create PostScript File for Later Distilling. After you save and close the Preferences dialog box, QuarkXPress exports a PostScript file instead of a PDF file when you follow the steps in the "Exporting a press-ready PDF" section in this chapter. Just be sure to switch it back before you want to export a PDF file from QuarkXPress!

Using Collect for Output

The Collect for Output feature collects your project, any linked pictures, the fonts it uses — everything necessary for someone else to open and edit your project in QuarkXPress, along with a helpful report about it.

TECHNICAL STUFF

Quark added the multiple layouts feature in version 6, and finally in QuarkXPress 2015 (five versions and 12 years later), Quark added the capability to collect all the layouts and their assets with the Collect for Output feature. Rejoice!

To use the Collect for Output feature, follow these steps:

1. **Choose File ⇨ Collect for Output to open the Collect for Output dialog box, shown in Figure 16-14.**

2. **Select any or all layouts you want to export.**

3. **Select all the check boxes under Collect, unless you have a specific reason not to.**

   If you deselect Layouts as Project, each layout will be exported as a separate QuarkXPress file.

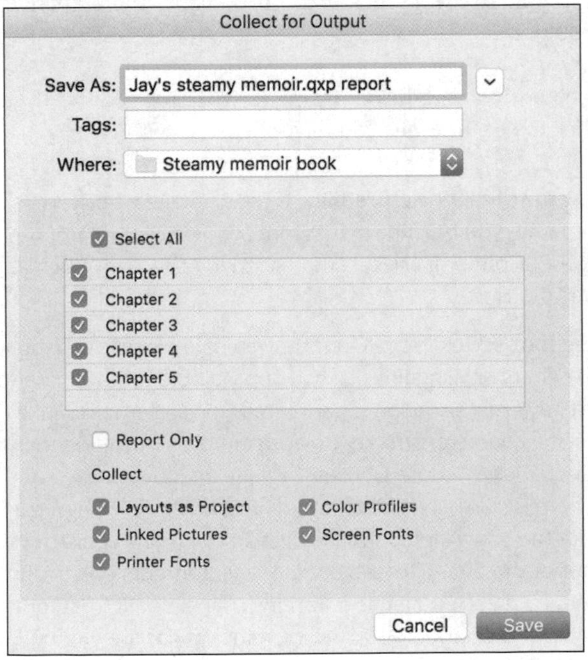

FIGURE 16-14: The Collect for Output dialog box.

Troubleshooting Your Print Results

Alas, sometimes despite your best efforts to dot all your *i*'s and cross every single one of your *t*'s, something goes awry. If your prints don't turn out the way you expect, read on for some ideas of what might be going wrong and how to fix them.

If your pictures look blurry or pixelated, try the following:

>> Check the resolution of the pictures you imported. Select one on the page and look in the Home/Classic tab of the Measurements palette. At the far right end of the bottom row is an Effective Image Resolution value (the icon looks like a grid of gray squares). If the resolution is lower than about 240 ppi and the print is blurry or pixelated, you need to either obtain a higher resolution image and reimport it or reduce the size of the picture box in QuarkXPress.

>> In the Pictures pane of the Print dialog box, make sure that you choose Normal and not Low Resolution in the Output drop-down menu.

TECHNICAL STUFF

The Effective Image Resolution is simply the original resolution of the image multiplied by the scaling factor used on that picture box. For example, if you import a 300 ppi picture and enlarge it to 200 percent, the Effective Image Resolution becomes 150 ppi. If you reduce it to 50 percent, the Effective Image Resolution becomes 600 ppi.

Another problem you might be having is with your fonts. If your fonts come out wrong, check to see whether you have these issues:

>> **Missing font in EPS picture files:** If you imported a picture in EPS format and it uses a font, you must have that font active on your computer when you print your layout or it will substitute with another font, such as the dreaded Courier.

>> **Missing font styles:** Not all fonts have a bold or italic variation (think about Zapf Dingbats or Wingdings). If you apply a bold or italic style to a font that doesn't have that variation, QuarkXPress may attempt to fake the effect by making the characters thicker (to appear bold) or leaning them over (to appear oblique). Choose Utilities ⇨ Usage and look at the Fonts pane. If a font has a warning triangle next to it like the one shown in Figure 16-15, select it and click the Show First button. Select an offending character on your page and look at the Character tab of the Measurements palette. If the Bold or Italic button is engaged and it has a warning triangle on it, that font doesn't have that style, and QuarkXPress is faking it for you, as shown for Zapf Dingbats in Figure 16-15.

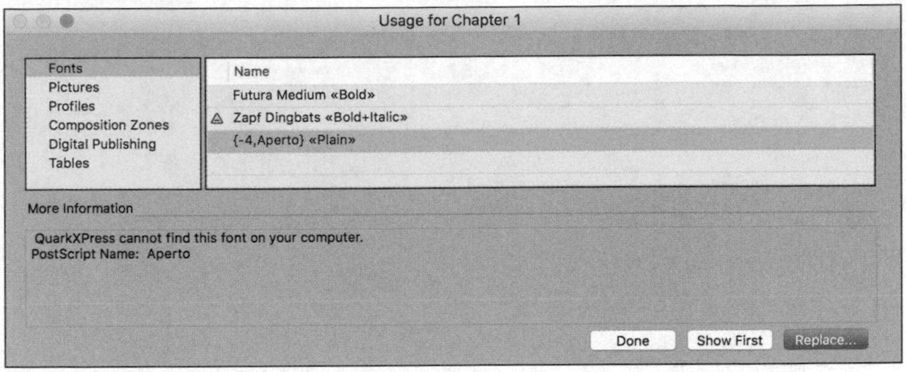

The following table shows the Usage dialog box:

	Name
Fonts	Futura Medium «Bold»
Pictures	⚠ Zapf Dingbats «Bold+Italic»
Profiles	{-4,Aperto} «Plain»
Composition Zones	
Digital Publishing	
Tables	

Usage for Chapter 1

More Information

QuarkXPress cannot find this font on your computer.
PostScript Name: Aperto

Done   Show First   Replace...

FIGURE 16-15:
The Fonts pane of the Usage dialog box.

REMEMBER

This chapter highlights the most important and common settings in the Print dialog box. For a complete explanation of absolutely everything, see my "QuarkX-Press 8 Essential Training" at Lynda.com. The features in version 8 are practically identical to those in QuarkXPress 2016.

Chapter **17**

Going Digital: PDF, Hyperlinks, ePUB, and HTML5 Animations

Producing a QuarkXPress project for digital media is like pushing a ball of spaghetti: Most of it winds up where you want it, but some of it doesn't. It's not Quark's fault; the digital media landscape changes every day. Instead, it's up to you to figure out where you want to go with your project and then adjust it for that output.

In this chapter, you find out how to export your QuarkXPress layout in several digital formats, and how to set up your document to take advantage of the unique capabilities of each. You learn to add bookmarks and hyperlinks to PDFs, prepare your layout for exporting to reflowable ePub and Kindle e-book formats, and export to PDF and fixed-layout e-book formats. The chapter also tells you how to add HTML5 interactivity and animations to your layout, and how to export it as an HTML5 publication. In addition, I introduce you to creating native mobile apps using Quark's App Studio. But first, I provide a quick explanation of how to export your pages as images to use on websites, social media outlets, and other publications.

Here we go!

Exporting Pages as Images

When you need to create an image of one or more pages in your QuarkXPress layout, you can print and scan them, or you can export them to PDF and open the PDF in Photoshop. A much easier way is available, though: You can export them as images. Just follow these steps:

1. **Choose File ⇨ Export ⇨ Image.**

   The Export Pages as Images dialog box appears.

2. **Choose a location for your exported image(s), choose which page(s) you want to export, and then click the Options button.**

   The Export Image Options dialog box appears, as shown in Figure 17-1.

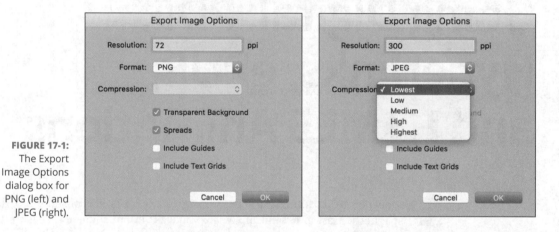

FIGURE 17-1:
The Export Image Options dialog box for PNG (left) and JPEG (right).

3. **In the Export Image Options dialog box, enter a resolution and choose a format: PNG or JPG.**

4. **If you choose JPG format, use the Compression drop-down menu to choose a level of compression.**

   To create a higher-quality image, choose a lower level of compression.

5. **Select the check boxes for the things you want to include in the image:**

   - **Transparent Background:** PNG supports transparent backgrounds, so this option creates a transparent background for any item that has a background of "none," including the empty areas of your page.

   - **Spreads:** If your layout uses Facing Pages, this option outputs all the pages in a spread as one image.

- **Include Guides:** Includes the guides used on your page, which normally don't print. Use this to show a colleague where the guides are.

- **Include Text Grids:** Includes the text grids on pages and in text boxes, which normally don't print. Use this to show a colleague the text grids on your pages.

6. **Click OK to export your image.**

Exporting to PDF

PDF has become the *de facto* standard for sharing complex documents with people who don't have the application you used to create them. It also has powerful interactive features such as bookmarks and hyperlinks that you can generate directly from QuarkXPress.

Creating a PDF file

To export your QuarkXPress layout in PDF format, follow these steps:

1. **Open the Export as PDF dialog box, shown in Figure 17-2, in one of these ways:**

   - Choose File ⇨ Export ⇨ Layout as PDF.

   - Control-click (Mac) or right-click (Windows) in an empty area of the page or pasteboard and choose Export ⇨ Layout as PDF from the context menu that appears.

   - At the bottom of the project window, click the Export arrow, which appears at the left of the horizontal scroll bar. Then choose Layout as PDF.

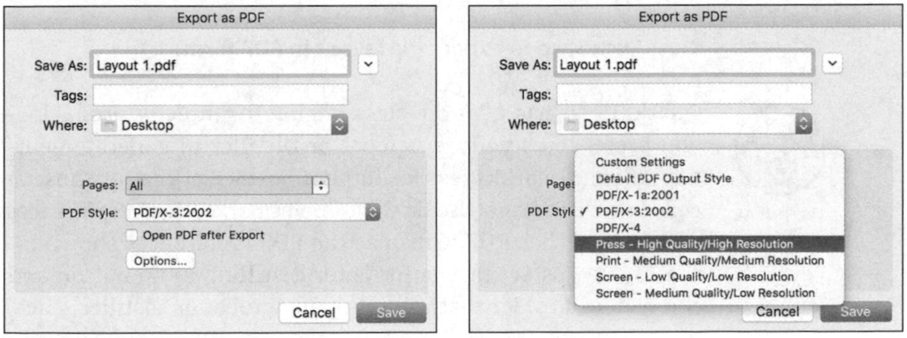

FIGURE 17-2:
The Export as PDF dialog box, with PDF Style drop-down menu exposed (right).

2. **Enter the pages you want to export in the Pages field.**

3. **Choose a preset from the PDF Style drop-down menu.**

4. **(Optional) Select the Open PDF after Export check box to automatically open the exported PDF in your default PDF reader application.**

5. **To examine or customize the PDF Export settings, click the Options button.**

   The PDF Export Options dialog box, shown in Figure 17-3, appears with the default settings for the Screen PDF Style (left) and with the Hyperlink Appearance options selected (right).

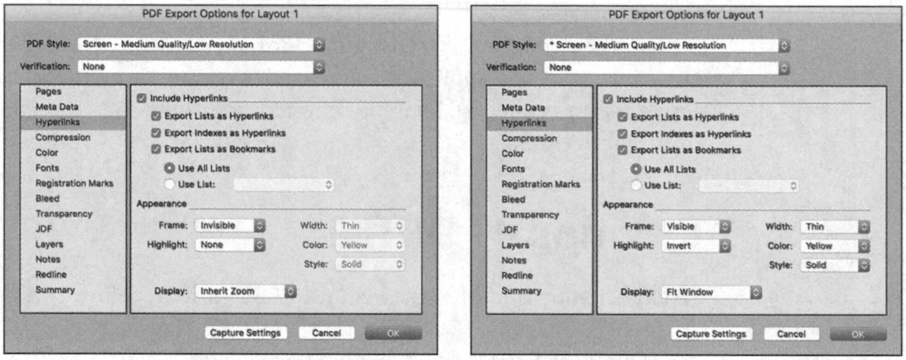

FIGURE 17-3: The PDF Export Options dialog box.

6. **Change any of the hundreds of options for your PDF file.**

   In the example in Figure 17-3, the Appearance options are changed to alter the appearance of the hyperlinks in the PDF, and to fit the exported PDF into the PDF reader application's window when it opens.

7. **If you need to cancel the PDF export to make changes to the layout, click the Capture Settings button.**

   QuarkXPress will remember the changes the next time you open the Export as PDF dialog box.

8. **Click Save to export the layout in PDF format.**

QuarkXPress has a world-class engine for directly producing PDFs. However, if you prefer to use Adobe Acrobat or Distiller to generate your PDF, you can also export your QuarkXPress layout as a PostScript file for those applications to process into PDF format. To do that, open QuarkXPress Preferences, and in the Application area, click PDF to display the PDF Preferences shown in Figure 17-4. Select the Create PostScript File for Later Distilling radio button and optionally choose the Watched Folder that you set up in Acrobat or Distiller. Click OK, and from then on, when you choose Export ⇨ Layout to PDF, QuarkXPress will export a PostScript file instead of a PDF.

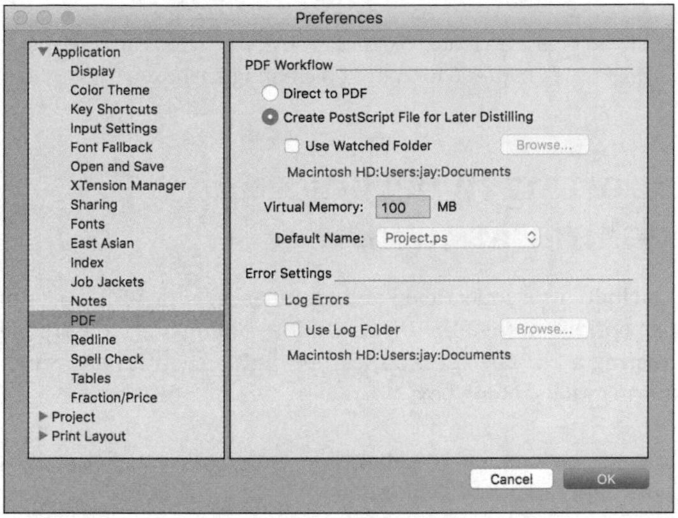

FIGURE 17-4:
The PDF area of the Preferences dialog box.

The Preferences dialog box shows:

Application
- Display
- Color Theme
- Key Shortcuts
- Input Settings
- Font Fallback
- Open and Save
- XTension Manager
- Sharing
- Fonts
- East Asian
- Index
- Job Jackets
- Notes
- **PDF**
- Redline
- Spell Check
- Tables
- Fraction/Price
- ► Project
- ► Print Layout

PDF Workflow
- ○ Direct to PDF
- ● Create PostScript File for Later Distilling
  - ☐ Use Watched Folder   Browse...
  - Macintosh HD:Users:jay:Documents
- Virtual Memory: 100 MB
- Default Name: Project.ps

Error Settings
- ☐ Log Errors
  - ☐ Use Log Folder   Browse...
  - Macintosh HD:Users:jay:Documents

Cancel   OK

TIP

To control the way QuarkXPress names your exported PDF files, open QuarkXPress Preferences, and in the Application area, click PDF to display the PDF Preferences shown in Figure 17-5. Choose a naming style from the Default Name drop-down menu.

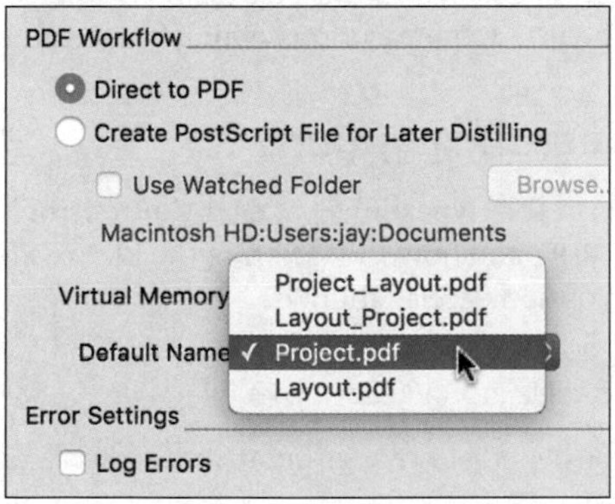

FIGURE 17-5:
The Default Name options in the PDF area of the Preferences dialog box.

PDF Workflow
- ● Direct to PDF
- ○ Create PostScript File for Later Distilling
  - ☐ Use Watched Folder   Browse.
  - Macintosh HD:Users:jay:Documents
- Virtual Memory
- Default Name
  - Project_Layout.pdf
  - Layout_Project.pdf
  - ✓ Project.pdf
  - Layout.pdf

Error Settings
- ☐ Log Errors

Using Interactive PDF Features

>> If you create Hyperlinks in QuarkXPress, you can include them when you export the layout to PDF format. See the next section, "Exporting hyperlinks and bookmarks to PDF," for more on hyperlinks.

>> If you use the List feature in QuarkXPress, your lists — for example, your table of contents — can also be converted to PDF bookmarks, hyperlinks, or both. See Chapter 6 for more on Lists.

>> If you create an index in QuarkXPress, the index can be hyperlinked in the PDF. See Chapter 6 for more on creating an index.

Exporting hyperlinks and bookmarks to PDF

To include hyperlinks, lists, and an index in your PDF, you simply need to select those options in the PDF Export Options dialog box (refer to Figure 17-3). See the "Creating a PDF file" section, earlier in this chapter, for more details on the PDF Export Options dialog box.

The next sections tell you about the options you need to consider if you want to export hyperlinks and bookmarks.

Choosing a PDF Style

The only preset PDF Styles that include hyperlinks are Screen – Medium Quality/ Low Resolution and Screen – Low Quality/Low Resolution. If your PDF is destined for onscreen viewing, just use one of these Screen PDF Styles and you'll be good to go. If you need the images in your PDF to have higher quality, use Print – Medium Quality/Medium Resolution instead and select all the Hyperlinks options in the Hyperlinks section of the PDF Export Options dialog box, as shown in Figure 17-3.

Setting PDF Appearance options

The Appearance options in the Hyperlinks pane let you control how the hyperlinks display in the exported PDF, and how the PDF fills the PDF reader window when it opens. The Appearance options are as follows:

>> **Frame:** Places a rectangle around each hyperlink.

>> **Highlight:** Makes the hyperlinks change appearance when a reader moves the mouse over them.

>> **Width, Color, and Style:** Determine the appearance of the frame.

>> **Display:** Tells the PDF reader application how to display the page when it opens. Inherit Zoom uses the current zoom level in QuarkXPress; Fit Window fits the entire page in the PDF reader window; Fit Width fits the page width; and Fit Length fits the page length.

Exporting an entire book to PDF

If you're using the Books palette while building a multichapter book, as shown in Figure 17-6 (see Chapter 6 for more on building a book), you can export all the chapters as one PDF. To do that, follow these steps:

1. Select all the chapters or make sure that no chapters are selected.

2. Make sure that the Single File check box is selected.

3. Click the Export as PDF button or choose Export Book as PDF from the Books palette menu.

4. Choose your PDF options as explained in earlier sections and click Save.

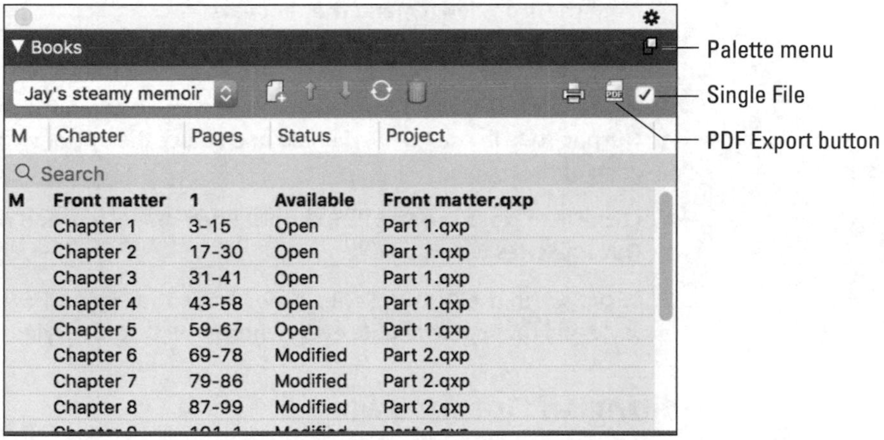

FIGURE 17-6: The Books palette with no chapter selected.

Labels pointing to the palette: Palette menu, Single File, PDF Export button

Palette contents:

M	Chapter	Pages	Status	Project
M	Front matter	1	Available	Front matter.qxp
	Chapter 1	3–15	Open	Part 1.qxp
	Chapter 2	17–30	Open	Part 1.qxp
	Chapter 3	31–41	Open	Part 1.qxp
	Chapter 4	43–58	Open	Part 1.qxp
	Chapter 5	59–67	Open	Part 1.qxp
	Chapter 6	69–78	Modified	Part 2.qxp
	Chapter 7	79–86	Modified	Part 2.qxp
	Chapter 8	87–99	Modified	Part 2.qxp

Creating and Editing PDF Output Styles

The PDF Export dialog box includes PDF Output Styles to cover the most common situations, but you can also create your own when exporting a PDF or any time in the Output Styles dialog box.

Creating an Output Style while exporting a PDF

To create a new PDF Output Style while exporting a PDF, follow these steps:

1. Choose File ⇨ Export as PDF.

The PDF Export dialog box opens.

2. Click the Options button in the PDF Export dialog box and select the options you want from each of the panes.

3. Choose New PDF Output Style from the PDF Style drop-down menu.

4. Enter a name for your new PDF Output Style in the Name field.

The style will appear everywhere PDF Output Styles can be used.

Creating an Output Style using the Output Styles dialog box

To create a new PDF Output Style by using the Output Styles dialog box, follow these steps:

1. Choose Edit ⇨ Output Styles to open the Output Styles dialog box.

2. In the Edit Output Styles dialog box, click the New button and choose PDF from the drop-down menu that appears.

This opens the Edit PDF Output Style dialog box.

3. In the Edit PDF Output Style dialog box, enter a name for your PDF Output Style in the PDF Style field and select the options you want from each of the panes.

4. Click OK to close the Edit PDF Output Style dialog box and return to the Output Styles dialog box.

5. Click Save in the Output Styles dialog box to save your new PDF Output Style and make it available everywhere PDF Output Styles can be used.

Editing an Output Style

To edit an existing Output Style, follow these steps:

1. Choose Edit ⇨ Output Styles to open the Output Styles dialog box.

2. In the Edit Output Styles dialog box, select the PDF Output Style you want to edit and click the Edit button.

This opens the Edit PDF Output Style dialog box.

3. In the Edit PDF Output Style dialog box, you can change the name of your PDF Output Style in the PDF Style field and select the options you want from each of the panes.

4. Click OK to close the Edit PDF Output Style dialog box and return to the Output Styles dialog box.

5. Click Save in the Output Styles dialog box to save the edits to your PDF Output Style and make it available everywhere PDF Output Styles can be used.

Deleting, sharing, and importing

Here are a few more tasks you might need to accomplish:

>> **To delete an existing Output Style:** Follow the steps in the previous instructions, but click the Delete button instead.

>> **To export your Output Styles to share with others:** Follow the steps in the previous instructions, but click the Export button instead. (You can select multiple Output Styles by holding down the Command or Ctrl key while clicking on the Output Styles you want to export.) In the Save dialog box that appears, enter a name for your exported Output Style, choose a location on your hard drive to save it, and click the Save button.

>> **To import Output Styles given to you by others:** Follow the steps in the previous instruction, but click the Import button instead. In the dialog box that appears, navigate to the Output Styles file you want to import and click the Open button. The Output Styles contained in the exported Output Styles file are added to the Output Styles in your copy of QuarkXPress.

Fixing Common PDF File Problems

When exporting your QuarkXPress layout to PDF, you may sometimes get unexpected results. Some common problems and their solutions are explained next.

Font embedding issues

The TrueType font format includes a flag that lets font developers disallow the font's inclusion in an exported PDF. Not many fonts have that flag enabled, but if yours does, that font will never be embedded into a PDF.

If you really need to use that particular font, you need to track down that font's developer or distributor and ask whether a version is available that does allow embedding into PDFs.

Image issues

If the images in your exported PDF are blurry or pixelated, one of these issues arose:

>> **The original image has too little resolution.** To fix the problem, you can acquire a higher resolution version of the image and relink it in QuarkXPress.

To do that, choose Utilities ⇨ Usage to open the Usage dialog box, click Pictures in the left pane to display all the pictures used in your layout, select the image, click the Update button, and navigate to the new image file. If you don't have a higher-resolution version of the image, you can reduce the scale percentage of the image on the page by reducing the size of the picture box and its content (as explained in Chapter 13).

>> **You chose a PDF Output Style that downsamples your images to a resolution lower than you expected.** To fix this problem, you can do one of two things: Reexport using a PDF Output Style higher up in the PDF Style drop-down menu in the Export as PDF dialog box; or click the Options button in the Export as PDF dialog box, click Compression in the right-hand pane, and type a new value into the DPI field next to the Resolution drop-down menu.

Printer's marks and bleed

If your exported PDF includes a *page bleed* (page items extending past the edge of the page border) or crop and registration marks, it's because you chose a PDF Output Style named Press or one with PDF/X in the name. If you don't want crop and registration marks, don't use one of output those styles; or you can click the Options button and then do the following: In the Registration Marks pane, set the Mode to Off, and in the Bleed pane, set the Bleed Type to Page Items.

Creating Hyperlinks

You can attach a *hyperlink* to a selection of text or to any item on the page so that when users click it, they're taken to a different location in the document, taken to a web page, or prompted to create a new email message. In QuarkXPress, all the destinations of hyperlinks live in the Hyperlinks palette. You manage hyperlinks in ways that are similar to managing colors or style sheets. When you export your project to PDF, EPUB, HTML5, or any other digital format, your hyperlinks are included.

Creating destinations

A *destination* is a general term for the location a hyperlink takes you to. A destination can be one of three types:

>> **URL:** Points to a resource on the web

>> **Page:** Points to a page in the layout

>> **Anchor:** Points to a place or item on a page in the layout

Just as colors and style sheets do, each destination has a name. You can name a destination anything you like. For example, if you have a destination using the URL `http://www.quark.com`, you could name it "Quark website."

To create a destination, follow these steps:

1. **Choose Window ⇨ Hyperlinks to display the Hyperlinks palette, shown in Figure 17-7.**

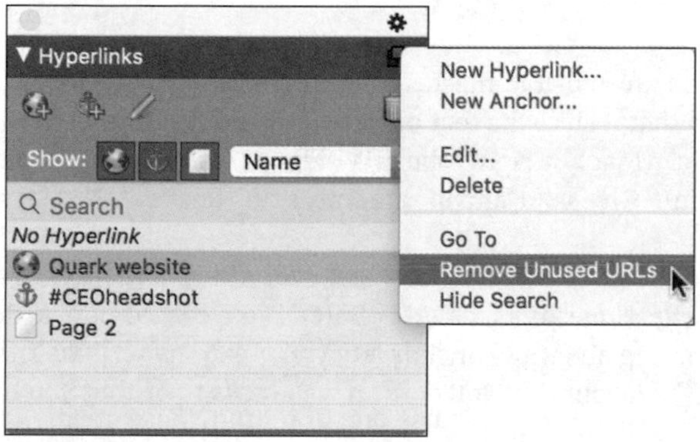

FIGURE 17-7:
The Hyperlinks palette.

2. **Click the New Hyperlink button or choose New Hyperlink from the palette menu to display the New Hyperlink dialog box, shown in Figure 17-8.**

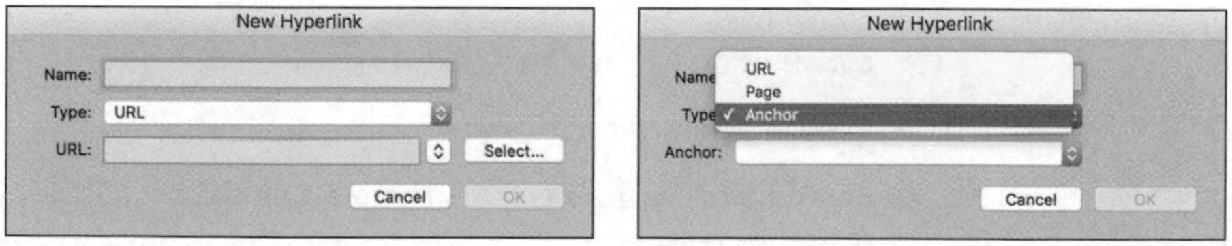

FIGURE 17-8:
The New Hyperlink dialog box.

Then choose one of these options:

- **To create a URL destination:** Choose URL from the Type drop-down menu. Then type in the URL and give your destination a name. To save yourself some typing (and errors), use the up/down arrows next to the URL field to choose from http://, https://, ftp://, and mailto: (yep, you can make a hyperlink that launches an email client and addresses a message).

- **To create a Page destination:** Choose Page from the Type drop-down menu and choose a page number from the Page drop-down menu.

- **To create an Anchor destination:** Choose Anchor from the Type drop-down menu and choose an anchor from the Anchor drop-down menu. (See the next section to learn how to create an anchor.)

3. **Click OK.**

TIP

If you want to create multiple new destinations, press Shift while you click OK, and the New Hyperlink dialog box will remain open.

Creating anchors

An anchor is an invisible marker that you attach to a selection of text or a page item. To do that, select the text or item and then choose Style ⇨ Anchor ⇨ New, or Control-click (Mac) or right-click (Windows) and choose Anchor ⇨ New from the context menu. Give your anchor a name.

TIP

To create an "empty" anchor, deselect everything and then click the New Anchor button in the Hyperlinks palette. Later, you can assign a destination for the anchor. Creating an empty anchor lets you create hyperlinks that point to anchors in parts of the layout that you don't have access to or that you haven't created yet.

Assigning hyperlink destinations

To assign a hyperlink destination to a selection of text or a selected item on the page, do one of the following:

>> Click the destination in the Hyperlinks palette.

>> Choose Style ⇨ Hyperlink and select the destination.

>> Control-click (Mac) or right-click (Windows) and choose Style ⇨ Hyperlink from the context menu.

Creating a hyperlink on the fly

You can also create a hyperlink by selecting text or an item and then choosing Style ⇨ Hyperlink ⇨ New (or Control-click on the Mac or right-click in Windows and then choose Hyperlink ⇨ New from the context menu). This displays the New Hyperlink dialog box, shown in Figure 17-8. Use the steps described in the "Creating destinations" section, earlier in this chapter, to create a new destination. When you do, you create a destination that is added to the project's list of destinations. You may want to edit its name to something you'll recognize at a later time.

Editing and appending destinations

To edit your list of destinations, choose Edit⇨Hyperlinks to open the Hyperlinks dialog box, shown in Figure 17-9. Here's what you can do in the Hyperlinks dialog box:

>> **View hyperlinks:** Just as with colors or style sheets, a project's destination list may contain destinations that are not currently used in the project. To view only the hyperlinks used (or not used), choose an option from the Show drop-down menu.

>> **Limit the list to only the URLs, Pages, or Anchors:** Choose an option from the Show drop-down menu.

>> **Edit a destination:** Click Edit.

>> **Import hyperlink destinations from a different QuarkXPress project:** Click Append and navigate to that project file.

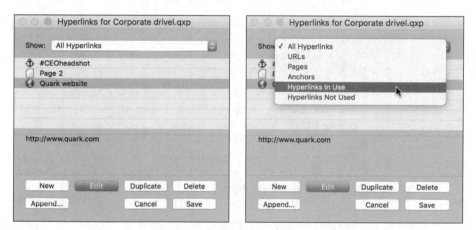

FIGURE 17-9: The Hyperlinks dialog box.

Formatting hyperlinks

Hyperlinked text is automatically underlined and colored according to the color chosen in QuarkXPress Preferences. By default, hyperlinks are blue. To choose a different color, open the Preferences dialog box by choosing QuarkXPress⇨Preferences (Mac) or Edit⇨Preferences (Windows) and under the Print Layout or Digital Layout section in the left pane, click General to view the layout's General preferences. There, click the color swatch next to Hyperlink Color to open the color picker and change the color.

You can also change the appearance of one selected hyperlink. To do so, simply change its attributes in the Measurements palette or apply a character style.

Navigating using the Hyperlinks palette

You can also use the Hyperlinks palette to navigate to destinations in the active QuarkXPress layout and on the web. With nothing selected on the page, double-click a destination in the Hyperlinks palette. (Or, select the destination and choose Go To from the Hyperlinks palette menu.) If you double-click a page destination or anchor, you are taken to that location in the active layout. If you double-click a URL, you are taken to that URL in your web browser.

Understanding Digital Publishing Formats

QuarkXPress let you export projects in several digital publishing formats: ePub, Kindle, HTML5 Publication, and App Studio. Your choice of output format will partly be determined by the experience you want your reader or customer to have:

>> Do you want to include multimedia content, such as video, slide shows, and interactivity?

>> Do you need to control the layout of the pages, or can you allow your readers to determine the font size and style for themselves?

Another factor is the amount of effort you want to put into creating your project. Have you already completed your project and want to convert it to a digital publishing format, or are you starting from scratch?

Platform compatibility may also be an issue. Do you need people to read your work on an Amazon Kindle device, an ePub reader, or in a web browser? Here is the lowdown on compatibility:

>> **Reflowable ePub:** Compatible with all ePub Readers (including Apple's iBooks) and Google Chrome.

>> **Fixed-layout ePub:** Dependent on the ePub Reader's capabilities, especially if it contains interactivity.

>> **Kindle:** Compatible with black-and-white Kindle devices and Kindle reader apps on desktop computers.

>> **HTML5 Publications:** Can be viewed using modern versions of Internet Explorer, Safari, Google Chrome, and Firefox.

>> **App Studio:** App Studio is Quark's online service that lets you create publication apps for iPad, iPhone, Kindle Fire, and Android devices.

This book doesn't teach you how to use App Studio to create an iPad, iPhone, Kindle Fire, or Android app from your QuarkXPress project. The important thing to know is that anything you can create in a QuarkXPress digital layout can be exported to a native app, and you can enrich it to include further bells and whistles. You upload it to Quark's online App Studio Portal and use the portal to export the app with its content. Because App Studio is intended as a tool for distributing publications, you can create and publish new "issues" for your apps, and those issues will then be available to the app. To learn more about App Studio, see Quark's "Digital Publishing with QuarkXPress 2016" (`http://files.quark.com/download/documentation/QuarkXPress/2016/English/Digital_Publishing_with_QXP_2016_EN.pdf`).

Table 17-1 can help you determine which format to target with your project:

TABLE 17-1   ## How to Choose an E-Book Format

	Kindle eBook	ePub	HTML5 Publications
Description	A format that lets you publish in the Amazon Kindle store	A standard book-centric format supported by many readers	A standard HTML5-based format supported by all major modern web browsers
Best for	Text-savvy books	Books	Online brochures, catalogs, magazines, and any other web content
Reader	Kindle	Kindle, Nook, Google, Apple iBooks	Any standards-compliant web browser like Google Chrome, Mozilla Firefox, Safari, and more.
Layout arrangement	Determined by Kindle	Reflow ePub: Determined by ePub reader application Fixed-layout ePub: Designed in QuarkXPress	Designed in QuarkXPress
Content	Text and pictures	Reflow ePub: Text, pictures, audio, video Fixed-layout ePub: Text, pictures, video, slide shows, HTML interactivity, and more	Text, pictures, video, slide shows, HTML interactivity, and more
Distribution	Amazon Kindle store	Apple, Barnes & Noble, Amazon, any third-party ePub distributor, or your own website	Your own web server

Creating Projects for ePub, Kindle, HTML5, and App Studio

The process of creating a QuarkXPress project for any digital format is the same for all formats — you simply use all the features in QuarkXPress that can export to your intended output format, and then you export your project.

REMEMBER

If you intend to output to reflowable ePub or Kindle format, you can use either a print layout or a digital layout in QuarkXPress. All other output formats require using a digital layout.

Converting a print layout to a digital layout

If you already have a print layout, duplicating that layout and converting it to a digital layout is super easy. Just follow these steps:

1. **Open the print layout and choose Layout ⇨ Duplicate to display the Duplicate Layout dialog box, shown in Figure 17-10.**

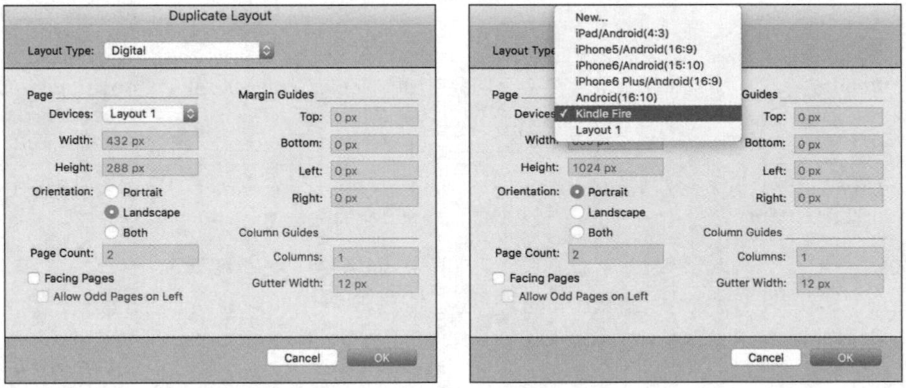

FIGURE 17-10:
The Duplicate Layout dialog box (left), with the Devices menu exposed (right).

2. **Choose Digital from the Layout Type drop-down menu.**

3. **In the Devices drop-down menu, choose a device.**

By default, the new digital layout uses the dimensions of your original print layout, but you can change the dimensions to match a standard size for a particular device that you select from the Devices drop-down menu. Devices include popular iOS, Android, and Kindle smartphones and tablets.

4. **In the Orientation section, select one of the radio buttons to choose an orientation.**

You can choose Portrait, Landscape, or Both. If you choose Both, two new layouts are created: one that duplicates the content and orientation of your Print layout; and a second, blank layout with the opposite orientation.

Creating a digital layout

To create a new digital layout:

1. **Choose File➪ New➪ Project to open the New Project dialog box, shown in Figure 17-11.**

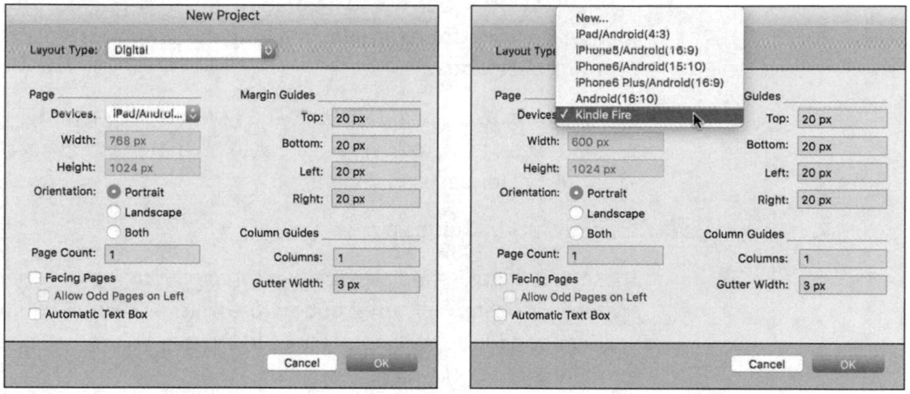

FIGURE 17-11:
The New Project dialog box (left) with the Devices menu exposed (right).

2. **Choose Digital from the Layout Type drop-down menu.**

3. **Choose a device from the Devices drop-down menu.**

The Width and Height fields are automatically filled in for the chosen device.

4. **In the Orientation section, select one of the radio buttons to choose an orientation.**

If you select Both, QuarkXPress will automatically create two layouts, one with a Portrait orientation and one with a Landscape orientation, which is mainly useful for using App Studio to create an app from your project. QuarkXPress displays the new project in a split view so that you can work with both views of the layout at the same time. To learn more about working with split windows, see the section that explains splitting a window in Chapter 2.

TECHNICAL STUFF

When you let QuarkXPress create both a portrait and landscape layout for your digital project, those layouts are part of a "layout family" that can share content. For more information, see "Synchronizing content between orientations," later in this chapter.

5. **In the Page Count field, enter how many pages you think you'll need.**

Don't worry: You can add and remove pages later.

6. **If your layout will have left and right pages (as in a magazine), select the Facing Pages check box.**

This setting enables you to have different margins and Master Pages for the left- and right-facing pages. If you know that your layout will require having odd page numbers (1, 3, 5, and so on) on the left-facing pages, select the Allow Odd Pages on Left check box. Normally, you keep this deselected.

7. **If you want QuarkXPress to be able to add new pages automatically as your text grows (for example, in a long document), select the Automatic Text Box check box.**

This setting places a text box within the margins of the master pages and applies that text box to every page based on that master page. (You can learn all about master pages in Chapter 5.)

8. **Set the Margin Guides as needed.**

These special guides indicate the "live" area of your layout, where your main content will be (text, pictures, and so forth). Items such as your page numbers, headers, and footers will normally be in the margin area, so be sure to leave room for them if you plan to use them.

9. **If your layout will have several columns, enter the number of columns in the Columns field under Column Guides.**

The Gutter Width field determines the space between the columns. QuarkXPress then does the math for you and places guides within the margins on each page, as necessary for the number of columns and gutter width you entered. If you enabled the Automatic Text Box check box (see Step 7), the text box will have these columns as well; otherwise you need to set the number of columns for each text box manually.

10. **Click OK.**

A project containing a default digital layout is created.

Synchronizing content between orientations

When you let QuarkXPress create both a portrait and landscape layout for your digital project, those layouts are part of a "layout family" that can share content. For example, if you create a table of contents on page 2 of the vertical layout for the iPad, you can instantly share that table of contents and copy it to page 2 of the horizontal layout for the iPad. You may need to reposition or resize the content in the other layouts, but it helps ensure that that content remains consistent everywhere it's used. For more information about shared content, see Chapter 7.

To instantly share selected items from one member of a layout family to all others, choose Item ⇨ Copy to Other Layouts. This converts all selected boxes into shared content and places copies of them on the same page of other layouts in the layout family. Options include:

>> **Same Position:** Puts the copies in the same position relative to the upper-left corner of the page, if possible.

>> **Use Relative Positioning:** Puts the copies in the same position relative to the page size and overall shape.

Adding Interactivity to Digital Layouts

You can use the HTML5 palette to add a variety of types of interactivity to a digital layout, including slide shows, movies, buttons, sound, and HTML. The tools in the HTML5 palette are also handy for creating presentations and banner ads for websites.

In a digital layout, choose Window ⇨ HTML5 to open the HTML5 palette, shown in Figure 17-12. This palette lets you name and add interactivity to whichever item is selected in your layout.

REMEMBER

Picture boxes, text boxes, anchored boxes, and no-content boxes support different kinds of interactivity. Options that are not available for the selected item are disabled.

The list at the bottom of the palette shows all the interactive objects in the active layout, including each enrichment type, object's name, and page number. Click the disclosure triangle at its left to expose the Interactive Objects list, as shown in Figure 17-12. Double-click any object to navigate to it.

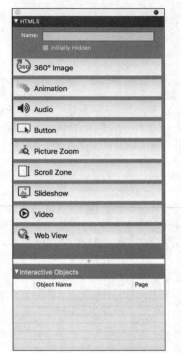

After you apply interactivity to a box, the application adds an icon to the box to show what kind of interactivity it has. To view these icons, make sure there's a check mark next to Visual Indicators in the View menu, which indicates that it's turned on. If there is no check mark, choose Visual Indicators in the View menu to turn it on, which adds the check mark. The icons match the icons in the HTML5 palette.

Creating a 360° image

A 360° image combines a series of images taken at fixed intervals around an object to create a single interactive image. The 360° image can auto rotate, and the user can grab the image and rotate it as well.

You can use pictures in PNG, JPEG, GIF, TIFF, and EPS formats. To create a 360° image, follow these steps:

1. **Select the picture box that you want to contain the 360° image.**

2. **In the HTML5 palette, click 360° Image to display the options shown in Figure 17-13.**

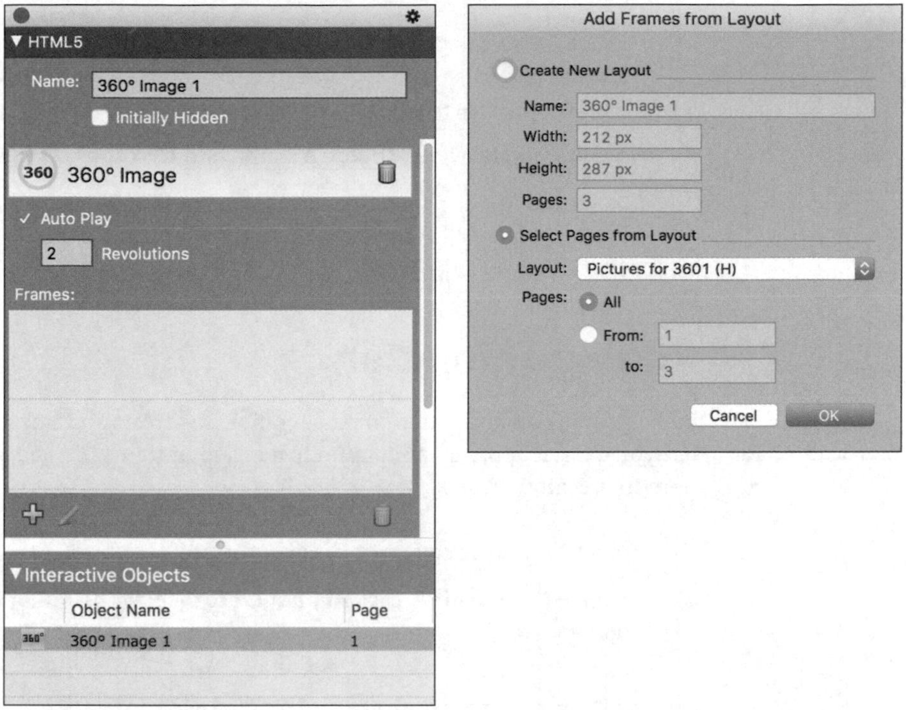

FIGURE 17-13:
The 360°
Image options
(left) and Add
Frames from
Layout dialog
box (right).

3. **(Optional) Enter a name for the 360° image in the Name field.**

This name displays in the Interactive Objects area at the bottom of the palette.

4. **If you want the 360° image to be initially invisible, select the Initially Hidden check box.**

5. **To allow the 360° image to initially rotate automatically, select the Auto Play check box.**

The Revolutions field lets you specify how many times the 360° image should automatically rotate when the image is first viewed. After the image completes the number of automatic revolutions, the user can manually rotate the 360° image.

6. **To add frames to the 360° image, click the Add Frames (+) button.**

The following options appear:

- **Add Frames from Picture Files:** Lets you add picture files as frames to the image. Press Shift to select multiple contiguous files or Command/Ctrl to select multiple noncontiguous files.

- **Add Frames from QuarkXPress Layout:** Displays the Add Frames from Layout dialog box, shown in Figure 17-13, which lets you add pages from a

QuarkXPress layout as separate frames. This is handy if you want to store your images in a layout in the same project. You can create a new layout here or choose pages from an existing layout.

7. **To edit a single frame, choose a frame and click the Edit (pencil) button.**

The picture file will open in the default application for editing that type of file on your computer. When you're finished editing, resave the picture file and it will update in QuarkXPress.

Adding animation

You can apply an animation to move individual boxes and lines around your page, but you cannot apply an animation to a group of items. To add an animation to an item in a Digital layout:

1. **Select the object you want to apply the animation to.**

2. **In the HTML5 palette, click Animation to display the options shown in Figure 17-14.**

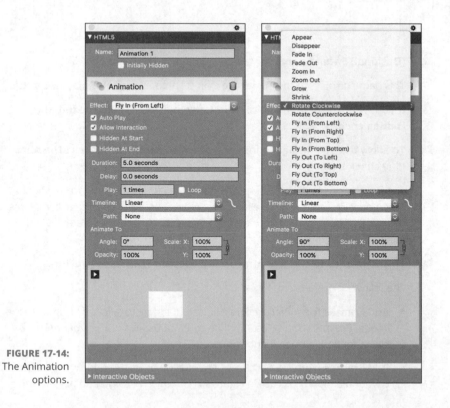

FIGURE 17-14:
The Animation options.

3. (Optional) Enter a name for the animation in the Name field.

This name displays in the Interactive Objects area in the bottom of the palette.

REMEMBER

Throughout QuarkXPress, a thing on a page is called an *item* . . . except for when it's used in animations. Then it's called an *object,* probably because computer programmers commonly use *object* to refer to a thing that can be manipulated.

4. In the Effect drop-down menu, choose the action you want the animation to perform.

For example, an object can fade in or out over time, appear or disappear, grow or shrink, rotate, or fly in from or out to any page edge.

5. To allow the animation to initially play automatically, select Auto Play.

6. To allow the viewer to interact with the animation, select Allow Interaction.

7. If you want the animation to be initially invisible, select Hidden at Start.

8. If you want the animation to become invisible after playing, select Hidden at End.

9. Use Duration to specify how much time it takes for the animation to occur.

10. Use Delay to specify how long of a delay there should be before the animation begins to play.

11. Use Play to specify the number of times the animation is played, or select Loop to cause the animation to play repeatedly.

12. In the Timeline drop-down menu, specify the timeline for the animation.

For example, you can choose to have the animation start slowly and speed up (Ease In), or slow down at the end (Ease Out).

13. (Optional) Use the Path drop-down menu to specify a path the animation will follow.

To use this feature, you need to already have a path on the page that you gave a name to in the HTML5 palette. Its name will then appear in the Path drop-down menu. However, the object will only travel on a straight line between the start and end points of the path, from left to right, with the center of the object positioned on top of those end points.

14. Set the following options in the Animate To section of the palette to determine the object's ending point:

- **Angle:** The rotation angle that the object completes during the animation.

- **Opacity:** The opacity the object should have at the end of the animation.

- **Scale: X** and **Scale: Y:** If you want the item to grow or shrink during the animation, enter the final scale percentages to apply.

15. **To preview the animation, click the Play (triangle) button.**

If the object moves along a path, you can preview that movement by clicking the Preview HTML5 Publication icon (it looks like a small globe) at the left of the project's bottom (horizontal) scroll bar.

Adding audio

You can associate an .mp3 audio file with a picture box. When the user views the layout, the box is replaced with audio controls that allow the sound to be played. You can also configure sound files to play in the background and to continue playing when the user changes pages.

TIP

You can start and stop the playback of audio files with actions. For more information, see "Working with interactivity actions," later in this chapter.

WARNING

Only one audio file can play at a time. If one sound is playing and another sound starts, the first sound is paused.

To add audio to a Digital layout, follow these steps:

1. **Select the picture box you want to replace with the audio controls.**

2. **In the HTML5 palette, click Audio to display the Audio options, shown in Figure 17-15.**

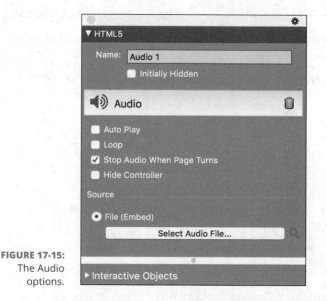

FIGURE 17-15: The Audio options.

3. **(Optional) Enter a name for the audio controller in the Name field.**

   This name displays in the Interactive Objects area in the bottom of the palette.

4. **If you want the audio item to be initially invisible, select the Initially Hidden check box.**

5. **To make the audio play automatically when the page it is on displays, select the Auto Play check box.**

   Auto Play for audio and video is not supported on mobile devices.

⚠ **WARNING**

6. **To make the audio play repeatedly, select the Loop check box.**

7. **To make the audio stop playing when the user goes to a different page, select the Stop Audio When Page Turns check box.**

8. **If Stop Audio When Page Turns is selected, you can hide the default audio controls by selecting the Hide Controller check box.**

9. **To choose an audio file, click the Select Audio File button and navigate to the audio file on your computer.**

10. **To finish configuring the audio item, click a different item or a blank part of the layout.**

Adding a button

To add a button to a Digital layout, follow these steps:

1. **Select the rectangular picture box you want to make into a button.**

2. **In the HTML5 palette, click Button to display the Button options, shown in Figure 17-16.**

3. **(Optional) Enter a name for the button in the Name field.**

   This name displays in the Interactive Objects area in the bottom of the palette.

4. **If you want the button to be initially invisible, select the Initially Hidden check box.**

5. **To add an action for the button, click the Add Action (+) button.**

   The Action drop-down menu appears, as shown in Figure 17-16.

6. **Choose an action from the Action drop-down menu, shown in Figure 17-16, then use the controls below the Action menu to configure the action.**

   You can add multiple actions to the same button. For more information about these actions, see "Working with interactivity actions," later in this chapter.

7. **To finish configuring the button, click a different item or a blank part of the layout.**

FIGURE 17-16:
The Button
options.

Adding a zoomable picture

A zoomable picture initially displays in a box, but takes over the entire screen when double-tapped. You can use this feature to add an animated pan-and-zoom effect to an image, or allow it to be zoomed and panned directly in its box.

Digital layouts support interactive pictures in PNG, JPEG, GIF, TIFF, and EPS formats. To add an interactive picture to a Digital layout, follow these steps:

1. **Select the picture box that contains the picture you want to make zoomable.**

2. **In the HTML5 palette, click Picture Zoom Button to display the Picture Zoom options, shown in Figure 17-17.**

3. **(Optional) Enter a name for the zoomable picture in the Name field.**

    This name displays in the Interactive Objects area at the bottom of the palette.

4. **If you want the zoomable picture to be initially invisible, select the Initially Hidden check box.**

5. **To allow the user to double-tap to switch back and forth between cropped view and full-screen view, select the Allow Fullscreen check box.**

FIGURE 17-17:
The Picture
Zoom options.

6. **To allow the user to zoom in and out with pinch gestures, select the Allow Pinch Zoom check box.**

7. **To allow the user to pan around in the picture with one finger, select the Allow Panning check box.**

8. **To make the picture pan and/or zoom when it first displays, select the Animate Pan and Zoom check box.**

   Make the following choices for your pan/zoom animation:

   - **Duration:** Lets you control how long the pan/zoom lasts. At the end of this duration, the picture stops and stays in its final position.

   - **Start and Stop:** These buttons allow you to set the beginning and ending crop. Click Start and scale/position the picture for the initial position, then click Stop and scale/position the image for the final position.

9. **To finish configuring the zoomable picture, click a different item or a blank part of the layout.**

Adding a scroll zone

A scroll zone is a scrollable area on a page. The content for the scrollable area comes from a different layout (the scrollable layout). After you set up a scroll zone, you can populate it with any combination of QuarkXPress items — for example, a long run of text, a large panoramic picture, or a series of interactive elements. You can then use that scrollable layout in multiple layouts within a layout family.

To set up a scroll zone for a digital layout, follow these steps:

1. **Navigate to a layout that is part of a layout family.**

2. **Draw a picture box to represent the size and the location of the scroll zone and then select the box.**

3. **In the HTML5 palette, click Scroll Zone to display the Scroll Zone options, shown in Figure 17-18.**

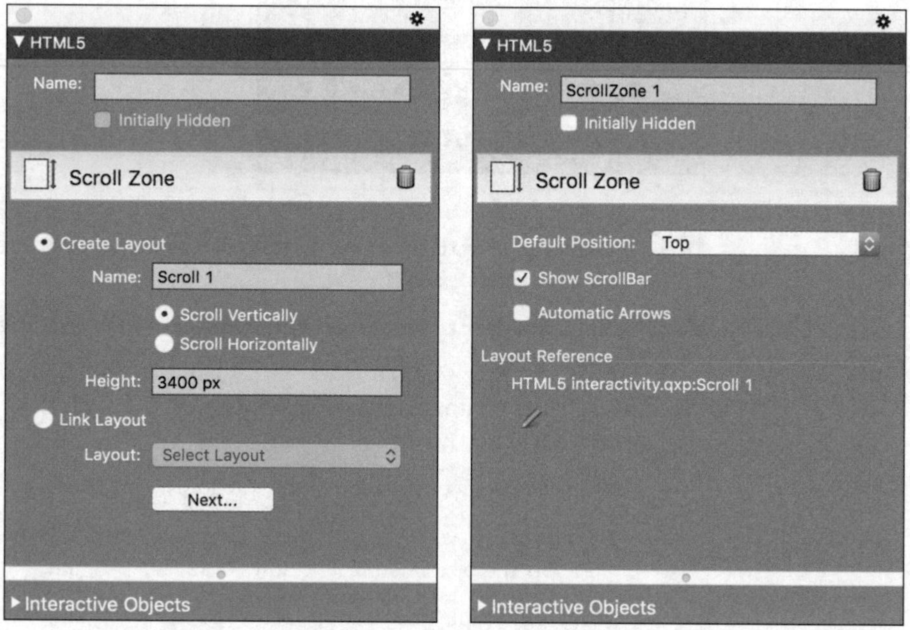

FIGURE 17-18: The Scroll Zone options (left) and after clicking the Next button (right).

4. **(Optional) Enter a name for the scroll zone in the Name field.**

   This name displays in the Interactive Objects area at the bottom of the palette.

5. **Choose whether you want to create a layout or link to an existing layout to serve as the scrollable layout:**

   - **If creating a new layout:** Click Create Layout and enter a name for the layout in the Name field. You can decide whether you want to create a horizontal or vertical scrollbox. A vertical scrollbox can be as long as you want it to be; a horizontal scrollbox is restricted to one page. Enter the height of the scrollable layout in the Height field.

   - **If linking to an existing layout in the active project:** Click Link Layout and choose that layout's name from the Layout drop-down menu. The size of the selected box is adjusted to fit the layout.

6. **Click Next.**

The HTML5 palette displays the controls shown in Figure 17-18.

7. **Specify the position of the scroll bar:**

- Choose Top or Bottom if scrolling vertically.

- Choose Left or Right if scrolling horizontally.

8. **To provide scroll bars as a visual cue that the area is scrollable,** select the Show ScrollBar check box.

9. **To automatically display arrows that indicate the direction in which the scroll zone can be scrolled, select the Automatic Arrows check box.**

10. **To edit the scrollable layout, click the Edit (pencil) button under Layout Reference.**

11. **To finish configuring the scroll zone, click a different item or a blank part of the layout.**

Adding a slide show

Slideshows may include both picture files and pages from QuarkXPress layouts. To add a slideshow to a digital layout, follow these steps:

1. **Select the picture box you want to contain the slide show.**

2. **In the HTML5 palette, click Slideshow to display the Slideshow options, shown in Figure 17-19.**

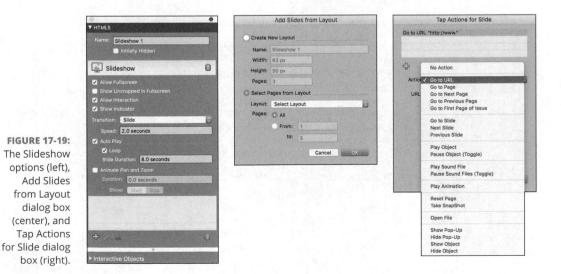

FIGURE 17-19: The Slideshow options (left), Add Slides from Layout dialog box (center), and Tap Actions for Slide dialog box (right).

3. (Optional) Enter a name for the slide show in the Name field.

This name displays in the Interactive Objects area in the bottom of the palette.

4. If you want the slide show to be initially invisible, select the Initially Hidden check box.

5. To allow the user to switch a slide to full-screen mode and back by double-tapping it, select the Allow Fullscreen check box.

6. To display slides uncropped when the slide show is in full-screen mode, select the Show Uncropped in Fullscreen check box.

If this check box is not selected, the slides use their picture-box crop in full-screen mode.

7. To allow the user to interact with the slide show, select the Allow Interaction check box.

8. To disable slide show indicators, deselect the Show Indicator check box.

By default, the option is selected to show slide show indicators.

9. Choose a style from the Transition drop-down menu to use when one slide transitions to the next.

The options are None, Slide, Fade, or Flip.

10. Enter a value into the Speed field to specify how long each transition lasts.

11. To make the slide show start playing immediately when the user displays the page, select the Auto Play check box.

If this box is deselected, the user must manually change the slides with finger swipes or with buttons.

12. To have the slide show play indefinitely, select the Loop check box.

If this box is not selected, the slide show will stop playing at the last slide.

13. To control how long each slide is on the screen, enter a value into the Slide Duration field.

14. To make the slide pan and/or zoom at the beginning of its display, select the Animate Pan and Zoom check box.

Then make these choices for the animation:

- **Duration:** Lets you control how long the pan/zoom lasts. At the end of this duration, the slide stops and stays in its final position until the next slide is displayed.

- **Start and Stop:** These buttons allow you to set the beginning and ending crop of each image. Click Start and scale/position the picture for the initial position; then click Stop and scale/position the image for the final position.

15. **To add a slide, click the Add Slide (+) button at the bottom of the slide list and choose one of these options:**

    - **Add Slides from Picture Files:** Lets you add picture files to the slide show. You can use picture files in PNG, JPEG, TIFF, PDF, and EPS formats. You can use the Shift or Command (Mac) or Ctrl (Windows) key to select multiple files.

    - **Add Slides from QuarkXPress Layout:** Displays the Add Slides from Layout dialog box, shown in Figure 17-19. This dialog box lets you add pages from a QuarkXPress layout to the slide show. You can create a new layout or choose pages from an existing layout.

16. **To edit a slide, select it and click the Edit (pencil) button.**

    If the slide is a picture file, that files opens in the default image editing application. If the slide is a page from a QuarkXPress layout, the layout opens and scrolls to that page.

17. **To execute an action when the user taps a slide, select it and click the Tap Actions for Slide button (it looks like a clapperboard) at the bottom of the HTML5 palette to display the Tap Actions For Slide dialog box shown in Figure 17-19.**

18. **To add an action, click the Add Action (+) button.**

    The Action drop-down menu activates.

19. **Choose the action you want from the Action drop-down menu and configure it the way you want it.**

    For more information on configuring from this drop-down menu, see the "Working with interactivity actions" section, later in this chapter.

20. **To set the cropping for a slide, select the slide's icon in the list and then scale and reposition the preview of the slide in the picture box.**

21. **To delete a slide, select the slide's icon in the list and click the trash can icon.**

22. **To finish configuring the slide show, click a different item or a blank part of the layout.**

Adding a video

To add a video to a digital layout, follow these steps:

1. **Select the picture box you want to contain the video.**

2. **In the HTML5 palette, click Video to display the Video options, shown in Figure 17-20.**

FIGURE 17-20:
The Video
options.

3. **(Optional) Enter a name for the picture in the Name field.**

   This name displays in the Interactive Objects area in the bottom of the palette.

4. **If you want the video to be initially invisible, select the Initially Hidden check box.**

5. **To make the video play automatically when the page it is on displays, select the Auto Play check box.**

   Auto Play for audio and video is not supported on mobile devices.

WARNING

6. **To make the video switch to full-screen mode as soon as it begins to play, select the Full Screen Only check box.**

7. **To make the video play repeatedly, select the Loop check box.**

8. **To hide the default video controls, select the Hide Controller check box.**

   Note that if you want the user to be able to control the movie, you will need to provide a way of controlling the video with actions.

9. **To hide the play button, select the Hide Play Button check box.**

10. **To specify the location of the video, click an option in the Source area, as follows:**

- **To use a local video file:** Click File (Embed) and then click the button and select the video file.

- **To use a video from a URL:** Click URL and enter the URL in the field.

- **To use a video file from YouTube or Vimeo:** Click YouTube/Vimeo, then paste the URL of the video in the src= field. (To get this value for a Vimeo or YouTube video, Control-click [Mac] or right-click [Windows] the video and then choose Get Embed Code or Copy Embed Code. Copy the code and paste it into a text editor, then copy the portion of the code that looks like this: `http://www.[site].com/embed/XXXXXX`, and paste it into the src= field in QuarkXPress. The XXX part of the fake code used here represents the strange combination of letters and numbers that YouTube/Vimeo uses to name each video file.)

TECHNICAL STUFF

Digital layouts support only H.264 video at up to 720p, 30 frames per second, Main Profile level 3.1, with AAC-LC stereo audio at up to 160 Kbps per channel, 48kHz, in the `.mp4` file format.

11. **To finish configuring the video, click a different item or a blank part of the layout.**

TIP

You can start and stop the playback of video files with actions. For more information, see "Working with interactivity actions," later in this chapter.

Adding a web view

You can use a web view to include changeable content (such as ads) or custom interactivity to a digital layout. You can use a web view to display HTML, PDF, Word, Excel, PowerPoint, RTF, and several other types of files. To add a web view to a digital layout, follow these steps:

1. Select the picture box to contain the web content.

2. In the HTML5 palette, click Web View to display the Web View options, shown in Figure 17-21.

3. Optionally, enter a name for the web view in the Name field.

This name displays in the Interactive Objects area at the bottom of the palette.

4. If you want the web view to be initially invisible, select the Initially Hidden check box.

5. To allow the user to interact with the content, select the Allow User Interaction check box.

FIGURE 17-21:
The Web View
options.

6. **To specify the location of the content, click an option in the Source area, as follows:**

   ● **To use a local file:** Click File (Embed). Put the file and any other files it uses (such as pictures) into a folder by themselves; then click the Select File button and select the file. To ensure that links work, all files in the folder that contains this file will be added to the article.

   ● **To use a URL:** Click URL and enter the URL in the field.

7. **Click Select Image in the Offline Image area and choose a picture file if the content in the web view is not embedded.**

   This lets you specify a PNG or JPEG image to display when an Internet connection is not available. The pencil and trash can icons under this button let you edit or delete the offline image from this web view.

8. **To finish configuring the Web view, click a different item or a blank part of the layout.**

Working with interactivity actions

Actions let you add interactivity to items in a Digital layout. The actions include:

>> **No Action:** Does nothing

- ➤ **Go to URL:** Navigates to a URL when the user touches or clicks the selected item (For Button interactivity, you can also add a geolocation value for the Go to URL action.)

- ➤ **Go to Page:** Jumps to a different page

- ➤ **Go to Next Page:** Jumps to the next page

- ➤ **Go to Previous Page:** Jumps to the page before this one

- ➤ **Go to First Page of Issue:** Jumps to the first page in the issue

- ➤ **Go to Slide:** Displays the specified slide of the slide show

- ➤ **Next Slide:** Displays the next slide of the slide show

- ➤ **Previous Slide:** Displays the previous slide of the slide show

- ➤ **Play Object:** Starts playing the audio or video object

- ➤ **Pause Object (Toggle):** Pauses and resumes the playing of the audio or video object

- ➤ **Play Sound File:** Plays a sound file

- ➤ **Pause Sound Files (Toggle):** Pauses and resumes the playback of all sound files

- ➤ **Show Pop-Up:** Displays a pop-up view containing either the content of a QuarkXPress layout in the same project file or the content of an external file

- ➤ **Hide Pop-Up:** Hides the currently displayed pop-up

- ➤ **Show Object:** Shows the specified object (if it is hidden)

- ➤ **Hide Object:** Hides the specified object (if it is visible)

- ➤ **Open:** Lets you open files and display them within your application

- ➤ **Play Animation:** Starts playing the specified animation

- ➤ **Reset Page:** Resets the page so that all animations are set back to their starting position

- ➤ **Take Snapshot:** Takes a snapshot (screenshot) of the page and saves it in the default image folder of the device

Publishing to ePub and Kindle

ePub and Kindle formats support both Fixed and Reflow views:

- ➤ **Fixed:** Similar to PDF in that it mimics your original layout — however complex it may be. It's appropriate for books whose layout is arguably as important as the pictures and text, such as cookbooks, travel books, and children's books.

>> **Reflow:** The traditional e-book view: full screen, with an adaptive layout and resizable text. It's appropriate for novels, how-to books, and other text-heavy publications.

Exporting to Fixed view format for ePub and Kindle

Exporting a digital layout in Fixed view format for ePub or Kindle is almost as easy as exporting a PDF: Choose File ⇨ Export ⇨ Layout as ePub (or Kindle). The key is that your layout must be a digital layout and not a print layout. If your current layout type is Print, you can quickly duplicate it and change its type to Digital by following the steps outlined in the "Converting a print layout to a digital layout" section, earlier in this chapter.

TIP

Unless you have specific reasons to change the options in the Export dialog box, choose Default ePub/Kindle Output Style and enjoy your new ePub/Kindle book.

Creating a Reflowable view e-book for ePub and Kindle

Before exporting your layout to Reflowable ePub or Kindle format, you need to identify the parts and pieces of your text and pictures and use the Reflow Tagging palette to place them into one or more Reflow Articles. If you've consistently applied Style Sheets to text, you'll have relatively little work to do. If you haven't, you probably lost some efficiency while creating your book and now have extra work to do.

TIP

If you format your book using only one long story that spans multiple text boxes, and you anchor all your pictures and captions in the text flow, exporting to Reflowable ePub or Kindle is a breeze! For more on anchoring items in text, see Chapter 14.

WARNING

Before beginning the process of creating Reflow articles, complete your book. If you change the book's content after adding it to articles, those changes will not show up in the article.

TIP

When you export a layout as an ePub or Kindle e-book, QuarkXPress will always export the first page of the layout as an image and use it as a cover of your e-book. Therefore, be sure that page one is your book cover.

The Reflow Tagging palette, shown in Figure 17-22, lets you tag text and pictures for Reflow, and reorder components within an article. The palette may contain one or more articles. Each article may contain one or more picture boxes, as well as stories that span multiple text boxes.

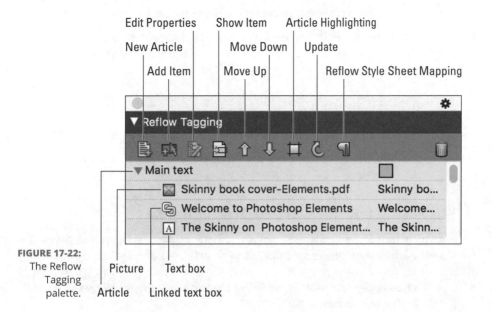

FIGURE 17-22:
The Reflow
Tagging
palette.

You have two ways to create Reflow articles:

>> **From a selection:** This approach lets you select the specific boxes you want included in the Reflow article. This approach is best if the layout has a lot of content that you don't want to include in the Reflow output.

>> **From pages:** This approach copies everything into the Reflow article. This approach is best if all or almost all of the content in the layout should be included in the Reflow output. (Content from master pages such as headers and footers, and content on page one is ignored.)

TIP

If you find it useful for organization, you can create one article for each chapter or section, but it's not necessary. However, because a page break occurs between each article, you can create a new article to force an important page break.

Read on to find out the details of creating Reflow articles.

Creating a Reflow article from a selection

To create a Reflow article from a selection, follow these steps:

1. Select the content you want to add to a Reflow article.

2. You have several ways to create a Reflow article, including:

- Choose Item⇨Digital Publishing⇨Add to Reflow⇨New Article. QuarkXPress creates a new Reflow article and inserts all the text and pictures in the selected boxes.

- Click New Article in the Reflow Tagging palette and then click Add Item. QuarkXPress adds the selected content.

3. To change the name of the new article, select it and click Edit Properties.

The Edit Properties dialog box opens and you can type a new name into the Name field.

Creating a Reflow article from pages

As mentioned previously, you can also create a Reflow article from pages. To add all the content on one or more pages to an article or articles, follow these steps:

1. Choose Layout⇨Add Pages to Reflow to display the Add Pages to Reflow dialog box, shown in Figure 17-23.

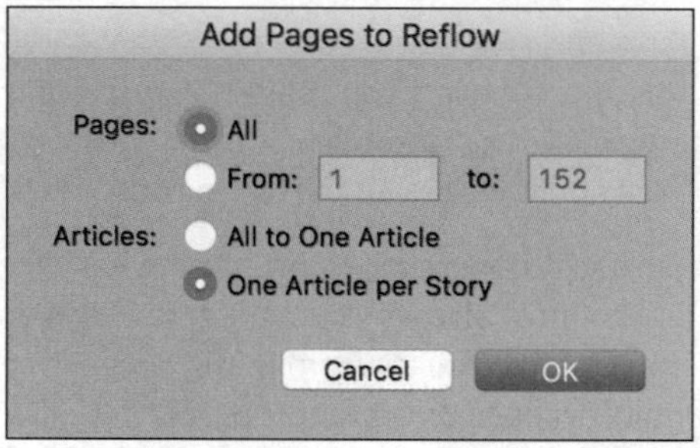

FIGURE 17-23: The Add Pages to Reflow dialog box.

2. Select a radio button in the Pages section to choose whether you want to add all the pages in the layout or only a specific range, and select a radio button in the Articles section to choose whether you want all the pages to go into the same article, or to create a separate article for each story.

3. Click OK.

QuarkXPress creates the necessary Reflow articles and inserts all the content from the selected pages into them.

4. **To change the name of the new article, select it and click Edit Properties.**

The Edit Properties dialog box opens and you can type a new name into the Name field.

TIP

To highlight components that have been tagged for Reflow, click the Article Highlighting button on the Reflow Tagging palette.

Adding content to a Reflow article

You have two ways to add content to an existing Reflow article:

>> Select one or more picture or text boxes and then choose Item ➪ Digital Publishing ➪ Add To Reflow ➪ *your reflow article name*.

>> In the Reflow Tagging palette, select the target Reflow article and then select one or more picture or text boxes and click Add Component.

TIP

To add a full-page image to an ePub layout that is to be viewed in iBooks, be sure that its dimensions are 1024 × 768 (or 2048 × 1536 for Retina).

Reordering components in a Reflow article

Each text box, story, or picture that you add to a Reflow article is added as a component. When you let QuarkXPress add items to an article, they may not appear in the correct order. To change the order of components in a Reflow article, follow these steps:

1. **In the Reflow Tagging palette, click the disclosure triangle to the left of the target Reflow article.**

The Reflow article expands to show the components inside it.

2. **From the list of components under the Reflow article you just expanded, select the component you want to move.**

3. **Drag and drop the component up or down in the Reflow Tagging palette or use the Move Up or Move Down buttons to reposition the component.**

Reflow style sheet mapping

When exporting to Reflow ePub format, you can choose to map (convert) the existing paragraph and character style sheets to different style sheets. This is useful if you want the text in your e-book to be formatted differently from your QuarkXPress layout, or if you need your exported style sheets to match the names of custom CSS styles you intend to use in your book. If you don't understand any of this, don't worry — most people don't use this feature.

1. **In the Reflow Tagging palette, click the Reflow Style Sheet Mapping button to display the Reflow Style Sheet Mapping dialog box, shown in Figure 17-24.**

Reflow Style Sheet Mapping

Paragraph Style Sheet	Mapped Reflow Paragraph Style Sheet	
¶ Byline (Author)	Byline (Author)	⬍
¶ Figure	Figure	⬍
¶ Figure Caption	Figure Caption	⬍
¶ Figure Credit	Figure Credit	⬍
¶ footer	footer	⬍
¶ heading 1	heading 1	⬍
¶ Headline	heading 1	⬍

Character Style Sheet	Mapped Reflow Character Style Sheet	
A FollowedHyperlink	FollowedHyperlink	⬍
A Hyperlink	Hyperlink	⬍
A mainfont2	mainfont2	⬍
A MS Word CharStyle 1	Emphasis	⬍
A MS Word CharStyle 2	Normal	⬍
A MS Word CharStyle 3	Normal	⬍
A MS Word CharStyle 4	Normal	⬍

☐ Show Used Style Sheet Only   [Reset All] [Cancel] [OK]

FIGURE 17-24:
The Reflow Style Sheet Mapping dialog box.

2. **Select the Show Used Style Sheet Only check box to list only the style sheets used in the current project.**

The list of style sheets is reduced to only those that have been applied to text in your layout.

3. **For each paragraph and character style sheet you would like to reassign when exporting, select the existing style sheet in the left column and choose a new style sheet from the drop-down menu in the right column.**

These style sheets are applied only when you export the Reflow ePub.

Click Reset All to remove all your choices and reset mapping to the defaults.

TIP

If your digital layout has multiple overlapping picture boxes and graphic text boxes whose appearance you need to maintain, you can streamline your export by grouping the boxes (to group them, select them and choose Item ⇨ Group) and then at the far right end of the Measurements palette select the Convert to Graphic on Export check box for the group. If you don't group those boxes, each one exports as a separate HTML element. If you group them, they export as a single graphic object. However, because the text is converted to a graphic, readers won't be able to search for it using the search feature in their e-book reader.

TIP

Creating a table of contents for ePub or Kindle

When you export a layout to ePub or Kindle format, you can create the table of contents in two ways:

>> Use the order of the Reflow articles, with one table of contents entry for each Reflow article.

>> Use the Lists feature in QuarkXPress to create a list to use as the table of contents, as explained in Chapter 6.

To control how the table of contents is created during export, click the Options button in the Export as ePub/Kindle dialog box to display the ePub/Kindle Export Options dialog box, shown in Figure 17–25. Here's how to work with this dialog box:

>> **To use the Reflow article names as your table of contents:** Select the Use Reflow Article Names radio button under Table of Contents.

>> **To use a list you built in QuarkXPress as your table of contents:** Select the Use List as TOC Palette radio button under Table of Contents and then choose the List you want to use from the drop-down menu below that.

>> **To enter a custom name for the first page of your book (which is always the cover):** Select the Custom radio button under Name of Cover Entry in TOC and enter the name you prefer. (By default, the table of contents lists it as "Cover.")

>> **To enter a custom name for your table of contents page title:** Select the Custom radio button under Title Text for HTML TOC and enter the name you prefer. (By default, the title of the table of contents page is "Contents.")

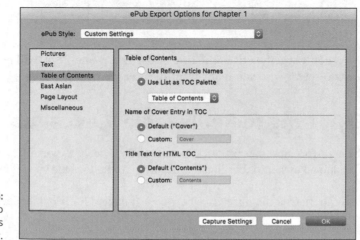

FIGURE 17-25: The ePub Export Options dialog box.

Working with e-book metadata

When you export an e-book, invisible *metadata* (information *about* the book that isn't necessarily *in* the book, such as the author, publisher, description, and custom keywords) travels along with it so that potential buyers and current users can discover information about the book. This metadata is also where book distributors retrieve your book's title, author, publisher, copyright, ISBN, language, and description — so it's important to make sure that all this data is correct.

To add or edit metadata for the currently open layout, choose Layout ⇨ eBook Metadata to display the eBook Metadata dialog box, shown in Figure 17-26.

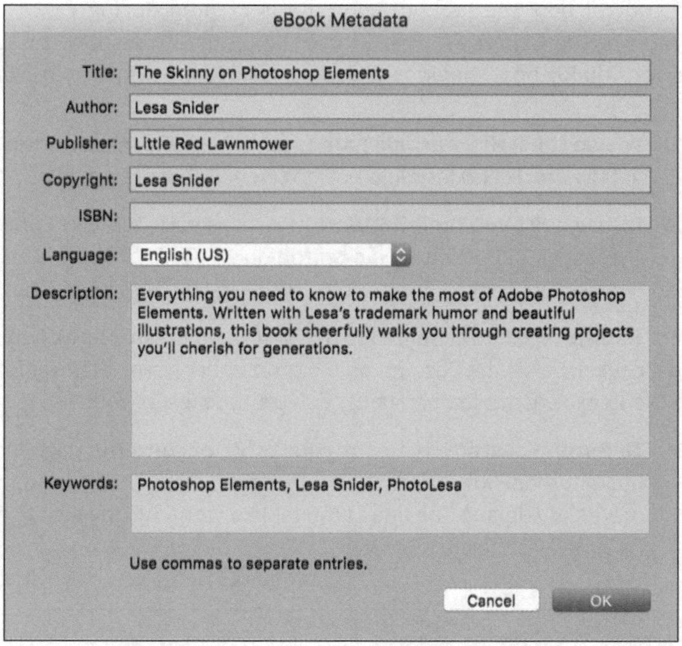

eBook Metadata

Title:	The Skinny on Photoshop Elements
Author:	Lesa Snider
Publisher:	Little Red Lawnmower
Copyright:	Lesa Snider
ISBN:	
Language:	English (US)
Description:	Everything you need to know to make the most of Adobe Photoshop Elements. Written with Lesa's trademark humor and beautiful illustrations, this book cheerfully walks you through creating projects you'll cherish for generations.
Keywords:	Photoshop Elements, Lesa Snider, PhotoLesa

Use commas to separate entries.

Cancel   OK

FIGURE 17-26:
The eBook Metadata dialog box.

REMEMBER

If you don't specify a title, the title of the exported e-book will be "Created with QuarkXPress" — so you really want to enter the title of the book!

Exporting to Reflowable View ePub

The ePub format supports both Fixed and Reflow views. Exporting to Fixed View ePub is explained earlier in this chapter. Exporting to Reflowable view is explained next.

REMEMBER

To recap, here is the difference between Fixed and Reflowable views:

>> **Fixed:** Similar to PDF in that it mimics your original layout — however complex it may be. It's appropriate for books whose layout is arguably as important as the pictures and text, such as cookbooks, travel books, and children's books.

>> **Reflow:** The traditional e-book view: full screen, with an adaptive layout and resizable text. It's appropriate for novels, how-to books, and other text-heavy publications.

To export your QuarkXPress layout to a Reflowable View ePub book, follow these steps:

1. **Choose File ➪ Export ➪ Layout as ePub to display the Export as ePub dialog box.**

2. **Type a name for your book in the Save As field.**

3. **If eBook Type area is available, select the Reflow radio button so that your e-book is exported as Reflowable view instead of Fixed view.**

4. **Choose an output style from the ePub Style drop-down menu or click the Options button.**

    The Default ePub Output Style in QuarkXPress works for most books. Unless you have a specific reason to change the export options, there's no reason to click the Options button — other than curiosity.

    If you click the Options button, the ePub Export Options dialog box displays, as shown in Figure 17-27.

FIGURE 17-27:
The ePub
Export Options
dialog box.

5. **Make any changes you deem necessary in the ePub Export Options dialog box and click OK to return to the Export as ePub dialog box.**

6. **Click the Save button and choose a location for your exported ePub file.**

Exporting to Reflowable View Kindle

To export to Kindle format, you need to have Amazon's KindleGen application on your computer. The first time you export to Kindle format, QuarkXPress asks you to locate KindleGen. If you don't have it, a button will appear in the Export for Kindle dialog box to have QuarkXPress download it for you.

When you have the KindleGen application on your computer, follow these steps to export your project to Kindle format:

1. **Choose File⇨Export⇨Layout as Kindle to display the Export as Kindle dialog box.**

2. **In the Save As field, enter a name for your e-book.**

3. **If the eBook Type area is available, select the Reflow radio button so that your e-book is exported as Reflowable view instead of Fixed view.**

4. **Choose an output style from the Kindle Style drop-down menu or click the Options button.**

   The Default Kindle Output Style in QuarkXPress works for most books. Unless you have a specific reason to change the export options, there's no reason to click the Options button — other than curiosity.

   If you click the Options button, the Kindle Export Options dialog box displays, with features similar to those in Figure 17-27.

5. **Make any changes you deem necessary in the Kindle Export Options dialog box and click OK to return to the Export as Kindle dialog box.**

6. **Click the Save button and choose a location for your exported Kindle file.**

7. **Click Save.**

Creating HTML5 Publications

Exporting your digital layout as an HTML5 publication is an easy way to reproduce your QuarkXPress layout as a web app that's viewable in any web browser. However, you need to be able to host websites on a server you control. If that sounds like you, choose File⇨Export⇨Layout as HTML5 Publication. In the Layout as HTML5 Publication dialog box that appears, select a location for the files and click the Export button.

Yep, it's really that easy. For details on how to configure the exported web app, see Quark's "Digital Publishing with QuarkXPress 2016" (http://files. quark.com/download/documentation/QuarkXPress/2016/English/ Digital_Publishing_with_QXP_2016_EN.pdf).

Even without a web server, you can preview your HTML5 publication in your computer's web browser. To do that, go to the bottom of the QuarkXPress window and, at the left of the horizontal scroll bar, click the Preview HTML5 Publication icon. It looks like a small Earth and is visible only on digital layouts.

5

The Part of Tens

IN THIS CHAPTER

» **Building interactive publications**

» **Key commands for tools**

» **Mind-blowing XTensions**

» **AppleScripts (Mac only)**

» **Documentation from Quark**

» **Tips & Tricks book**

» **Online resources**

Chapter **18**

Ten QuarkXPress Workflow Resources

QuarkXPress has a thriving ecosystem that includes third-party XTensions (plug-ins), free tools from Quark, free training videos, websites, a Facebook group, and forums. You may be surprised at the unique and valuable opportunities in the following sections.

Quark's Free QuarkXPress Document Converter

QuarkXPress Document Converter is a stand-alone application that converts legacy documents (QuarkXPress 3, 4, 5, and 6) to the new format (QuarkXPress 9.1), which lets you open these documents in QuarkXPress 10 or later. It can convert multiple documents at one time, including entire folders and subfolders, without overwriting the original files.

The easiest way to obtain this utility is to choose Convert Legacy Files from the Help menu in QuarkXPress.

WARNING

When you open a converted legacy document in QuarkXPress 2016, it uses the text flow engine introduced in QuarkXPress 9 — therefore, your text may reflow.

TIP

If you've ever encountered the dreaded "Pasteboard XT" warning, you'll appreciate this: QuarkXPress Document Converter removes the bogus warning that the Pasteboard XT XTension is required to open a document.

TECHNICAL
STUFF

If your legacy QuarkXPress project includes a Web or Interactive (Flash) layout, you won't be able to open it in QuarkXPress 10 or higher. QuarkXPress Document Converter removes web layouts and Flash layouts from projects, so you can use any existing print layouts.

App Studio

App Studio is Quark's online service that lets you create HTML5-based publication apps for iPad, iPhone, Kindle Fire, and Android devices. Anything you can create in a QuarkXPress digital layout can be exported to a native app, and you can enrich it to include further bells and whistles such as map coordinates *(geolocation)*, hotspots and pop-ups, HTML5 widgets, page flips, and vertical scrolling pages and text boxes.

To use App Studio, you upload your QuarkXPress project to Quark's online App Studio Portal and use the portal to export the app with its content. (Amazingly, you can even upload an InDesign document, a PDF, or even an XML file if you have the skills.) Because App Studio is intended as a tool for distributing publications, you can create and publish new issues for your apps, and those issues will then be available to the app.

To learn more about App Studio, visit its website (http://www.appstudio. net) and read Quark's "Digital Publishing with QuarkXPress 2016" (http:// files.quark.com/download/documentation/QuarkXPress/2016/English/ Digital_Publishing_with_QXP_2016_EN.pdf).

Key Commands for Tools

To quickly switch from one tool to another, press its corresponding key on your keyboard — when you're not typing in a text box, of course! Table 18-1 shows the keyboard commands.

TABLE 18-1 **Keyboard Equivalents for Switching among Tools**

Tool	Windows	Mac OS X
Item tool	V	V
Text Content tool	T	T
Text Linking tool	T	N
Text Unlinking tool	T	N
Picture Content tool	R	R
Rectangle Box tool	B	B
Oval Box tool	B	B
Starburst tool	B	B
Composition Zones tool	L	B
Line tool	P	L
Orthogonal Line tool	P	L
Bézier Pen tool	P	P
Add Point tool	P	P
Remove Point tool	P	P
Convert Point tool	P	P
Scissors tool	P	P
Select Point tool	P	P
Freehand Drawing tool	P	P
Table tool	G	G
Zoom tool	Z	Z
Pan tool	X	X

XTensions That Will Blow Your Mind

For more than 25 years, the publishing professionals at XChange U.S. & U.K. have advised QuarkXPress users on XTensions that make specific tasks more productive. Visit their website — or better yet, give them a call for experienced advice on whether they know of a timesaving solution for the tasks that you most often tackle:

https://www.xchangeus.com or +1-877-940-0600

https://www.xchangeuk.com or +44 (0) 345-259-0255

Xdata

Xdata lets you automate the building of pages by using placeholders and then importing data from an external file — perhaps from a database. The result can be as simple as an old-fashioned mail merge (name, address, and so on) or it can involve numerous if/then relationships between sales history, variable images, prices, and other calculations.

You create a QuarkXPress "template" that defines how you want the information to look, then Xdata imports and automatically formats data you've exported from a database or spreadsheet. In addition, Xdata can import specific pictures that are cited in the template and the data file. It can manipulate text from inside individual data fields and create directory-style headers and footers on each page or spread.

Xdata is also fantastic for creating lengthy documents containing lots of similar items, such as catalogs, financial, and legal reports, conference guides, abstracts, real estate guides, trader and swap magazines, classified advertising, timetables, phone books, course listings, and TV guides.

Xcatalog

Xcatalog lets you create bidirectional links between a QuarkXPress document and an external database. You can link any picture or text element, from a single character to a phrase or paragraph or entire story. It's excellent for making sure that you've included the absolute latest pictures, text, and prices in a catalog or directory.

JoLetter XTension

JoLetter lets you create advanced mail merge projects such as personalized letters. It works with tab-separated and `.csv` text files exported from any spreadsheet or database application and is available for $129 at `www.jolauterbach.com`.

MadeToPrint

MadeToPrint lets you combine all the settings for a printing job into a selectable item. This lets you (or an inexperienced coworker) easily print the same document to a laser printer, color proofer, or imagesetter, and export to PDF or EPS with all the correct settings. You can even make a group of settings for several different printers, and send a document to all the printers at one time — or to a printer and simultaneously to PDF, PostScript, EPS, InDesign, or a QuarkXPress collect-for-output.

You can also build nearly any kind of imposition (rearranging pages so that they can be printed by a commercial printer), from simple booklets to complex brochures, catalogs, and books. In addition, you can optionally break a print job into separate pages, which is helpful when printing long documents that may otherwise choke or slow the printer. When exporting to PDF, you can access Adobe Distiller's settings from within the Print dialog box. (See Chapters 16 and 17 for more on exporting to PDF.) MadeToPrint can also generate a job slug or a new name for the output file based on several variables including date and time, user, page(s), and the last modification's date and time.

Image Info XT

Image Info XT adds a tiny palette that displays lots of useful information about a selected picture, such as its resolution and (more important) Effective Resolution, dimensions, file size, file format, color space, color profile, date and time of last modification, location on your hard drive, QuarkXPress Layer, status, and the QuarkXPress page number. The palette lets you edit the original image, display the image file in your computer's file system, and relink the picture box to a different picture. It's available for $10 at `www.creationauts.com`.

Arabic XT

Arabic XT lets you set bidirectional type in the Arabic, Farsi, Hebrew, Jawi, and Kurdish languages, without requiring an Arabic operating system. You can create text that flows either right to left or left to right, and paragraphs that flow in opposite directions. It supports Arabic and roman script in the same document, with automatic Kashida insertion.

Badia Software's XTensions (Mac only)

Available at www.badiasoftware.com, here are some of Badia's exceptional and affordable XTensions for Mac users:

>> **BigPicture** gives you get instant access to detailed image information, complete picture lists, a unique search and relink engine, plus powerful tools for updating, revealing, opening, renaming, replacing, and moving multiple links. $80.

>> **ContactPage Pro** is the easiest way to create professional-looking contact sheets of images with captions. You can use ContactPage Pro to create picture catalogs, proof sheets, photo books, or anytime you need to quickly browse or print pictures with full descriptive text captions. $60.

>> **Duplica** allows you to sample and apply text and item attributes using multiple Clipboards. Simply choose the attributes you want to copy and then paste them in other parts of the document in one single step. $70.

>> **Exportools Standard** automates exporting individual document pages or spreads into separate files. It can also export groups of pages and selections, extract all the document text, and even split documents with their corresponding image links. $70.

>> **Exportools Professional** allows you to output multipage documents as single-page or multipage files. With more than a dozen types of formats to choose from, Exportools Professional is the only tool you need to export pages, spreads, and text and images for print, web, or portable devices, and it costs $120.

>> **FullMeasure** provides Text tools (text count, copy fitting, special characters, text export, case conversions), complete picture information, reference points, nudge controls, and document information. $60.

>> **IDML Import** lets you easily import IDML files created with Adobe InDesign into QuarkXPress. It will build all document pages and spreads; import colors and graphics, master pages, style sheets, and layers; create all text boxes, picture boxes, vector shapes, tables, frames, and groups; and format text stories. You can buy it for $70.

PDF Importer XT

QuarkXPress currently imports only one page at a time from a PDF file. If you want to import multiple pages at one time, get PDF Importer XT from Creationauts. This XTension lets you choose which pages to import from a PDF: selected pages or only the even or odd pages. When importing the PDF, it creates a new QuarkXPress page for each page in the PDF and optionally converts its objects to native QuarkXPress items. This XTension is available for $20 at www.creationauts.com.

ID2Q

Markzware's ID2Q lets you convert Adobe InDesign files to QuarkXPress format. When you're handed an InDesign document that really should have been built in QuarkXPress, this XTension can save you tons of time and frustration. Intricate details of the InDesign document are instantly converted and re-created within QuarkXPress, including page positioning, fonts, styles, images, text attributes, tables, layers, blends, runarounds, linked text boxes, anchored boxes, and colors. You can find it http://markzware.com.

ID Util (Mac only)

Markzware's ID Util is a utility for Mac users that can export all the text from an Adobe InDesign document, with its styling. When you just need to grab the text from an InDesign document, get this $20 utility from www.markzware.com.

AutoCorrectXT

AutoCorrectXT adds an auto-correct feature and can correct user-defined typing errors as well. In addition, the XTension lets you create "boilerplate" text — words or phrases that someone can insert by typing a few characters. It supports many languages and is available at http://athenasoftsolutions.com.

Other Affordable Workflow Tools

Although the following products aren't XTensions for QuarkXPress, they can be quite helpful for QuarkXPress users.

Quite Imposing Plus

This plug-in for Adobe Acrobat rearranges the pages in a PDF so that they can be correctly printed in spreads and signatures on a printing press, or as a booklet on a desktop printer. It has tons of professional imposition features. You can find it at https://www.xchangeus.com.

JoJo (Mac only)

If you need to open a QuarkXPress document in the version that created it (instead of the most current version on your Mac), drag and drop the document over the dock icon of JoJo. Get it at www.jolauterbach.com.

AppleScripts (Mac Only)

QuarkXPress includes a bunch of AppleScripts for Mac users. To run a script, choose it from the Scripts menu (which looks like a paper scroll). To add new scripts, place them into the Scripts folder in the QuarkXPress application folder. Here are some of the most useful:

Box Tools submenu:

>> **Add Crop Marks** places crop marks around the selected box.

>> **Make Caption Box** creates a caption box (text box) below the selected box.

Grid submenu:

>> **By Dividing a Box** creates a grid of boxes based on the dimensions of the selected box.

Images submenu:

>> **Copy to Folder** saves a copy of the picture in the selected picture box to a specified folder.

>> **Fldr to Select PBoxes** imports picture files from a specified folder into selected picture boxes. Pictures are imported in alphabetical order.

Picture Box submenu:

>> **Crop Marks & Name** places crop marks around the active picture box and enters the name of the picture file into a text box below the picture box.

>> **Place Name** enters the name of a picture into a text box below the picture box that contains the picture.

>> **Set All Bkgnd None** changes the background color of every picture box in the layout to None.

>> **Set All Bkgnd** changes the background of every picture box in the layout to a specified color and shade.

Saving submenu:

>> **Each Page as EPS** saves each page of the layout as an individual EPS file with a color TIFF preview.

Special submenu:

>> **Open Apple Events Scripting PDF** opens "A Guide to Apple Events Scripting. pdf." This PDF file contains detailed information about writing AppleScript scripts for QuarkXPress.

>> **Open QuarkXPress Folders** opens your choice of folders within the QuarkXPress folder.

Stories submenu:

>> **Link Selected Text Boxes** links selected text boxes. The text chain order is based on the stacking order of the text boxes.

>> **Unlink Selected Boxes** breaks the links between selected text boxes while retaining the position of the text in the text chain.

Tables submenu:

>> **Row or Column Color** applies a specified color and shade to every other row or column in a table.

Typography submenu:

>> **Make Fractions** converts all instances of numbers on either side of a slash (for example, 1/2) into formatted fractions.

Documentation from Quark

Quark keeps the current versions of documentation for QuarkXPress 2016 at the following web page: `http://www.quark.com/Support/Documentation/QuarkXPress/2016.aspx`. Here are some of the most useful:

>> Getting Started with QuarkXPress 2016

>> A Guide to QuarkXPress 2016

>> What's New in QuarkXPress 2016

>> A Guide to XPress Tags 2016

>> QuarkXPress 2016 Known and Resolved Issues

>> A Guide to Apple Events Scripting

>> Digital Publishing with QuarkXPress 2016

>> Keyboard Command Guide: Mac OS X

>> Keyboard Command Guide: Windows

The Skinny on QuarkXPress Tips & Tricks

This affordable e-book series of tips and tricks covers a wide variety of techniques and tools in QuarkXPress. Other titles in the series cover tools you may also use, such as Photoshop and Lightroom. Get it at `http://www.theskinnybooks.com`.

Online Resources

Quark actively participates in a number of online presences, including the supremely helpful ones that follow:

Planet Quark

I was the editorial director of *Planet Quark* (`http://www.planetquark.com`) from its beginning in 2007 through February 2014. The 2,600+ stories I wrote and edited cover a variety of topics related to desktop publishing, but since then, the stories are almost exclusively about QuarkXPress.

Quark's Facebook group

Join this members-only Facebook group for power users of QuarkXPress. Questions are answered by informed members and Quark employees at `https://www.facebook.com/groups/quarkxpress/`.

QuarkXPress YouTube channel

This YouTube channel offers a collection of short videos about specific features in QuarkXPress, as well as longer videos highlighting groups of new features in new releases. Go to `https://www.youtube.com/user/QuarkXPressTV`.

Quark Forums

This online forum has lots of questions and answers from QuarkXPress users, as well as users sharing experiences. You can read everything without registering, but to post a message you must register. You can find the forum at `http://forums.quark.com`.

IN THIS CHAPTER

» **Talking with a commercial printer**

» **Avoiding scroll bars**

» **Sharing rather than copying**

» **Making use of the built-in calculator**

» **Making style sheets quickly**

» **Using Auto Save and Auto Backup**

» **Customizing QuarkXPress**

Chapter **19**

Ten Do's and Don'ts When Using QuarkXPress

This book explores hundreds of detailed topics, but if I had to choose ten easy-to-forget-but-extremely-useful things to remember, the ones in this chapter, dear reader, would be them. *Namaste.*

Do Talk with Your Commercial Printer

All print projects begin and end with the printer. That's because only printers know their limitations and the thousands of ways a project can be improved without increasing cost. Chat with the printer before you start your project, discussing your goals and budget. The printer may even have a Job Jackets file (explained in Chapter 7) that will set your project up correctly before you even begin — and it will drastically reduce the possibility that your file will have problems at the end.

Don't Use Scroll Bars

Instead of using the scroll bars to pan around your layout, use the Grabber Hand. Just hold down the Option (Mac) or Alt (Windows) key and then click anywhere on the page and drag. To move to a different page, press Shift+Page Up or Shift+Page Down on your extended keyboard. (If you work with multipage documents, investing in a keyboard with Page Up, Page Down, Home, and End keys will pay you back almost immediately.)

If you use this panning technique along with Command-0 (Mac) or Ctrl+0 (Windows) — and that's zero, not the letter 0 — to change your view to Fit In Window, as well as Shift-Control-drag (Mac) or Ctrl+drag (Windows) to zoom into an area, your efficiency will improve by 1,000 percent.

To recap, memorize these navigation techniques:

>> **Mac:** Shift-Control-drag to zoom into an area. Option-drag to pan around. Command-0 to Fit in Window.

>> **Windows:** Ctrl+drag to zoom into an area. Alt+drag to pan around. Ctrl+0 to Fit in Window.

Do Temporarily Switch to the Item Tool

When you need to move an item as you're editing its content, you don't need to switch from the Content tool to the Item tool. Just hold down the Command (Mac) or Ctrl (Windows) key to temporarily use the Item tool. When you release the Command or Ctrl key, your cursor reverts back to the Content tool.

Don't Copy When You Can Share

Whether you're using one layout or multiple layouts, if any possibility exists that an item you're about to copy will be updated later on, use the Sharing features explained in Chapter 7. That way, if you update the item anywhere in your project, it gets updated everywhere.

Do Use the Built-In Calculator

Every field in the Measurements palette can do math for you. If you need to reduce an item by half, type /2 or *.5 after the current value. If you need to move an item by a specific amount, type + or − after the current value and then type the distance to move it. You can use any unit, so to change a value by 2 points, type **2pt**. Use **p** for picas, **mm** for millimeters, " for inches, and so forth.

Do Make Style Sheets Quickly

The fastest and most intuitive way to make a style sheet is to format some text the way you want it to look and then click the New (+) button in either the Paragraph or Character Style Sheet palette. A new Style Sheet is created with all the formatting of the selected text.

Do Use Keyboard Shortcuts to Size Pictures and Text

To scale a picture to fit its box, press Shift-Option-Command-F (Mac) or Shift+Alt+Ctrl+F (Windows). In other words, mash down the three modifier keys that surround the Z key and press F.

To increase the size of a picture inside its box by 5 percent, get the Picture Content tool and press Shift-Option-Command-> (Mac) or Shift+Alt+Ctrl+> (Windows). To decrease, use < instead.

To increase the point size of selected text by 1 point, use those same shortcuts.

To increase leading by 1 point, press Shift-Command=' (Mac) or Shift+Ctrl+' (Windows) — and that's an apostrophe at the end. To decrease leading by 1 point, press Shift-Command-; (Mac) or Shift+Ctrl+; (Windows) — and that's a semicolon at the end. To increase/decrease by 1/10 point instead, add the Option (Mac) or Alt (Windows) key.

Trust me: When adjusting pictures and text, these shortcuts will become your best friends.

Don't Scale Pictures below the DPI You Need for Output

When scaling a picture, keep an eye on the Effective DPI field in the Home/Classic tab of the Measurements palette. (It's on the bottom row, far right, and looks like a grid of gray squares.) If the value gets below 240 dpi, the picture could pixelate when printing. In that case, import a higher-resolution original image or find a way to reduce the size of the picture on the page.

Do Use Auto-Save and Auto-Backup

If your computer is prone to crashing, select the Auto Save check box in the Open and Save pane of QuarkXPress Preferences. Your projects then save themselves at the interval you specify there. If you want to keep copies of your project as it evolves, select the Auto Backup check box in that same pane and tell it how many revisions to save. Each time you manually save your project, QuarkXPress will then create a new copy for you to continue your work and keep the old ones intact. (*Note:* In any case, even if you don't enable Auto Save or Auto Backup, QuarkXPress 2016 silently saves a backup of your last ten opened documents. You find them in the Quark Backup folder that QuarkXPress creates for you in the Documents folder on your hard drive.)

Do Customize How QuarkXPress Works

After you use QuarkXPress for a while, poke around in its Preferences. Here are some of the changes that may increase your productivity:

>> Change the width of the Pasteboard (Display pane).

>> Make your own keyboard shortcuts (Key Shortcuts pane).

>> Change the language format of Quotes and turn on/off Smart Quotes (Input Settings pane).

>> Enable Auto Save & Auto Backup (Open and Save pane).

>> Control which attributes are included by default when Sharing an item (Sharing pane).

>> Turn Font Previews on or off in menus (Fonts pane).

>> Enable East Asian text functionality (East Asian pane).

>> Control Index styling (Index pane).

>> Automatically evaluate layouts using Job Jackets (Job Jackets pane).

>> Change appearance of Notes (Notes pane).

>> Change Project/Layout naming scheme for exported PDFs (PDF pane).

>> Ignore numbers and Internet addresses when spell checking (Spell Check pane).

>> Change appearance of fractions and prices (Fraction/Price pane).

>> Verify pictures when opening a project (General pane in the Project section).

>> Turn Auto Page Insertion on or off (General pane in the Layout section).

>> Change default Ruler unit of measurement (Measurements pane in the Layout section).

>> Change appearance of Small Caps, Superscript, and Subscript (Character pane in the Layout section).

>> Change everything about tables you create with the Table tool (Table Tool pane in the Tools section of the Layout section).

>> Change the snap distance to guides, and whether they are in front of page items or behind them (Guides & Grid pane in the Layout section).

>> Change default Soft Proofing profile (Color Manager pane in the Layout section).

Appendix

Chart of Features Added in QuarkXPress 7 and Up

If you skipped a version or two of QuarkXPress, you're not alone — but you've missed some efficiency-enhancing improvements. Here is a complete list of the new features introduced since version 7.

Feature Comparison

User Experience	7	8	9	10	QX2015	QX2016
Modern, intuitive interface (OS X)	No	No	No	Yes	Yes	Yes
Modern, intuitive interface (Windows)	No	No	No	No	No	Yes
Trackpad gesture support*	No	No	No	No	No	Yes
Search in palettes	No	No	No	No	Yes	Yes
Native Cocoa Application*	No	No	No	Yes	Yes	Yes
HiDPI and Retina Display Support	No	No	No	Yes	Yes	Yes
Customize keyboard commands*	No	No	No	No	Yes	Yes
Xenon Graphics Engine	No	No	No	Yes	Yes	Yes
Next Generation Palettes	No	No	No	Yes	Yes	Yes

*Mac OS X feature only

(continued)

(continued)

	7	8	9	10	QX2015	QX2016
Full Screen Experience*	No	No	No	Yes	Yes	Yes
Set default tool preferences from existing objects	No	No	No	Yes	Yes	Yes
Custom Color Schemes*	No	No	No	Yes	Yes	Yes
Palette grouping/ palette sets	Yes	Yes	Yes	Yes	Yes	Yes
Dockable palettes	No	No	No	Yes, Mac only	Yes	Yes
Keyboardable measurement palette* (for example, Command+M)	No	No	No	Yes	Yes	Yes
Resizeable measurement palette (large/small)	No	No	No	No	No	Yes
Output	**7**	**8**	**9**	**10**	**QX2015**	**QX2016**
Direct PDF export (without distiller)	Yes	Yes	Yes	Yes	Yes	Yes
Pass-Through Transparency of native objects	No	Yes	Yes	Yes	Yes	Yes
Pass-Through Transparency of PDF	No	No	No	Yes	Yes	Yes
PDF/X-1a and PDF/X-3 Export	Yes	Yes	Yes	Yes	Yes	Yes
Direct PDF/X-4 Export	No	No	No	No	Yes	Yes
Export layers in PDFs	No	Yes	Yes	Yes	Yes	Yes
Export as Image	No	No	No	Yes	Yes	Yes
Export a book as a single PDF	No	No	No	Yes	Yes	Yes
Host-based separations	Yes	Yes	Deprecated	No	No	No
In-RIP separations and Composite output	Yes	Yes	Yes	Yes	Yes	Yes

*Mac OS X feature only

Color Management	7	8	9	10	QX2015	QX2016
ICC-based color management	Yes	Yes	Yes	Yes	Yes	Yes
Support for ICCv2	Yes	Yes	Yes	Yes	Yes	Yes
Support for ICCv4	No	No	No	No	Partial	Yes
Layout Experience	**7**	**8**	**9**	**10**	**QX2015**	**QX2016**
Page size larger than 1.20m / 48"	No	No	No	No	Yes	Yes
Create custom page sizes	No	No	No	No	Yes	Yes
8000% Zoom	No	No	No	Yes	Yes	Yes
Format Painter	No	No	No	No	Yes	Yes
Display crisp image previews of bitmap images	No	No	No	Yes	Yes	Yes
Display crisp image previews of PDF and AI	No	No	No	Yes	Yes	Yes
Display crisp image previews of EPS	No	No	No	No	Yes	Yes
Dynamic Guides / Smart Guides	No	No	No	Yes	Yes	Yes
Convert imported AI/EPS/PDF to native objects	No	No	No	No	No	Yes
Layers	Yes	Yes	Yes	Yes	Yes	Yes
Layers on Master Pages	No	No	No	No	Yes	Yes
Text on a path	Yes	Yes	Yes	Yes	Yes	Yes
Bézier illustration tools	Yes	Yes	Yes	Yes	Yes	Yes
Color picker (iDropper)	No	No	No	No	No	Yes
Two- color gradients	Yes	Yes	Yes	Yes	Yes	Yes

*Mac OS X feature only

(continued)

(continued)

Multi-color gradients	No	No	No	No	No	Yes
Full Screen Color Browsing*	No	No	No	Yes	Yes	Yes
Adaptive Resolution	No	No	No	Yes	Yes	Yes
Advanced Image Control Palette	No	No	No	Yes	Yes	Yes
Print Preview	No	No	No	Yes	Yes	Yes
Page Navigator*	No	Yes	Yes	Yes	Yes	Yes
Flip shapes horizontally and vertically	No	No	No	Yes	Yes	Yes
Fit box to image	No	Yes	Yes	Yes	Yes	Yes
Fit box to text	No	No	No	No	No	Yes
Space/Align	Yes	Yes	Yes	Yes	Yes	Yes
Space/Align with key item	No	No	No	Yes	Yes	Yes
Find/Change for text	Yes	Yes	Yes	Yes	Yes	Yes
Find/Change supports breaking/non-breaking characters	No	No	No	No	No	Yes
Item Styles and Item Find/Change	No	Yes	Yes	Yes	Yes	Yes
Trim Preview	No	No	Yes	Yes	Yes	Yes
View Sets	No	No	Yes	Yes	Yes	Yes
Guide Manager Pro	No	Yes	Yes	Yes	Yes	Yes
Dedicated orthogonal line tool	No	No	No	Yes	Yes	Yes
Scale images smaller than 10% and larger than 1000%	No	No	No	Yes	Yes	Yes
Scale images up to 5000%	No	No	No	No	Yes	Yes

Mac OS X feature only

Scale by inputting a percentage	No	Yes	Yes	Yes	Yes	Yes
Relink images in Usage Dialog	No	No	No	No	Yes	Yes
Designer-controlled Automation	**7**	**8**	**9**	**10**	**QX2015**	**QX2016**
Conditional Styles	No	No	Yes	Yes	Yes	Yes
Bullets and Numbers	No	No	Yes	Yes	Yes	Yes
Callouts	No	No	Yes	Yes	Yes	Yes
ShapeMaker	No	No	Yes	Yes	Yes	Yes
ImageGrid	No	No	Yes	Yes	Yes	Yes
Linkster	No	No	Yes	Yes	Yes	Yes
Cloner	No	No	Yes	Yes	Yes	Yes
Tables (designed tables) with page wrap	No	No	Yes	Yes	Yes	Yes
Fast, inline tables with page wrap	No	No	No	No	Yes	Yes
Tables Styles (for inline tables)	No	No	No	No	Yes	Yes
Footnotes	No	No	No	No	Yes	Yes
Endnotes	No	No	No	No	Yes	Yes
Cross-referencing	No	No	No	No	No	Yes
Variables (print date, creation date, for example)	No	No	No	No	Yes	Yes
Variables can line-wrap	No	No	No	No	No	Yes
References	No	No	No	No	Yes	Yes
Running headers	No	No	No	No	Yes	Yes
Indexes and tables of contents	Yes	Yes	Yes	Yes	Yes	Yes

*Mac OS X feature only

(continued)

(continued)

Text and Typography	7	8	9	10	QX2015	QX2016
Unicode and OpenType support	Yes	Yes	Yes	Yes	Yes	Yes
Support for stylistic sets (OpenType)	No	No	No	No	No	Yes
Glyphs palette	Yes	Yes	Yes	Yes	Yes	Yes
Copy Textstyle Tool (eyedropper tool for text)	No	No	No	No	Yes	Yes
Highlight Missing Font	No	No	No	Yes	Yes	Yes
Story Editor	No	No	Yes	Yes	Yes	Yes
Preset and customizable hanging characters	No	Yes	Yes	Yes	Yes	Yes
Several baseline grids	No	Yes	Yes	Yes	Yes	Yes
Additional East Asian baseline grid setup options	No	No	No	Yes	Yes	Yes
Advanced character spacing; Mojigumi setup controls	No	No	No	Yes	Yes	Yes
Additional East Asian text and typography setup controls	No	No	No	Yes	Yes	Yes
Digital Publishing	**7**	**8**	**9**	**10**	**QX2015**	**QX2016**
Unified App Studio and e-book layout	No	No	No	No	No	Yes
HTML5 Animations for apps	No	No	No	Yes	Yes	Yes
HTML5 Animations for e-books	No	No	No	No	Yes	Yes
Create tablet and smartphone apps	No	No	Yes	Yes	Yes	Yes

*Mac OS X feature only

Feature	7	8	9	10	QX2015	QX2016
Reflowable e-book export in ePub and Kindle format	No	No	Yes	Yes	Yes	Yes
Use Style Sheets to export CCS Styles for e-books	No	No	No	No	Yes	Yes
Fixed-layout e-book export in ePub and Kindle format	No	No	No	No	Yes	Yes
Justification, run-around, drop caps, and so on. in ePub and HTML5	No	No	No	No	No	Yes
Create HTML5 Publications	No	No	No	No	No	Yes
Collaboration	**7**	**8**	**9**	**10**	**QX2015**	**QX2016**
Books and Collaboration	Yes	Yes	Yes	Yes	Yes	Yes
Add all layouts of a project to a book	No	No	No	Yes	Yes	Yes
Redlining	No	No	No	Yes	Yes	Yes
Notes	No	No	No	Yes	Yes	Yes
Job Jackets	Yes	Yes	Yes	Yes	Yes	Yes
Job Jackets in XML format	No	No	No	Yes	Yes	Yes
Job Jackets can contain a default dictionary	No	No	No	No	Yes	Yes
Auxiliary dictionary editable (XML)	No	No	No	No	Yes	Yes
Import/Export hyphenation exceptions	No	No	No	Yes	Yes	Yes
Composition Zones	Yes	Yes	Yes	Yes	Yes	Yes
Synchronized content	Yes	Yes	Yes	Yes	Yes	Yes

*Mac OS X feature only

(continued)

(continued)

Import/Export	7	8	9	10	QX2015	QX2016
Import PDF	Yes	Yes	Yes	Yes	Yes	Yes
Paste objects from Illustrator or MS Office as native objects	No	No	No	No	No	Yes
Import/export hyphenation exceptions	No	No	No	Yes	Yes	Yes
Legacy Word import (DOC)	Yes	Yes	Yes	Yes	No	No
Legacy Excel import (XLS)	Yes	Yes	Yes	Yes	No	No
Word import (DOCX)	Yes	Yes	Yes	Yes	Yes	Yes
Excel import (XLSX)	Yes	Yes	Yes	Yes	Yes	Yes
Native Illustrator file (AI) import	No	Yes	Yes	Yes	Yes	Yes
Native Photoshop file (PSD) import	Yes	Yes	Yes	Yes	Yes	Yes
Import footnotes/ endnotes from DOCX (MS Word)	No	No	No	No	Yes	Yes
Collect for Output across all layouts	No	No	No	No	Yes	Yes
Open PDF automatically after exporting	No	No	No	No	Yes	Yes
Downsave one version	Yes	Yes	Yes	Yes	Yes	Yes
Open legacy documents (3.1 up to 6) directly	Yes	Yes	Yes	Via Document Converter	Via Document Converter	Via Document Converter
Open legacy documents (7 and higher) directly	Yes	Yes	Yes	Yes	Yes	Yes
Easily convert Print layout to fixed-layout ePub	No	No	No	No	Yes	Yes
Easily convert Print layout to HTML5	No	No	No	No	No	Yes

*Mac OS X feature only

Other	7	8	9	10	QX2015	QX2016
Anchored Boxes without limit	No	No	Yes	Yes	Yes	Yes
QR Code Creator	No	No	No	Yes	Yes	Yes
Spotlight support (for all versions)	No	No	Yes	Yes	Yes	Yes
QuickLook support	No	No	Yes	Yes	Yes	Yes
Global file format	No	Yes	Yes	Yes	Yes	Yes
Support for 35+ languages	Passport Edition only	Yes	Yes	Yes	Yes	Yes
East-Asian (right-to-left) support built-in	No	No	No	Yes	Yes	Yes
Free technical support (60 days after purchase)	No	No	No	Yes	Yes	Yes
Attractive technical support plans available for purchase	No	No	No	Yes	Yes	Yes
Upgrade	**7**	**8**	**9**	**10**	**QX2015**	**QX2016**
Upgrade to QuarkXPress 2016 available	Yes	Yes	Yes	Yes	Yes	Yes
Reduced upgrade price when upgrading to QX2016	No	No	No	No	Yes	n/a
Platform support	**7**	**8**	**9**	**10**	**QX2015**	**QX2016**
Cross-platform licensing (OS X and Windows)	Yes	Yes	Yes	Yes	Yes	Yes
Dual-activation (install on two machines)	Yes	Yes	Yes	Yes	Yes	Yes
64-bit application	No	No	No	No	Yes	Yes
Drag-and-drop installation*	No	No	No	No	Yes	Yes
Mac OS X Mavericks (10.9)	No	No	Yes	Yes	Yes	Yes

*Mac OS X feature only

(continued)

(continued)

	7	8	9	10	QX2015	QX2016
Mac OS X Yosemite (10.10)	No	No	No	Yes	Yes	Yes
Mac OS X El Capitan (10.11)	No	No	No	No	Yes	Yes
Runs on 32-bit flavors of Windows	Yes	Yes	Yes	Yes	No	No
Windows 7 (64 bit)	No	Yes	Yes	Yes	Yes	Yes
Windows 8 and 8.1 (64 bit)	No	No	Yes	Yes	Yes	Yes
Windows 10 (64 bit)	No	No	No	No	Yes	Yes

*Mac OS X feature only

Index

shading
  pictures, 253
  text color, 173
Shape submenu, 51, 52
ShapeMaker dialog box, 29,
    56–60
Share Multiple Items dialog box,
    132
Shared Item Properties dialog
    box, 130–131, 134–135
shared layout, defined, 130
sharing
  color setups, 290
  Composition Zones, 133–137
  content, in layout family, 327
  items, 130–133
  Job Jackets, 137–138
  overview, 129
  tips for, 368
shortcuts, keyboard. *See*
    keyboard shortcuts
Show Object action, 343
Show Pop-Up action, 343
Single File check box, Books
    palette, 120
Single Layout Mode, 17
skewing
  boxes, 70
  pictures, 252
  text boxes, 144
  text in box, 148
Skip button, Check Spelling
    palette, 214
slab serif fonts, 161
slideshows, 337–339
Small Caps style, 180–181
smooth point, Bézier shape,
    48, 49
Smoothness option, text
    runarounds, 268
Snap to Guides feature, 90
Snap to Page Grids feature, 90
soft proofing layouts, 288–289

Source setups, copying, 290
Spacing control, ShapeMaker
    dialog box, 57
special characters, 176–180, 210
special effects, text, 174–176
spectrophotometers, 287
spell-checker, 28. *See also* Check
    Spelling palette
spelling, choosing language for,
    182
Spirals tab, ShapeMaker dialog
    box, 58
Split All Paths option, Merge or
    Split Paths menu, 95
Split Outside Paths option,
    Merge or Split Paths menu,
    94, 95
split views, 39–40
splitting
  items, 93–95
  table cells, 239, 243
spot color, 277–278, 281
Spreads option
  Export Image Options dialog
    box, 310
  Print dialog box, 294
stacking order, 80–81
Starburst tool, 44
Static Text content variable, 219
Status column, Books palette,
    123
stories, 151, 213–214
Story Editor, 207, 216–217
stretching text, 174
Style menu, 25, 262, 279
style sheets
  appending, 199
  applying, 199–201
  Character, 176, 201
  context menu for, 30, 31
  creating, 195–197, 369
  deleting, 199
  importing, 153

mapping for Reflowable view,
    347–348
No Style, 198
Normal, 198
overview, 195
replacing, 199
updating, 198
Style Sheets palette, 32,
    195–196, 200
styles
  Composition Zones items, 136
  Item Styles feature, 96–100
  line, 47
  type, 170
Stylistic Sets, OpenType fonts,
    172
Suitcase Fusion, Extensis, 162
Summary pane, Print dialog box,
    300
Super Step and Repeat feature,
    74, 75–76
Superior style, 180
Superscript style, 180
Suppress Output feature, 35,
    72–73, 87
Suppress Picture Output
    feature, 73, 261–262
suppressed item, defined, 27
swashes, font, 171
symmetrical point, Bézier shape,
    48, 49
synchronization
  chapter settings, 121–122
  content, in layout family, 327
  of items, 130–133
  overview, 16, 129

T

Tab Order option, Table
    Properties dialog box, 231
Table Break Properties dialog
    box, 244–245
Table Link dialog box, 233–235

About the Author

Jay J. Nelson has used QuarkXPress almost daily since 1988 when he managed one of America's first prepress service bureaus. He became a Quark Authorized Trainer and then owned a Quark Authorized Training Center. For the next 21 years, Jay was the editor and publisher of *Design Tools Monthly*, a widely respected executive summary of graphic design news.

Jay was a keynote speaker at Quark's launch of QuarkXPress 7 and 8, and is the author and presenter of the training video included with QuarkXPress 7. He has also reviewed every version of QuarkXPress for *Macworld/PCWorld* magazine since version 8.

Jay has publishing in his blood and is the third generation in his family dedicated to the process of producing books, newspapers, and magazines. He is the author of "Jay Nelson's Guide to Self Publishing" and is the publisher of The Skinny Book series of eBooks. He also contributes regularly to *Macworld* and *Photoshop User* magazines. Earlier in his career, Jay owned a graphic design studio and training company, and managed a printing company. He knows a lot about digital publishing, fonts, and font management. Follow Jay on Twitter: @jaynelson.

Dedication

For my grandfather Sven Alfred Nilsson, who came to the United States from Sweden at the age of 17 and learned English by typesetting for newspapers — for the rest of his life. He may not have been a nice man, or a good husband or father, but I respect his fortitude and choice of trade.

Acknowledgments

I am deeply grateful to Lesa Snider, my loving partner in life's adventures, for showing me with her own spectacular books how to be a great writer — a goal I still hope to achieve. Heartfelt thanks also to Matthias Guenther at Quark for providing invaluable technical editing and supporting all my Quarkian quests and questions; to Gavin Drake at Quark for supporting Planet Quark when I was its editorial director and for including me in many Quark adventures; to Sarah Rector at Quark for tirelessly handling all my odd requests over the years; to Susan Christophersen for softly sculpting my writing's rough edges to produce a much happier book for our readers; to Steve Hayes at Wiley for helping me shape the original outline of this book; to all the readers of *Design Tools Monthly* for supporting my work during the 21 years it was in print; to Terri Stone, Jackie Dove, Susie Ochs, and Roman Loyola at *Macworld* for asking me to write reviews of the recent releases of QuarkXPress; to Erin Livers, my partner at Arts & Letters when we taught countless QuarkXPress classes to budding publishers; to Tami Stodghill at XChange and Cyndie Shaffstall at The PowerXChange for endless support around XTensions; to Tim Banister and Dan Logan at Quark for letting me help shape the product in a small way; to Peter McClard for his insanely creative XTensions that ultimately were absorbed into QuarkXPress; and to the millions of users of QuarkXPress around the world who have joined me on this crazy journey.

My appreciation also goes to the original titans of desktop publishing: Paul Brainerd for Aldus PageMaker, James Von Ehr for Altsys Fontographer and Free-Hand, Tim Gill for QuarkXPress, Chuck Geshke and John Warnock for PostScript and Adobe Illustrator, and the brothers Thomas and John Knoll for Photoshop. These titans created desktop publishing for the voiceless around the world at a time when printing presses were owned by only a few rich men. And of course to Steve Jobs for enlightening an entire generation on the power of typography and the supreme value of design.

Publisher's Acknowledgments

Executive Editor: Steve Hayes

Project Manager and Copy Editor: Susan Christophersen

Technical Editor: Matthias Guenther

Editorial Assistant: Serena Novosel

Sr. Editorial Assistant: Cherie Case

Production Editor: Antony Sami

Cover Image: mandritoiu/Shutterstock